# CIM

## STUDY TEXT

Certificate

# Marketing Fundamentals

*First edition 1994*
*Fifth edition April 1998*

*ISBN 0 7517 4067 5 (previous edition 0 7517 4055 1)*

***British Library Cataloguing-in-Publication Data***
*A catalogue record for this book*
*is available from the British Library*

*Published by*

*BPP Publishing Limited*
*Aldine House, Aldine Place*
*London W12 8AW*

*http://www.bpp.co.uk*

*Printed in Great Britain by*
*WM Print Ltd*
*Frederick Street*
*Walsall*
*West Midlands WS2 9NE*



*BPP would like to thank Professor Geoff Lancaster for his contributions to previous editions of this Study text.*

*We are grateful to the Chartered Institute of Marketing for permission to reproduce in this text the syllabus, tutor's guidance notes, past examination questions and specimen examination paper of which the Institute holds the copyright. The suggested solutions to both the specimen paper questions and the past examination questions have been prepared by BPP Publishing Limited.*

*Contents*


| | Page |
|---|---|
| **PREFACE** | (v) |
| **INTRODUCTION**<br>How to use this Study Text - syllabus - tutor's guidance notes - the examination paper - study checklist | (vi) |
| **PART A: THE MARKETING CULTURE** | |
| 1 The evolution of the marketing concept | 3 |
| 2 Environmental and quality issues | 31 |
| 3 The strategic implications of a marketing orientation | 62 |
| **PART B: THE MARKETING TOOL** | |
| 4 Marketing research | 89 |
| 5 Product | 106 |
| 6 Price | 141 |
| 7 Place | 166 |
| 8 Promotion | 185 |
| **PART C: COMBINING THE MARKETING MIX** | |
| 9 Combining the marketing mix | 221 |
| **PART D: CUSTOMER CARE** | |
| 10 Customer care | 257 |
| **ILLUSTRATIVE QUESTIONS** | 275 |
| **SUGGESTED SOLUTIONS** | 278 |
| **GLOSSARY** | 315 |
| **INDEX** | 293 |
| **ORDER FORMS** | |
| **REVIEW FORM & FREE PRIZE DRAW** | |

## PREFACE

You're taking your professional CIM exams in the coming year and you want to pass first time.

Here's why BPP's study package is the professional solution.

### The BPP Study Text

The BPP Study Text gives you the knowledge and application techniques you need.

- We show you the syllabus and analyse the papers set so far - so that you know what you're up against. We consult the examiner to make sure we - and you - are on the right track.
- Each chapter takes you through the syllabus in a structured, methodical way. You can check you've mastered the theory by tackling the *Exercises* and the *Test Your Knowledge* quiz featured in each chapter.
- *Case Examples* from real companies show how the theory is applied - and they are useful for exam answers, too.
- A bank of *Illustrative Questions*, at least one per chapter, lets you put your skills into practice.
- A *Glossary* and *Index* offer a ready reference.

### *Marketing Fundamentals* Study Text: April 1998

This BPP Study Text for *Marketing Fundamentals* has been written specifically for the syllabus, taking account of the exams set so far.

#### *New in the April 1998 edition*

- New feature: **Exam focus points**. Exam focus points show you what the examiner is interested in, how topics have been covered in the past, and how you can tackle exam questions in future. You will find exam focus points throughout this text.
- New and updated case examples.

### Practice and Revision: further help from BPP

The other vital element of BPP's study package is the *Practice & Revision Kit*, produced in association with Nottingham Trent University. The 1998 Kit is packed with exam-style questions (including all the exam papers from December 1994 to December 1997) with full model answers written by experienced tutors. The Kit offers you the vital practice you need at unbeatable value for money. See the *Order Form* at the end of this Study Text for more details.

### Help us to help you

Your feedback will help us improve our study package. Please complete and return the *Review Form* at the end of this Study Text; you will be entered automatically in a Free Prize Draw.

### A final word

We've done our best to make our study package smart, focused and friendly. Of course, exam success is ultimately up to you - and following our professional approach will help you pass.

*BPP Publishing*
*April 1998*

For information about the products and services offered by BPP Publishing and other businesses in the BPP Holdings plc group, visit our website. The address is:

http://www.bpp.co.uk

## HOW TO USE THIS STUDY TEXT

This Study Text has been designed to help students and lecturers to get to grips as effectively as possible with the content and scope of *Marketing Fundamentals.*

Syllabus coverage in the text is indicated on pages (viii) and (ix) by chapter references set against each syllabus topic. Syllabus topics are also identified within each chapter of the text. It is thus easy to trace your path through the syllabus.

As a further guide - and a convenient means of monitoring your progress - we have included a *study checklist* on page (xiv) on which to chart your completion of chapters and their related illustrative questions.

### Chapter format and contents

Each *chapter* of the Study Text is divided into *sections.*

- An *introduction* places the subject of the chapter in its context in the syllabus and the examination.
- The text gives clear, concise topic-by-topic coverage.
- *Exercises* reinforce learning, confirm understanding and stimulate thought.
- Case examples show you how the theory applies in real life.
- A *chapter roundup* at the end of the chapter pulls together the key points.
- *Exam focus points* show you how the subject is examined.
- A *test your knowledge* quiz helps you to check that you have absorbed the material in the chapter.

Some features of the Study Text are worth looking at in more detail.

### Exam focus points

Exam focus points show how a topic covered in the text has been or might be examined. Some exam focus points are short reminders which flag when and how topics have been examined before. Others are more extensive and show how you might have tackled a particular question in a recent exam.

### Exercises

Exercises are provided throughout the text to enable you to check your progress as you work through the text. A suggested solution is usually given, but often in abbreviated form to help you avoid the temptation of merely reading the exercise rather than actively engaging your brain.

### Case examples

Case examples can be found throughout. They describe marketing as it is practised in the 'real world'. The case examples support and challenge what has been written in the text. As you study for the exams, develop your own file of examples to cite in your answers. At the end of each Part of the text, you will find a more extended case example.

### Chapter roundup and Test your knowledge quiz

At the end of each chapter you will find two boxes. The first is the *Chapter roundup* which summarises key points. The *Test Your Knowledge* quiz in the second box serves a number of purposes.

- *Use it after the chapter roundup*. It can be glanced over quickly to remind yourself of key issues covered by the chapter.
- *Use it as a quiz*. Try doing it mentally on the train in the morning to check how well you remember what you have read the night before.
- *Use it to revise*. Shortly before your examination sit down with pen and paper and try to answer all the questions fully.

### Illustrative questions

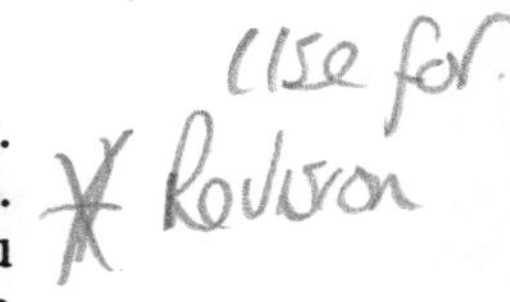

Each chapter refers to an illustrative question in the bank at the back of the Study Text. Initially you might attempt such questions with reference to the chapter you have just covered. When you are more confident try the question without referring to the Text. Only when you have attempted each question as fully as possible should you refer to the suggested solution to check and correct your performance.

### Glossary and Index

The glossary defines key terms and the comprehensive index helps you locate key topics.

> **A note on pronouns**
>
> On occasions in this Study Text, 'he' is used for 'he or she', 'him' for 'him or her' and so forth. Whilst we try to avoid this practice it is sometimes necessary for reasons of style. No prejudice or stereotyping according to sex is intended or assumed.

## SYLLABUS

### Aims and objectives

- to provide students with an understanding of the development of marketing and its changing role within a variety of organisations
- to provide students with an awareness of the various tools of the marketer, an appreciation of their strengths and weaknesses and the skills necessary to use them effectively and creatively at an operational level, in the process of identifying, influencing and satisfying demand
- to ensure students understand the synergy of impact achievable through modifying the marketing mix and positioning product and service offerings to meet the needs of clearly identified market targets
- to introduce students to the importance of both planning and control in the management of the marketing activity

### Learning outcomes

Students will be able to:

- understand the importance of customer care and be able to make proposals for assessing, improving or maintaining customer care levels
- recognise the role of marketing in business, understand the development of marketing and appreciate its implications for the organisation and be able to make clear recommendations for making effective cultural change within the organisation
- apply their working knowledge of the individual elements of the marketing mix to enable them to appreciate and criticise current marketing activities of organisations
- recognise the differences involved in marketing products and services

### Indicative content and weighting

| | | Covered in Chapter |
|---|---|---|
| **1** | **The marketing culture (20%)** | |
| 1.1 | Evolving orientation of organisations, the development of the marketing concept and its distinction from sales and product orientated organisations | 1 |
| 1.2 | Future modifications to the concept as organisations take on board environmental, legal and quality issues | 2 |
| 1.3 | The strategic implications of a marketing organisation. Developing and growing a marketing activity within the organisation. Over-viewing the marketing process | 3 |
| **2** | **The marketing tool (50%)** | |
| 2.1 | Overview of the marketing research process and its importance in identifying and analysing customer needs | 4 |
| 2.2 | Organising to provide effective marketing data, the role of information systems and the function of external agancies | 4 |
| 2.3 | The product/service portfolio – the mix of products and benefits they offer (functional, physical and symbolic benefits). The role of packaging | 5 |
| 2.4 | The nature of a product/service, its characteristics and life cycle | 5 |

| | | |
|---|---|---|
| 2.5 | New product development and PLC modifications as a way of expanding or extending the offering | 5 |
| 2.6 | The importance of price and its determinants | 6 |
| 2.7 | Models to help with pricing decisions based on cost, competition and demand (including breakeven analysis, marginal costing and price elasticity) | 6 |
| 2.8 | Distribution channels and alternative approaches to distribution – cost v control | 7 |
| 2.9 | The creative use of availability as a source of competitive advantage including Just In Time | 7 |
| 2.10 | Understanding the communication process and the elements of the promotional mix | 8 |
| 2.11 | The notion of segmentation as a means of targetting customers | 3, 5 |
| **3** | **Combining the marketing mix (20%)** | |
| 3.1 | How the mix changes at different stages of PLC and to meet the needs of different market places | 9 |
| 3.2 | Differences between goods and services. The 7 Ps of service marketing | 9 |
| **4** | **Customer care (10%)** | |
| 4.1 | Assessing and monitoring levels of customer care and its importance within TQM | 10 |
| 4.2 | Practical approaches to improving the standard of customer care and marketing's role within that | 10 |

## TUTOR'S GUIDANCE NOTES

> The following notes were published in the *Tutor's Manual* in 1994. The updated manual published in September 1997 contained a marking guide to a particular exam sitting. We have retained the 1994 version for your reference.

The aim of this paper is to test candidates' understanding of the basic precepts of marketing with the emphasis being upon understanding rather than merely memory.

The paper has been designed in two main parts – A and B, weighted 40% and 60% respective with the second section being sub-divided.

Part A is compulsory and this puts candidates in a tactical problem solving situation through the medium of a short scenario, or may or occasion give students an article or information on which they will be asked to comment.

Part B is a choice of three from six [nine, before June 1996] and this tests candidates on the broader issues of marketing and some specialist issues.

The paper is therefore more practically inclined. Tutors are, therefore, encouraged to capitalise on the experience of course members already engaged in marketing through the medium of seminar discussion. Marketing professionals should, wherever possible, be introduced to add practical input to discussions and lectures. Nevertheless, it is realised that some candidates will still lack knowledge of practical apllication, be this first- or second-hand. Such candidates should be encouraged to read case material in marketing textbooks and to ensure that they are up-to-date in matters pertaining to marketing prior to the examination. Such current affairs material can be witnessed in the 'quality' press and appropriate technicl and professional journals.

The questions are designed such that candidates who demonstrate an understanding of marketing fundamentals and can appreciate how these principles work in a practical setting should satisfy the requirements for this examination.

In order to score high marks candidates should, in addition to demonstrating a sound basic understanding, distinguish themselves along a number of criteria:

- use of appropriate examples or otherwise demonstrate a good appreciation of reality
- show evidence of creative thinking in relation to the problems set
- produce answers which adhere to the specific questions set, in a clear, concise and objective manner

Candidates who demonstrate such qualities as those outlined above will be rewarded over and above the pass criteria. Those who demonstrate basic textbook knowledge and basic ability of application will only achieve a pass.

## Assessment methods and format of the paper (from June 1996)

| | Number of marks |
|---|---|
| Part A: compulsory (number of questions varies) | 40 |
| Part B: marketing's broader remit (3 from 6) | 60 |
| | 100 |

(*Note*. Before the June 1996 exam, candidates had a choice of 9 questions in Part B.)

Time allowed: 3 hours

## Analysis of past papers

The analysis below shows the topics covered in exam papers set so far and the specimen paper.

### December 1997

*Part A* (compulsory)

1 A watch manufacturer is considering a major innovation
 (a) How to exploit an innovative product
 (b) Pricing strategy, sales growth and high development costs

*Part B* (3 questions)

2 Distribution and marketing
3 Packaging
4 Price setting
5 Social responsibility
6 Product life cycle
7 Segmentation and targeting

### June 1997

*Part A* (compuslory)

1 A jewellery maker is 'product-led'
 (a) What might be the benefits of a customer orientation?
 (b) How should the firm identify changing needs and wants of retailers and customers?

*Part B* (3 questions)

2 Price setting: alternatives to 'cost plus'
3 High pressure sales techniques and customer care
4 Marketing mix for goods and services
5 Product life cycle: pros and cons
6 Job description for communications manager
7 Controllable elements of marketing activities

### December 1996

*Part A* (compulsory)

1 Advising a bio-technology company on a new product
 (a) Ways of marketing and segmentation
 (b) Developing elements of the marketing mix

*Part B* (3 questions)

2 New product development: innovative/replacement/imitative
3 Pricing policy guidelines
4 Development of a marketing research system
5 Customer care for engineering company
6 Marketing management and the social perspective
7 Service marketing: the 7Ps

*June 1996*

*Part A* (compulsory)

1 Major product innovation
  (a) Implications for existing manufacturers
  (b) Pricing policy

*Part B* (3 questions)

2 Customer orientation
3 Tasks to be done by a new marketing research department
4 Implications of Just-in-Time
5 Communications and the marketing mix
6 Differences between marketing and sales
7 Relevant marketing mix for two companies (out of a choice of four)

*December 1995*

*Part A* (compulsory)

1 Growing better bananas: changing marketing mix for growers, importers and retailers; customer needs

*Part B* (3 questions)

2 Pricing for computer software
3 Remuneration of an insurance sales force: salary or commission?
4 New products for growth
5 Researching new markets
6 Selling in the promotional mix
7 Mission statement and marketing implications
8 Lean manufacturing, Just in Time, and marketing implications
9 Customer care officer's job specification
10 Promotion: pull versus push

*June 1995*

*Part A* (compulsory)

1 Analyse a company's approach to pricing and promotion

*Part B* (3 questions)

2 The role of the marketing manager in a medium-sized manufacturing company
3 Pricing of contract cleaning services
4 Overview of the marketing research process
5 Marketing vs selling
6 Customer care in a despatch department
7 New product development
8 Application of product or service portfolio analysis in aiding planning
9 The qualities required of senior marketing managers
10 Job specification for a post dealing with promotional activity

*December 1994*

*Part A* (compulsory)

1 Marketing an innovation. Combining marketing and research

*Part B* (3 questions)

2 Changing to marketing orientation
3 Marketing satisfying needs v marketing creating needs
4 Advantages and disadvantages of changing to a distribution agent
5 Screening new products
6 Price competition - advantages and disadvantages
7 Role of advertising and sales promotions
8 Monitoring and improving standards of customer care
9 Logistical systems as a means of controlling costs
10 Pricing decisions

## STUDY CHECKLIST

This page is designed to help you chart your progress through the Study Text, including the illustrative questions at the back of it. You can tick off each topic as you study and try questions on it. Insert the dates you complete the chapters and questions in the relevant boxes. You will thus ensure that you are on track to complete your study before the exam.

| | | Text chapters | Illustrative questions | |
|---|---|---|---|---|
| | | *Date completed* | *Question numbers* | *Date completed* |
| | **PART A: THE MARKETING CULTURE** | | | |
| 1 | The evolution of the marketing concept | | 1-3 | |
| 2 | Environmental and quality issues | | 4,5 | |
| 3 | The strategic implications of a marketing orientation | | 6 | |
| | **PART B: THE MARKETING TOOL** | | | |
| 4 | Marketing research | | 7,8 | |
| 5 | Product | | 9-11 | |
| 6 | Price | | 12,13 | |
| 7 | Place | | 14-17 | |
| 8 | Promotion | | 18-22 | |
| | **PART C: COMBINING THE MARKETING MIX** | | | |
| 9 | Combining the marketing mix | | 23 | |
| | **PART D: CUSTOMER CARE** | | | |
| 10 | Customer care | | 24 | |

# Part A
## The marketing culture

# Chapter 1

# THE EVOLUTION OF THE MARKETING CONCEPT

**This chapter covers the following topics.** *Syllabus reference*



| | | Syllabus reference |
|---|---|---|
| 1 | History of marketing | 1.1 |
| 2 | The marketing concept | 1.1 |
| 3 | Marketing orientated strategy | 1.1 |
| 4 | The business system | 1.1 |
| 5 | What is marketing management? | 1.1 |
| 6 | Marketing and the environment | 1.1 |
| 7 | The marketing mix | 1.1 |



### Introduction

Marketing is both a philosophy for business organisations and also a functional area of management located within a departmental structure. The *marketing concept* means focusing on customer needs. In practice, this consumer orientation should permeate every part of a business if it is to succeed. The theory of marketing involves modifying the 'marketing mix' variables of product, price, place and promotion which will be discussed throughout this text. This chapter aims to give an overview of the marketing concept including the various marketing environments and the scope of marketing.

Once you have finished this chapter, you should understand the following.

(a) Marketing has developed in parallel with business as a whole, becoming more complex and more sophisticated.

(b) Marketing has become increasingly important for business, and business has become 'marketing led', rather than sales or production led, as in the past.

(c) The marketing concept has also developed over time, helping to create a corporate culture where the customer really does come first. This is reflected in the way marketing is organised within the company structure.

(d) The marketing mix is introduced here, and developed in depth in the rest of the text.

## 1 HISTORY OF MARKETING

1.1 The idea of marketing grew out of systems of trade and exchange. When a society becomes capable of producing a surplus (that is, more than is necessary for subsistence), this may be traded for other goods and services. In early societies trade was person-to-person, a barter system, exchanging goods for other goods. As societies develop, trade takes place using an agreed medium of exchange, usually money.

1.2 The production of goods before the industrial revolution was usually small scale and aimed at *local* customers. During the industrial revolution, production became organised into larger units. Towns grew bigger and trade increased as people became more dependent on buying rather than producing these goods themselves. Producers and the markets in which they sold gradually became geographically distinct and separated from each other, rather than confined to remote localities. Before the industrial revolution buyers had direct contact with sellers and so producers were in a good position to know their customers' needs and wants. Later, when buyers lived some distance from producers, it became necessary for producers to find out what products buyers wanted and what product attributes were desired.

### Exercise 1

In Tesco, *Clubcard* and similar schemes award points for sums spent over a minimum amount. The points can later be turned into money-off vouchers. Is this just to encourage people to spend more or, in the light of what you have just read, does it have other purposes?

### Solution

Tesco gave two motives: it wanted to 'say thank you to customers' and recreate the kind of relationship that existed between consumers and local shops half a century ago. The latter point is the important one. Tesco will be able to build a sizeable database of customers' names, addresses and shopping habits. It can then exploit this by, say, targeting its own-brand baked beans at customers who are known to purchase branded beans; find out more about why one family buys its wines and spirits from the supermarket and another does not.

The success of this approach is demonstrated in the way most of the other big supermarket chains have introduced their own 'loyalty cards'.

As you will learn when you read on, it is only relatively recently that producers have once again realised the importance of knowing and caring for the customer.

1.3 Mass production techniques increased the volume and range of goods on the market. Increased productivity also resulted in lower unit costs. The opening up of 'mass' markets created high demand so that until very recently many business problems centred on production and selling rather than marketing, since it was more important to produce *enough* of a product to satisfy strong demand and thinking about 'customer needs' was secondary.

1.4 This was exacerbated in the UK because of its historical pre-eminence in industry and trade. Great Britain dominated world trade up until the First World War. The United States, Japan and Germany then took much of Britain's share in the market for manufactured goods. Present day UK businesses have to compete effectively. Marketing enables them to identify customer needs and to create products that satisfy those needs.

1.5 At present, many markets are saturated, and, for most products and services, excess supply rather than excess demand is the problem. In these circumstances, the focus has switched from 'how to produce enough' (supply factor) to 'how to increase demand' (demand factor). Marketing techniques have grown out of this switch in orientation.

1.6 Simple mass marketing techniques were first applied to selling fast-moving consumer goods such as washing powder, toothpaste and groceries. From a simple set of methods concentrating on advertising and sales, marketing methods have become wide ranging, complex and scientific. Marketing techniques have grown in importance as competition and consumer choice have increased. Marketing methods are seen as a key factor in the success or failure of a product.

1.7 Some areas, such as services and industrial markets, are only now becoming marketing orientated. However, what *is* marketing orientation? The next section aims to answer this question and to discuss the marketing concept in more detail.

## 2 THE MARKETING CONCEPT

*Examined 6/97, 6/96, 12/95*

2.1 There are many definitions of marketing. Here we will consider two which will provide insight into how marketing is used in practice.

2.2 *Definition 1*

> 'Marketing is the management of exchange relationships.'

This emphasises the role of marketing in relating to the world outside the organisation. All relationships which cross the boundary between the organisation and the outside world, especially when they relate to customers, need to be managed. The organisation will be judged by customers, suppliers, competitors and others according to their personal experience. How often have you been put off an organisation by the manner of a telephone operator, or the tone of a receptionist's voice? These contacts are vital in creating a positive image for the organisation with customers and the public.

2.3 *Definition 2*

> 'Marketing is concerned with meeting business objectives by providing customer satisfactions.'

This definition is important because it stresses the importance of the customer, and more particularly, customer satisfaction. When people buy products or services they do not simply want the products, they also want the benefits from using the products or services. Products and services help to solve a customer's problems. It is the solution to these problems that customers are buying.

2.4 A market orientated organisation will have:

(a) a *focus* on meeting the needs of customers which have been clearly identified; and

(b) a *structure and processes* of operation which are designed to achieve this aim. Rather than just employing a marketing manager or a market research department, *all of the company's activities must be co-ordinated around the needs of the customer* when making decisions about what to produce and subsequently how and where the product or service is to be made available to the target consumer.

Underlying all of this is the belief that a market orientation is essential to the long-term profitability of the company.

2.5 In summary, the marketing concept has these elements:

(a) customer orientation;
(b) a co-ordination of market led activities;
(c) a profit orientation, but not-for-profit organisations often employ marketing too (for example, churches or organisations such as the Boy Scouts).

---

**Exercise 2**

How might a profit orientation undermine attempts to *co-ordinate* market-led activities?

**Solution**

The production function might try to increase profits by reducing costs. The marketing function might try to increase profits by emphasising the quality of the product. Lower costs *and* higher quality might not be achievable.

---

2.6 The activities and philosophy of market orientated companies contrast sharply with *production orientated* and *sales orientated* organisations.

Peter Doyle provides a useful distinction between these viewpoints.

(a) 'A *production orientation* may be defined as the management view that success is achieved through producing goods of optimum quality and cost, and that therefore, the major task of management is to pursue improved production and distribution efficiency.'

(b) 'A *sales orientation* is the management view that effective selling and promotion are the keys to success.'

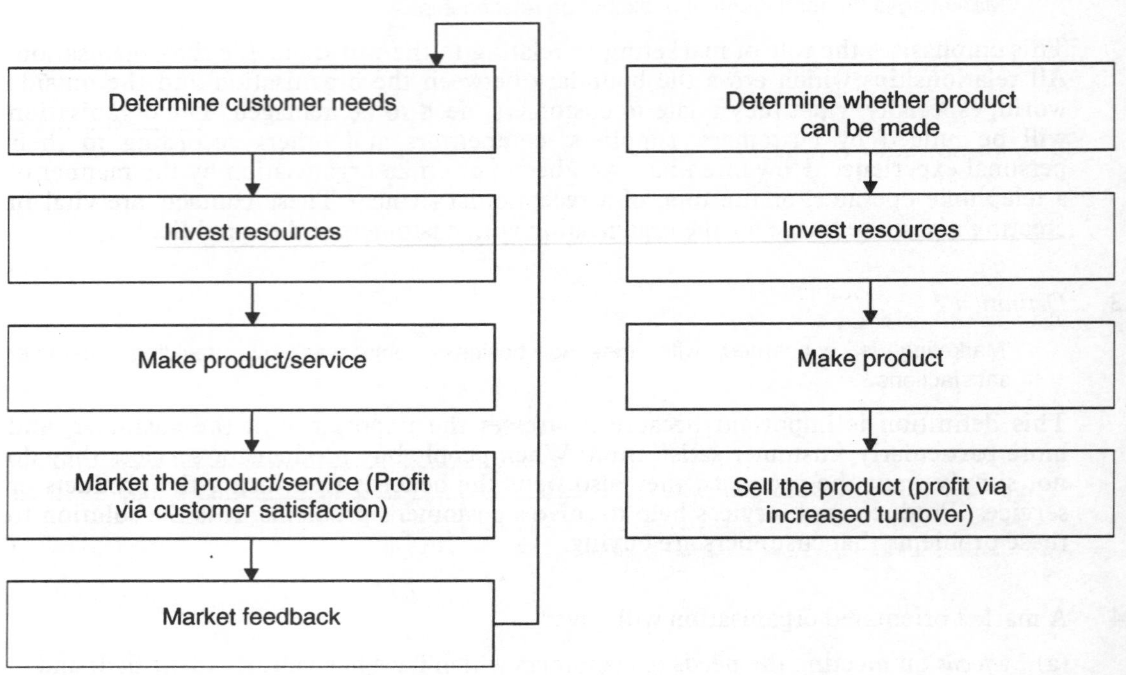


**Exam focus point**

The difference between marketing and selling featured in the June 1995 exam (see Q4 *Marketing and selling* in our Practice & Revision Kit) and also in June 1996 (see Q6 *Selling vs marketing* in our Practice & Revision Kit). One way of tackling this answer is to talk not only about the different jobs that marketers and sales peole do, but about the different orientations outlined above. The issue also surfaced in the June 1997 mini-case (Q92 *Christmas Gems* in our Practice & Revision Kit).

## Customer orientation

2.7 The truism that 'without customers, you don't have a business' remains the logic for maintaining a customer orientation. Satisfying customers' needs at a profit should be the central drive of any company.

2.8 In contrast to following a market orientation however, many companies adopt a *sales orientation*. Here, the tendency is to make the product first and then to worry about whether it will sell. Underlying this philosophy is a belief that a good sales force can sell just about anything to anybody.

2.9 Theodore Levitt distinguishes between sales and marketing orientations in terms of the place of the customer in the marketing process.

> 'Selling focuses on the needs of the seller; marketing on the needs of the buyer. Selling is preoccupied with the seller's need to convert his product into cash; marketing with the idea of satisfying the needs of the customer by means of the product and the whole cluster of things associated with creating, delivering and finally consuming it.'

2.10 The marketing concept suggests that companies should focus their operations on their customers' needs rather than be driven solely by the organisation's technical competence to produce a particular range of products or services, or a belief in the sales force.

2.11 Research into the preference of beer drinkers in the North of England revealed that the *appearance* of the product was a very important source of satisfaction. A common local saying claimed that 'You drink with your eyes'. Popular beers have to *look* as well as *taste* right.

2.12 If new products and services are developed with an inadequate regard for customer requirements, the result will be the need for an expensive selling effort to persuade customers that they should purchase something from the company that does not quite fit their purpose. Repeat purchase is also less likely.

2.13 According to Peter Drucker: 'the aim of marketing is to make selling superfluous'. If the organisation has got its marketing right, it will have produced products and services that meet customers' requirements at a price that customers accept. Little or no sales effort will be needed - in theory!

### Exercise 3

Quality Goods makes a variety of widgets. Its chairman, in the annual report, boasts of the firm's 'passion for the customer'. 'The customer wants quality goods, and if they don't get them they'll complain won't they?'

Is this a marketing orientated firm?

### Solution

No. A mere absence of complaints is not the same as the identification of customer needs. The firm, if anything, has a product orientation.

## Co-ordinating marketing activities

2.14 A true marketing orientation requires a co-ordinated marketing effort. This covers market research to identify customer needs, market-led product development, sales promotion and advertising to ensure that customers know of the existence of the product and its benefits, effective distribution and delivery to ensure availability, and market-based pricing.

2.15 Marketing orientated companies consequently need the following organisational characteristics for an integrated marketing effort.

(a) Marketing functions are identified and co-ordinated under a single executive (market research, product-market planning, advertising and promotion, sales and distribution).

(b) Direct, formal communications are established between the marketing function and executives responsible for development, design and manufacturing, and finance. This ensures direct linkage between market needs and production decisions.

2.16 If marketing effort is directed at making *long run* profits the whole organisation clearly benefits. In the short term, however, many companies will set sales maximising objectives for the sales force. High *sales*, of course, do not necessarily guarantee high *profits*.

2.17 These two positions are represented as follows.

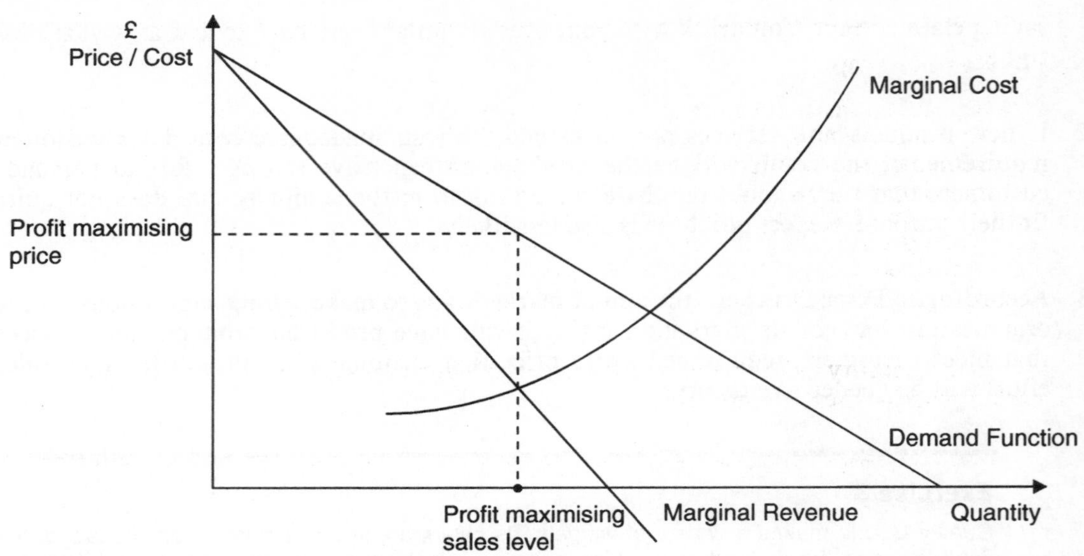


PROFIT MAXIMISATION, where marginal revenue = marginal cost

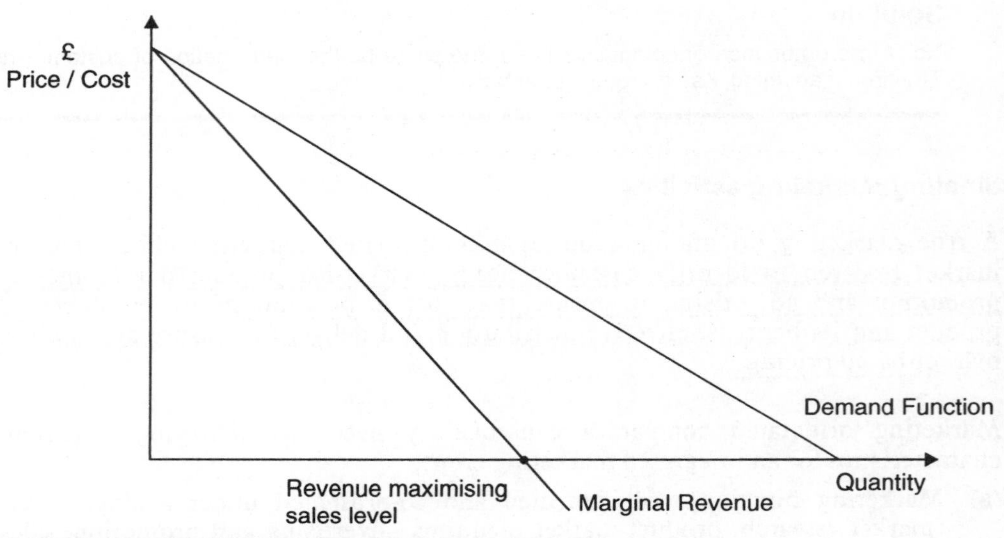


REVENUE MAXIMISATION, where marginal revenue = zero

2.18 If the sales force is directed solely to maximise sales volume, then it may wish to reduce prices or attempt to offer speedier delivery. There will be a greater incentive to reduce prices and disrupt planned production at the cost of overall profitability. Under these circumstances there is likely to be frequent and unhelpful conflict between production and sales departments with an inevitable loss of customer service. Profit margins will fall.

2.19 However, when the sales force is motivated to maximise *profit* rather than sales, it will only wish to make extra sales if this is profitable for the company. The impact on profits will be taken into account before offering a price cut. Similarly, the costs of disrupting production will be considered when deciding whether or not to make a delivery promise that would involve rescheduling production of the next batch of the product.

2.20 Marketing performance must be judged by profit and return on investment - not by volume of sales. The wider implications of marketing decisions must be recognised. If sales are an end in themselves, conflicts with the production departments are almost inevitable.

2.21 Top management must ensure that the marketing department and in particular the field sales force is clear about the objective of increasing corporate profits.

### Case example

The UK subsidiary of Landis and Gyr, the Swiss multi-national, has a rule whereby the sales department can make changes to the production plan without penalty for up to six weeks before manufacture. After this date the sales department's budget must carry all the costs of disrupting the line. The six week period was determined as being a reasonable lead time within which an efficient production system should be able to accommodate change without incurring significant extra costs. Naturally, the appropriate length of such a lead time will be determined by the particular technology being employed in the manufacturing process.

2.22 Using profitability as the benchmark for performance also acknowledges the role of the market place as the ultimate arbiter of success.

### Exercise 4

A customer contacts your company and asks whether it can make a completely silent washing machine. This is not possible with current technology. What is your reaction?

### Solution

Firstly, establish the demand for completely silent washing machines. If demand is sufficiently widespread it is worth trying to address the problem. However, you must find out, by talking to customers, what the *real* problem is - perhaps that the sound travels to other rooms and wakes the baby or annoys the neighbours. There may well be product modifications, or add-on products, that can minimise this problem.

## The marketing concept in practice

*Examined 12/94*

2.23 The term 'marketing' has only come into general use in business since the 1960s. Before that, most companies had a sales department but not a marketing department. The increasing use of 'marketing' rather than 'sales' in job titles does not necessarily mean that all such companies are becoming more marketing orientated. A study by Professor Peter Doyle, funded by the Chartered Institute of Marketing in 1987, concluded that:

> 'British chief executives increasingly recognise the need to make their companies more marketing orientated. But boards of directors are still dominated by a financial outlook and most lack a professional approach to strategy and market innovation.'

2.24 Doyle's study is a good indication of the degree of acceptance of the marketing concept within British industry. A questionnaire was mailed to the chief executives of all the 'Times 1,000' companies, of whom 365 responded. These were classified according to the orientation which the answers revealed.

CORPORATE PHILOSOPHIES

| | % |
|---|---|
| Production orientated | 10 |
| Sales orientated | 21 |
| Marketing orientated | 50 |

Doyle concluded that the remaining 19% of companies responding could best be classified as having a financial orientation, by which he meant:

> 'the management view that success is about using assets and resources to optimise profit and return on capital employed.'

2.25 Even though the marketing concept, and the attempt to match goods to consumer needs, is widely accepted, there will always be a need for an effective sales force. The need to convince the customers that they should buy the company's products arises because it is highly unlikely that their market needs can be exactly satisfied. Also, they may not be aware of the needs which the product satisfies. The sales force will therefore have to overcome the following problems.

(a) The organisation is unlikely to be the only potential supplier. It will therefore be necessary to convince customers to buy from the company and not from a competitor who may also have attempted to match the customer's needs and wants.

(b) Customers may need to be reassured about the benefits of owning or using the company's product or service. In industrial markets buyers will require evidence that technical specifications and appropriate industry standards are met.

(c) It may not be feasible to meet the exact requirements of each specific customer. When mass production techniques are targeted at the average customer's requirements, it may be that no individual's needs are actually satisfied.

(d) Customers' requirements might have changed since market-led production decisions were made. In markets for basic commodities, customer requirements are stable over considerable periods. Other markets are very dynamic and consumer needs change quickly. Markets subject to rapid changes in taste or fashion, such as clothing, leisure and entertainment, are particularly prone to rapid obsolescence.

2.26 Although there will always be the need for a sales force, sales effort will be more successful if products and services meet market needs. A market-led approach will make what is on sale more acceptable to customers. Salesmen are no longer left trying to persuade potential buyers to change their perceptions of what they need. More productive activities such as developing leads and providing better customer service and identifying changes in customer requirements to which the organisation needs to respond can be pursued.

2.27 All good sales presentations are customer orientated. Instead of merely cataloguing a series of product features, the intelligent salesperson concentrates on promoting the benefits that will be derived from the company's product or service. The DIY enthusiast is not necessarily interested in the technical specification of a power drill's electric motor. Whilst this might be the pride and joy of the company's research and development team, the customer is only really interested in finding a *solution* to a range of DIY tasks, for a way of getting a series of 3/16 inch holes to fix some brackets, for example. The good salesperson will ensure that the potential purchaser is assured that using the product will provide the particular benefits sought. In industrial markets such benefits might include the cost reductions that can be gained using the company's products, the reliability of deliveries and product quality.

### Exercise 5

What went wrong in the following cases?

(a) Company A printed 10,000 T-shirts bearing the legend 'England - World Cup 1994'.

(b) The marketing literature for Company B's new toaster proudly proclaims that it has a 2kw element heating to a temperature of 300º.

(c) Company C, which makes electronic personal organisers, has a stand in the computer department of W H Smith's.

### Solution

Think about (a) and (b) for yourself, in terms of what you have just read. For (c), where in Smith's might have been a more appropriate location for the stand?

## Problems in introducing the marketing orientation

2.28 When a sales or product orientated organisation decides to become marketing orientated, there are a number of issues that need to be addressed. Firstly, the organisation should understand what marketing orientation actually means.

2.29 How a company reacts to problems will depend on its orientation. If a company is not marketing orientated then it will possess a product or sales orientated attitude at present. To adopt the marketing concept major organisational, structural and cultural changes will need to happen.

2.30 In changing to a marketing orientated company, the organisation will have to consider products, logistics, level of service and marketing techniques, with the customers' needs as priority considerations. This will require dedication and commitment from every member of the company. Every member of the organisation will have to consider the customer *before* decisions are made rather than making sales or products as a priority.

2.31 Problems may arise within the structure of the company. Sales and product orientated firms do not require the same degree of 'working together' as a marketing orientated company. Requiring production, personnel and marketing, for example, to work towards the same goals will be a difficult task for management and, before a change in the culture of the organisation has been achieved, many conflicting situations will first have to be resolved.

2.32 According to how the change process is organised, when progressing to marketing orientation there may be a state of confusion within the company. The marketing department will take on a larger role with more responsibilities, therefore a full understanding and effective communication is vital.

2.33 Problems will arise if managers do not adopt a marketing philosophy and build it into their culture and mission. Commitment from management is the beginning of adoption from all departments and without total dedication as a whole, changing to a market orientated organisation will be unsuccessful. Customer needs are a priority and until this is recognised by the company as a whole, it will stay as a product or sales orientated business.

## 3 MARKETING ORIENTATED STRATEGY

3.1 So far our consideration of the marketing concept has concentrated on tactical issues - the day to day marketing activities of a company. At this level it is possible to argue that, under certain circumstances, a sales orientation might be preferable. After all, people do buy things that they have little need of after persuasive selling. A particular company may have an effective sales force, but be unable to comprehend or respond to customer needs. Such a company may well be profitable operating a sales orientation, but find it difficult and costly to change towards a customer needs focus.

3.2 On the longer term consequences of ignoring market needs, however, the case for adopting a marketing orientation appears to be overwhelming. Theodore Levitt's seminal article *Marketing Myopia* appeared in the Harvard Business Review in July-August 1960, arguing that a market orientation should determine the longer term strategic direction of companies. If managers perceive the company's business solely in technical and production terms, products will be perceived according to their physical properties. In an industry where competitors probably share similar technical competences, everyone will appear to produce similar products.

3.3 *Marketing Myopia* begins with this bold statement:

> 'Shortsighted managements often fail to recognise that in fact there is no such thing as a growth industry.'

Levitt's argument is that there are clearly large numbers of growth *markets* derived from society's needs, but the *industries* that serve these needs at a particular time may well decline in the face of competition if another industry's new technology better matches the growing market's needs.

3.4 Levitt illustrates his argument with examples of vision blinkered by the production concept of competing for business in a particular industry. The following question is posed.

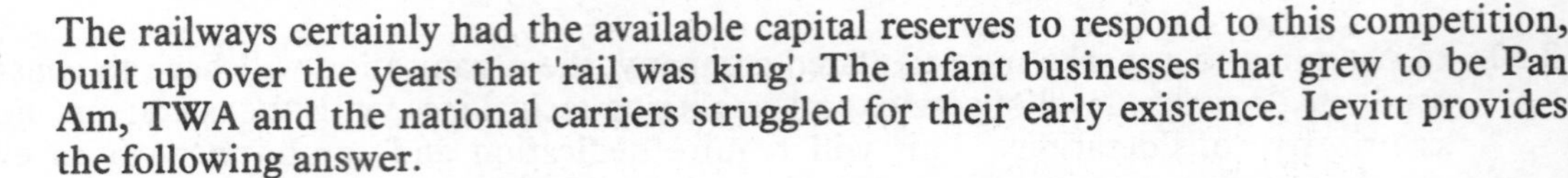

> Q Why did the American Railways not respond to the airlines and trucking companies that eventually took away the railroad's passenger and freight business?

The railways certainly had the available capital reserves to respond to this competition, built up over the years that 'rail was king'. The infant businesses that grew to be Pan Am, TWA and the national carriers struggled for their early existence. Levitt provides the following answer.

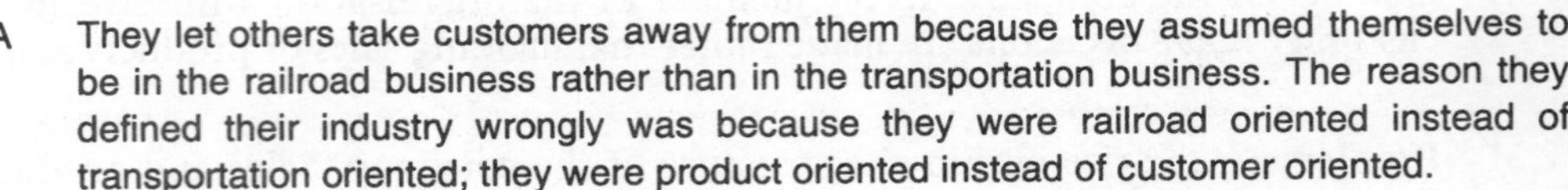

> A They let others take customers away from them because they assumed themselves to be in the railroad business rather than in the transportation business. The reason they defined their industry wrongly was because they were railroad oriented instead of transportation oriented; they were product oriented instead of customer oriented.

The railway industry went into decline even though the transportation market continued to grow by leaps and bounds. By adopting an 'industry focus' the railways did not take on the new enterprises which they did not see as being any part of the railroad business.

3.5 Not all North American railways followed such a 'myopic' stance. Canadian Pacific saw its role in the transportation market clearly, expanding into trucking, shipping and airlines, later moving into telecommunications and telex to adopt the most suitable technology for transporting data. Today Canadian Pacific is one of the world's largest transportation businesses.

3.6 The strategic message is clear. A marketing orientation focuses on the needs of the customer. If these needs change, or a better technology emerges that more closely attends to these needs, the company will be responsive; such events are its business. Responding to such changes is the only way for the company to survive. The marketing concept, as the basic philosophy that underpins corporate strategy, is therefore widely accepted.

3.7 Even if the need to respond to change is accepted, adherence to a production orientation can produce costly mistakes.

---

### Case example

In the late 1950s and early 1960s the American car market was under threat from import penetration, with the Volkswagen Beetle making the most significant inroads.

General Motors, the largest American motor manufacturer, reacted in a way which betrayed the production orientation followed by the company. GM's four main 'badges', used to segment the market place, are:

(a) Cadillac - the super luxury market
(b) Pontiac - the executive range
(c) Buick - middle range
(d) Chevrolet - value for money and young driver segment

The *physical* product characteristics of a VW Beetle might include:

(a) small (by US standards);
(b) rear engined;
(c) air cooled engine (therefore noisy);
(d) minimal instrumentation.

This was the product to which GM was losing sales. Chevrolet, the corresponding wing of the company, set about making just such a product. Naturally the new small car was to be powered by an air cooled rear engine and it would have very basic instrumentation. GM were ill-prepared for this venture. The company was under pressure from senior management to produce the new car quickly. The smallest available engine block was a flat six cylinder that was still very heavy for a relatively small car. The new engine also needed to be air cooled as that was what the customers were buying. To achieve this, Chevrolet mounted a large fan that sat on top of the engine driving air vertically down on to the cylinder heads. To drive this large fan a long fanbelt was added that took the power from the crankshaft via a right angle pulley.

The new car was launched as the Chevrolet Corvair. Its design caused a number of serious problems. The stresses on the fan belt frequently led to either the belt breaking or the bracket holding the right angle pulley fracturing. The car was so noisy that the sound of these mechanical failures could not be heard. Naturally, with minimal instruments the driver could not sense that the engine was now rapidly overheating until, as often happened, the engine either seized or caught fire. To compound these problems, the weight distribution on such a small car with a very heavy rear engine caused difficulties. For safe driving the rear tyres had to be pumped up rock hard whilst the front tyres were kept soft.

After a number of fatal accidents, the consumer activist Ralph Nader produced *Unsafe at Any Speed*, which recounted the story of the Chevy Corvair. The book made little impact until General Motors, unwisely, sued and lost. Nader was established as the leader of the American consumer movement.

3.8 What would have happened if GM had followed a marketing orientation and had attempted to find out why people were buying the Beetle rather than looking at the Beetle's product features? Key consumer benefits might have included:

(a) reliability;
(b) economy;
(c) affordability;
(d) ease of parking.

### Exercise 6

How many products can you think of today that serve the same purpose and yet bear very little *physical* similarity to each other?

## The marketing concept: a critical review

*Examined 12/94*

3.9 Not all commentators accept that the use of the term *marketing* rather than *selling* represents a real shift in basic philosophy. Some suggest that this simply reflects the fact that bringing in revenue is now more complex. It makes sense to use advanced techniques in advertising and market research that were previously unavailable. Others argue that today's 'sophisticated' consumers are more critical and more aware than their forefathers. So-called 'marketing techniques' are simply a continuation of the same old process of persuasion in order to sell products.

3.10 The most strident advocate of this view is the economist J K Galbraith who has summarised his views as follows.

> 'So called market orientated companies have merely adopted more sophisticated weapons for selling the product.'

3.11 Approval of the marketing concept is not universal even amongst those who accept that it represents a real change in philosophy and practice. Thus, the uncritical acceptance of marketing orientation as the established wisdom within both the commercial and academic communities has, itself, been the subject of debate.

3.12 There are two main arguments against the influence of the marketing concept.

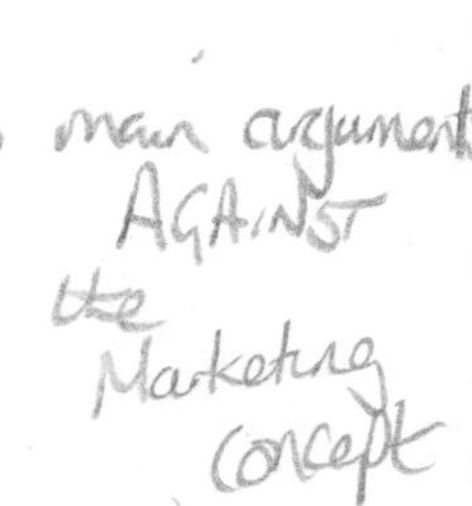
Two main arguments
AGAINST
the
Marketing
concept

(a) Organisations develop a bias that favours marketing activities at the expense of production and technical departments. As a result, insufficient energies go into the development of technical improvements which could offer a more appealing product.

(b) Secondly, apart from attending to customers' current needs, organisations must focus on future customer requirements. Slavishly focusing new product development on satisfying immediate *customer* perceptions of what is needed can, the argument runs, stifle real innovation.

3.13 These points are forcibly made by Bennett and Cooper.

> 'A market orientated R & D strategy necessarily leads to low risk product modifications, extensions, and style changes. Product proliferation, a disease of the seventies, has been

one result. Market driven new product ideas will usually result in the ordinary. Market researchers have become expert at encouraging consumers to verbalise their wants and needs, but people tend to talk in terms of the familiar, about what is around them at a particular moment. For example, ask a commuter what new product ideas he would like to see in the area of rapid transit and, chances are, he will list a number of improvements to his bus or subway system - tinted glass windows, air conditioning, better schedules, and the like. Rarely will he be able to think in terms of totally new and imaginative urban transportation systems. The latter are the domain of the engineer, scientist and designer.'

### Exercise 7

Imagine you are a consumer being asked what features you would like to see if you were buying a new television set:

(a) in the early 1960s;
(b) in the early 1990s.

What is your response?

3.14 The value of the marketing orientation is illustrated in the following case.

### Case example

Eurostar is losing £180 million a year on its London to Paris and Brussels services. Passenger numbers are 40 per cent (about 3.5 million people) short on targets set by parent London & Continental Railways (LCR). And even the most optimistic assessment says it will not break even until 2001 – two years after it was scheduled.

The competing interests of LCR's eight shareholders has been criticised as contributing both to the over-inflated targets it used to secure the Eurostar contract, and to the inconsistency in its advertising and business strategies.

A fast link from central Paris to central London, without air travel delays, should surely be a winner. How could a company involved in this project so significantly fail to meet its targets? City sources, as well as people in the ad industry, have singled out a misguided marketing strategy as the crux of its woes.

"It gave away too many discounts," said one analyst. "Once it had done that it found it increasingly difficult to raise the price."

A senior ad agency source says that the price discounting worked against the message it was putting across in its advertising. "It was made into an aspirational brand through its advertising and marketing. But because it was most relevant to business class travellers it has forfeited everything that made it sexy and exciting in pursuit of passengers."

Personnel changes have also affected Eurostar's consistency. Mark Furlong was seconded from Virgin to be marketing director but moved back to Virgin last November. Commercial director Ian Brookes left to rejoin Virgin in October last year. The arrival of Hamish Taylor as managing director from British Airways 12 months ago was designed to bring more consistency to the marketing effort.

Taylor says the company will develop the leisure market, which makes up about 80 per cent of its business, through product enhancements such as special ski trains, and targeting new customers outside the South East where most of the advertising has run in the past. He is also looking to create a consistency over the business and leisure markets.

"It should have been more confident in marketing the success of Eurostar," says a source close to the company. "The whole Channel Tunnel rail link has been dominated by engineers and finance departments and nobody has ever worked out the potential and what was needed to meet targets. It sacrificed the brand advertising for the short-term need to fill trains cheaply," says the source.

(*Adapted from The Economist*, 10/6/96)

3.15 General Electric, one of Rolls Royce's major competitors, made its commitment to the marketing concept as long ago as 1952.

'(The marketing concept) ... introduces the marketing man at the beginning rather than at the end of the production cycle and integrates marketing in each phase of business. Thus, marketing, through its studies and research, will establish for the engineer, the design and manufacturing man, what the consumer wants in a given product, what price he is willing to pay, and where and when it will be wanted. Marketing will have authority in product planning, production scheduling, and inventory control, as well as in sales distribution and servicing of the product.' (*1952 Annual Report: US General Electric Company*)

### Exercise 8

What would be the effects of introducing a marketing approach to a charity?

### Solution

(a) The reasons for the organisation's existence ('what business are we in?') should be expressed in terms of the 'customer'.

(b) Marketing research should be used to find out:

  (i) who needs help, and in what ways, and how satisfactory is the current help provided;

  (ii) where funds should be raised, and what the best approaches should be;

  (iii) which political figures are susceptible to 'lobbying' and how such lobbying should best be conducted.

(c) 'Target markets' would be identified for charitable acts, fund-raising and influencing.

(d) The charity might also wish to promote an image to the public, perhaps by means of public relations work.

(e) The management of the charity will be aware that they are in competition for funds with other charities, and in competition with other ways of spending money in trying to obtain funds from the public. It should organise its 'sales and marketing' systems to raise funds in the most effective way. (Some years ago the Band Aid charity recognised the potential of telemarketing - ie telephone 'selling' - to raise funds.)

### Customers' wants and needs

3.16 Critics of marketing have accused it of creating unnecessary wants and needs in customers. This is based on a misconception of its nature: the basic principle of marketing is that marketing satisfies customer needs and does not create unnecessary ones. A company which produced products and then tried to create a market for them would be in trouble very quickly: no person can be persuaded to buy something that he does not really want. Marketing can, however, influence buying behaviour, which is complex in its motivations and outcomes.

### Exam focus point

A question in the December 1994 paper (Q3 *Unnecessary needs* in our Practice & Revision Kit) covers precisely this point. To answer it, though, you need a bit more knowledge of buyer behaviour. This debate will go on and on.

## 4 THE BUSINESS SYSTEM

4.1 In looking at how marketing fits into business operations, we will consider three essential systems: distribution, information and the flow of influence.

### The distribution system

4.2 In exchange for payment, goods and services flow from producers to customers through a distribution system. This system has a large number of components, such as credit terms, delivery, insurance, price/discounts/margins and storage.

4.3 The distribution system can be *long* or *short*. Customised industrial goods are often supplied direct from producers to customers. But when international trade is involved, a longer distribution system may involve importers, exporters, agents, wholesalers and retailers.

4.4 The distribution system may be owned by the producer or may be independent. So, for example, a building society's distribution system is its branch network. This is a *short* system. On the other hand, a producer of low value plastic toys may export them in the first instance using a freight forwarder. The overseas buyer may be a wholesaler who then sells to shopkeepers who finally sell to the end consumers. This is a *long* system.

4.5 Customers may be final consumers of the product or service or they may be organisational buyers who in turn are producers of other goods and services for which the purchased item is a component.

### The information system

4.6 Information flow is essential in marketing. Before a customer orientated firm makes and supplies goods or services, it will want to ensure that they meet customers' needs. In other words, it needs information about customer behaviour first. If distributors are independent, the producer also needs to be aware of their needs. The producer needs a flow of information from its market and distribution system. This information should then be used by the firm to construct its product (or service) offering, expressed as a bundle of customer satisfactions.

4.7 The flow of information from the producing firm to its market is referred to as a *marketing flow*. The elements of this marketing flow are price information, product/service information, promotion/advertising information, distributor information and selling information. Together these make up the *marketing mix* for the product or service. The art of marketing is to blend these elements into a unified whole which presents the market with a clear, distinctive product, which offers something different from its rivals. This clear overall message is the product's USP: its *unique selling proposition*.

### Flow of influence

4.8 Business flows do not operate in isolation. Each part of the process has influences on it.

(a) The actions of producers and distributors are influenced by competitors. Each competitor is striving for (competitive) advantage, trying to get ahead of its rivals.

(b) Customer behaviour is influenced by a whole range of factors. People are members of groups and members of organisations and may be influenced by cultural, social, psychological and practical factors.

4.9 To obtain an accurate picture, the whole business system must be considered within its environment. It may be influenced by the following.

(a) *Political and legal factors*, eg employment legislation, advertising laws, legislation affecting sales and purchasing and credit controls.

(b) *Economic influences*, eg income levels, employment levels, the rate of inflation and growth rates in the economy.

(c) *Social influences*, eg friends and family, fashions, politics, and political influences such as voting intentions and attitudes to the EU, South Africa and the Commonwealth.

(d) *Technological influences*, eg information technology, new forms of leisure, robotics and computer aided manufacturing/design (CAM/CAD).

These so called 'PEST' factors will be dealt with later in this chapter in more detail.

## Case example

Tesco has long demonstrated that it has something of a grasp of the way things are moving in UK markets. Politically, too, its antennae look fairly acute – witness this week's news that it will be one of the first to take a major initiative under the Government's welfare-to-work. programme.

The supermarket chain will start recruiting the long-term unemployed in the new year in a pilot scheme at its Cheshunt HQ and in stores at Harlow, Stevenage and on Tayside. During a programme that can be expected to run throughout 1998, Tesco will, it hopes, provide some 1,500 jobs through the scheme.

Not all the recruits will be eligible for the welfare-to-work £60-a-week subsidy provided by the Government, but the TUC made it clear on Monday that the Tesco initiative is very much in keeping with what is now known as the New Deal programme, which means getting people back to work.

Another, albeit cynical, way of looking at it would be to observe that these people could be returned to unemployment after six months, having collected the Government subsidy.

Furthermore, the £4 billion raised for the scheme could be spent through companies that are expanding anyway.

I have no idea whether Tesco is eligible for or is a beneficiary of any of the myriad development funds that are available for expansion in central Europe, but it is undoubtedly the case that the region not only offers untold retail market opportunities but also a comparatively cheap workforce.

(George Pitcher in *Marketing Week, 11/12/97)*

## What is the scope of marketing?

4.10 The table below (adapted from Neil Borden's) shows a list of the types of marketing decision. This is a 'typical' list for a 'typical' organisation. Different organisations operating in different markets will have different organisational structures and so will depart from this list.

**Elements of the marketing mix**

| *Marketing decision* | *Policies and procedures relating to:* |
|---|---|
| Product planning | Product lines to be offered - qualities, design, detailed contents etc<br>The markets in which to sell - to whom, where, when and in what quantity<br>New product policy - research and development programme |
| Branding | Selection of trade marks and names<br>Brand policy - individual or family brand<br>Sale under private brand or unbranded |
| Pricing | The level of premiums to adopt<br>The margins to adopt - for the trade, for direct sales |
| Channels of distribution | The channels to use between company and consumer<br>The degree of selectivity amongst distributors and other intermediaries<br>Efforts to gain co-operation of the trade |
| Selling personnel | The burden to be placed on personal selling<br>The methods to be employed (1) within the organisation and (2) in selling to intermediaries and the final consumer |
| Advertising/marketing communications | The amount to spend - the burden to be placed on advertising<br>The copy platform to adopt (1) product image desired, (2) corporate image desired<br>The mix of advertising - to the trade, through the trade to customers |

| *Marketing decision* | *Policies and procedures relating to:* |
|---|---|
| Promotions | The burden to place on special selling plans or devices directed at or through the trade<br>The form of these devices for consumer promotions, for trade promotions |
| Servicing | Providing after sales service to intermediaries and to final consumers (such as direct mail offers) |

4.11 Customer orientation does not mean that the marketing department can rule the roost over other departments in a company. It must develop relationships with other important departments, as discussed in the next section.

## 5 WHAT IS MARKETING MANAGEMENT?

*Examined 6/95, 12/96*

5.1 The marketing mix is the means by which the aims of marketing management are achieved. It involves analysis, planning and control.

### Analysis

5.2 A marketing orientation begins and ends with the customer. Thus analysis in marketing management involves identifying, for example, who are the customers, why do they buy and are they satisfied with it, having bought it? This process includes *market research* which is covered in more detail in Chapter 4. The process can include quantitative analysis (How many customers? What is our market share? How many competitors?) and qualitative analysis (Why do people buy? What are their motivations, attitudes, personality?).

5.3 In sophisticated companies, market information is integrated into a *marketing information system* which can be used by managers in making marketing decisions. *Decision support systems* use such information to develop effective marketing decision making.

### Planning

5.4 Marketing management also uses the information from marketing analysis to develop the organisation's marketing response - the *strategic marketing plan*.

The strategic marketing plan will involve:

(a) identification of selected target markets;
(b) forecasting future demand in each market;
(c) setting the levels of each element of the marketing mix for each target market.

### Control

5.5 The third main component of marketing management is control of the ways in which the marketing plan is implemented. Control involves setting quantifiable targets and then checking performance against these targets. If necessary, remedial action is taken to ensure that planned and actual performance correspond.

5.6 Marketing organisation within a company's organisational structure involves a range of problems.

### The development of marketing departments

5.7 Although every organisation is different, common patterns appear in the structure of organisations. Departments of marketing are widely thought to have evolved from sales departments. Traditionally all marketplace issues would have been the responsibility of a sales director who would typically report direct to senior management. Marketing orientation was probably absent. At this point, the organisation would usually have been production or sales orientated. When the need for a marketing orientated approach became more apparent a marketing director might appear in parallel to the sales director, but each would have two separate functional departments.

5.8 Organisational structures have generally moved from a sales department to a marketing department. With fuller recognition of the marketing approach to business, sales and marketing may become a single department, with sales as a sub-group within marketing as opposed to marketing being a sub-group within sales.

5.9 At present, the marketing department plays a key role in co-ordinating marketing activities. The marketing manager has to take responsibility for planning, resource allocation, monitoring and controlling the marketing effort. In order to ensure that the marketing effort has maximum effectiveness, this co-ordinating role is crucial, involving co-ordination of marketing efforts for different products in different markets as well as ensuring that individual marketing campaigns are themselves co-ordinated and consistent. As such, the marketing function tends to be thought of as a staff management function with a co-ordinating role, rather than a line management function.

## Organising marketing departments

5.10 The organisational role and form of marketing departments will continue to vary. There is no one format which can be described as 'best' or 'most effective'. The existing organisational structure, patterns of management and the spread of the firm's product and geographical interests will all play a part in determining how it develops. Whatever the format, the marketing department must take responsibility for four key areas:

(a) functions (promotion, pricing etc);
(b) geographical areas;
(c) products;
(d) markets.

These four areas of responsibility will provide insight into how the different forms of marketing department may arise.

### *Functional organisation*

5.11 The department is headed by a marketing director who is responsible for the overall co-ordination of the marketing effort. A number of functional specialists such as a market research manager and a sales manager are found in the second tier of management and they take responsibility for all related activities across all products and markets. This format has the benefit of great simplicity and administrative directness. It allows individuals to develop their particular specialisms, but also imposes a burden on the marketing director who has to co-ordinate and arbitrate activities to ensure the development of a coherent marketing mix for elements of the product range.

5.12 With a limited product portfolio, the burden on the marketing director may not be a problem. As the range of products and markets expands, however, it will tend to become less efficient. There is always the danger that a particular product or market may be neglected because it is only one of many being handled by a single manager who will find it difficult to play a specialist role for all products.

### *Geographical organisation*

5.13 This is an extension of the functional organisation. Responsibility for some or all functional activities is devolved to a regional level, through a national manager. This type of organisation is more common in firms operating internationally where the various functional activities need to be broken down for each national market or group of national markets.

*Product-based organisation*

5.14 Product managers are responsible for specific products or groups of products. This type of approach is likely to be particularly appropriate for organisations with very diverse product assortments or with a very extensive range of products.

5.15 The individual product manager develops plans for specific products and ensures that products remain competitive, drawing on the experience and guidance of functional managers. The product manager is effectively responsible for all the marketing activities relating to a particular product group and consequently needs skills in promotion, pricing and distribution. This approach allows the individual product managers to develop considerable experience and understanding of particular product groups and as such may be effective within a rapidly changing competitive environment. Because they have to undertake a variety of functional activities, the danger is that they will become 'jacks of all trades and masters of none'. In spite of this, the product-based approach is becoming increasingly important because the benefits of managers with expertise related to specific product groups is seen to outweigh the costs associated with a loss of functional specialisation.

*Market management*

5.16 This is a variant on the product management structure. Instead of individual managers taking responsibility for particular products they will instead take responsibility for particular markets. When an organisation sells a variety of different products into particular markets, the understanding of the product is perceived to be slightly less important than the understanding of the market. So managers with knowledge and experience of a particular market are more valuable.

*Matrix management*

5.17 Matrix management can be thought of as an integration of the product and market management approaches. In an organisation dealing with a variety of products in a variety of markets the product-based approach will require managers to be familiar with a wide variety of different markets, while the market-based approach will require managers to be familiar with a wide variety of products. In either case, however, expertise may not be fully or efficiently utilised. The matrix-based system combines the two. A series of managers deals with markets and a further series deals with products. The market managers will take responsibility for the development and maintenance of profitable markets while the product manager will focus on product performance and profitability. The system involves these being interlinked. Each product manager deals with a variety of market managers and each market manager deals with a variety of product managers.

5.18 Although this system may seem to resolve the dilemma of choosing the best form of organisation for a marketing department, it presents certain problems. It is extremely costly, employing large numbers of managers. There are also possible conflicts between product and market managers to consider and, particularly, the issue of who should take responsibility for certain activities. Should the sales force be product or market based and who should take responsibility for pricing?

*Divisional marketing organisation*

5.19 As well as the organisation of marketing within a unitary organisation, of course there are many organisations where the larger product groups are developed into separate divisions (what is often called a multi-divisional or 'M' form organisation). These divisions will have a high degree of autonomy, but ultimately are responsible to a head office. Here, marketing activity will often be devolved to divisional level (see below) although this is not invariable since some marketing decisions will naturally remain the responsibility of corporate headquarters. The extent of corporate involvement can vary from none at all to extensive. No particular level of corporate involvement is more desirable than another; however, it is often suggested that corporate involvement will tend to be more extensive in the early stages of the organisation's development when the divisions are individually quite weak, but as divisions strengthen, corporate involvement in marketing begins to decline.

## Relationship with other departments

5.20 It can be claimed (and often is by marketing managers) that marketing involves every facet of the organisation's operations. The philosophy of a customer orientation, central to marketing, can be argued to be a central business function which is a prerequisite to success. It is easy to get carried away with this argument and thus to understate the role of finance, production, personnel and other business functions. A strongly held conviction by the marketing department that customer orientation is all important can lead to conflict with other departments.

5.21 The table below shows potential conflicts which can arise with other departments in the organisation. Again this can only be a typical list and is intended as a warning of potential dangers. The top management of the organisation needs to take a strong line on any conflicts which arise and to ensure that departmental heads have clear instructions as to the organisation's priorities.

*Summary of organisational conflicts between marketing and other departments*

| *Other departments* | *Their emphasis* | *Emphasis of marketing* |
|---|---|---|
| Engineering | Long design lead time<br>Functional features<br>Few models with standard components | Short design lead time<br>Sales features<br>Many models with custom components |
| Purchasing | Standard parts<br>Price of material<br>Economic lot sizes<br>Purchasing at infrequent intervals | Non-standard parts<br>Quality of material<br>Large lot sizes to avoid stockouts<br>Immediate purchasing for customer needs |
| Production | Long order lead times and inflexible production schedules<br>Long runs with few models<br>No model changes<br>Standard orders<br>Ease of fabrication<br>Average quality control<br>Tight quality control | Short order lead times and flexible schedules to meet emergency orders<br>Short runs with many models<br>Frequent model changes<br>Custom orders<br>Aesthetic appearance |
| Inventory management | Fast moving items<br>Narrow product line<br>Economic levels of stock | Broad product line<br>Large levels of stock |
| Finance | Strict rationales for spending<br>Hard and fast budgets<br>Pricing to cover costs | Intuitive arguments for spending<br>Flexible budgets to meet changing needs<br>Pricing to further market development |
| Accounting | Standard transactions<br>Few reports | Special terms and discounts<br>Many reports |
| Credit | Full financial disclosures by customers<br>Lower credit risks<br>Tough credit terms<br>Tough collection procedures | Minimum credit examination of customers<br>Medium credit risks<br>Easy credit terms<br>Easy collection procedures |

*Source*: Philip Kotler, 'Diagnosing the marketing takeover', *Harvard Business Review*, Nov-Dec 1965 (70-72)

5.22 A continual problem is the relation between research and development (R&D) and marketing. This has already been touched on in this chapter in the context of objections to the marketing concept.

(a) Part of the problem might be cultural. To the marketing department, the R&D department is filled with scatty boffins; to the R&D department, the marketing department would be full of intellectually vacuous wideboys. Furthermore the R&D department may have an 'academic' or university atmosphere, as opposed to a commercial one.

(b) Part of the problem is organisational. If R&D consumes substantial resources, it would seem quite logical to exploit economies of scale by having it centralised.

(c) Finally, marketing work and R&D work differ in many important respects. R&D work is likely to be more open-ended than marketing work.

5.23 That being said, there are many good reasons why R&D should be more closely co-ordinated with marketing.

(a) If the firm operates the marketing concept, then the 'identification of customer needs' should be a vital input to new product developments.

(b) The R&D department might identify possible changes to product specifications so that a variety of marketing mixes can be applied.

---

**Exercise 9**

This is a question that you can discuss with colleagues, or perhaps even write an essay on, based on what you have learned in this chapter.

The phrase 'the customer is always right' was introduced into the retail trade in the 1930s by H Gordon Selfridge, who started up the department store that still bears his name. 'Whatever the true rights and wrongs of the situation, it was to be assumed that the customer was always right.' (*Brewer's Dictionary of 20th Century Phrase and Fable*)

Do you think Selfridge was ahead of his time, or was his concept not the same thing as the 'marketing concept'?

---

## 6 MARKETING AND THE ENVIRONMENT

*Examined 12/96*

### The micro environment: the market environment

6.1 Earlier sections have highlighted the importance of an organisation understanding its operating environment. This understanding enables it to exploit changing market conditions, which is the essence of a successful marketing strategy. The *micro environment* includes all factors which impact directly on a firm and its activities in relation to a particular market or set of markets in which it operates. It also incorporates any internal aspects of the organisation (such as corporate culture) which may influence the development of a marketing strategy. We will consider the market environment and the internal environment in turn.

6.2 The nature of the market environment is outlined in the diagram below. The market environment comprises all aspects of a market which affect the company's relationship with its customers and the patterns of competition. Its importance should not be underestimated, not only because it has a major impact on the operation of a business, but also because the business can, in part, control and change it. Suppliers, distributors, consumers, competitors and interest groups have all been identified as key elements of the market environment.

6.3 Understanding the interactions and the behaviour of these groups enables the firm to use its marketing strategies to encourage loyalty, obtain preference from suppliers/distributors, and influence what competitors do and what consumers think. Equally, through the development of corporate image, it can influence the way the business is perceived by various interest groups. Understanding of and reactions to the market environment can be a key factor in ensuring longer term competitive success.

*The micro environment*

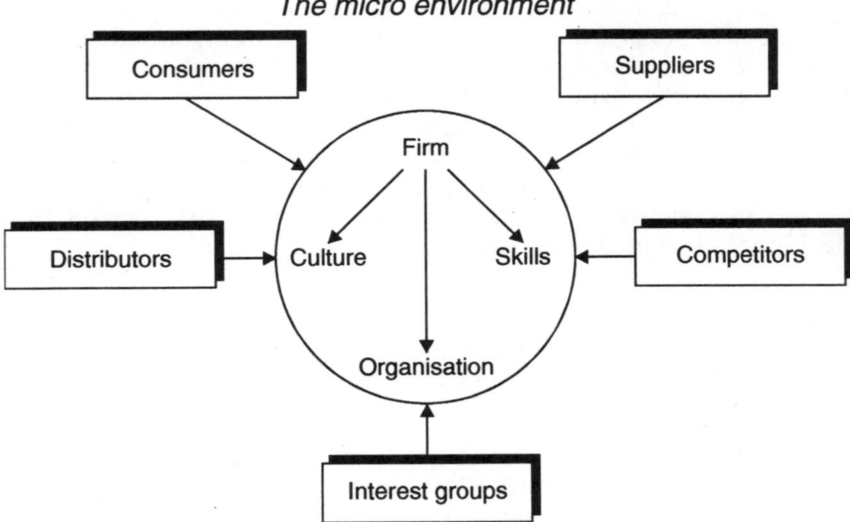


We will now consider each of the key elements of the market environment in turn.

*Suppliers*

6.4 Organisations need information about the number, size and bargaining strength of their suppliers; their ability to guarantee regular supplies, stable prices and quality.

*Distributive network*

6.5 Although the nature and structure of the distributive network is generally treated as a marketing mix variable which can be controlled by an organisation, it is also part of the market environment. There are few instances where a market is so new that there are no existing distribution systems. Normally these systems are in place, and they will impose constraints on what an organisation can do, partly because of consumer familiarity with existing systems and partly because of the degree of market power held by the distribution network. For example, in the UK food industry the decisions taken by food manufacturers are heavily influenced by the market power of the large supermarket chains.

*Consumers*

6.6 Understanding consumers is clearly of considerable importance when developing a marketing strategy. As we shall see later, it bears on many aspects of marketing decisions.

*Competition*

6.7 Marketing as an aid to establishing a competitive position in the market place has already been stressed; any organisation must develop an awareness and understanding of its competitors, their strengths and weaknesses and the essence of their strategic approach.

*Interest groups*

6.8 Finally, any analysis of the market environment must accommodate the role of interest groups (sometimes referred to in marketing literature as 'publics'). These are groups whose opinions and attitudes may affect the success or otherwise of a business. An understanding and awareness of the attitudes of these groups will enable the business to consider how best to present itself to them.

## The micro environment: the internal environment

6.9 The internal environment is where the firm can exercise greatest control because it is here that it possess greatest knowledge. Nevertheless, as was emphasised above, it should not be overlooked because the internal capabilities of the organisation are a key factor in generating marketing success. The analysis of the internal environment rests on an understanding of the nature of the *corporate culture* - the attitudes and beliefs of personnel at all levels. Strategies appropriate for an organisation with a culture orientated towards rapid innovation and risk-taking may be quite different from those available to a company orientated towards high quality and an exclusive image, or those pursued by an organisation which sees itself as a low risk, market follower with a reliable, if traditional product range.

6.10 Understanding the strengths and weaknesses of the structure of the company, and of the personnel within the company are equally important. Internal structures may be changing to reflect the increased pressures of a competitive market place.

6.11 *Marketing audits* help an organisation (and the individuals involved in the planning process) to understand the internal environment. A marketing audit is simply a systematic analysis and evaluation of the organisation's marketing position and performance. It may cover all activities which are either directly or indirectly connected with the marketing function, or it can simply focus on specific products/markets or specific marketing functions. Further distinctions may be drawn between audits at the corporate level, at the divisional level or at the level of the product/market.

6.12 The audit will focus on all the relevant marketing activities, but the following may be singled out as being of particular importance.

### *Marketing capabilities*

6.13 The audit considers in which aspects of marketing the company may be considered to have particular strengths and weaknesses. We may want to know the following.

(a) How flexible/responsive is the organisation of the marketing department?
(b) What is the company's image/reputation?
(c) How strong are particular product lines?
(d) What is the extent of brand loyalty among customers?

Although these assessments are subjective, their importance cannot be understated because they will often form the basis of future marketing campaigns.

### *Performance evaluation*

6.14 This involves comparing the actual achievements of marketing with what was expected - are sales meeting forecasts? Is the message being communicated to the target group? Is the product reaching consumers? This evaluation will identify weaknesses and strengths of current marketing campaigns and processes which can then be modified for this product and for products in the future.

### *Competitive effectiveness*

6.15 This focuses on the source of an organisation's competitive advantage. Analysis requires understanding competitors, the markets they are targeting and the particular features they use to their advantage, and how our product is *differentiated* from those of our competitors.

6.16 There are a number of tools available for marketing audits. Note that the marketing audit should be systematic, should canvass a wide variety of opinions and is frequently based on data gathered by questionnaire surveys.

## The macro environment

6.17 The macro environment is concerned with broad trends and patterns in society as a whole which may affect all markets, but will be more relevant to some than others. Changes in the environment, if identified and carefully analysed, will form the basis for evolving marketing strategies, identifying profitable products and determining the best routes to reach consumers. Careful monitoring of this environment can enable an organisation to identify threats to its business and will enable it to adopt a proactive rather than a reactive stance in the action it takes.

6.18 The macro environment can be described in terms of four key components: political/legal, economic, social/cultural, and technological (PEST factors). The diagram below shows these factors.

*The total environment*

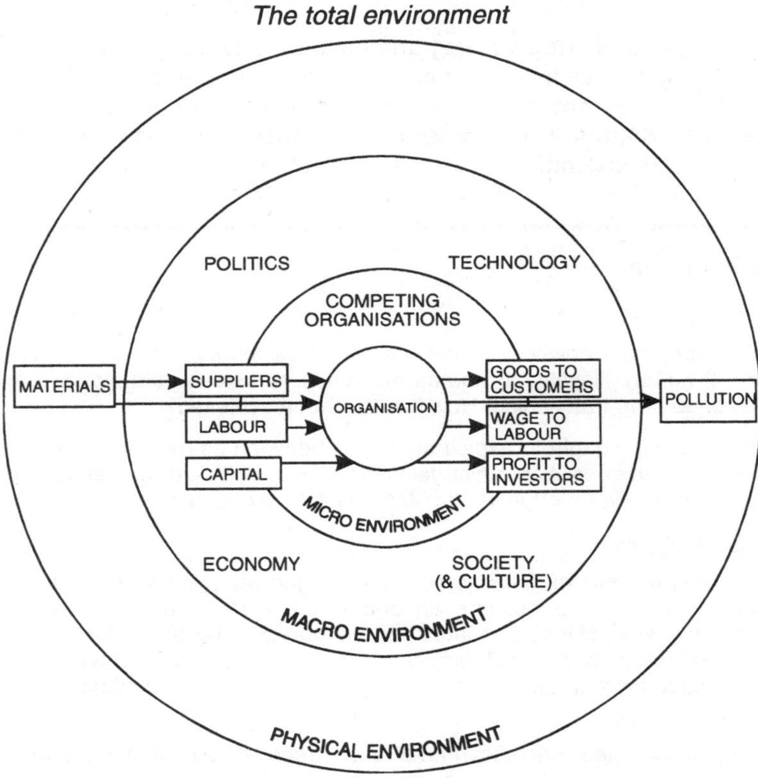


### *The political/legal environment*

6.19 The political/legal environment involves the interaction between organisations and government or regulatory bodies. It includes legal restrictions which governments impose to regulate the pursuits of businesses in a formal sense as well as the equally important but less formal aspects of government relations with industry such as government attitudes to business and willingness to support initiatives. Increasingly, international developments, including the EU (European Union), need to be considered in the context of the legal environment.

### *The economic environment*

6.20 Economic conditions are perhaps the key component of the macro environment. Developments within the economy which are likely to have an impact on businesses either directly or as a result of their impact on consumer spending are obviously of critical significance to any business. Key aspects of the economic environment would include inflation, unemployment, economic growth, consumer income and wealth, interest rates, balance of payments and currency fluctuations.

*The social/cultural environment*

6.21 The social/cultural environment includes demographic change and changing attitudes and perception. The UK, like many other developed countries, has an ageing population, and this of course has many implications for organisations. The changing role of women may also have implications for the marketer. For instance, as more women work, more convenient shopping times have been developing. This is a very wide-ranging set of factors, however, and may involve many different issues.

*The technological environment*

6.22 The technological environment refers to the way in which technology (both the level and the rate of change) will affect the way an organisation undertakes its business.

6.23 When developing marketing strategy any business needs to consider both the micro and macro environmental factors. A successful marketing strategy needs to fit in to the external operating environment, but remain consistent with internal attitudes and capabilities. To illustrate this, one trend that affects businesses, consumerism, will be looked into in further detail.

---

## Case example

*Sony*

In 1994, Sony was nowhere in the video games market; by 1997, it had become market leader. 12 million Playstation games machines had been sold worldwide, while Sega (7m) and Nintendo (4m) trail behind. How has this been achieved?

Sony's marketing sought to exploit synergies between its hardware and software operations, combining expertise in electronics technology with software marketing know-how developed through Sony Music Entertainment (SME), its record company.

*Entering the market*

Sony ignored the market initially, but after Shigeo Maruyama, VP of SME, won a Nintendo machine at a party, he became an enthusiast, and decided that he wanted to produce software for the machine, and launched several popular titles. This gave the company an initial involvement in the distribution of Nintendo software, while at the same time the semiconductor division of the company was making semiconductor chips for the same machine.

Entry into the games machine market was preceded by intensive and meticulous market research; it was decided that the best chance of breaking in would be by launching an advanced machine at the point when the market for Nintendo 'Super Famicon' had become saturated.

Because of the company's technical expertise, production of an advanced machine was not the biggest hurdle. Although Sony was a globally recognised brand, research showed that it had no 'street credibility' in video games. Sony Computer Entertainment (SCE) decided, therefore, to underplay the Sony name and emphasise the Playstation brand in TV advertising.

*Distribution*

As part of the same strategy, it was decided not to sell the Playstation at consumer electronics retailers. Market research in Japan had shown that consumers do not buy video games machines at consumer electronics retailers but at discount stores and specialist video games stores. This unprecedented move triggered protests from shops which normally carried Sony's consumer products.

Fortuitously, Sega's introduction of the Saturn, one month before the launch of the Sony machine, established the superiority of 32 bit technology amongst consumers. Clever promotional work (public relations and publicity in the media) managed to create the common perception that the battle for the 32 bit market was going to be between Sega and Sony, however, wrong-footing Nintendo from the start.

At the same time, the company transferred marketing expertise from SME to SCE, shifting the strategic emphasis from the technology, and the hardware, to the software, which executives from the music division knew would drive the sales of the Playstation. It was decided to sell the games machine at a low enough price to attract consumers, even if this meant losing money initially.

This emphasis on software also encouraged SCE to court independent software producers with more attractive licensing deals than competitors were prepared to offer. Software producers which had been important to the success of the Super Famicon began to shift their allegiance from Nintendo to Sony as a consequence, and the success of the Sony strategy was assured.

*(Adapted from the Financial Times, 7/3/97)*

---

### Ethics/consumerism

6.24 The importance of customer care has been acknowledged as a result of the growth of consumerism. In the UK a number of consumer rights have been recognised in law, including the following.

(a) The right to be informed of the true facts of the buyer-seller relationship, for example:

(i) the true cost of loans (APRs must now be published in any advertisement for loans);

(ii) truth in advertising (watchdog bodies vet any advertisement and consumers complain about advertisements to the Advertising Standards Authority).

(b) The right to be protected from unfair exploitation or intrusion. Consumers' trust in organisations must not be abused. For example, the sale of mailing lists to third parties can lead to consumers receiving vast quantities of 'junk' mail.

(c) The right to a particular quality of life. This right is focused increasingly on environmental protection making suppliers aware of the implications of their actions on the eco-system, and the quality of water, air etc.

6.25 Marketers are increasingly responsive to these consumerist pressures to maintain a good image and reputation with customers and other important publics. This may militate against aggressive marketing tactics; the need to consider the best interests of customers should be paramount in a marketing strategy. The long-term view is necessary rather than attempting to maximise short-term profits.

## 7 THE MARKETING MIX

*Examined 12/96*

7.1 The concept of a *marketing mix*, sometimes known as the *marketing offer*, was first used by Professor Neil Borden of Harvard Business School in 1965, who summarised the concept of the marketing mix as:

> 'a schematic plan to guide analysis of marketing problems through utilisation of:
>
> (a) a list of the important forces emanating from the market which bear upon the marketing operations of an enterprise; and
>
> (b) a list of the elements (procedures and policies) of marketing programmes.'

7.2 Borden formulated a check list of the market forces bearing upon the marketing mix, changes in any one which should lead to a review of the marketing mix and adjustments to take account of new market conditions.

7.3 These market forces are as follows.

(a) The *motivation* of consumers, their buying habits and their attitudes towards products or services in the market.

(b) *Trade motivation* and attitudes, trade structure and practices.

(c) *Competition analysis* requires answers to the following questions.

(i) Is this based on price or non-price actions?

(ii) What choice is available to customers in terms of products, price and service?

(iii) What is the relation between supply and demand?

(iv) What is the company's size and strength in the market?

(v) How many firms operate in the market?

(vi) Is market power becoming more or less concentrated?

(vii) Are there any substitute products or services?

(viii) Are competitors developing new products, pricing strategies or sales promotions?

(ix) Are competitors' attitudes or behaviour changing?

(x) How is the competition likely to react to any of the company's proposed plans?

(d) *Government controls* over the following.

(i) Products (eg government standards - BSI, prohibitions and health and safety legislation)

(ii) Pricing (eg on government contracts, measures to control inflation)

(iii) Competitive practices (eg referrals to the UK Monopolies and Mergers Commission, EU rulings on fair competition, USA Sherman anti-trust legislation)

(iv) Advertising and promotion (eg restrictions on advertising tobacco, gambling and alcohol, limits on the advertising spend on ethical drugs, cooling off periods after signing contracts for personal loans)

7.4 Borden's original (very broad) formulation of the marketing mix includes market forces which are not under the control of the company, and management's response of changes in the company's marketing activities.

7.5 The current, most common, definition of the marketing mix concentrates on the variables under the firm's control that the marketing manager manipulates in an attempt to achieve tactical marketing objectives.

7.6 Marketing mix variables are usually expressed in the form of the *four Ps* of product, price, place and promotion. These four variables are the heart of a marketing plan. Marketing mix variables are highly interactive however; a decision relating to one variable is very likely to have an effect on other elements of the mix. A highly co-ordinated approach is needed if the company is to arrive at the most effective blend of factors.

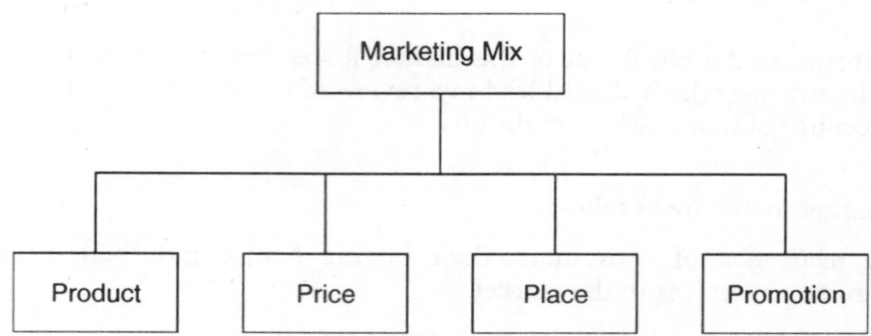

7.7 The four Ps of the marketing mix are often described as 'the controllables', to distinguish elements of marketplace operations that an organisation can influence as opposed to those that are beyond its control. 'Uncontrollables' includes competitor's actions, government policy, general economic conditions and so on. The Hammerite fiasco, however, was caused by factors that should have been entirely within the organisation's control.

---

### Exam focus point

Q7 *Social perspectives* in our Practice & Revision Kit was set in December 1996. It proposed that marketing not only had to satisfy the needs of the *individual* consumer, but also had to take account of the wider social perspective. From a marketing point of view, such a perspective can be justified. It provides an opportunity for segmentation, it pre-empts changes in the law and it also creates an environment in which business can flourish in the long term.

---

## Chapter roundup

- In this first chapter we have looked at the *marketing*, *sales* and *production* orientations and discussed why the marketing orientation has gradually come to be accepted as the most appropriate and the most likely to be successful.
- We have seen how this has resulted in increased importance for the *marketing department*, and we have looked at ways of organising the marketing function in an organisation.
- Finally, we have looked in outline at the factors within the remit of the marketing department; the micro, macro and internal environments and the *four Ps*.
- So far we have considered a well established theory of what marketing is, and how it should be done. It is a *dynamic* discipline however.
- In the past few years marketing, along with the whole of business practice, has been profoundly affected by two new movements: environmentalism and the 'quality' movement. We turn in the next chapter to consider the ways in which marketing practices have been influenced by these two very different factors.

## Test your knowledge

1 Why did mass production lead to the development of the marketing orientation? (see para 1.5)
2 Give two definitions of marketing. (2.2, 2.3)
3 What is a sales orientation? (2.6) How does it differ from a market orientation? (2.9)
4 Why might sales maximising objectives result in lower profit margins? (2.18)
5 Why did Levitt say 'there is no such thing as a growth industry'? (3.3)
6 Where did General Motors go wrong in developing the Chevy Corvair? (3.7, case example)
7 What are the two main arguments against the marketing concept? (3.12)
8 Differentiate between long and short distributive systems. (4.3, 4.4)
9 What are PEST factors? (4.9)
10 What are the advantages of functional organisation for a marketing department? (5.11)
11 What are the disadvantages of matrix management? (5.18)
12 Why should a firm analyse its market environment? (6.3)
13 Name a technique useful in analysing a firm's internal environment. (6.11)
14 Why should a firm take note of consumerist pressures? (6.25)
15 List the market forces bearing upon the marketing mix. (7.3)

**Now try illustrative questions 1 to 3 at the end of the Study Text**

# Chapter 2

# ENVIRONMENTAL AND QUALITY ISSUES

**This chapter covers the following topics.**



| | | *Syllabus reference* |
|---|---|---|
| 1 | Environmental issues | 1.2 |
| 2 | The implications for business | 1.2 |
| 3 | Green marketing practices | 1.2 |
| 4 | The origins and nature of the quality movement | 1.2 |
| 5 | Quality and customers | 1.2 |



## Introduction

These issues, environmentalism and the quality movement, reflect, more than anything else, the significance of the central tenet of the marketing concept - both are founded on an absolute necessity to respond to consumers' needs. Only a short time ago, the relevance of both to many product and service areas would have been dismissed out of hand - as an obsession for a few zealots, but little else.

All that has changed, in a very short period of time. It has changed because companies now realise that, in order to compete, one must be aware of what it is about the product or service that is important to the consumer. The quality movement has insisted that founding the total process of identifying, producing and selling what the consumer wants around this single focus is the only way towards satisfied, and increasing numbers of customers; better profits; and consequently, survival and then prosperity in an increasingly tough and competitive marketplace.

Those same discerning, quality conscious, sophisticated consumers are also looking at how products and services fit into a society which is becoming more and more anxious about the possible consequences of heedless and escalating consumption. Public awareness of the connections between industrial production, mass consumption and environmental depletion and damage is higher than it has ever been, with scientific information flooding out through the mass media and sometimes generating profound public reaction. Food scares, when badly handled, have caused great damage to primary producers and retailers in the UK food sector; when handled well (as, for instance, in the scare over the mineral water Perrier), little damage to sales is caused and the company may even emerge with an enhanced reputation.

Modern marketing practice, then, needs to reflect awareness of these issues, and is being changed by these issues and the resulting practices that are recommended.

Once you have finished this chapter you should understand the following.

(a) Environmental and legal issues will affect the marketing concept more and more in the future; they have already had a significant impact.

(b) Quality issues are very important in a marketing context; consumers are increasingly sophisticated in their demands for better quality products.

## 1 ENVIRONMENTAL ISSUES

*Examined 12/96*

1.1 The marketing concept will undoubtedly be increasingly affected by environmental issues in the future. There is already a considerable impact on marketing policies. In 1990, 26% of all new products marketed in the USA were using a 'green' approach. In the past there has been a tendency to regard marketing, and business activities in general, as antithetical to the concept of 'green-ness', but now it is being recognised that the two are complementary, in many ways.

## Green concerns

1.2 The modern green movement, although arising from concerns over pollution and overpopulation which are centuries old, was given major impetus by studies carried out in the 1970s into the effects of massive growth on the finite resources of the Earth. The possible consequences were underlined by disruptions in the supply of oil and other raw materials caused by wars and economic conflicts. Initial predictions of impending disaster failed to produce a significant change in public opinion, and policymaking on green issues was largely stalled.

1.3 From the mid-eighties onwards, however, a series of ecological disasters (eg the Chernobyl nuclear reaction) reawakened public concerns and sparked general public fears about environmental dangers. Pressure groups, agencies and prominent individuals began to play a part in bringing these issues to the public attention. Consumers are now aware (through the mass media) of the importance of green issues, and at the same time products and services, and the ways in which they are marketed, are changing to reflect this growing consumer awareness. There has been a slight backlash against green campaigners, typified by Channel 4's *Against Nature* early this year. However, if anything, these concerns have been intensified. The forest fires destroying rain forests in Indonesia have been linked to uncontrolled and unregulated logging.

### Exercise 1

In recent years 'green' issues have come into considerable prominence. How have green issues affected the way in which products are marketed?

### Solution

There are many points to make because every stage of a product's life is affected by environmental issues - how it is made, what is made of, how it gets to the customer, what it is used for, what is the effect of its use, and how it is disposed of. 'Green' issues have affected the *product* itself ('ozone-friendly', 'dolphin-friendly'), its *packaging* (recyclable), its *price* (organically produced vegetables are more expensive, for example), and its *promotion* (BMW got a good deal of mileage out of the appealing idea that their cars are almost totally recyclable for the next generation of car drivers).

## The green movement

1.4 The green movement is concerned with humanity's relationship to the environment. A major focus of this is concern about the damage to nature and living things which has come about as a consequence of exploitation of natural resources and modern ways of living. This is expressed through philosophical ideas such as:

(a) stewardship and paternalism;
(b) humanism;
(c) conservationism;
(d) environmentalism;
(e) animal rights and welfare; and
(f) pacifism.

1.5 A major concern is with the study of *ecology* which is concerned with the systems of plant and animal life which exist, and the relationships between them. Major themes of this way of thinking include the following.

(a) The environment is a web of complex interconnected living systems.
(b) Everything, including pollution, goes somewhere into this system.
(c) The balance of nature reflects a natural wisdom which is benign.
(d) All exploitation of nature will ultimately have a cost.

## Green economics

1.6 Conventional economics, according to green thinkers, has failed to deal with the problems of our modern economy. Concentration on labour and capital, rather than land - a legacy of the booming Victorian industrialism which generated such a demand for economics as a modern science - has resulted in a devaluing of the land resource. Economists have not, in the past, placed any price on natural resources such as land or the ozone layer. They are seen as 'free' or worthless, since they play no apparent role in economic activity. Pricing mechanisms, of course, undervalue these resources in favour of manufactured goods, which have a clear derivation from factors such as labour and raw materials availability.

1.7 This 'production orientation', which focuses on products rather than people, is held to be another shortcoming of economics, since it leaves out notions such as 'quality of life' and consumer satisfaction.

1.8 According to green critics, standard economics fails to differentiate the growth-generation of the goods and services produced in response to society's need to replace and renew, for the consequences of decay and destruction, and positive growth. Also, markets do not inhibit pollution; this is only limited by statute. Consumers, however, are assumed to have endlessly expandable and insatiable desires which provide the assurance of constantly expanding markets.

1.9 Green economists have tried to put together an economics based on alternative ideas. These include:

(a) monetary valuation of economic resources;
(b) promoting the quality of life;
(c) self reliance;
(d) mutual aid;
(e) personal growth; and
(f) human rights.

1.10 The *green agenda* is seen by many of its proponents to involve a return to non-material values, partly at least as a reaction to the materialism of the late 20th century in the developed world. Green politics and green values are thought to extend far beyond simple conservation. Political parties in many parts of the world are now embracing green causes, and developing policies which see environmental stress not as a discreet problem, but as a symptom of underlying problems in the institutions which have developed within our modern world. Local concerns, such as pollution, are seen to relate to global issues such as the destruction of the rainforests and the ozone layer. Green groups are now distinct entities, calling on support from a wide spectrum within society, rather than elite, intellectual or marginal 'crank' groups.

1.11 The engagement of powerful mainstream political parties, public figures and interest groups with these issues has seen them fully incorporated into establishment debates. Mass concern is certainly evident, and polls in all developed countries reveal that concern for the environment is likely to be a significant factor in voting habits for the majority of the population from now on. Topics on the green agenda which are likely to generate public concern would include protection of the natural environment (global warming, deforestation etc) and also human environments (population growth, poverty, health etc).

## Which environmental issues will impact upon businesses?

1.12 Environmental impacts may be *direct*:

(a) through changes affecting costs or resource availability;

(b) through impact on consumer demand;

(c) through affecting power balances between competitors in a market - for instance, environmental damage may place some competitors at a disadvantage because of additional operating costs to clean up the product or processes, or affect the availability of raw materials and so on;

(d) legislative change may well affect the environment within which businesses operate.

Finally, *indirect* impacts may manifest themselves in, for example, pressure form customers or staff as a consequence of concern over environmental problems.

1.13 Among the environmental issues which are likely to be seen as relevant to businesses are the following.

(a) *Resource depletion* may influence business operation through impacts on the availability of raw materials through damage to soil, water, trees, plant-life, energy availability, mineral wealth, animal and marine species.

(b) *Genetic diversity* may not seem immediately important for business, but in fact the development of many important new plants, animals, medicines and the new bio-technology which enables commercially valuable materials of all kinds to be synthesised, depends crucially on the availability of wild species from which resources of all kinds can be drawn. In the development of high-yielded and disease-resistant plants, for example, wild species are a critical resource.

(c) *Pollution concerns* are of course at the centre of most worries about the environment.

(i) Businesses are finding themselves under more and more pressure to curtail the impacts of their activities on the *water table*, the *seas* and the *oceans*. Concern over the quality of drinking water, to which this has been linked, has generated a massive increase in the size of the bottled water market in the UK. In the late 1980s, growth rates were around 20% per annum.

(ii) The *quality of air* has been much discussed, owing to the effect of motor car exhaust, and the general impact of road vehicles - clearly this may well have a bearing upon distribution policies.

(iii) Concerns about the *pollution of land*, through landfill policies and the long-term damage wrought by industry upon the land it occupies, are all likely to require some policy changes over the next few years.

(iv) *Noise pollution* is also likely to become more important, and this can have far reaching impacts on the operation of all manner of businesses.

### Businesses and pollution

1.14 In order to take action to remedy these problems, the *polluter pays principle* was adopted by the OECD in the early 1970s. It aims to relate the damage done by pollution involved in the production of goods and services to the prices of those goods. The intention is to deter potential polluters by making it uneconomic to produce goods and services which also create pollution. The principle has been broadly accepted and has been a major factor in reaction to major pollution incidents, such as large-scale oil and chemical spills.

#### Case example

*Acid rain*, which has been linked to large-scale damage to forests throughout northern Europe, and acidification of water supplies and fish-bearing lakes and rivers, has generated massive bills. However, it has not been possible to establish direct culpability, so that the polluter pays principle has not enabled Swedish foresters or Finnish farmers to claim from British industrialists or Russian power stations. So large are the bills involved, and so clear are the impacts on the natural environment and agri-systems, that political pressures to constrain the effects of industrial production have increased enormously.

### Exercise 2

Can you think of further examples of environmental issues which have caused concern in recent years?

### Solution

Similar alarms have been expressed about *ozone depletion*; alternatives to CFCs are being developed to act as solvents in the electronics industry, and coolants in refrigerators. The use of CFCs for blowing polystyrene foam used as insulation by the building industry has been banned in some countries and is being phased out in many others.

*Waste* is causing just as much alarm, whether it is nuclear waste from power stations or industrial or domestic waste in landfill sites. This is increasingly becoming the target of legislation by national governments to control in the domestic arena, and is the subject of new international agreements, arrived at by governments concerned, for example, about the effects of waste dumping on marine life, and on the beaches of many different countries.

*Recycling* is already widespread, and the demand for products and packaging made from recycled materials, or from materials which lend themselves to recycling is increasing steadily. Car manufacturers such as Mazda and Citroen are using plastic components to reduce vehicle weight, and recycling used components.

In addition to these concerns about the impact of production and consumption on the environment, there are also related concerns about the ways in which these affect *human and animal welfare*. The mistreatment of animals in food production, and concern of the inhumanity of certain kinds of animal husbandry techniques has produced a strong reaction amongst consumers. Vegetarianism is on the increase in the UK, and this has had a significant impact on the demand for meat, amongst other changes. There has also been an impact on the sales of cosmetics and other products in which animals are used in product testing.

Related to this, there have been a whole series of *food scares*, some of which have been related to the ways in which food is produced. Obviously, concerns about food safety and dietary health are closely linked to the ways in which chemicals and drugs are used in intensive husbandry and crop production, as well as the forms of feeding which have been employed. The scare over 'mad cow disease' (bovine spongeform encephalopathy) has been linked to the use of recovered proteins from waste meat products in the production of animal feed, although this is still controversial.

All the above can have a very direct impact on aspects of marketing. You might also have thought of problems relating to climatic changes, energy resources and social issues in general. A more extended consideration of social issues can be found in Peattie (1991) and Elkington and Burke (1990).

## Green pressures on business

1.15 Pressure for better environmental performance is coming from many quarters. Consumers are demanding a better environmental performance from companies. In recent surveys, it has been demonstrated that around three-quarters of the population are applying environmental criteria in many purchase considerations. A survey by *Which?* magazine found that 90% of the sample had considered green issues in relation to their consumption on at least one occasion within the past year. They also claimed to be prepared to pay a premium for green products.

*Green pressure groups*

1.16 Green pressure groups have increased their influence dramatically since the late 1980s. Membership of the largest 13 green groups in the UK grew to over 5 million, with staff of over 1,500. This includes the National Trust.

1.17 Groups have typically exerted pressure through three main types of activity.

(a) *Information based*: gathering and providing information, mounting political lobbies and publicity campaigns.

(b) *Direct action*: varying from peaceful protests and the semi-legal activities of organisations such as Greenpeace through to the environmental terrorism of more extreme organisations.

(c) *Partnership and consultancy*: groups here aim to work with businesses to pool resources and to help them improve environmental performance.

1.18 *Employees* are increasing pressure on the businesses in which they work for a number of reasons - partly for their own safety, and partly in order to improve the public image of the company.

1.19 *Legislation* is increasing almost by the day. Growing pressure from the green or green-influenced vote has led to mainstream political parties taking these issues into their programmes, and most countries now have laws to cover land-use planning, smoke emissions, water pollution and the destruction of animals and natural habitats.

1.20 Part of this increased pressure is coming from the *media.* Large scale disasters and more technical, less dramatic issues such as global warming have become common themes for newspaper and television stores, and have generated very widespread public awareness of the issues concerned. Surveys found that coverage of these issues increased by a factor of 10 between 1985 and 1989.

1.21 As a result, the criteria applied by the public at large, and investors in particular have undergone change. *Ethical investment* has grown in popularity, standing at round £200 million in the late 1980s.

1.22 *Environmental risk screening* has become increasingly important. Companies in the future will become responsible for the environmental impact of their acquisitions. As a consequence, many are now checking out the environmental as well as the business and financial profile of enterprises which they might wish to acquire.

**Case example**

Direct action by consumers can have a very immediate impact. During 1995, Greenpeace activists boarded Shell's decommissioned oil rig, Brent Spar, in an attempt to force the company to reconsider the decision to sink the rig in mid-Atlantic rather than demolish and dispose of it on land. Shell's U-turn on the matter was prompted to a great extent by the beginnings of a consumer boycott of its products in Europe, particularly in Germany. Deutsche Shell was caught out very badly, underestimating as it did the level of public feeling on the subject. It was forced to abandon a high-profile corporate environmental and community project advertising campaign which it had just launched.

However, this case also demonstrated the importance of getting your information right. Greenpeace was forced to apologise eventually because it had substantially overestimated the amount of dangerous pollutants still contained within the Brent Spar rig.

## Social responsibility and sustainability

1.23 Green marketing is founded on two main ideas: one is a response to and responsibility for the community; the other is sustainability - the idea that we must be aware of the need for resources to be marshalled and monitored so that the environment can continue to provide inputs and absorb the products of consumption.

1.24 Social responsibility is based on two ideas.

(a) *The moral and ethical responsibilities of businesses*

Businesses must exist within a society which they depend on for continued existence. While businesses control many of the resources available to society, the majority of the population actually contribute to the production of wealth, and justice demands that they share in its benefits. On the other hand, society should not be asked to solve and pay for those problems which businesses cause, without help from those businesses, which have a moral obligation to assist in their solution. Businesses and business people are also socially prominent, and must be seen to be taking a lead in addressing the problems of society.

(b) *The benefits to business of 'enlightened self-interest'*

In the long term, a business's concern over the possible damage which may result from certain types of business activity will safeguard the interests of the business itself. In the short term, responsibility is good for the image of the company - it is a very valuable addition to the public relations activities of a business. In addition, as pressure for legislation grows, 'self regulation' can avoid potentially disadvantageous campaigns.

1.25 Opponents of these ideas, such as Milton Friedman, argue that social responsibility is not part of a company's remit, since it should only be concerned to protect the interests of its shareholders, rather than protect society's interests. Friedman believes that, since unfettered market forces are most likely to produce the greatest degree of affluence, this is what will provide the basis for social welfare programmes. More extreme proponents of this view in the USA even succeeded, in some stages, in having businesses legally prevented from making charitable donations.

1.26 A company's responsibility to society involves the following elements.

(a) Economic responsibilities
(b) Legal responsibilities
(c) Ethical responsibilities (for example, product safety, labelling)
(d) Discretionary responsibilities (corporate donations to charity)

1.27 The degree of morality and legality involved in the social responsibilities of a company may take a number of different forms.

A business may be strictly operated on principles which strive to be:

(a) *moral and legal* (eg the Body Shop);

(b) *immoral and legal* (eg selling arms to brutal military dictators);

(c) *moral but illegal* (eg publishing stolen but revealing documents about government mismanagement);

(d) *immoral and illegal* (eg the drugs trade, employing child labour).

1.28 Many modern companies are publishing the terms under which they choose to operate as a 'code of ethics', although this may well be published under different titles (such as a code of conduct, principles of conduct, guidelines, operating principles, company objectives or a staff handbook). Such principles, when widely disseminated and made accessible to employees, form a valuable basis for developing effective and sensitive policies in relation to environmental issues.

### Case example

The National Consumer Council urged the Government to ban some health claims about food, such as 'nature's way to reduce cholesterol' or 'essential for healthy living'. The proliferation of health messages is confusing consumers, and may, it is believed, be obscuring official advice about a healthy, balanced diet.

Information on labels has led to confusion, and claims about unfamiliar or new foods are virtually meaningless to consumers. Terms such as transfatty acids, Omega 3, taurine, hydrogenated fats, or lactobillus bulgaricus were mystifying, according to a report produced by the NCC, and many carefully qualified claims ('may help maintain a healthy heart' were rejected along with the strange ingredients). One pensioner commented 'Its no good if you've got to have a degree to understand it'. Although short claims and symbols were better received, they often failed to provide sufficient information. The more customers had to read the label, the more they were likely to become suspicious of the claims, or reject them as a 'marketing ploy'. Strict controls about the way these messages are being used has now become vital, the report concluded. The Food and Drink Federation said that these kinds of products were often at the cutting edge of new technological developments, but admitted that the communication of their benefits needed to be improved considerably.

*(Adapted from The Financial Times, January 1997)*

1.29 *Sustainability* involves developing strategies so that the company only uses resources at a rate which allows them to be replenished in order to ensure that they will continue to be available, while at the same time emissions of waste are confined to levels which do not exceed the capacity of the environment to absorb them. In relation to the development of the world's resources, policies based on sustainability seek:

(a) to pursue equity in the distribution of resources;
(b) to maintain the integrity of the world's ecosystems;
(c) to increase the capacity of human populations for self-reliance.

### Case example

Every marketer seeks to differentiate their product or service from competitors, and the Cooperative Bank is an example of differentiating through something more abstract than product or service, but nonetheless real organisational values. The Bank promised its consumers that it would behave in a socially responsible and ethical way, not lending money to repressive regimes, or being involved in business activities which damaged the environment and so on. The end benefit to the consumer is emotional rather than fiscal or directly practical. Why was this policy adopted, and what were its consequences?

For many years personal banking has been dominated by the 'big four' banks, who hugely outspent the Coop in advertising. In the late eighties, personal current account losses were outweighing gains, customer profile was slipping downmarket and identity was becoming blurred. In deciding on a new strategy, the Coop had to choose between positioning itself as another mainstream bank, or finding a way to differentiate itself.

Two factors were crucial in the decision, Firstly, taking on the major banks would require funds which it did not have. Secondly, the bank already had a latent point of difference in ethics. It was owned by the Cooperative Society, not by financial interests in the City; it already had contacts with Community Action Groups, the Labour and Liberal parties and various other 'non-establishment groups', while at the same time the Bank's code of conduct meant that it had no relationships with politically or environmentally unsound organisations.

The decision was taken to capitalise on this heritage, and the bank repositioned itself as 'the bank committed to the responsible sourcing and distribution of funds'.

The results were dramatic. Current account closures fell by 21% and account openings increased by 6% year on year. The proportion of new account openings who were ABC1 increased from 40% to 51% in the same period, and the average size of deposits rose by 9%.

That this is directly attributable to the new ethical marketing is reinforced by the fact that during this time there were no advantageous movements in price, no changes in product, 200 branch closures and a completely unchanged 'share of voice' relative to other advertising for banking services (1%). At the same time, the total market actually declined, and the percentage of customers coming through the Cooperative movement actually fell, suggesting that these new customers were coming from somewhere else. Ethics had been a hugely successful commercial factor for the company. *(Adapted from ADMAP, May 1996)*

## Environmental standard BS7750

1.30 By the early nineties, it became clear that, for many major companies, environmental protection had become a key strategic issue for the remaining years of the century. Industry was now bracing itself for a potential flood of harsh new environmental legislation relating to:

(a) product standards;
(b) plant design standards;
(c) waste reduction and recycling;
(d) civil liability for environmental damage;
(e) environmental impact studies;
(f) packaging; and
(g) eco-labelling.

1.31 Emphasis is moving away from 'end of pipe' pollution control to preventing problems at source. Laws setting standards for products such as packaging materials and manufacturing processes are likely to become more prominent. Faced with growing legislation and public pressure, companies have begun to develop new standards themselves. These are referred to as 'environmental management systems'.

Potential benefits include:

(a) reduced insurance premiums;
(b) easier conformance with environmental legislation;
(c) reduced fines for infringing regulations;
(d) cost savings through more efficient resource use;
(e) improved public relations;
(f) reduced likelihood of environmental accidents;
(g) increased staff motivation;
(h) improved ability to attract and retain staff. (*Grayson*, 1992)

1.32 The world's first standard for environmental management systems, BS7750, developed by the British Standards Institution, follows in the footsteps of the increasingly successful, although controversial, quality standard BS5750 (now ISO9000). BS7750 is now being followed by a European regulation, the *European Eco-Management and Audit* regulation.

1.33 BS7750 provides the basis for a structured, documented system. According to the *Environment Business Supplement* (1992) the main characteristics are that it is:

(a) *generic*: it can be applied to all kinds of organisations;

(b) *pro-active*: to prevent problems at source;

(c) *on-going*: directed towards continual improvement;

(d) *voluntary*: there is no legal requirement to adopt the standard and no specified performance targets;

(e) *systems-based*: involves carefully documented procedures and policy directives.

1.34 Implementing a system which conforms to the standard involves the following stages.

(a) Carrying out a preparatory environmental review.

(b) Defining and documenting the organisation's environmental policy.

(c) Defining an appropriate managerial structure, including the appointment of a management representative with overall responsibility for these areas.

(d) Maintaining registers of environmental regulations and environmental effects.

(e) Setting objectives and targets which must include a commitment to continual environmental improvement, prioritised, quantified and set in timescales.

(f) Formulating an environmental management programme. This will:

  (i) describe the procedures and activities planned to achieve stated targets and objectives; and

  (ii) define responsibilities for achieving them.

(g) Preparing an environmental management manual and documentation.

(h) Preparing documentation, assigning responsibilities and planning operational control procedures for controlling activities and processes which have the potential to affect the environment.

(i) Establishing a record system to enable confirmation that the system is operating.

(j) Setting up an environmental audit system which periodically documents how well the organisation's systems are performing.

(k) Establishing an environmental review system which involves a periodic assessment of the continuing suitability and effectiveness of the environmental management system.

1.35 The new European Union regulation, the *Eco-Management and Audit* scheme, aims to promote continual improvement in environmental performance by requiring participating companies to establish environmental protection system, carry out regulation, systematic audits of the performance of the system, and provide information about this in a public statement. This will be a voluntary scheme, and will not be applied to service organisations.

1.36 At present, response to BS7750 is fragmentary. Many companies feel that ISO9000 (the 'quality' standard) accomplishes many of the same objectives, and are more relevant to the situation of companies involved in, for example, the grocery sector. Yet environmental issues are being taken very seriously indeed by companies in many different sectors.

**Exercise 3**

Environmental matters are often in the news. Over (say) the next month, cut out items from (good) newspapers or make notes from any relevant TV or radio items or programmes which are concerned with environmental matters. Consider the implications for the marketing function of the business, government department etc concerned.

## 2 THE IMPLICATIONS FOR BUSINESS

2.1 'Green marketing' brings a new factor into the traditional nexus of the modern business person. The environment is now part of the 'triangle' involving company, customer and competitor. Environment creates a 'magic diamond'.

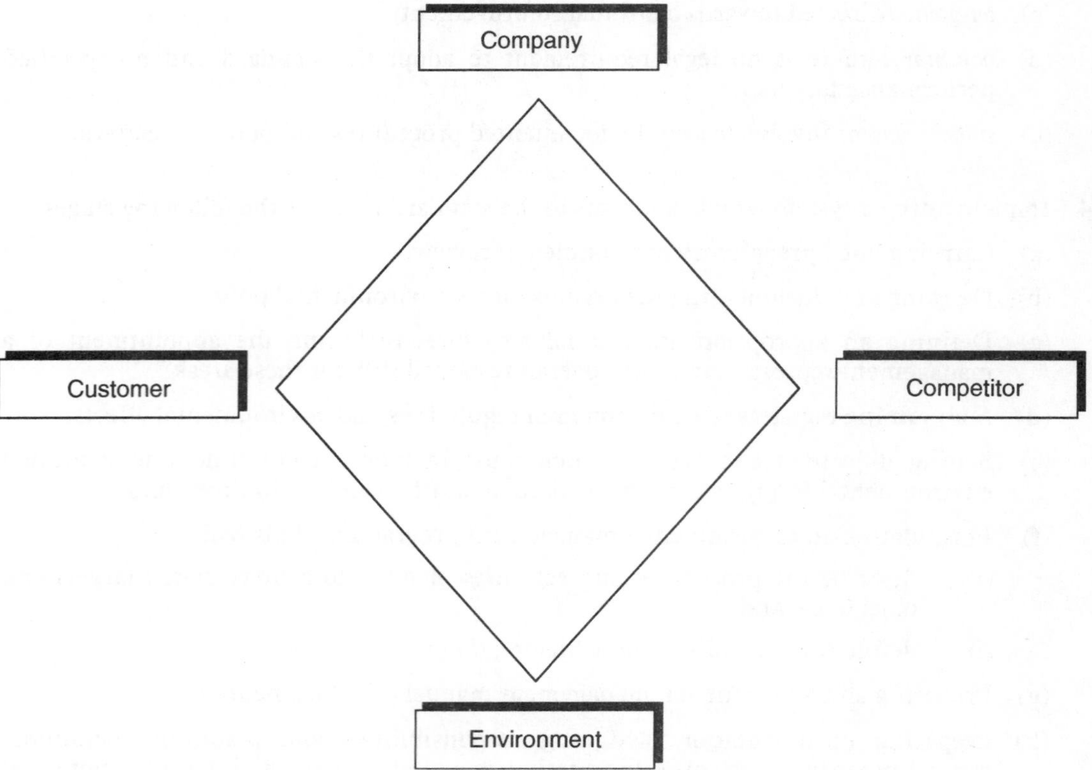


2.2 As the previous section emphasised, there are strong reasons for bringing the environment into the business equation. But the strongest reason is the consumer, and the need to make responsiveness to, and responsibility for, the consumer the central principle of marketing activity.

2.3 The 'green consumer' must be the driving force behind changes in marketing and business practices. If new practices do not meet consumer needs, they will fail.

2.4 *Green consumption* can be defined as the decisions directly or indirectly related to consumer choice and usage which involve environmentally-related beliefs, values, attitudes, behaviour or choice criteria. That this is important is evident from:

(a) surveys which indicate increased levels of environmental awareness and concern;
(b) increasing demand for, and availability of, information on environmental issues;
(c) green product concepts and green substitute products;
(d) value shifts from consumption to conservation;
(e) effective PR and marketing campaigns by environmental charities and causes.

Nevertheless, of course, levels of green-ness vary across the population.

## Segmenting the green market

2.5 Profiles of green consumers show that the force of green concern varies according to product class, prevailing market conditions, attitudes and beliefs about the product in question. Many consumers have not resolved the complex, confusing and often contradictory messages which are being sent out by various interest groups in this area. Broadly, females are more environmentally-aware then males, and families with children (particularly young children) are more likely to be concerned about making green consumption choices. The evidence also shows that consumers are taking the issue on board, and are becoming both more aware and more sophisticated in their approach.

2.6 Marketing Diagnostics has developed a typology of green consumers which identifies four main groups.

(a) *Green activists* (5-15% of the population) are members/supporters of environmental organisations.

(b) *Green thinkers* (30% includes activists) seek out green products and services, and look for new ways to care for the environment.

(c) *Green consumer base* (45-60%) is anyone who has changed their behaviour in response to green concerns.

(d) *Generally concerned* (90%) claim to be concerned about green issues.

2.7 A behaviourally-based *psychographic typology* by Ogilvy and Mather involves a range of factors. Four categories of consumers are identified in terms of tendencies and characteristics.

(a) *Activists* (16%) are:

(i) aware of the issues;
(ii) likely to buy green products;
(iii) concerned for their children;
(iv) optimistic about technological change;
(v) people oriented;
(vi) home owners with children;
(vii) Conservative voters;
(viii) likely to be upmarket consumers.

(b) *Realists* (34%) are:

(i) the youngest group - those with young children;
(ii) worried about the environment;
(iii) consider profit and environmental protection as conflicting;
(iv) are pessimistic about a solution;
(v) are sceptical about a 'green bandwagon';
(vi) vote Labour.

(c) *Complacents* (28%) are:

(i) upmarket consumers with older children;
(ii) are optimistic - about mankind, business and government;
(iii) see this as someone else's problem;
(iv) are not very conscious of green issues;
(v) are right wing politically.

(d) *Alienated* (22%):

(i) less well educated, downmarket consumers;
(ii) young families/senior citizens;
(iii) unaware of green issues;
(iv) see greenness as a fashion or a fad;
(v) are pessimistic about a solution;
(vi) are left wing politically.

2.8 Studies show that consumer behaviour varies in green-ness according to the information which is available to them about the product, the regularity of purchase, the price-sensitivity of the purchase involved, their degree of brand loyalty to existing brands, the availability of substitutes and the credibility of green products which are available. The importance of this issue, and the different factors which are impelling marketers to take it on board, will force a new role for the marketer, in which a greater account is taken of the world outside the company and its priorities; but also in how the company functions internally, and what role the marketer plays in linking these different aspects.

2.9 A successfully green marketer needs:

(a) to understand the consumer's wants and needs;

(b) to understand the environmental issues which are relevant to the company, customer, products and market environment;

(c) to evaluate the degree to which green product attributes fit consumer needs;

(d) to match price to consumer demand;

(e) to develop strategies which identify and effectively meet consumer needs and competitor challenges in relation to green issues;

(f) to promote the flow of environmentally-related information on consumers and product/service performance throughout the company.

### Exercise 4

Make a list of all the branded products you can think of which use 'green-ness' as a major selling point.

## 3 GREEN MARKETING PRACTICES

### Exam focus point

Green marketing featured in the December 1997 exam (the Test Paper of our Practice & Revision Kit). As well as having an interesting subject matter, the format of the question asked you for *notes for a talk*.

### Principles

3.1 How are we to resolve the seeming contradiction between the reduction in consumption which lies at the heart of the idea of green marketing, and the extra consumption which has been the primary aim of marketing as previously conceived? Green marketing begins from the premise that marketing *as such* is not environmentally unfriendly, and that the products and services with which it deals will necessarily become greener to reflect more general awareness of the need to counter the effects of environmental degradation and to develop sustainable management strategies.

3.2 A number of barriers have to be overcome.

(a) *Costs* are likely to be incurred with the need to develop new products and services.

(b) *Technical and organisational barriers* have to be overcome in developing, for instance, practical applications of green energy sources, and in reshaping organisations and their workforces into new ways of carrying out their workroles and promoting new attitudes to their jobs.

(c) At the moment, many of the problems which will need to be addressed are highly *complex*, and there seem to be *conflicts* between the various alternatives available. How do we choose between fuels which create acid rain, and those which produce atomic waste? What about the human consequences of dismantling environmentally unfriendly industries in areas where there are no alternative sources of employment?

(d) Many of the policies pursued by a particular enterprise will have implications for the environment in countries beyond *national boundaries*.

(e) Changes which promote beneficial effects, for example on the ozone layer, may well have *no visible effects* and may be resisted as a consequence.

(f) The fact that problems are generally created, and have to be treated, over a relatively *long time scale* also creates difficulties in promoting policies and mobilising groups to implement them.

3.3 One of the main problems faced by those seeking to implement these green policies is the *lack of certainty* about the nature of the problem, about the *effectiveness* of the remedies proposed, and about the *reactions* of the publics towards which the policies are ultimately directed. In some cases, companies have introduced supposedly environmentally friendly policies and products simply as a means of paying a token allegiance to the idea, or to try to garner extra sales from the gullible. One possible consequence of this is *moral fatigue*: as with other issues in the past, the public may become jaundiced and disenchanted with the whole idea, or sceptical about claims to greenness which are made, in various ways, by almost every manufacturer or service provider.

## Developing the policies

3.4 Green marketers argue that these policies are very close to the spirit of total marketing advocated by Peter Drucker and latterly by advocates of the Total Quality concept, where managerial principles are related strictly to the generation of customer satisfaction. This requires a particular kind of manager, treating all of the company's activities as a holistic entity, and seeking to rethink the ways in which corporate aims (traditionally the pursuit of customer satisfaction and profit through meeting a clearly defined need) can be reconciled with a responsible and sustainable means of achieving them. A new, green, managerial orientation is involved. This will include:

(a) rethinking the balance between efficiency and effectiveness;
(b) rethinking attitudes to and relationships with customers;
(c) rethinking the balance between our needs and our wants;
(d) redefining 'customer satisfaction';
(e) refocussing onto the long-term objective, rather than short or medium-term;
(f) 'less is more';
(g) rethinking the value chain; and
(h) new corporate culture(s).

## Processes for green marketing

3.5 This differs from conventional marketing in:

(a) the *information* which is fed into the process;

(b) the *criteria* against which performance is measured;

(c) the *values* against which objectives are set;

(d) the extent to which the process need to be *holistic*: to permeate and involve the whole organisation.

## Marketing information

3.6 At the heart of green marketing is an appreciation and thorough understanding of the ways in which the company impacts on the customer, the society and the environment. An audit of company performance is therefore essential.

3.7 Customer needs, and their sensitivities to particular environmental issues, need to be closely researched, along with the activities, strategies and policies of competitors. A typical model of analysis, such as the SCEPTICAL list, could be applied to green issues.

**S** ocial factors
**C** ultural factors
**E** conomic factors
**P** hysical environment
**T** echnological factors
**I** nternational factors
**C** ommunication and infrastructure factors
**A** dministrative and institutional factors
**L** egal and political factors

For each of these areas, we can examine which 'green issues' are raised for the company in question.

## Marketing planning

3.8 Marketing plans need to be re-considered in the light of new environmental priorities. Those areas which will require re-definition include:

(a) financial, strategic product/market and technical objectives;

(b) markets;

(c) strategies and action plans - including market share, customer satisfactions and competitor comparisons;

(d) performance and technical aspects of product performance and quality.

### *Performance*

3.9 All of these aspects will have to be fitted within a view of the company's performance which takes account of environmental responsibilities. In addition, the traditional criteria for evaluating success or failure, and the parameters within which they operate, may well have to be re-drawn.

### *Time*

3.10 Timescales also have to be lengthened considerably, since products are now evaluated in terms of their long term effects, as well as the impact of the processes by means of which they have been produced. Programmes designed to clean up environmental impacts often take a long time to become fully operational.

### *Judging success*

3.11 Getting marketing's four Ps (price, place, promotion and product) right leads to profit, according to orthodox ideas. Green marketing insists that the mix must be evaluated in terms of four Ss.

**S** atisfaction of customer needs

**S** afety of products and production for consumers, workers, society and the environment

**S** ocial acceptability of a product, its production and the other activities of the company

**S** ustainability of the products, their production and the other activities of the company

## Competitors and suppliers

3.12 Since greenness will be an important competitive factor, it will be important for companies to have information about their performance here in comparison with major competitors and to be assured that their suppliers are meeting green standards.

## A model of the green marketing process

3.13 As we have argued, the green marketing process requires the matching of those internal variables which the company can control with the strictures of the operating environment which the commercial decision-maker faces. Like conventional marketing, green marketing needs to sort out, not the four Ps of the conventional mix but a blend of internal and external factors. Peattie (1992) describes these as internal and external 'green Ps' to be used as a checklist to diagnose how well the company is succeeding in living up to targets for green performance.

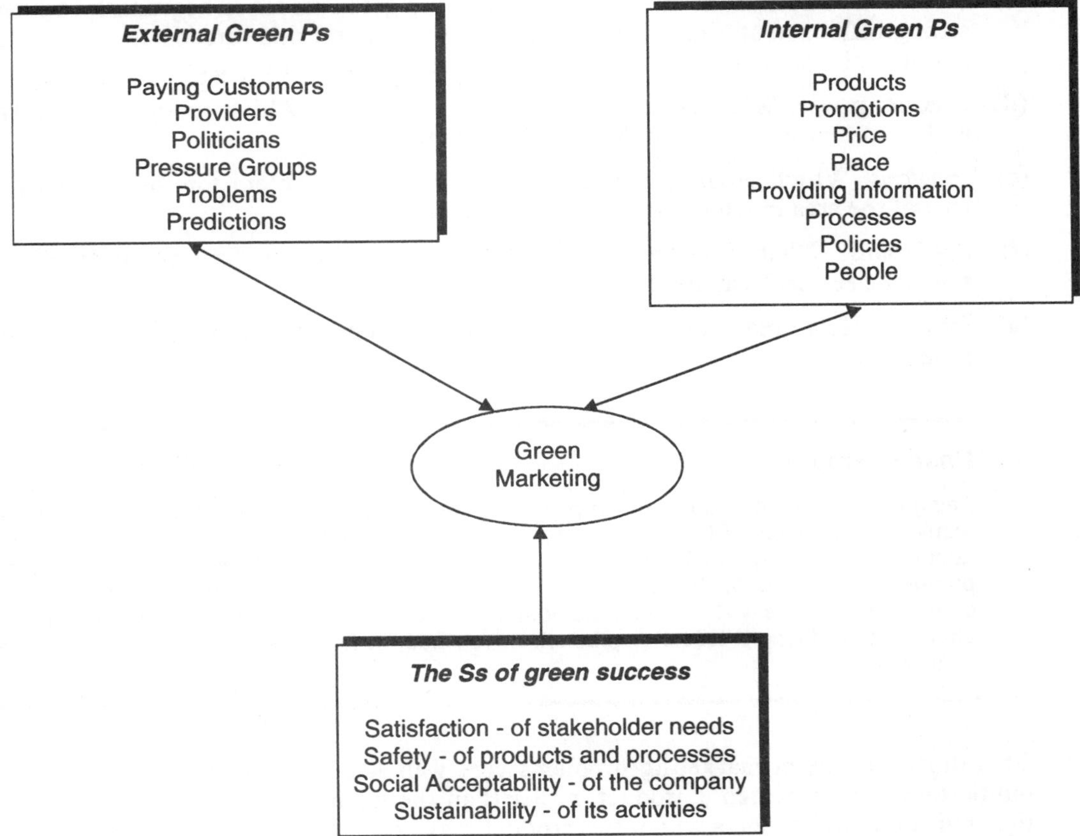


### *Analysing the process*

3.14 Inside the company, marketers need to attend to the following 'internal green Ps'.

(a) *Products*. A green audit needs to look at how safe products are in use, how safe they are when disposed, how long they last, and what are the environmental consequences of materials used in manufacturing and packaging the product.

(b) *Promotion*. Using green messages in promotion. Establishing standards of accuracy and reliability.

(c) *Price*. Prices set for green products must reflect differences in demand; price sensitivity is also an important issue.

(d) *Place*. How green are the methods by which distribution takes place?

(e) *Providing information*. This needs to be related to internal and external issues bearing on environmental performance.

(f) *Processes*. Energy consumed, waste produced.

(g) *Policies*. Do they motivate the work force, monitor and react to environmental performance?

(h) *People*. Do they understand environmental issues, and how the company performs in relation to these issues?

3.15 Outside the company, a different set of factors need to be addressed. These might be referred to as 'external green Ps'.

(a) *Paying customers*. What are their needs in relation to green products and services? What information are they receiving about green products?

(b) *Providers*. How green are suppliers of services and materials to the company?

(c) *Politicians*. Public awareness and concern over green issues is beginning to have a strong influence on the legislation which appears, and this directly impacts on the conduct of business. A modern organisation must make this part of its concerns.

(d) *Pressure groups*. What are the main issues of concern? Which groups are involved and what new issues are likely to concern them?

(e) *Problems*. Which environmental issues have been a problem for the company, or part of the area in which it works, in the past?

(f) *Predictions*. What environmental problems loom in the future? Awareness of scientific research can be strategically vital.

(g) *Partners*. How green are my allies? How are business partners perceived? Will this pose problems?

---

**Case example**

Being able to predict problems can produce great strategic advantages, but also some odd results. The problem of CFCs from aerosols and their effects on the ozone layer was known about from the early 1970s, and Johnson & Johnson abandoned the use of them in their products back in 1975. Consumer reactions to the problem began in the late 1980s, and of course the firm was well prepared, but found themselves in a very strange position, having to attach 'ozone friendly' labels to products which had, in fact, been modified more than ten years before!

---

3.16 This illustrates green marketing problems very well - action is vital at the time when public *perceptions* threaten a product, rather than the manufacturer simply dealing with the environmental dangers which the product may pose. Green marketing practices will have to deal with more and more of these problems, and the old assumption that these worries are simply a 'moral panic' which will run its course and disappear is surely now revealed as wishful thinking.

3.17 Nevertheless, resistance to green marketing within many companies is likely to remain strong. It may be necessary for marketers to *internally market* ideas for these changes. New products, new communications strategies and messages, new 'clean' plant and technology, new appointments of staff skilled in these areas, and very broad changes in organisational culture will all have to be 'sold' to powerful individuals and groups within organisations. Obviously, the internal politics of business organisations need to be taken into account by green practitioners.

3.18 Green marketing needs to be accepted not just into the present policies of the company, but into the way in which it plans and acts far into the future. It is necessary to institutionalise the ideas, and to change the culture of the company by:

(a) building a basis for understanding by setting up frameworks for disseminating information;

(b) formulating systematic plans for the implementation of green marketing;

(c) setting aside resources;

(d) requiring demonstrations of managerial commitment;

(e) encouraging participation and contributions throughout the company;

(f) sustaining an internal public relations programme which creates a healthy response to green ideas.

## How to be green in different business settings

3.19 Businesses, and the settings in which they operate, are endlessly varied, and general principles such as those which we have previously outlined can be of only limited use as a guide for managerial actions. Subdividing the settings within which businesses operate may enable us to identify principles which are more directly relevant.

Four main types can be identified.

(a) Primary industries
(b) Manufacturing industries
(c) Service industries
(d) Not-for-profit industries

3.20 Clearly, further subdivision is possible. Deciding on which green policies are relevant and appropriate for the individual firm must, however, ultimately rest on a careful appreciation of exactly how green issues relate to the circumstances of the particular firm.

### *Mix variations for different industries*

3.21 *Product.* For primary industries, products are often bulky and undifferentiated. One producer may well have only a single product or a small number in their portfolio. Manufactured goods are highly variegated in value, complexity and degrees of differentiation. Service and not-for-profit industries are offering intangible products which present particular marketing difficulties.

3.22 *Place.* Primary products are often bulky and perishable and, as a consequence, distribution is a key factor. The nature of the product, and the pure volume of the market, as for instance in foodstuffs, places particular demands on the technologies involved in storage and transportation, as in the case of food, for example, FMCGs (Fast Moving Consumer Goods) face very different distribution problems, given the variety and complexity of the market segments towards which they are targeted.

3.23 *Price.* Primary product prices are usually fixed in commodities markets. Food product prices are often the end product of complex support mechanisms. Prices set amongst manufacturers are typically cost-based, while services tend to be priced according to demand. Not-for-profit (NFP) organisations do not, as is commonly thought, simply aim to cover costs. Profits here mean better ability to function, and all manner of organisational gains.

3.24 *Promotion.* Promotional activity may be inappropriate and entirely ineffective for primary producers, and what is done tends to be generic. This contrasts strongly with the intensive promotional campaigns mounted by large scale producers of manufactured goods and service providers. NFP organisations are finding promotional campaigns and public relations to be increasingly important, but their funding and expertise in these areas is often severely limited.

### Case example

The barstool politician is a feature of every public house, but now, it seems, political statements are likely to come out of the pumps too. Small brewers in Britain are latching on to popular political causes.

The Isle of Skye Brewery produced 'Extortion Ale' for islanders protesting against the high tolls charged to cross the new Skye Bridge, and found a ready market amongst local publicans. 'Independence Ale' has been produced to appeal to Scottish Nationalist sentiments - albeit by the English-owned Moulin Brewery in Perthshire. The Grolsch-owned Ruddles Brewery found a huge success with its 'Rutland Independence Ale' to celebrate victory in the campaign to reestablish Rutland as England's smallest country.

Beers celebrating environmental issues also seem to be going down well. Beers such as 'Toxic Waste' and 'Acid Rain' have sold well in Somerset. On very different themes, 'GL' (Gay and Lesbian) Lager is selling in large amounts in Britain's homosexual pubs and clubs, raising £10,000 for AIDS-related charities in 1995. *(Adapted from The Economist, 20/4/96)*

### Exercise 5

Consider the environmental impact on marketing in the following contexts. You may want to investigate each of these areas and discuss them with fellow students or colleagues.

(a) Primary industries (eg food production)
(b) Consumer goods manufacturing
(c) Industrial or business to business production
(d) Retailing
(e) Service providers
(f) Not-for-profit sector
(g) Small businesses

## 4 THE ORIGINS AND NATURE OF THE QUALITY MOVEMENT

### Quality issues and marketing

4.1 Quality, in a variety of guises, has become increasingly important for managers in every part of modern business organisations. In Europe and the USA this has been generated by the very visible success of Pacific Rim economies, particularly the Japanese. Many analysts have argued that the central tenet of their business philosophy has been the ability to produce high quality goods closely in tune with the needs of the target market. Although this has been part of everyday conversation for many years, evidence shows that there is a clear connection between 'relative perceived quality' and business performance. Quality of goods or service relative to major competitors is the single most important factor in an enterprise's performance.

4.2 UK studies carried out by the British Institute of Management surveyed 100 leading businessmen, who identified 'building long-term relationships with key customers' and 'creating a more customer centred culture' as the most important factors for success. In this process, the overwhelming majority considered quality and customer satisfaction to be 'very important' and central to this pursuit was the need for a quality approach which was 'marketing led'.

4.3 In the past, quality has been approached by looking at processes of manufacturing and reducing the variability and waste which such systems can produce by using control systems, and introducing methods of checking to assure quality and reliability. The aim is to remove faults and substandard work.

4.4 More recently, approaches to quality developed in Scandinavia and the USA have emphasised the importance of marketing, particularly for the service industries. This approach insists that quality should only be seen from the perspective of the customer, since the customer is the only judge of what is to count as quality. In keeping with the most recent writing on quality systems in general, this services-marketing perspective is entirely appropriate for manufactured goods companies, breaking the inertia of a production-based philosophy.

### Exam focus point

Social responsibility and quality issues can be brought into many questions. In questions about packaging for example, you could mention recyclability – some governments now require that packaging is recycled. Recyclable packaging also reflects well on the organisation in the public eye.

## Multiple definitions

4.5 In everyday life, the term 'quality' is used in rather vague and nebulous ways. It is clear that it may mean very different things in boxing and ballet, in wine and water-skiing. We may know quality when we see it, but, it seems, not everyone agrees as to what it may involve in a single case, and it seems impossible to compare very different sorts of quality, between, say, food products and industrial machinery.

4.6 Definitions abound; it is difficult to reconcile or choose between them. Quality is variously described as:

'... conformance to specifications ...' (Deming, 1986)

'... fitness for use ...' (Juran, 1989)

'... conformance to requirements ...' (Crosby, 1979)

4.7 The British Standards Institution offers a formal definition in BS4778.

'... the totality of features and characteristics of a product or service that bear on its ability to satisfy stated or implied needs.' (BSI, 1987)

4.8 To understand what these definitions mean requires more than merely interpreting what seem to be simple and, in themselves, rather uninformative and vague statements. We therefore need to look more closely at the personalities of the quality movement, the authorities which dominate debate in this area.

### Exercise 6

The boss of Acme Umbrellas Ltd believes that customers want robust umbrellas, so he makes one *entirely* out of aluminium apart from some gold decoration. 'It is a bit heavy I suppose', he says, showing an example. 'But it's *perfectly* made, look at the gold pins and look at the flawless finish. Why don't people want it?'

### Solution

The *design quality* is poor, in that it does not meet customer requirements in an *appropriate* way. The umbrella is, however, perfectly made, so its *conformance quality* is *high*.

## The Quality Movement

4.9 This movement grew from the general alarm which spread throughout Europe and the US during the 1980s as previously successful manufacturing industries failed, while Japanese cars and electronic goods prospered. Japanese takeovers of failing western companies, and turnarounds based on the application of new managerial practices underlined the urgency of understanding what this new approach involved, and how it could be applied here in the UK.

## Why is this new approach needed?

4.10 According to a study carried out by the MIT Commission on *Industrial Productivity in the USA*, failure to compete amongst US and European companies is due to:

(a) outdated business strategies which emphasised finance and marketing to the detriment of manufacturing and adequate investment in human and physical capital;

(b) short time horizons and a preoccupation with short term financial results which inhibits investment in research and development;

(c) technological weaknesses in development and production, and an inability to fully capitalise on technological advances;

(d) neglect of human resources, and a failure to regard labour as anything other than a cost;

(e) failures of cooperation within the organisation so that internal barriers inhibit effective use of resources.

4.11 Poor management practices were the real stumbling block amongst the American firms. Japanese-owned US firms with the same workers and different management practices consistently outperformed home companies. The main differences were in the ways in which Japanese managers used the input of subordinates to determine and clarify goals and to implement work tasks. Workers in the new system are:

(a) more heavily involved in problem solving;
(b) better motivated; and
(c) more skilled, open to learning and flexible;

while companies using the new system are committed to a philosophy of continuous improvement through the participation of all employees.

4.12 There are several ways in which 'total quality' can be approached. Emphasis may be placed on:

(a) quality tools (for example, statistical process control or quality function deployment);

(b) problem solving (for example, spotting defects in production, service, quality circles etc);

(c) error prevention and 'building quality in'.

4.13 These approaches generally fall short of achieving objectives because they fail to bring about a total transformation of the way in which the organisation operates. It involves a cultural change, a change so radical that, for many companies, it will not be brought about unless they are facing a survival threat.

4.14 The principles of total quality management are an amalgam of the ideas of three main thinkers: W Edwards Deming, Joseph M Juran and Philip B Crosby. Each has their own version of how quality can be achieved.

## Deming

4.15 Originally a statistician, Deming worked for General Electric before the war when statistical quality control systems were being developed there. He taught quality control courses during the war, but mainly to engineers and middle managers. After the war, he passed on his ideas when invited to teach in Japan, where top managers were keen to take these new ideas on board. Twenty one executives taking his course represented 81% of the country's capital. His influence was profound, and he was lauded from the earliest days of his work there, receiving the nation's highest honour from the Emperor himself. Yet he remained virtually unknown in his own country even when Japanese products were generally recognised to have surpassed the quality of the western competition by the early 1970s. A TV programme by NBC in 1980 suddenly made him a household name in US boardrooms and he was finally invited to take his rightful part in the revitalisation of the industries of his homeland.

### *The Deming system*

4.16 The foundation of this system is the improvement of products and services by reducing uncertainty and variability in the design and manufacturing processes. Deming saw variability as the chief cause of poor quality, with failure to adhere to the original specifications in manufacturing producing product failure, and inconsistent service frustrating customers and damaging the firm's reputation. As a remedy, Deming proposes an unceasing cycle of product design, manufacture, test and sales, followed by market surveys to gain feedback, after which the cycle begins again with re-design.

4.17 According to Deming, higher quality leads to higher productivity which in turn produces long-term competitive strength. The Deming Chain Reaction proposes that less mistakes mean lower costs and higher productivity, because work does not have to be redone. This has obvious implications for the success of a company.

*The Deming Chain Reaction*

Improve quality → Decrease costs → Improve product-ivity → Increase market share → Stay in business → Provide more jobs and more jobs

4.18 Deming described this method in what he calls 'a system of profound knowledge'. This has four parts.

Appreciation for a system
Some knowledge of the theory of variation
Theory of knowledge
Psychology

4.19 We do not need to look at this theory in any depth here. We merely need to note that Denning produced an accessible methodology which incorporated these ideas in the famous table of *14 Points for Management*. These embody what he saw as the principles which lead to *quality*.

| *Deming's 14 Points for Management* | |
|---|---|
| 1 | Create and publish to all employees a statement of the aims and purposes of the company or other organisation. The management must constantly demonstrate their commitment to this statement. |
| 2 | Learn the new philosophy. |
| 3 | Understand the purpose of inspection. |
| 4 | End the practice of awarding business on the basis of price tag alone. |
| 5 | Improve constantly and forever the system of production and service. |
| 6 | Institute training. |
| 7 | Teach and institute leadership. |
| 8 | Drive out fear, create trust. Create a climate for innovation. |

9 Optimise toward the aims and purposes of the company the efforts of teams, groups, staff areas.

10 Eliminate exhortations for the workforce.

11 (a) Eliminate numerical quotes for production. Instead, learn and institute methods for improvement.

(b) Eliminate MBO (management by objectives). Instead, learn the capabilities of processes and how to improve them.

12 Remove barriers that rob people of pride and workmanship.

13 Encourage education and self improvement for everyone.

14 Take action to accomplish the transformation.

4.20 Deming's work remains controversial, since it calls for fundamental and sweeping changes in organisational culture, and attacks some of the traditional shibboleths of management. It has, however, been highly influential. When Ford became a Deming company in 1981, executives attended seminars given by Deming based on the 14 points, as well as visiting Japan to see the system in action. The following guiding principles were produced.

*Ford's Guiding Principles*

- *Quality comes first.* To achieve customer satisfaction, the quality of our products and services must be our number one priority.
- *Customers are the focus of everything we do.* Our work must be done with customers in mind, providing better products and services than our competition.
- *Continuous improvement is essential to our success.* We must strive for excellence in everything we do; in our products, in their safety and value; and in our services, our human relations, our competitiveness and our profitability.
- *Employee involvement is our way of life.* We are a team. We must treat each other with trust and respect.
- *Dealers and suppliers are our partners.* The company must maintain mutually beneficial relationships with dealers, suppliers and our other business associates.
- *Integrity must never be compromised.* The conduct of our company worldwide must be pursued in a manner that is socially responsible and commands respect for its integrity and for its positive contributions to society. Our doors are open to men and women alike without discrimination and without regard to ethnic original or personal beliefs.

4.21 The president of Ford commented at the time.

'The work of Dr Deming has definitely helped change Ford's corporate leadership. It is management's responsibility to create the environment in which everyone can contribute to continuous improvement in processes and systems. What stands out is that he helped me crystallise my ideas concerning the value of teamwork, process improvement and the pervasive power of the concept of continuous improvement.'

## Juran

4.22 Victor Juran's career has paralleled that of W Edwards Deming in many respects. Like Deming, Juran worked for Western Electric in the 1920s, as a corporate industrial engineer. In 1951 he produced his opus magnum the *Quality Control Handbook*, in print continuously since that time. He then taught quality to the Japanese, taking over from Deming, and played a significant role in the commercial successes which they subsequently enjoyed. His message is very similar.

4.23 Juran believes, with Deming, that lack of quality leads to competitive failure and huge costs, and that the only remedy for this is new thinking about quality which includes all levels of the management structure. The top level, he avers, is particularly in need of training on the importance of management for quality.

4.24 While Deming proposes fundamental cultural changes which strike at the very core of every organisation, Juran aims to fit his quality program into a company's current strategic planning with the minimum risk of rejection. Employees, he states, speak different languages in the different levels of an organisation, and this must be taken into account. While top managers speak the language of dollars, workers speak the language of things, and middle managers must be able to speak to both and mediate between them.

4.25 Quality issues, he states, must be rendered into the language which the various levels of the organisation can understand and deal with: the top level relating to quality via issues of accounting and analysis of quality costs, while the operational level relates to it through increasing conformance to specifications, through elimination of defects. As can be seen, this sits comfortably alongside most of the priorities and presuppositions which managers already have.

4.26 He defines quality as 'fitness for use'. There are four components to this.

(a) *Quality of design*: focusing on market research, the product concept and design specifications

(b) *Quality of conformance*: technology, manpower and management

(c) *Availability*: reliability, maintainability and logistical support

(d) *Field service*: promptness, competence and integrity

4.27 Quality is, he says, pursued on two levels:

(a) the mission of the firm as a whole; and
(b) the mission of each individual department within the firm.

4.28 Like Deming, Juran sees the pursuit of quality as a never ending cycle of market research, product development, design, planning for manufacture, purchasing, production process control, inspecting and testing. Once the product is sold, feedback is obtained, and this initiates the cycle once more.

4.29 Juran's ideas are focused around the *quality trilogy*. This is constituted by the following.

(a) *Quality planning*

(i) Identifying customers
(ii) Determining their needs
(iii) Developing product features to meet those needs
(iv) Establishing quality goals
(v) Setting short and long term strategic plans to reach those goals

(b) *Quality control*

(i) Determining what to control
(ii) Establishing units of measurement for objective evaluative data
(iii) Establishing standards of performance
(iv) Measuring actual performance
(v) Acting in response to the data

(c) *Quality improvement*

(i) Proving the need for improvement
(ii) Identifying specific projects for improvement
(iii) Organising to guide the projects
(iv) Diagnosing the problem areas
(v) Providing remedies

(vi) Providing evidence of the effectiveness of remedies
(vii) Providing control to maintain improvements achieved

4.30 Juran believes that it is the neglect and low priority given to quality planning and quality improvement which are the major weaknesses in western companies. Japanese companies have succeeded by implementing quality improvement programmes supported by massive management training and the enthusiastic commitment of top leadership. As a consequence, the Japanese experience demonstrates the value of this investment in terms of competitive advantage, reduced failure costs, higher productivity, smaller inventories and better delivery performance.

## Crosby

4.31 P H Crosby developed his ideas during a successful career at International Telephone and Telegraph (ITT), where he moved from line inspector to corporate vice-president over a period of 14 years. He describes his system in two sets of principles, the 'absolutes of quality management' and the 'basic elements of improvement'.

4.32 The 'absolutes of quality management' are as follows.

(a) *Quality means conformance to requirements, not elegance*

Crosby insists that quality is a series of requirements which must be clearly stated. It can then be communicated and measured to see if it has been achieved. These measurements will establish the presence or absence of quality. Absence of quality is a nonconformance problem or an output problem. How requirements are set is a managerial issue.

(b) *There is no such thing as a quality problem*

Problems arise in specific departments and must be identified by those departments. Quality, as well as a problem, is created in a specific department and is not the province of a specific 'quality' department within the organisation.

(c) *There is no such things as the economics of quality; it is always cheaper to do the job right first time*

Quality is free. Nonconformance costs money.

(d) *The only performance measurement is the cost of quality*

The cost of quality is the expense of nonconformance. While most companies spend almost 20% of their revenue on quality costs, a well run quality management programme can reduce this to less than 3%. A major part of the programme involves measuring and publicising the costs of poor quality, to focus managerial attention on this problem.

(e) *The only performance standard is zero defects*

Zero defects is a performance standard, with the theme 'do it right the first time'. This means concentrating on the prevention of defects rather than finding and fixing them.

4.33 This is, Crosby argues, a matter of concentrating, of applying the same standards we have in our private life to the way in which we approach the workplace. He asserts:

> 'Most human error is caused by lack of attention rather than lack of knowledge. Lack of attention is created when we assume that error is inevitable. If we consider this condition carefully and pledge ourselves to make a constant effort to do our jobs right the first time, we will take a giant leap towards eliminating the waste of rework, scrap and repair that increases cost and reduces individual opportunity.' (Philip Crosby, *Quality is Free,* 1979)

4.34 This is quite clearly different from the ideas of Juran and Deming, neither of whom would have placed this emphasis on the responsibility of the line worker when the majority of imperfections in the system of production are due to poorly designed equipment and systems which are beyond the control of the individual.

4.35 'Basic elements of improvement', the other aspect of his system, includes three themes:

(a) *determination*, or the commitment of management to this process;

(b) *education*, which involves transmitting the absolutes to the members of the organisation; and

(c) *implementation*, which should clearly specify the process whereby quality is to be established within the organisation.

4.36 This has proved a popular approach because it emphasises behaviour processes within organisations rather than simply the use of statistical techniques. At the same time, it does not stipulate what a programme will involve in fine detail. As a consequence, it can be fitted alongside existing corporate strategies with minimal disruption and tailored to the enterprise involved to accommodate all kinds of idiosyncrasies.

## 5 QUALITY AND CUSTOMERS

### Total Quality Management: the marketing implications

5.1 The indications are that from now on, quality will evolve around marketing-led developments. As the discussion of the main quality gurus demonstrates, such agreement as exists on the definition of what quality involves refers to customer needs: to deliver quality is to identify and produce what customers need. This is, recognisably, a close connection with the core of the marketing concept: to identify and meet customer needs at a profit.

### Total quality and total customer orientation

5.2 A *customer orientation*, seeking to satisfy the customer, is pursued in marketing by recognising that customers buy 'the sizzle, not the steak' - products are bought for the benefits they deliver; how customers can use the product to accomplish the things they want to do.

5.3 Feigenbaum (1983) identifies Total Quality Management (TQM) directly with the customer. TQM is defined as:

> '... the total composite product and service characteristics of marketing, engineering, manufacture and maintenance, through which the product and service in use will meet the expectations by the customer.'

5.4 What constitutes a 'quality product or service' must, it seems, be related to what the customer wants. Indeed, quality would have no commercial value unless it delivered customer benefit, since the key reason for aiming to produce quality products is to derive extra sales, to establish competitive advantage through tangible and generally perceived superiority in particular product or service features. All the gurus would agree that the customer must be the final arbiter of the quality which a product possesses.

5.5 From a marketing point of view, then, *quality is in the eye of the consumer*. This being so, marketing approaches to quality must accept the limitations which follow. If quality is meeting the requirements of the consumer, then it should be recognised that throughout and beyond all enterprises, whatever business they are in, is a series of 'quality chains'.

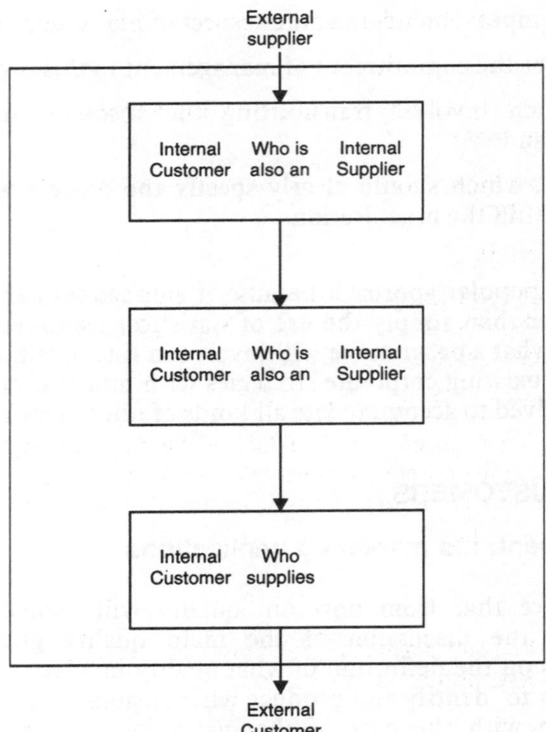


5.6 John Oakland argues that *meeting customer requirements* is the main focus in a *search for quality*. While these requirements would typically include aspects such as availability, delivery, reliability, maintainability and cost effectiveness, in fact the first priority is to establish what customer requirements *actually are*.

(a) If the customer is *outside* the organisation, then the supplier must seek to set up a marketing activity to gather this information, and to relate the output of their organisation to the needs of the customer.

(b) *Internal customers* for services are equally important, but seldom are their requirements investigated. The quality implementation process requires that all the supplier/customer relationships within the 'quality chain' should be treated as marketing exercises, and that each customer should be carefully consulted as to their precise requirements from the product or service with which they are to be provided. Each link in the chain should prompt the following questions.

*Of customers*

- Who are my immediate customers?
- What are their true requirements?
- How do or can I find out what the requirements are?
- How can I measure my ability to meet the requirements?
- Do I have the necessary capability to meet the requirements? (If not, then what must change to improve the capability?)
- Do I continually meet the requirements? (If not, then what prevents this from happening, when the capability exists?)
- How do I monitor changes in the requirements?

*Of suppliers*

- Who are my immediate suppliers?
- What are my true requirements?
- How do I communicate my requirements?
- Do my suppliers have the capability to measure and meet the requirements?
- How do I inform them of changes in the requirements?

5.7 It should be noted that this focus on the customer does pose a number of problems.

(a) *Quality is subjective*

(i) If quality is relative to customer expectations, it cannot be measured in an absolute sense.

(ii) Different customers will want, need or expect different things from the same product-type.

(b) *Quality is distinctive*

Product differentiation and highly segmented modern markets mean that the precise requirements of a particular market segment will impart an equally precise and differentiated definition of quality.

(c) *Quality is dynamic*

Expectations, and therefore definitions of quality, are highly dynamic: they change over time as a consequence of experience. A ratchet effect is highly likely, so that expectations will rise relatively easily, but will rarely and very reluctantly fall.

## Quality and gap analysis

5.8 If quality is the outcome, marketing processes are very clearly the main instruments by means of which this problem can be solved.

5.9 Parasuraman *et al* (1985) have applied 'gap analysis', developed within the services marketing field, to the realisation of quality in manufacturing and product marketing. It involves focusing on the potential gaps between identification, interpretation, specification, delivery and reaction to services. Customer satisfaction - solving the customer's needs in the delivery of a quality product or service - occurs when these are matched, and the gaps are minimised. Dissatisfaction (a poor quality product or service) occurs when these gaps are broad.

5.10 A key differentiating feature of service quality is that it is judged by the consumer not simply on the outcome of the service (what the service is intended to deliver) but in addition on the process of delivering the service (the way in which the service is delivered). In relation to services marketing, what is emphasised here is the *inseparability of services*: the fact that services are produced and consumed at the same time.

## Quality gaps

5.11 Gap analysis proposes that customer perceptions of the quality of a product or service are determined by the degree to which they believe it meets their expectations. These expectations are created from a variety of inputs. These would include physical aspects, service elements and other cues available.

5.12 Gap analysis sets out to measure levels of satisfaction, or dissatisfaction, to identify the source of dissatisfaction when it occurs and to eliminate it. Customer expectations, of course, refer to what *should* be delivered, rather than what they may believe will be delivered. The central issue is how customer expectations develop; what are the sources of unrealistic or inappropriate requirements?

5.13 Clearly, what expectations are raised depends on the way in which the organisation treats the customer. A company which is product-orientated starts with its own beliefs about what the customer expects and creates a specification to guide the production or creation process. The product or service which is delivered in this case reflects the company's perceptions of quality, rather than the customer's.

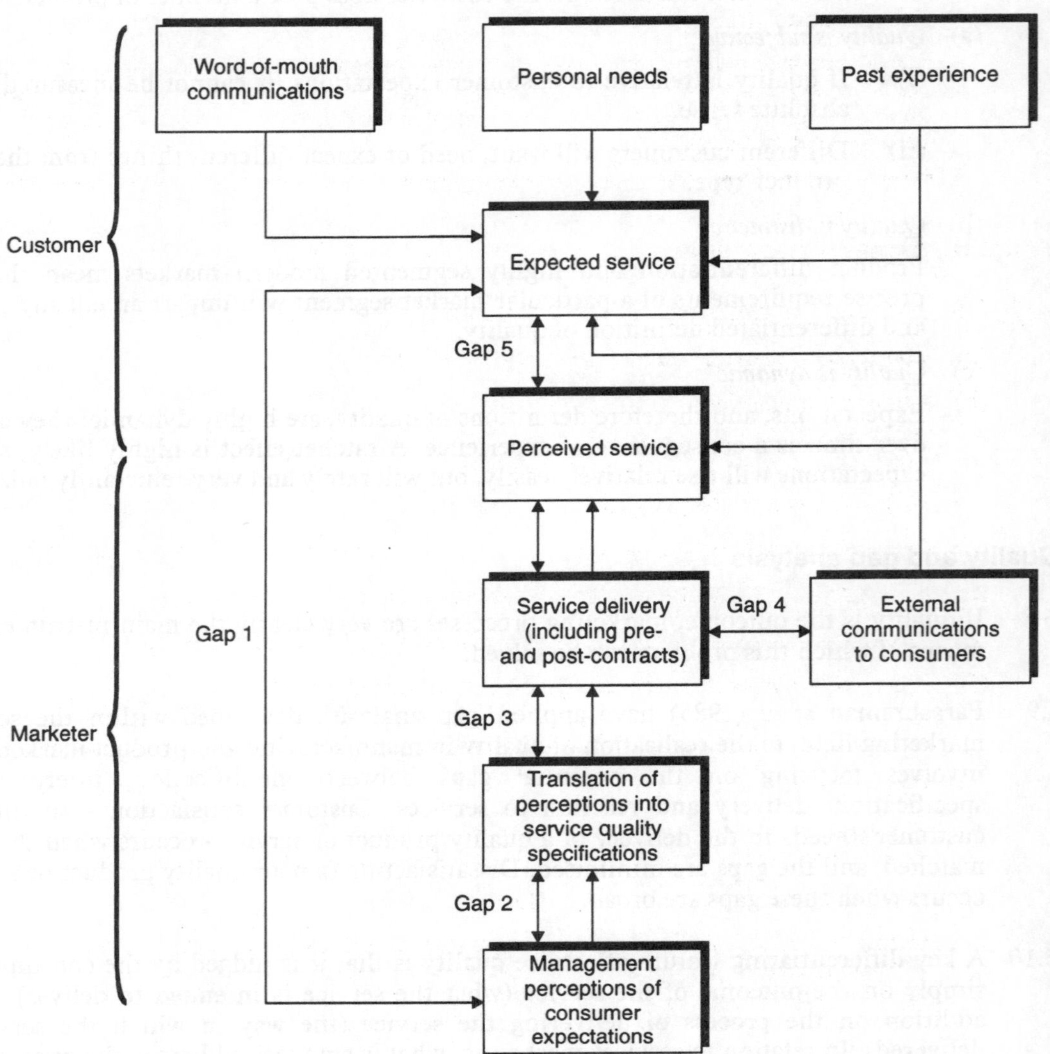


(Adapted from: Zeithaml, Parasuraman, Ber
*Delivering Quality Service*, 199

5.14 **The major factors which determine customer expectations and perceptions with regard to service quality are:**

**(a) word of mouth communications;**
**(b) personal needs; and**
**(c) past experience.**

5.15 **The 'gaps' which can cause dissatisfaction, are between:**

**(a) customer expectations and marketers' perceptions;**
**(b) marketers' perceptions and (service or product) quality specifications;**
**(c) quality specifications and delivery;**
**(d) delivery and external communications;**
**(e) perceived service/product and expected service/product.**

5.16 **A marketing orientation to a quality programme starts from the identification of what the customer expects. This is, of course, quite likely to be varied and the key to using this idea is to gather marketing intelligence using appropriate methodologies and making this information available, in an appropriate and useable form, to managers within the organisation.**

### Exam focus point

We will cover customer care in more detail later in the text. In any discussion about products, services and customer care you can bring in quality as the underlying principle. Quality is subjective, distinctive and dynamic and, ultimately, exists in the mind of the customer. So it is very relevant to the marketing mix.

## Mounting a quality programme

5.17 Successful programmes typically involve a number of key characteristics.

(a) *Total involvement:* a culture change is involved

(b) *Customer orientation:*

  (i) Who are our customers?
  (ii) What do they want?
  (iii) What are the obligations involved?

(c) *Quantified processes:* measurement is critical to monitor progress and improvement

(d) *Commitment* and leadership from top management

(e) *Strong process* (eg systems being implemented and strictly observed)

(f) *External customer objectives* are given the highest priority

### Exercise 7

You have just overheard the following conversation. The Board of a company are in a meeting and they are having a 'full and frank exchange of views' (ie a blazing row).

*Chairman:* Ladies and gentlemen, *please....*

*Marketing director: No,* he's said quite enough. Customers are *our* department, and all this TQM nonsense is just another, yes *another* example of those jargon-spouting boffins and bodgers in production trying to encroach on my turf! I *do* need resources. I don't need white-coated robots criticising the angles at which I fix the paper clips on to my reports!

*Chairman:* Ladies and gentlemen, *please....*

*Production director: No,* she's said quite enough. Marketing people couldn't give *one* hoot, let alone two, about quality and we all know it's quality that sells the goods. Remember, when we had to abandon our solar powered torch? State of the art, state of *the art* that was, and did they try and sell it? Did they?

*Chairman:* Ladies and gentlemen, *please.....'*

*Finance director:* 'No, they've both said quite enough. If all we get out of TQM is pointless rows like this, I might as well go back and count some more beans. At least it's *meaningful* and relaxing.

*Chairman:* Ladies and gentlemen! No, you've all said *quite* enough. I don't think any of you have grasped the point. I'd better get another management consultant in with a better flipchart.

What insights do each of the above characters have into TQM?

### Solution

The chairman has got the gist. All of them miss the point as to the nature of TQM. The marketing director has a point in that TQM *does* imply a blurring of functional boundaries, but the marketing director *ought* to be pleased that, if TQM is implemented, the marketing concept will be brought into product design. The production director still has not grasped the concept. His idea of quality is 'technical excellence' not fitness for use. The finance director ought to care, as TQM has meaningful cost implications. The row is not pointless: at least the issue is being discussed, which is a beginning.

## Quality and British Standards

5.18 Many companies have, or are striving to obtain, certification under BS EN ISO 9000. This is a nationally-promoted standard, only awarded after audit and inspection of the company's operations, which certifies that the company is operating to a structure of written policies and procedures which are designed to ensure that it can consistently deliver a product or service to meet customer requirements.

5.19 This is an important form of quality assurance, but you should be aware that there is a sharp distinction between BS EN ISO 9000, which emphasises effective documented *systems*, and TQM, which emphasises the importance of *attitudes* - enthusiasm and commitment to quality.

## Chapter roundup

- *Environmental issues* have become more important over the last 10-20 years, with the emergence of the green movement and green economics.
- Environmental issues will have a *direct* and *indirect* impact on both marketing practices and on businesses in a more general sense.
- Environmental *protection* is now a key strategic issue and businesses setting up environmental management systems will probably use the guidance given by BS7750 (as well as the quality standard ISO9000).
- The *green market* has become significant and it is possible to segment the market into activists, realists, complacents and alienated.
- Green marketing practices must overcome a variety of *barriers*. A new 'green' orientation is required in obtained marketing information, marketing planning and creating a green marketing process.
- As we can see, the heart of quality programmes are the need to define, research and respond to customer need. This is the *marketing orientation* at work. Quality programmes complement this core element with the *formulation of systems* which ensure sustained and consistent delivery of the desired processes and products. Further, their insistence on *commitment* from all parts of the organisation, on *monitoring and measurement* to check that the systems are working, and the requirement that the very top management should provide *leadership* on these issues, aims to take this consumer-driven approach to management from a broad principle which may lack practical implications, to the heart of a management philosophy which aims at nothing less than the transformation of the processes with which it is concerned.
- The full implications of the issues discussed in this chapter will become clearer as you work through the rest of the text.

## Test your knowledge

1 What are the major philosophical ideas on which the green movement is based? (see para 1.4)

2 What alternative ideas are encompassed by green economics? (1.9)

3 Differentiate between the direct and indirect impacts of environmental issues on marketing. (1.12)

4 Define 'sustainability'. (1.29)

5 What are the main characteristics of BS7750? (1.33)

6 How should an environmental management system be instituted under BS7750? (1.34)

7 How can the green market be segmented? (2.6)

8 What are the main barriers to green marketing practices? (3.2)

9 What are the 'four Ss' of the green marketing mix? (3.11)

10 List the 'internal green Ps' (3.14) and 'external green Ps'. (3.15)

11 Give some definitions of 'quality'. (4.6, 4.7)

12 Reproduce the Deming Chain Reaction. (4.17)

13 List Deming's 14 Points for Management. (4.19)

14 What is Juran's 'quality trilogy'? (4.29)

15 What are Crosby's absolutes of quality management? (4.32)

16 Define total quality management. (5.3)

17 Define gap analysis. (5.11, 5.12)

**Now try illustrative questions 4 and 5 at the end of the Study Text**

# Chapter 3

# THE STRATEGIC IMPLICATIONS OF A MARKETING ORIENTATION

**This chapter covers the following topics.** *Syllabus reference*



| | | Syllabus reference |
|---|---|---|
| 1 | Marketing strategy | 1.3 |
| 2 | The planning cycle | 1.3 |
| 3 | Marketing planning and strategy | 1.3 |
| 4 | Strategy formulation | 1.3 |
| 5 | Market segmentation | 1.3 |
| 6 | Positioning products and brands | 1.3 |
| 7 | The marketing plan | 1.3 |



## Introduction

Marketing was, until recently, seen as a distinct functional activity playing primarily a *tactical* role in business development. This view has been superseded by the recognition that marketing has a key *strategic* role. *Strategic planning* sets or changes the objectives of an organisation. *Tactical planning* is concerned with decisions about the efficient and effective use of an organisation's resources to achieve these objectives.

Modern consumers are more sophisticated and quality conscious than ever before. To deal with such rapid change, an organisation needs a planned approach to guide development in an increasingly uncertain business environment. Effective planning will enable any organisation to adopt a *proactive* stance to its markets, to anticipate changes and remain competitive. Plans must be flexible and adaptable in this age of uncertainty.

Once you have finished this chapter, you should understand the following.

(a) A marketing orientation has strategic implications for a company.

(b) The marketing process as a whole will become clear as this chapter offers an overview of marketing within the organisation.

(c) Developing and growing a marketing strategy requires planning at various levels.

## 1 MARKETING STRATEGY

*Examined 6/97*

1.1 *Corporate strategic plans* are intended to guide the overall development of an organisation. Marketing *strategies* will be developed within that framework. To be effective, these will inevitably be interlinked and interdependent with other functions of the organisation. The strategic component of marketing planning focuses on the direction which an organisation will take in relation to a specific market or set of markets in order to achieve a specified set of objectives. *Marketing planning* also requires an *operational* component which details specific tasks and activities to be undertaken in order to implement the desired strategy.

1.2 This approach ensures that marketing efforts are consistent with organisational goals, internally coherent and tailored to market needs and that the resources available within the organisation are systematically allocated.

### Strategies

1.3 Strategies develop at several levels. *Corporate strategy* deals with the overall development of an organisation's business activities, while *marketing strategy* focuses on the organisation's activities in relation to its markets. *Deliberate strategies* are the result of planning. *Emergent strategies* are the outcome of activities and behaviour which develop unconsciously but which fall into some consistent pattern.

In practice, most strategies are part deliberate and part emergent.

1.4 Strategic marketing has three key components:

(a) the designation of specific, desired objectives;
(b) commitment of resources to these objectives;
(c) evaluation of a range of environmental influences.

Note that the strategy does not just focus on organisational *efficiency*; it is more important that the organisation should be *effective*. *Efficiency* here relates to doing a task well, but *effectiveness* relates to doing the right task - having the right products in the right markets at the most appropriate times.

1.5 An organisation can only be effective if it is aware of and responsive to its environment. Marketing is by definition 'strategic', since successful marketing of a product requires that the firm has the right type of product and is operating in the right markets.

1.6 Strategy also has a dynamic component. To be truly effective the organisation should not only be 'doing the right things now', it needs to be aware of and prepared to anticipate future changes to ensure that it will also be 'doing the right things in the future'. Planning and strategy enable managers to think through the possible range of future changes, and hence be better prepared to meet the changes that actually occur.

---

### Exercise 1

Has your business got a formal 'corporate strategy'? Read it and think about its effects on marketing strategy.

---

## 2 THE PLANNING CYCLE

---

### Exam focus point

The issues raised in this chapter are most likely to be examined in the compulsory *mini-case*. You are given a short scenario describing a business and you might have to develop some ideas as to how it could market its products more effectively. For example, the June 1997 mini-case *Christmas Gems* (Q92 of our Practice & Revision Kit) covered the changing needs of customers and introducing a marketing orientation to the firm.

---

2.1 The link between the development of marketing strategies and marketing plans and overall corporate strategies and corporate plans will be made clearer if we consider their relative positions in the *planning cycle*. A typical planning cycle begins with the collection of information from all areas of the organisation. Financial and production data and also marketing research data will be gathered. Individual functional departments also provide an input to the corporate planning process. This phase is often described as *'bottom up' planning* since the main information flow is from lower to higher levels of management.

2.2 The second phase involves the organisation and analysis of the information to formulate an overall *corporate plan*. This will specify organisational objectives and means of achievement in the short, medium and long term. The plan outlines broad aspects of overall corporate development and provides a framework within which specific functions can develop their own plans. This phase is referred to as *'top down' planning* since the flow of information is now from senior to junior levels.

2.3 'Bottom-up' and 'top-down' planning enable corporate planners to provide a coherent structure for the organisation's development. This provides a framework to enable managers to think ahead and anticipate change and allows patterns of resource allocation within the organisation to be clearly identified. The plan also benefits from the specific experience of managers close to markets or functions within the organisation.

2.4 Although the planning cycle has been presented as having two discrete phases, in practice it is a continual process. Annual plans guide short-term developments, but are developed within the framework of medium and long-term plans which will themselves be updated as the operating environment changes.

## 3 MARKETING PLANNING AND STRATEGY

### Developing a marketing activity

3.1 A marketing plan should follow a logical structure:

(a) from historical and current analyses of the organisation and its market;

(b) on to a statement of objectives;

(c) then to the development of a strategy to approach that market, both in general terms and in terms of developing an appropriate marketing mix; and

(d) finally to an outline of the appropriate methods for plan implementation.

Implementation may appear at the end of any discussion of marketing plans. Arguably, the process of monitoring and controlling marketing activities is the most crucial factor in determining whether a plan is successful or not.

3.2 The main function of the plan is to offer management a coherent set of clearly defined guidelines, but at the same time it must remain flexible enough to adapt to changing conditions within the organisation or its markets. The stages in strategic planning are as follows.

Development of the organisation's mission statement
↓
Statement of objectives
↓
Situational analysis
↓
Strategy development
↓
Specific plans
↓
Implementation

### Company mission statement

*Examined 12/95*

3.3 The company mission statement is simply a statement of what an organisation is aiming to achieve through the conduct of its business; it can even be thought of as a statement of the organisation's reason for existence. The purpose of the mission statement is to provide the organisation with focus and direction.

3.4 Factors influencing the development of the mission statement include:

(a) corporate culture;
(b) organisational structure;
(c) product/market scope;
(d) customer needs;
(e) technology.

This approach forces managers to think of the customer groups and the particular set of needs/wants which the firm is looking to satisfy, and so is particularly relevant to marketing.

3.5 A mission statement can offer guidelines to management when considering how the business should develop and in which directions. With the benefits of a clear mission statement, future growth strategies can rely on what are regarded as distinctive competences and aim for synergies by dealing with similar customer groups, similar customer needs or similar service technologies.

### Case example

Here is part of a mission statement. How good do you think it is?

ROYAL MAIL: MISSION

As Royal Mail our mission is to be recognised as the best organisation in the world distributing text and packages. We shall achieve this by:

- excelling our Collection, Processing, Distribution and Delivery arrangements
- establishing a partnership with our customers to understand, agree and meet their changing requirements
- operating profitably by efficient services which our customers consider to be value for money
- creating a work environment which recognises and rewards the commitment of all employees to customer satisfaction
- recognising our responsibilities as part of the social, industrial and commercial life of the country
- being forward looking and innovative

## Statement of objectives

### Exam focus point

Mission was specifically examined in December 1995 (Q16 *Mission implications* of our Practice & Revision Kit). You were given Zeneca's mission statement – *outperforming* competitors in satisfying customer needs and in continuous improvement. The implications of this mission could be investment in people, investment for the long term, technological innovation and so on. Marketers might be involved in communication, researching the market and, perhaps as importantly, reminding the firm's strategists that the end-user and beneficiary of pharmaceutical products is not always the person who makes the purchase decision.

3.6 Objectives enter into the planning process both at the corporate level and at the market level.

(a) Corporate objectives define specific goals for the organisation as a whole and may be expressed in terms of profitability, returns on investment, growth of asset base, earnings per share and so on.

(b) These will be reflected in the stated objectives for *marketing* other functional plans. They will not be identical to those specified at the corporate level and need to be translated into market-specific marketing objectives. These may involve targets for the size of the customer base, growth in the usage of certain facilities, gains in market share for a particular product type and so on, but all must conform to three criteria: they must be achievable, they must be consistent and they must be stated clearly and preferably quantitatively.

### Situation analysis

3.7 Situation analysis requires a thorough study of the broad trends within the economy and society, as well as a detailed analysis of markets, consumers and competitors. *Market segmentation* is considered, and also an understanding of the organisation's internal environment and its particular strengths and weaknesses. Market research and external databases provide information on the external environment while an audit of the organisation's marketing activities provides information on the internal environment. A *marketing information system* may be used for processing and analysis, while SWOT analysis (see below) may be used to organise and present the results of such analysis.

### Strategy development

3.8 Strategy development links corporate and market level plans. Most large organisations will have important *resource allocation* decisions to make. Financial and human resources must be allocated in a manner consistent with corporate objectives. This process is a key component of corporate strategy and indicates how specific markets or products are expected to develop, enabling the development of *market level plans*.

3.9 Market specific plans relate to particular markets or, in some cases, particular products, but are closely tied to the corporate plan through the statement of objectives and the resource allocation component. Situation analysis must supply further information on patterns of competition, consumer behaviour and market segmentation, as input to the development of marketing objectives and market specific strategies.

3.10 Since marketing mix variables are under the control of the marketing department, development is guided by the need to ensure that the product's features, image, perceived value and availability are appropriate to the market involved.

3.11 Marketing expenditure rests on resource allocation decisions at corporate levels, but nevertheless a suggested budget and the way it is to be spent are required.

### Implementation

3.12 This requires an identification of the specific tasks, allocation of responsibility for those tasks and a system for monitoring their implementation. It may also include some elements of contingency planning. However well thought out the marketing plan may be, markets are dynamic. Planned activities may turn out to be inappropriate or ineffective and need a response - to modify the strategy as new information becomes available.

## 4 STRATEGY FORMULATION

4.1 In developing a marketing strategy, the company is seeking to meet the specific needs of its consumers and to do so more effectively than its competitors.

### SWOT analysis

4.2 This technique provides a method for organising information to identify strategic direction. The basic principle is that any statement about an organisation or its environment can be classified as a Strength, Weakness, Opportunity or Threat. An *opportunity* is simply any feature of the external environment which creates conditions which are advantageous to the firm in relation to a particular objective or set of objectives. By contrast, a *threat* is any environmental development which will present problems and may hinder the achievement of organisational objectives. What constitutes an opportunity to some firms will almost invariably constitute a threat to others.

4.3 A *strength* can be thought of as a particular skill or distinctive competence which the organisation possesses and which will aid it in achieving its stated objectives. A *weakness* is simply any aspect of the company which may hinder the achievement of specific objectives.

4.4 This information would typically be presented as a matrix of strengths, weaknesses, opportunities and threats. Effective SWOT analysis does not simply require a categorisation of information, it also requires some evaluation of the relative importance of the various factors. These features are only relevant if perceived to exist by consumers. Threats and opportunities are conditions presented by the external environment and they should be independent of the firm.

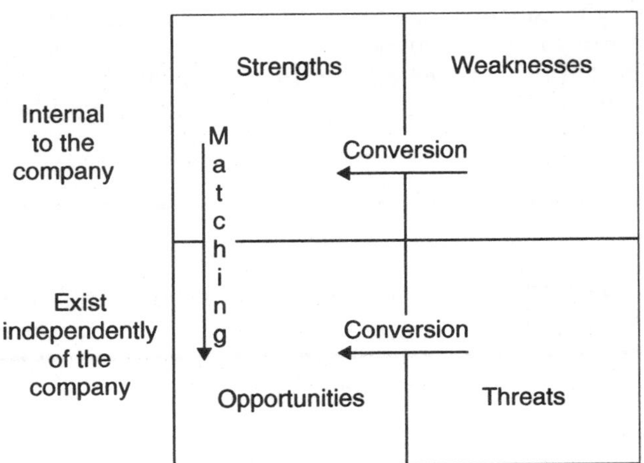


4.5 The two major strategic options from a SWOT analysis are as follows.

(a) *Matching* the strengths of the organisation to the opportunities presented by the market.

(b) *Conversion* of weaknesses into strengths in order to take advantage of some particular opportunity, or converting threats into opportunities which can then be matched by existing strengths.

---

## Case example

Although a well respected and successful company in the UK for more than forty years, Group 4 has been operating world wide since its founding in Sweden at the turn of the century. Its alarm systems, armoured vans and security systems were already a familiar sight on British streets, when it rocketed onto the front pages with the escape of eight prisoners in four weeks in the course of the company carrying out Prison Service contracts. Criticisms from prison officers and politicians reflected more on the controversial policy of privatisation than on the company involved, but the image of the company was clearly damaged. Their advertising and PR company, Broughton Jacques, decided to mount a campaign to counter the negative publicity.

The approach adopted was to tackle the issues head on, and use hard hitting advertising to limit the damage and focus on the range scale and variety of Group 4's business activity.

The tone adopted was mocking; sample headlines included 'Some facts about Group 4 which may have escaped you' . The company also commissioned research to evaluate the damage to the brand amongst buyers of security services in corporate companies. This showed that Group 4's identity had never been stronger, but that the image was poor. Advertising was commissioned in order to reach these decision makers and allay their fears. Target audiences were:

(a) policy makers (central and local government, home office), to win their confidence;

(b) opinion formers/pressure groups (journalists, unions), to win their confidence and empathy;

(c) existing Group 4 customers, to retain contacts and develop organic growth;

(d) potential Group 4 customers, to win market share at the expense of competitors; and

(e) Group 4 employees and the public, to generate renewed confidence.

Advertising was intended to convey information but also to capture attention and to build up into a strong overall campaign. The copy referred to the negative headlines, and sought to offer an alternative perception of the company. The marketing communication also devoted considerable attention to the personnel of the company since, in many ways, it was the employees who suffered most from the events surrounding the coverage. Internal communication was felt to be an essential part of the programme.

Overall, the objectives of the programme were achieved. Each of the five advertisements that was run reached a significant number of the target audience, and the campaign capitalised on high awareness of Group 4 amongst the target groups, while also improving the negative image. *(Adapted from Admap, June 1996)*

4.6 It is also necessary to consider more specific aspects of strategies: how best to compete, how to grow within the target markets etc. A number of analytical techniques can be used; not to offer definitive statements on the final form that a strategy should take, but rather to provide a framework for the organisation and analysis of ideas and information.

### Exercise 2

Can you (do you dare?) carry out a SWOT analysis on yourself? Try it with a group of friends and compare the results.

## Competitive strategies

4.7 Management must identify the way in which it will compete with other organisations and what it perceives as the basis of its competitive advantage. The American strategist Michael Porter argues that the strategy adopted by a firm is essentially a method for creating and sustaining a profitable position in a particular market environment. Profit depends first on the nature of its strategy and second on the inherent profitability of the industry in which it operates. An organisation in a basically profitable industry can perform badly with an unsuitable strategy while an organisation in an unprofitable industry may perform well with a more suitable strategy.

4.8 The profitability of an industry depends on five key features:

(a) bargaining power of suppliers;
(b) bargaining power of consumers;
(c) threat of entry;
(d) competition from substitutes;
(e) competition between firms.

4.9 A competitive strategy requires the organisation to decide whether to compete across the entire market or only in certain segments (*competitive scope*) and whether to compete through low costs and prices or through offering a differentiated product range (*competitive advantage*). Four strategies are possible; according to Ennew, Watkins and Wright, these are as shown here.

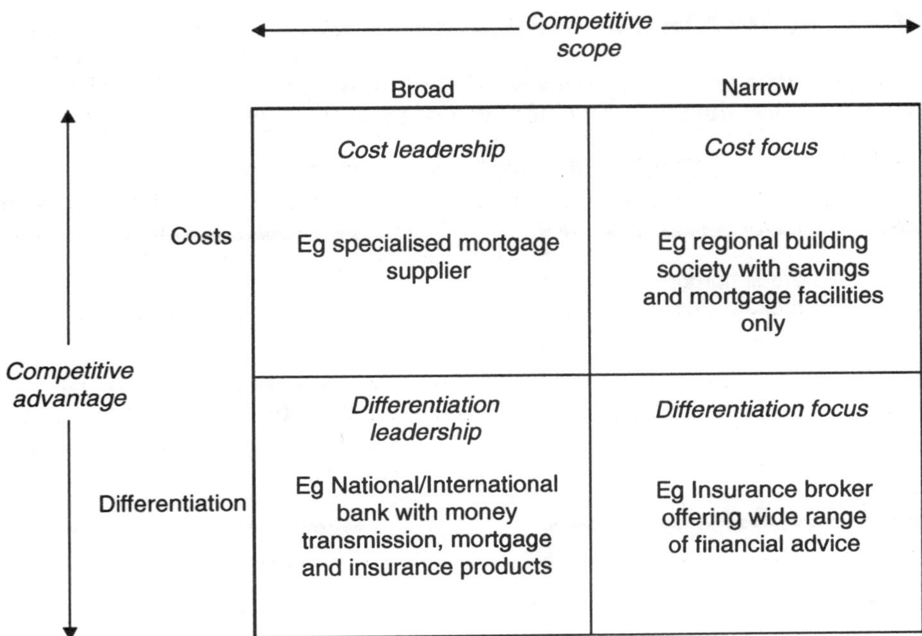


(a) *Cost leadership* attempts to control the market through being the low cost producer.

(b) *Differentiation* offers leadership or focus products which can be regarded as unique in areas which are highly valued by the consumer, creating customer loyalty which protects the firm from competition. The price premium must outweigh the costs of supplying the differentiated product for this strategy to be successful.

(c) *Focus/nicheing,* based on either costs or differentiation, aims to serve particularly attractive or suitable segments or niches.

An important feature of this approach is the need to avoid being 'stuck in the middle' - trying to be all things to all consumers. The firm trying to perform well on costs and on differentiation is likely to lose out to firms concentrating on either one strategy or the other.

## Growth strategies

*Examined 12/95*

4.10 Ansoff's Product/Market matrix suggests that the growth strategy decision rests on whether to use new or existing products in new or existing markets. This produces four possible options.

(a) *Market penetration*

This involves selling more of the existing products in existing markets. Possible options are persuading existing users to use more; persuading non-users to use; or attracting consumers from competitors. This is only a viable strategy where the market is not saturated.

(b) *Market development*

This entails expanding into new markets with existing products. These may be new markets geographically, new market segments or new uses for products.

(c) *Product development*

This approach requires the organisation to develop modified versions of its existing products which can appeal to existing markets. By tailoring the products more specifically to the needs of some existing consumers and some new consumers the organisation can strengthen its competitive position.

(d) *Diversification*

Diversification (new products, new markets) is a much more risky strategy because the organisation is moving into areas in which it has little or no experience. Instances of pure diversification are rare and use as a strategic option tends to be in cases when there are no other possible routes for growth available.

## 5 MARKET SEGMENTATION

*Examined 12/96*

5.1 Customers differ in various respects - according to age, sex, income, geographical area, buying attitudes, buying habits etc. Each of these differences can be used to segment a market.

*Steps in the analysis of segmentation*

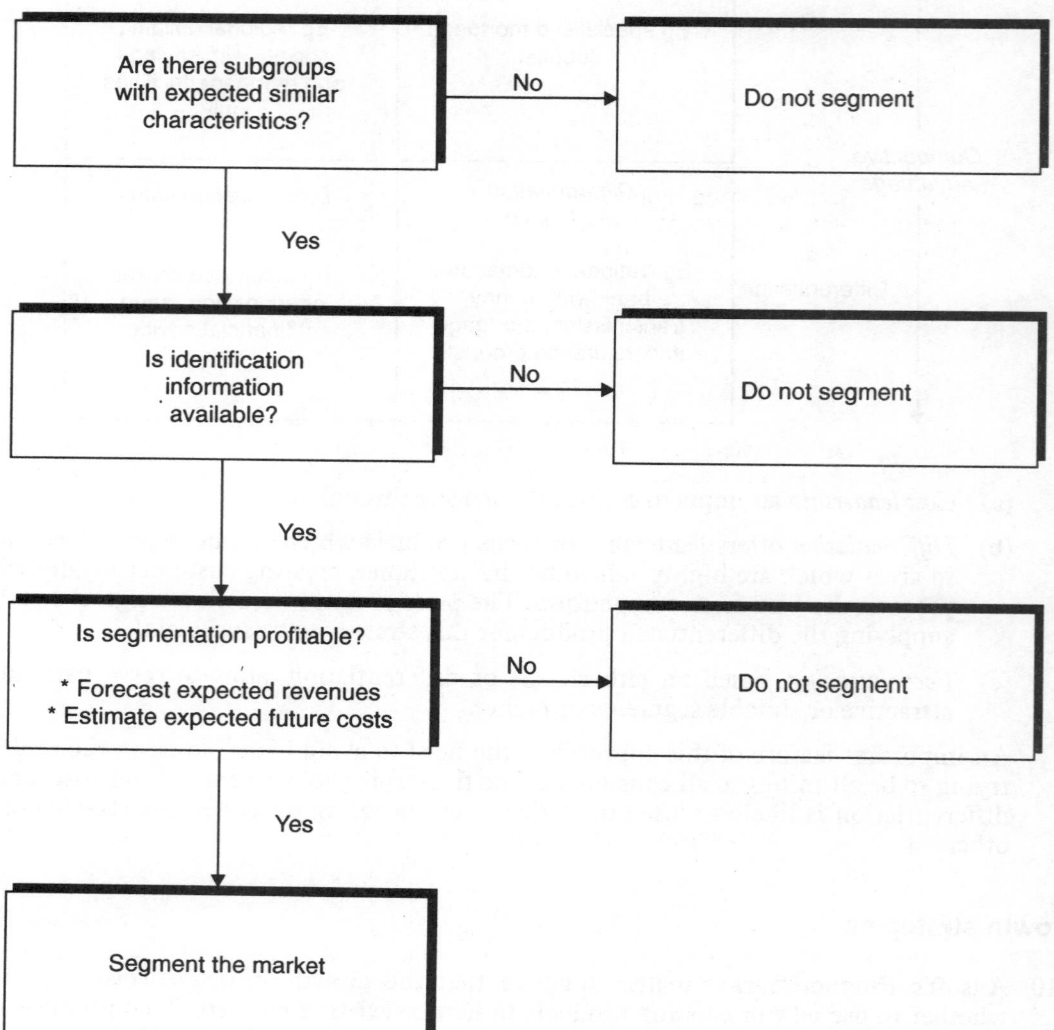


### Market segmentation and marketing planning

5.2 Market segmentation is based on the recognition of the diverse needs of potential buyers. Different customer attitudes may be grouped into segments. A different marketing approach is needed for each market segment.

5.3 Market segmentation involves:

> 'the subdividing of a market into distinct and increasingly homogeneous subgroups of customers, where any subgroup can conceivably be selected as a target to be met with a distinct marketing mix.' (Tom Cannon, *Basic Marketing: Principles and Practice*, 1980)

5.4 The important elements in this definition of market segmentation are as follows.

(a) Each segment consists of people (or organisations) with common needs and preferences, who may react to 'market stimuli' in much the same way.

(b) Each segment can become a target market with a unique marketing mix.

5.5 A total market may occasionally be homogeneous but this is rare. A segmentation approach to marketing succeeds when there are identifiable 'clusters' of consumer wants in the market.

### Exercise 3

Suggest how the market for umbrellas might be segmented.

### Solution

The market for umbrellas might be segmented according to the sex of the consumer. Women might seem to prefer umbrellas of different size and weight. The men's market might further be subdivided into age (with some age groups buying few umbrellas and others buying much more) or occupation (eg professional classes, commuters, golfers). Each subdivision of the market (each subsegment) will show increasingly common traits. Golfers, for example, appear to buy large multi-coloured umbrellas.

### Case example

One of the reasons for the growth in fast food has been the rise in the number of small and single person households, often not adequately catered for by manufacturers. Chicken Tonight, the UK's most popular brand of wet cooking sauces, is predicting a major growth in the dynamic wet cooking sauce market following the launch of unique two serving jars, and the addition of new recipes to its family sized range.

The reason for this change is the growing number of one and two person households, which already account for 62% of UK dwellings, and the belief that these will offer the key to continued growth in the wet cooking sauce market. The brand launched a range of unique serves-two jars to maximise the potential offered by the 1.8 million smaller households which do not currently buy wet cooking sauces. Why is this likely to be a profitable marketing move?

First, because the new jars are ideally suited to the consumer profile of independent retailers and forecourts, as well as major multiples. Many of the small household buyers obtain foods from these sources. Retailers will be encouraged to stock these products using introductory discounts and the brand will be supported by intensive advertising, which will also make it attractive to these retailers.

Second, this is an untapped market and this size of jar is intended to stimulate trial of the product at minimum outlay. Recipes also reflect the growing popularity of flavours found in the takeaway food market, such as garlic and curry.

The product will, then, provide an opportunity for small households to buy the product at locations where it would previously have been unavailable, and also allow larger households to try the new flavours, which will also be available in the family size jars. This new product launch, is achieving a number of marketing objectives very effectively within the same product concept. *(Adapted from The Grocer, 14/9/96)*

## The bases for segmentation

5.6 There are many different bases for segmentation; one basis will not be appropriate in every market, and sometimes two or more bases might be valid at the same time. One 'segmentation variable' might be 'superior' to another in a hierarchy of variables.

5.7 Typical market segments are as follows.

(a) *Geographical area:* for example, the needs and behaviour of potential customers in South East England may differ from those in Scotland or Italy.

(b) *End use:* for example, paper used in office will vary in quality depending on whether it is used for formal letters and reports, informal working or for typewriter carbon copies. 'Use' in the consumer market might refer to leisure or work use.

(c) *Age*

(d) *Sex*

(e) *Family size* or *family life cycle*

(f) *Income*

(g) *Occupation*

(h) *Education*

(i) *Religion* or *religious sect*

(j) *Race*

(k) *Nationality*

(l) *Social class*

(m) *Lifestyle*

*Lifestyle dimensions*

| *Activities* | *Interests* | *Opinions* | *Demographics* |
|---|---|---|---|
| Work | Family | Themselves | Age |
| Hobbies | Home | Social issues | Education |
| Social events | Job | Politics | Income |
| Vacation | Community | Business | Occupation |
| Entertainment | Recreation | Economics | Family size |
| Club membership | Fashion | Education | Dwelling |
| Community | Food | Products | Geography |
| Shopping | Media | Future | City size |
| Sports | Achievements | Culture | Stage in lifecycle |

(Joseph Plummer, *'The Concept and Application of Lifestyle Segmentation'*, *Journal of Marketing*, January 1974)

(n) *Buyer behaviour:* the usage rate of the product by the buyer, whether purchase will be on impulse, customer loyalty, the sensitivity of the consumer to marketing mix factors (price, quality and sales promotion).

### Case example

Heinz has more than 50% of the canned market for soups, with cream of tomato accounting for 15% by itself. This suggests they are doing an awful lot right, but their marketing department is not content. Heinz undertook extensive research to enhance its understanding of the role and use of soups in the home, and consumer behaviour at the point of purchase. A new segmentation strategy grew out of this.

People shop the 'category fixture' in sequence, the research showed, beginning with 'store cupboard' varieties - standard soups bought to replace items used since they last shopped, to maintain a stock level at home. Next in the sequence come large diced soup, bought to provide a smaller number of substantial working meals, then dietary and low calories soups, bought as an indulgent treat, and finally condensed soups, mainly used as a cooking ingredient. This suggested that the category fixture (soups) had to be made more logical and less fragmented.

Heinz decided to discontinue a number of sub ranges in standard soups. These had originally been launched as a point of difference, but the research showed that consumers were confused by them, and did not differentiate between standard and sub brands as manufacturers did. Working with Safeway, who shared their research data, the company was able to test and confirm these findings. The research teaming of Heinz and Safeway was also able to develop effective strategies to cater for wide regional variances. The segmentation of the market enabled them to cater for distinctive regional preferences in varieties, brands and pack sizes. Safeway and Heinz space planning managers developed fixtures which best matched the consumer's needs and also optimised profitability.

*(Adapted from The Grocer, September 1996)*

5.8 Segmentation may be based on the use or usefulness of the product. The market for various foods, for example, can be segmented into 'convenience foods', such as frozen chips and TV dinners, or 'wholesome foods'.

*Segmentation of the toothpaste market*

| *Segment name* | *Principal benefit sought* | *Demo-graphic strengths* | *Special behavioural character-istics* | *Brands dispropor-tionately favoured* | *Personality character-istics* | *Lifestyle character-istics* |
|---|---|---|---|---|---|---|
| **The sensory segment** | Flavour, product appearance | Children | Users of spearmint flavoured toothpaste | Colgate, Stripe | High self-involvement | Hedonistic |
| **The sociables** | Brightness of teeth, breath freshness | Teens, young people | Smokers | Macleans, Ultra Brite, Thera-med | High sociability | Active |
| **The worriers** | Decay prevention | Large families | Heavy users | Crest | High hypochon-driasis | Conser-vative |
| **The indepen-dent segment** | Price | Men | Heavy users | Brands on sale | High autonomy | Value-oriented |

## Segmentation of the industrial market

5.9 Segmentation can also be applied to an industrial market based on, for instance, the nature of the customer's business.

5.10 Components manufacturers specialise in the industries of the firms to which they supply components. In the motor car industry, there are companies which specialise in the manufacture of car components.

(a) *Magazines and periodicals.* In this market the segmentation may be according to:

(i) sex (Woman's Own);
(ii) social class (Country Life);
(iii) income (Ideal Home);
(iv) occupation (Accountancy Age, Computer Weekly);
(v) leisure interests;
(vi) political ideology;
(vii) age ('19', Honey);
(viii) lifestyle (Playboy).

(b) *Sporting facilities.* Segmentation may be according to:

(i) geographical area (rugby in Wales, skiing in parts of Scotland, sailing in coastal towns);

(ii) population density (squash clubs in cities, riding in country areas);

(iii) occupation (gymnasia for office workers);

(iv) education (there may be a demand from ex-schoolboys for facilities for sports taught at certain schools, such as rowing);

(v) family life cycle or age (parents may want facilities for their children, young single or married people may want facilities for themselves).

5.11 Segmentation in any particular market is a matter of 'intuition' or 'interpretation'. The examples in the previous paragraph merely suggest a few bases for segmentation in each case.

### Case example

*Marketing Week* (5 July 1996) analysed the results of the Childwatch Monitor survey.

'The survey shows that it is not enough for a channel to be given a child till the age of seven - by the age of 11 it will have changed its viewing habits, and by 13 and 15 it will have done so again. It measures "claims" of viewing, so a certain amount of street-cred must be allowed for. But it shows TV channels are segmenting the child and youth market in the same way comics and magazines do.'

The survey results were summarised as follows (for cable and satellite).

| *Age* | *Sex* | *Most popular channel(s)* |
|---|---|---|
| 7-8 | Both | Carlton Network |
| 9-10 | Both | Nickelodeon |
| 11-12 | Girls | MTV |
| 11-12 | Boys | Nickelodeon |
| 15-16 | Girls | MTV, Sky Movies |
| 15-16 | Boys | Sky Sports, Sky Movies, MTV, Sky One, The Movie Channel |

## Target markets

5.12 Trying to sell to every buyer is neither practicable or effective. The marketing management of a company may therefore choose one of the following policy options.

(a) *Undifferentiated marketing*: this policy is to produce a single product and hope to get as many customers as possible to buy it; that is, ignore segmentation entirely.

(b) *Concentrated marketing*: the company attempts to produce the ideal product for a *single* segment of the market (eg Rolls Royce cars, Mothercare mother and baby shops).

(c) *Differentiated marketing*: the company attempts to introduce several product versions, each aimed at a different market segment (for example, the manufacture of several different brands of washing powder).

5.13 The major disadvantage of *concentrated marketing* is reliance on a single segment of a single market. On the other hand, specialisation in a particular market segment can give a firm a profitable, although perhaps temporary, competitive edge over rival firms.

5.14 The major disadvantage of *differentiated marketing* is the additional cost of marketing and production (more product design and development costs, the loss of economies of scale in production and storage, additional promotion costs and administrative costs and so on). When the costs of further differentiation of the market exceed the benefits from further segmentation and target marketing, a firm is said to have 'overdifferentiated'. Some firms have tried to overcome this problem by selling the same product to two market segments.

5.15 The choice of marketing strategy will depend on the following factors.

(a) How far can the product and/or the market be considered homogeneous? Mass marketing may be 'sufficient' if the market is largely homogeneous (eg safety matches).

(b) Will the company's resources be overextended by differentiated marketing? Small firms may succeed better by concentrating on one segment only.

(c) Is the product sufficiently advanced in its 'life cycle' to have attracted a substantial total market? If not, segmentation and target marketing is unlikely to be profitable, because each segment would be too small in size.

5.16 The potential benefits of segmentation and target marketing are as follows.

(a) *Product differentiation*: a feature of a particular product might appeal to one segment of the market in such a way that the product is thought better than its rivals.

(b) The seller will be more *aware* of how product design and development may stimulate further demand in a particular area of the market.

(c) The resources of the business will be used more *effectively*, because the organisation should be more able to make products which the customer wants and will pay for.

5.17 We have looked at the strategic implications of market segmentation here. We will look at more practical aspects of how markets are segmented in Chapter 5.

---

### Case example

'When your biggest brand launch in three decades succeeds only on its price – especially when you have spent an estimated £20 million on advertising it – something has gone wrong.

This is the situation facing the UK's biggest tobacco manufacturer Gallaher, which launched its mid-market cigarette brand Sovereign more than 18 months ago in an effort to claw back market share from Imperial's buoyant Lambert & Butler brand.

But despite throwing millions of pounds at Sovereign in promotion and advertising, Gallaher has failed to crack the quality-economy sector of the market.

Gallaher now finds itself with a brand it is treating as premium product in terms of ad spend (estimated at £2 million a month), on which it is making only small own-label margins.'

(*Marketing Week* 4 December 1997)

---

## 6 POSITIONING PRODUCTS AND BRANDS

---

### Exam focus point

The relationship between segmentation and targeting was covered in the December 1997 exam (in the Test Paper in our Practice & Revision Kit). Segmentation is a way of analysing customers so that groups of individuals with similar characteristics can be identified. Targeting involves selecting one or more customer groups and satisfying them with a marketing mix.

---

6.1 Brands can be positioned against competitive brands on *product maps*. These are defined in terms of how buyers perceive key characteristics of the product.

6.2 Yoram Wind identifies a comprehensive list of these characteristics.

(a) Positioning by specific product features, eg price or specific product features
(b) Positioning by benefits, problems, solutions, or needs
(c) Positioning for specific usage occasions
(d) Positioning for user category, eg age, gender
(e) Positioning against another product, eg comparison with market leader
(f) Product class disassociation, eg organic food, lead-free petrol
(g) Hybrid basis, eg user and product features

---

### Exercise 4

Give an example for each of Yoram Wind's list of key characteristics.

### Solution

(a) *Positioning by specific product features.* Most car advertisements stress the combination of product features available and may also stress what good value for money this represents.

(b) *Positioning by benefits, problems, solutions, or needs.* Pharmaceutical companies position their products to doctors by stressing effectiveness and side effects. Other examples include Crest, which positions its toothpaste as a cavity fighter, and DHL, which uses its worldwide network of offices as a basis for its positioning.

(c) *Positioning for specific usage occasions.* Johnson's Baby Shampoo is positioned as a product to use if you shampoo your hair every day, and Hennessy Cognac is for special occasions.

(d) *Positioning for user category.* Examples here include 7-Up's use of the Fido Dido character to target urban adolescents. Age has been used as a basis for positioning by Saga Holidays, by many breakfast cereal producers (compare the target markets for Kellogg's Rice Krispies and Special K) and by Affinity shampoo for women over 40.

(e) *Positioning against another product.* Although Avis never mentions Hertz explicitly in its advertising, its positioning as Number 2 in the rent-a-car market is an example of positioning against a leader.

(f) *Product class disassociation.* Lead-free petrol is positioned against leaded petrol.

(g) *Hybrid basis.* The Porsche positioning, for example, is based on the product benefits as well as on a certain type of user.

6.3 A basic perceptual map is to plot brands in perceived price and perceived quality terms.

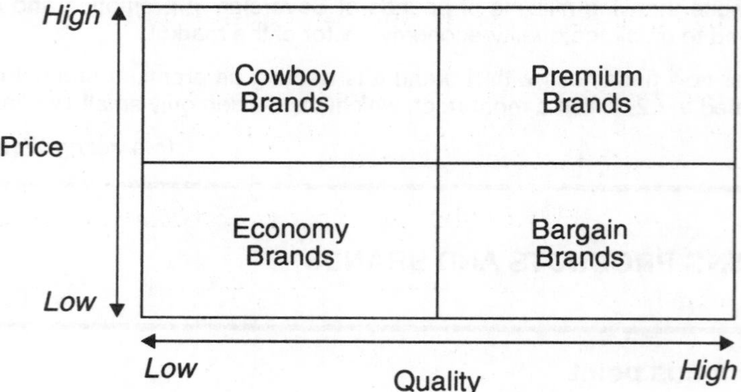


6.4 Price and quality are important elements in the marketing mix. Most consumers will not see them as independent variables. A 'high' price will usually be associated with high quality and equally low price with low quality. Thus, while everybody would like to buy a bargain brand, there is a problem to overcome. This is a question of belief: will customers accept that a high quality product can be offered at a low price?

### Exercise 5

Where would you place MFI in the quality/price map?

### Solution

MFI would claim to be in the 'bargain' quadrant. Many potential customers think that they are at the lower end of the economy segment. MFI's practice of frequent sales and discounts has the effect of overcoming at least some of the difficulties resulting from individuals using price as a surrogate for assessment of quality. Thus the price label shows the higher pre-discounted price and the low sale price. The assumption is that customers will use the pre-sale price to confirm promotional claims about quality.

6.5 Public concern about the use of promotional pricing ('prices slashed') has led to the introduction of restrictions on the use of these techniques. Stores now have to provide evidence that the promotion is part of a genuine 'sale' - that is, the product must have been offered for sale at the price which is cited as the original, within a specified time.

## Identifying a gap in the market

6.6 Market research can determine where customers perceive competitive brands are located in relation to each other.

Resturants in Anytown

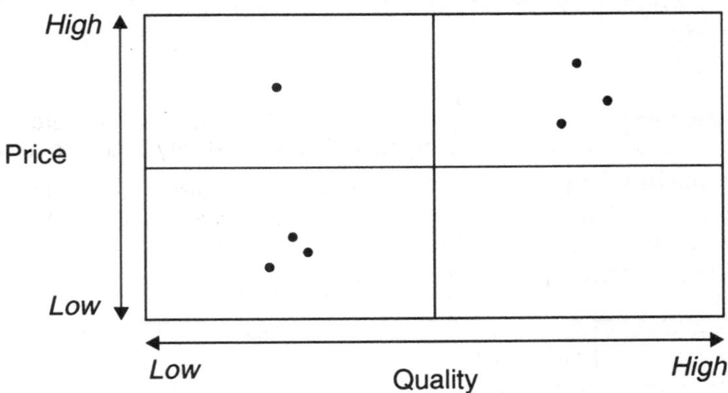


6.7 In the hypothetical model above, there appears to be a gap in the market for a moderately priced reasonable quality eating place. This is shown between clusters in the high price/high quality and the low price/low quality segments.

6.8 Perceptual maps can also plot how customers perceive competitive brands performing on key product user benefits. Kotler's hypothetical examples consider the various products that serve the US breakfast market.

Product-positioning map: Breakfast market

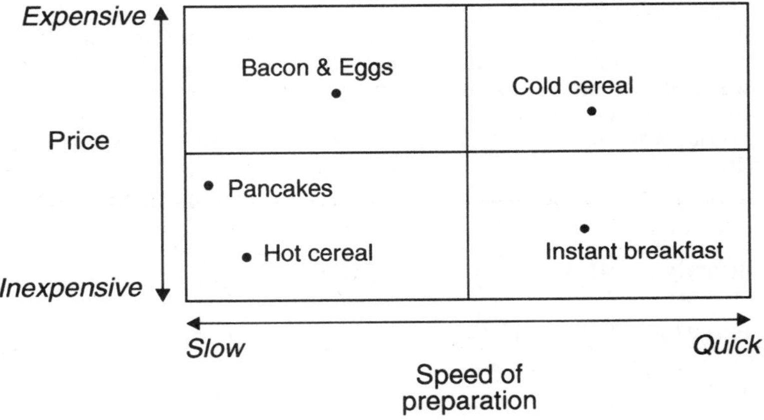


6.9 Within the market (for breakfast foods), a producer might be interested in entering the instant breakfast market. It would then be advisable to plot the position of the various instant breakfast brands.

Brand-positioning map: Instant breakfast market

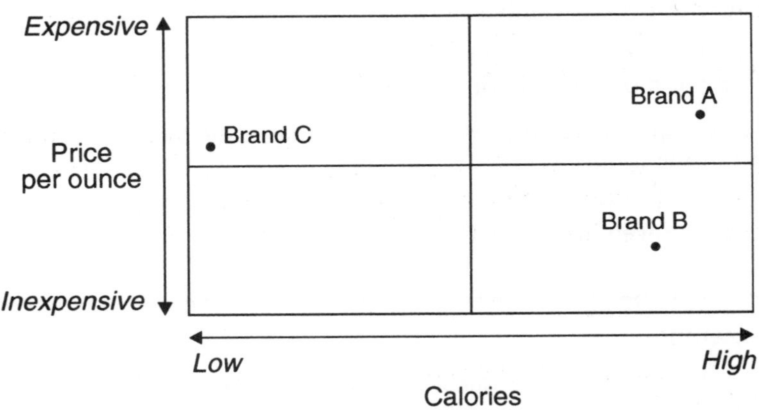

6.10 The above analysis now shows an apparent gap for a modest priced slimmers brand. Once again, it would be necessary to establish whether or not there is sufficient demand for such a product.

## Competitive positioning

6.11 Competitive positioning concerns 'a general idea of what kind of offer to make to the target market in relation to competitors' offers' (Kotler). Important considerations in competitive positioning are product quality and price, and Kotler identified a 3 × 3 matrix of nine different competitive positioning strategies.

| *Product* | *High price* | *Medium price* | *Low price* |
|---|---|---|---|
| *High* | Premium strategy | Penetration strategy | Superbargain strategy |
| *Medium* | Overpricing strategy | Average quality strategy | Bargain strategy |
| *Low* | Hit and run strategy | Shoddy goods strategy | Cheap goods strategy |

### Exam focus point

Q90 *Setag Industries* of our Practice & Revision Kit was set in June 1996. Setag is a watch manufacturer. You had to assess the potential effect of an important product innovation on the industry as a whole. A key question is whether the whole market would be affected or only a *segment* of innovators. The firm then had to consider a positioning for the new innovation – pricing policy was required in detail, but remember that price reflects the overall positioning of the offer.

## Fragmented industries and market segmentation

6.12 The fragmentation of industries and proliferation of market segments tends to occur when the following conditions apply.

(a) There are low entry barriers, and so new firms can enter the market relatively easily.

(b) There are few economies of scale or learning curve effects, and so it is difficult for big firms to establish a significant overall cost leadership.

(c) Transport and distribution costs are high, and so the industry fragments on a geographical basis.

(d) Customer needs vary widely.

(e) There are rapid product changes or style changes, which small firms might succeed in reacting to more quickly than large firms.

(f) There is a highly diverse product line, so that some firms are able to specialise in one part of the industry.

(g) There is scope for product differentiation, based on product design/quality differences or even brand images.

### Case example

Show stopping vehicles at the Geneva motor show seem to indicate that, even for the luxury car maker, the future is small. While small cars have been bread and butter for volume manufacturers such as VW and Ford, they represent a huge leap for Mercedes Benz and

BMW, both of which have built their reputations on big expensive luxury vehicles. Why have they shifted?

Three factors have been crucial.

(a) The need to break free from an ageing customer base
(b) The need to escape from limited growth prospects
(c) The need to avoid high manufacturing costs

The average age of Mercedes drivers is 60, and although the BMW driver is in his 40s this is creeping up too. Both companies have tried to diversify into markets which are wider and have younger consumers, such as station wagons or coupes, but this has been a limited success. Although both companies have also diversified into slightly cheaper models, growth in their main markets of US and Europe is limited, while rising affluence in Asia and South America can only provide limited growth. Competition at the top end of the market is stiffening and manufacturing costs at home are rising.

Both companies have increased manufacturing abroad, and will expand their activities here. But the competitive pressures in the luxury car business have convinced them that they must do more than just diversify within their niche to generate long term sales and profits. Helmut Werner, ex Chairman of Mercedes Benz commented: 'You have to keep growing or profits will be eradicated', while BMW's chairman commented: 'To do nothing would be fatal.'

BMW was able to move into this market with the acquisition of Rover, which already possessed great expertise in the small car market via the Mini. Mercedes decided to develop their own small car. The A class will take the company into the second biggest segment of the European car market, while the Smart, a tiny two seater intended for urban use, is being developed with SMH the company behind SWATCH.

A delicate balance is involved in this move. It is possible that the high class image which has given it the widest profit margins in the European car industry will be damaged by this move into cheaper categories, while the success of both of these innovative and unconventional models is by no means assured. The risk with the extremely radical Smart is extremely high, and the 'brand values' of Mercedes could be badly damaged by a flop.

BMW have an easier task, since they can work through Rover, already an established name in this market. Branding is therefore taken care off, but the company involved is still losing money. Have they made the right move?

Conventional wisdom sees this as a gamble which they may well lose. The chairman of a rival company argues that the Class A is commercially risky, and the Smart seems likely to be a disaster because it is so unconventional. BMW, in the meantime, will take ten expensive years to put Rover right. Both will, therefore, fail in their attempts to enter these new markets.

Others argue that the outcome can only be positive. According to Chris Will, Motor Industry Analyst at Lehman Brothers in London, 'Whether they succeed or not, it shows the managements of Germany's car companies have become more realistic about the pressures on their industry.' *(Adapted from the Financial Times, 17/3/97)*

## 7 THE MARKETING PLAN

7.1 The marketing plan in detail consists of several inter-related decisions.

(a) *Sales targets* must be set for each product and each sales division (with sub-targets also set for sales regions, sales areas and individual salesmen). Sales targets may be referred to as sales quotas.

(b) The *total marketing budget* must be set.

(c) Given an overall marketing budget, resources (cash) must be *allocated* between:

  (i) salaries and other staff costs;

  (ii) above the line expenditure (advertising);

  (iii) below the line expenditure (sales promotion items, price reduction allowances etc).

(d) The overall sales target set by top management will incorporate *sales price decisions*; but within the formulation of the marketing plan there is likely to be some room for manoeuvre and an element of choice in the pricing decision. In other words, top management will decide on a 'rough pricing zone' and a specific price within this zone will be fixed later within the marketing plan.

(e) Expenditure on marketing will also be allocated to different products or services within the organisation's product or service range. Some products might justify additional marketing expenditure; whereas others, nearing the end of their life cycle, may lose a part of their previous allocation.

7.2 Market plan decisions (sales targets, total marketing expenditure budget, the marketing mix and the allocation of expenditure to products) are the main elements of *marketing programming*.

### The marketing budget

7.3 Top management must set an overall sales strategy and a series of sales objectives; only then should a more detailed marketing plan be prepared.

7.4 There are three types of annual budget planning for a marketing budget.

(a) *Top-down planning*: the setting of goals for lower management by higher management.

(b) *Bottom-up planning*: employees set their own goals and submit then to higher management for approval.

(c) '*Goals down - plans up*' *planning*: a mixture of the two styles; top management sets overall goals and employees formulate plans for achieving those goals. This is well suited to the formulation of sales budgets.

7.5 When budgeting for sales revenue and selling costs, variables are many and difficult to estimate. Setting budgets and budgetary control on the marketing side is different from the more 'mechanical' approach which can be adopted with other budgets.

7.6 A sales and marketing budget is necessary because:

(a) it is an element of the overall strategic plan of the business (the master budget) which brings together all the activities of the business;

(b) where sales and other non-production costs are a large part of total costs, it is financially prudent to forecast, plan and control them;

(c) since selling rests on uncertain conditions, good forecasts and plans become more important. If budgets are to be used for control, the more uncertain the budget estimates are, the more budgetary control is necessary.

### Matching forecast demand with estimated available capacity

7.7 One of the problems in setting budgets is matching the forecast demand from customers with the estimated available capacity. There are three aspects to this problem.

(a) It is difficult to make an accurate forecast of demand.

(b) It is difficult to predict available capacity accurately too, given uncertainties about factors of production, operating conditions and performance.

(c) There are often practical difficulties in matching demand with capacity (seasonability, variations in demand).

7.8 In order to match demand with capacity, management must be flexible, and be prepared to take action:

(a) to suppress demand if it exceeds capacity, by raising prices, for example;

(b) to stimulate demand if there is excess capacity, such as by advertising or price reductions;

(c) to reduce excess capacity by selling off surplus assets;

(d) to supplement production when there is undercapacity by subcontracting work to other organisations, and perhaps to take steps to increase capacity (by acquiring new premises, equipment and labour, or by negotiating for more overtime from existing employees).

### The advertising budget decision

7.9 Setting an advertising budget is based on the theory of *diminishing returns*. For every extra £1 of advertising spent, the company should earn an extra £x of profit. Further expenditure on advertising is justified until the marginal return £x diminishes to the point where £x < £1.

7.10 Unfortunately, the marginal (ie extra) return from additional advertising cannot be measured easily in practice because:

(a) advertising is only one aspect of the overall marketing mix;

(b) advertising has some long-term effect, which goes beyond the limits of a measurable accounting period;

(c) where the advertising budget is fixed as a percentage of sales, advertising costs tend to follow sales levels and not vice versa.

7.11 Advertising budgets are often set by using rule of thumb methods or by taking competitor activity into consideration.

7.12 Recommended practice for fixing advertising cost budgets, however, would involve the use of:

(a) *empirical testing* (for example, in a mail order business or in retail operations, since it may be possible to measure the effect of advertising on sales by direct observation);

(b) *mathematical models* using data about media and consumer characteristics, desired market share, and using records of past results. Regression analysis can be conducted to find out the likely cost of advertising (through several media) to achieve a given target.

### Control

7.13 Once the plan has been implemented, the task of management is to control the use of resources. This may involve:

(a) a comparison of actual sales against the budget;

(b) a comparison of actual marketing costs against the budgeted expenditure levels and against actual sales;

(c) analysis of the profitability of individual products, and distribution outlets;

(d) strategic control, ie checking whether the company's objectives, products and resources are being directed towards the correct markets.

### Allocation of costs

7.14 The allocation of *direct selling costs* to products, type of outlet and so on is fairly straightforward, but *indirect costs* such as administration overheads must be allocated on an arbitrary basis (such as to products by value of sales). This aspect of cost allocation should be carefully considered when deciding whether to eliminate an unprofitable expenditure from selling or distribution.

(a) The cost of distributing goods to a distant area may seem to be relatively unprofitable; but if, by not selling the goods in this area, there will be unused production capacity, the products which are produced and sold will have to bear a higher proportion of fixed costs which will still be incurred.

(b) The allocation of fixed selling costs to products may make a product seem unprofitable, but the product may still be making a *contribution* to those fixed costs.

## Overviewing the marketing process: marketing audits

7.15 Top management is responsible for ensuring that the company is pursuing optimal policies with regard to its products, markets and distribution channels. Carrying out this responsibility is known as strategic control of marketing, and the means to apply strategic control is the *marketing audit*.

7.16 Although not compulsory a marketing audit should:

(a) be conducted regularly;

(b) take a comprehensive look at every product, market, distribution channel, ingredient in the marketing mix and so on;

(c) be carried out according to a set of predetermined, specified procedures: it should be systematic.

The 'auditors' should be independent of the marketing function.

## The audit procedure

7.17 A marketing audit should consider the following areas.

(a) The *marketing environment*: markets, customers, competitors, PEST factors.

(b) *Marketing objectives and plans*: related to resources, and allocation of resources, implementation procedures, organisation.

(c) *Marketing activities*: sales factors, product review, distribution etc.

## Chapter roundup

- In this chapter we have looked at marketing strategy and at tactical methods for maximising sales, most notably segmentation. We concluded by looking at the components of the marketing plan and at how managers can assess the effectiveness of their strategy and detailed plans by the use of marketing audit.
- Use of strategic planning enables organisations to be *effective*, not just efficient. Information is gathered and used to develop a corporate plan, covering short, medium and long-term goals and acting as a framework within which specific functions such as marketing can develop their own plans.
- Techniques used in strategy formulation include situation and SWOT analysis. The latter enables an organisation to choose whether to *match* its strengths to available opportunities or to *convert* its weaknesses into strengths or its threats into opportunities.
- *Competitive strategies* can only be developed after thorough evaluation of an organisation's industry and involve deciding:
    - whether to compete across the whole market or only in certain segments (*competitive scope*);
    - whether to compete through low costs/prices or by offering a differentiated product range (*competitive advantage*).
- The Ansoff Product/Market matrix is used to determine *growth strategies*. It produces four strategies: market penetration or development, product development and diversification.
- *Market segmentation* should result in increased total sales and profits because products/services will be more likely to appeal to the target segments and pricing policy can be more sophisticated. There are many possible bases for segmentation. Some relate to the target consumer and others to the product. Practical aspects of market segmentation are covered in Chapter 5.
- Product/brand positioning may be determined in several ways, most commonly by highlighting specific product features, including price. Price and quality are very important in consumer perceptions of a product and analysis of existing products in a market can be used to identify gaps.
- The *marketing plan* should include:
    - sales targets;
    - total marketing budget analysed between above the line, below the line and other items.

  *Budgeting* is an essential financial discipline but a particularly tricky problem in marketing given the difficulty in determining both likely demand and likely cost of achieving a given sales target. The rules of thumb commonly used in setting promotional budgets (such as a percentage of budgeted or past sales or profit) are unsatisfactory because they are arbitrary.
- *Marketing audits* are a means of applying strategic control to ensure that marketing policies are optimal. They should be carried out regularly, comprehensively and as far as possible objectively. The audit should consider the marketing environment, existing marketing objectives and plans, and marketing activities.

## Test your knowledge

1 What is an emergent strategy? (see para 1.3)

2 Outline the stages in strategic planning. (3.2)

3 What is situation analysis? (3.7)

4 What do the letters in SWOT analysis stand for? (4.2)

5 What five factors affect the profitability of an industry? (4.8)

6 A cost focus strategy attempts to control the market through being the low cost producer. True or false? (4.9)

7 Differentiate between market and product development. (4.10)

8 Diversification is a low risk strategy. True or false? Give reasons for your answer. (4.10)

9 When should market segmentation be used? (5.1)

10 List as many bases for market segmentation as you can. (5.7)

11 What is concentrated marketing? (5.13) What are its risks? (5.13)

12 A bargain brand is perceived as low price, high quality. True or false? (6.3)

13 What seven conditions tend to give rise to fragmentation of industries and proliferation of market segments? (6.12)

14 What is above the line expenditure? (7.1)

15 Why is a sales and marketing budget necessary? (7.6)

16 List the problems encountered in setting a sales budget. (7.7)

17 What should be the scope of a marketing audit? (7.17)

**Now try illustrative question 6 at the end of the Study Text**

## MARKETING FUNDAMENTALS IN ACTION

*For most Parts of each Study Text, we take a look at the subject matter covered in the light of real companies, either to offer more detail or to give an understanding of the wider corporate context.*

*Nike* is a marketing icon that deserves continuing success, claims Andrew Seth (*Marketing Business*, January 1998). Nike's achievement is staggering: £6 billion of sales, and the swoosh is a universal symbol. The lessons of single-minded focus and driving the brand right through the business are those we learnt at Lever two decades ago, when Phil Knight founded his sports company in Portland, Oregon.

His vision of branding is comprehensive – be in no doubt that Nike is brand-led. Knight knew what his brand needed, and the benchmarks – Coca-Cola, Sony and Rolls-Royce – to measure it against.

The market is identified with precision, the method is rational and thorough, while emotionally, the approach used to target consumers through the youth subculture of music and leisure is irresistibly empathetic.

The approach is overtly competitive, aggressive when it needs to be. Like the 1960s appeal of Sinatra's *I did it my way*, Nike found brilliant ways to put across their more militant 1980s and 1990s version, "Winning your own way".

Nike was determined to build a better product, with levels of R&D not previously seen in sports goods. A recognisable point of difference was the "waffle" sole: coupled with better cushioning, attractive design and constant, churning, Japanese-level innovation, Nike was able to bring more than 300 new shoe designs to market each year.

Nike needs low cost because it has set itself a huge task – to become the world's best sports goods company. To do this, it must supply sports shoes that satisfy a wide range of physical and psychological aspirations, often at apparently astronomic prices, for what used to be the cheapest mass market footwear.

Good marketing involves complete congruence between internal and external communication. Nike exemplifies this perfectly. Its internal communications emanate from a Portland office that could be a cathedral or a stylish university campus if it wasn't its HQ. Elitism, self-belief, an established heritage (built partly around the prematurely-deceased athlete Steve Prefontaine), and an acknowledgement of heroism are key factors. The external messages are consistent. The heroes are given high visibility, and what heroes they are.

Inevitably, even the best companies in the world have problems. Nike has had its share – not least in the widespread reaction among US communities, including students and literate consumer groups, to Nike's East Asian factory conditions.

No company, however consistent, however committed its leadership, will find life plain sailing for ever and Nike hit some choppy water in the second half of 1997. Commentators suggest its market is saturated, draw attention to its exposure from high prices, express concern about its interference with sporting contracts, even suggest the swoosh could go negative.

# Part B
## The marketing tool

# Chapter 4

# MARKETING RESEARCH

**This chapter covers the following topics.** *Syllabus reference*



| | | Syllabus reference |
|---|---|---|
| 1 | Types of marketing research | 2.1 |
| 2 | In-house vs external agencies | 2.2 |
| 3 | Marketing research procedure: secondary data | 2.1 |
| 4 | Marketing research procedure: primary data | 2.1 |
| 5 | Marketing information systems | 2.2 |



## Introduction

Marketing decisions are made under conditions of uncertainty and risk. Marketing research aims to reduce risk by providing information about the factors involved and possible outcomes of particular actions.

Important decisions frequently have to be taken and, in order to reduce risk, management needs relevant and comprehensive information. It is the task of marketing research to provide this information.

Marketing research is defined as involving the investigation of factors related to the marketing activities of a company.

'Market research' and 'marketing research' are often used interchangeably, however.

(a) 'Market research' involves gathering information about the market for a particular product or service (typically, consumer attitudes, existing product usage etc).

(b) 'Marketing research', according to the American Marketing Association is 'the systematic gathering, recording and analysing of data about problems relating to the marketing of goods and services' and so includes research on the effects of pricing, advertising and other marketing decision variables.

Once you have finished this chapter, you should understand the following.

(a) The marketing research process is important in identifying and analysing customer needs.

(b) The organisation for the collection of marketing research data will require an effective information system.

(c) External agencies may be used to collect marketing research data, although larger organisations may have their own in-house departments.

## 1 TYPES OF MARKETING RESEARCH

*Examined 6/96*

1.1 Marketing research may include the following specific types of research.

(a) *Market research* includes:

- (i) analysis of the market potential for existing products;
- (ii) forecasting likely demand for new products;
- (iii) sales forecasting for all products;
- (iv) study of market trends;
- (v) study of the characteristics of the market;
- (vi) analysis of market shares.

(b) *Product research* includes:

- (i) customer acceptance of proposed new products;

(ii) comparative studies between competitive products;
(iii) studies into packaging and design;
(iv) forecasting new uses for existing products;
(v) test marketing;
(vi) research into the development of a product line (range).

(c) *Price research* includes:

(i) analysis of elasticities of demand;
(ii) analysis of costs and contribution or profit margins;
(iii) the effect of changes in credit policy on demand;
(iv) customer perceptions of price (and quality).

(d) *Sales promotion research* includes:

(i) motivation research for advertising and sales promotion effectiveness;
(ii) analysing the effectiveness of advertising on sales demand;
(iii) analysing the effectiveness of individual aspects of advertising such as copy and media used;
(iv) establishing sales territories;
(v) analysing the effectiveness of salesmen;
(vi) analysing the effectiveness of other sales promotion methods.

(e) *Distribution research* includes:

(i) the location and design of distribution centres;
(ii) the analysis of packaging for transportation and shelving;
(iii) dealer supply requirements;
(iv) dealer advertising requirements;
(v) the cost of different methods of transportation and warehousing.

The most important of these are product and market research, which we will now examine in more detail.

### Exam focus point

These tasks were covered in a June 1996 question (Q24 *In-house research* of our Practice & Revision Kit). This list would have been useful to ensure you covered all the possibilities.

## Product research

1.2 This aspect of marketing research attempts to make product research and development customer-oriented. Product research is concerned with the product itself, whether new, improved or already on the market, and customer reactions to it.

### Exercise 1

Where might the ideas for new products come from? Try to think of likely sources within and outside the firm.

### Solution

The possibilities are endless, but you might have thought of research and development personnel; marketing and sales personnel; competitors; customers; ideas springing from new scientific or technological discoveries.

1.3 New ideas are screened by specialists (market researchers, designers, research and development staff etc) and rejected if they:

(a) have a low profit potential or insufficient market potential;
(b) have a high cost and involve high risk;
(c) do not conform to company objectives;

(d) cannot be produced and distributed with the available resources.

Ideas which survive the screening process will be product tested and possibly test marketed to indicate how well the product will sell if produced for a wider market.

1.4 Product research may examine:

(a) product form and attributes in relation to consumer tastes and needs; and
(b) competitive products and existing products in the company portfolio.

1.5 Product research also includes the need to keep the product range of a company's goods under review as a way of *reducing costs* by eliminating unprofitable lines; by extending custom by diversification; finding *new segments* by adapting products or their uses; and finding new uses for existing products, to extend a product range. Uses for plastics and nylon, for example, have been extended rapidly in the past as a result of effective research.

---

**Exercise 2**

Without going into the detail of individual brands, can you think of some broad product areas where this kind of extension has been apparent in recent years?

**Solution**

Again, there are many possibilities. You might have thought of the vast expansion in the range of uses for man-made materials such as plastics or nylon. Or you might cite the proliferation of computer hardware: whereas twenty years ago computer usage was confined to the mainframe installations in large companies, nowadays even very small organisations have a PC or two to streamline their operations.

---

1.6 Information about competitors' product ranges and their new or improved products is important if the company is to maintain a competitive edge.

## Market research

1.7 Market research information can be collected directly (for example, from sample market results or questionnaires filled in by customers) or from secondary sources (such as analyses of past sales, or external information such as the *Nielsen Index*, which gives summary information on sales by products and geographical areas).

1.8 The quantity and quality of information provided by market research has an associated cost and the trade-off between cost and accuracy is important, particularly because risk cannot be eliminated. Market research can help to reduce the risk in decision making but, usually, the more accurate the information, the higher the cost. Market research should always be *cost effective*.

## Techniques of market research

1.9 *Market forecast* comprises the assessment of environmental factors, outside the organisation's control, which will affect the demand for its products/services.

(a) An *economic review* (national economy, government policy, covering forecasts on investment, population, gross national product, and inflation).

(b) *Specific market research* (to obtain data about specific markets and forecasts concerning total market demand).

(c) Evaluation of *total market demand* for the firm's and similar products - including such factors as profitability and market potential.

1.10 *Sales forecasts* attempt to predict how a product will sell when factors such as price and promotional activity are varied. Unlike the market forecast, a sales forecast concerns the firm's activity directly. It takes into account such aspects as sales to certain categories of customer, sales promotion activities, the extent of competition, product life cycle, performance of major products. Sales forecasts are expressed in volume, value and profit, and in the case of national and international organisations regional forecasts are usual, by product.

Research into potential sales will involve an estimate of the part of the market which is within the possible reach of a product.

1.11 Market research needs to consider trends in economic, fiscal, political and social influences which may affect supply and demand. In addition, demand changes in market sectors, geographical areas or other changes which are cyclical or seasonal.

## 2 IN-HOUSE VS EXTERNAL AGENCIES

2.1 Marketing research has been a growing source of organisation expenditure in recent years. Very few organisations believe that they can shoulder the cost of a large full-time staff of marketing research workers, especially a 'field force' of researchers spread around the country. It is quite probable, therefore, that:

(a) the organisation will have a small full-time marketing research department; and

(b) they will use the services of external marketing research consultants for specific projects. In addition to marketing research agencies, there are marketing research departments in many of the large UK advertising agencies.

### External agencies

2.2 An external agency would bring *expertise* in marketing research which an organisation might not be able to supply in-house, although it would need to liaise with the organisation through its marketing research department.

2.3 A further advantage of marketing research agencies is that they may bring together their general knowledge of a particular market and supply this information to all clients or subscribers. An example of such information provision is the Television Consumer Audit.

2.4 Often, outside research organisations are used for overseas research, not only because they can help overcome language difficulties, but also because of local expertise and speed of access of information.

2.5 In addition to external marketing research agencies a UK company is often able to obtain considerable help and advice and information from a variety of organisations including the following:

(a) overseas agents and distributors;
(b) banks;
(c) trade and professional organisations;
(d) Chambers of Commerce;
(e) Department of Trade and Industry;
(f) UK and foreign embassies and consulates; and
(g) academic institutions.

### In-house marketing research

2.6 The advantages of using an internal marketing department to conduct marketing research are as follows.

(a) *Confidentiality*

One of the problems in using outside agencies, particularly for sensitive topics such as new product launches, is the possibility of the information getting into the hands of competitors.

(b) *Cost*

It is often considered more cost effective to use internal personnel because, providing they are fully occupied, there is no need to add on a profit margin as is the case for external agencies.

(c) *Expertise*

Although external agencies may be aware of the latest and most sophisticated marketing research techniques, they may have less knowledge of the product/service, the market situation and the company's customers.

2.7 The organisation of the marketing research department should be in accordance with the needs of the company. Therefore, there is likely to be much variation depending on the emphasis placed on marketing versus sales and the other functional departments.

2.8 However, the marketing research manager would normally report to the marketing director and have reporting to him personnel responsible for desk research on the one hand and field research on the other.

2.9 The marketing research manager would also need to work closely with the rest of the marketing department, the sales department and indeed to have close links with customers.

---

**Case example**

PPP Healthcare, one of the UKs leading health care service operators has used a data warehousing system to slash its operating costs. In 1995 they realised that their mainframe based data system was costly and inadequate, employing teams of programmers in lengthy, complex operations to answer simple queries. A user friendly system was needed, and Malcolm Lambell, director of IT, turned to Sequent, a company used to providing off site data storage and interrogation systems. A data warehouse was established at Sequent headquarters in Tunbridge Wells, going 'live' at the beginning of 1996. This holds key information on claims, income and customers, and has revolutionised the way in which the company works with the hospitals which provide the health care for PPP customers. The company can now control its costs (which constitute 80% of its yearly income) much more effectively, and enables it to compete much more effectively. Services can be precisely tailored to deliver the most cost effective package, including, for example, new insurance packages linked to a specific hospital.

This has proved so effective that the £1m, cost of establishing the data warehouse has been recouped in the first year! *(Adapted from the Financial Times, February 1997)*

---

## 3 MARKETING RESEARCH PROCEDURE: SECONDARY DATA Examined 6/95, 12/95

3.1 Marketing research involves the following five stages.

(a) *Definition of the problem.* The marketing problem which management wishes to resolve must be properly defined. This usually involves careful consultation between managers and researchers to clarify the nature of the problem, and decide what information it is appropriate and possible to collect.

(b) *Design of the research.* Once the research team knows what problem it must help to resolve, it will establish the type of data, the collection method to be used, the selection of a research agency (if appropriate) and if a sample is to be taken, the design of the sample frame.

(c) *Collection of the data*

(d) *Analysis of the data*

(e) *Presentation of a report* which should then lead to a management marketing decision

3.2 Marketing research information is composed of secondary data and primary data. Primary data is discussed in Section 3 below.

3.3 Secondary data is 'data neither collected directly by the user nor specifically for the user, often under conditions that are not well known to the user' (American Marketing Association). The collection of secondary data for marketing research is sometimes known as *desk research*.

3.4 Desk research involves collecting data from internal and external sources.

(a) Records inside the firm, gathered by another department or section for its own purposes may be useful for the research task in hand. Internal data would include:

(i) production data about quantities produced, materials and labour resources used etc;

(ii) data about inventory;

(iii) data about sales volumes, analysed by sales area, salesman, quantity, price, profitability, distribution outlet, customer etc;

(iv) data about marketing itself, such as promotion and brand data;

(v) all cost and management accounting data;

(vi) financial management data relating to the capital structure of the firm, capital tied up in stocks and debtors and so on.

(b) Published information from external sources includes:

(i) publications of market research agencies, such as the Nielsen Index;
(ii) government statistics;
(iii) publications of trade associations;
(iv) professional journals.

3.5 Sources of secondary data for marketing vary according to the needs of the organisation.

3.6 The *government* is a major source of economic information and information about industry and population trends. Examples of UK government publications are:

(a) the Annual Abstract of Statistics and its monthly equivalent, the Monthly Digest of Statistics, containing data about manufacturing output, housing, population etc;

(b) the Digest of UK Energy Statistics (published annually);

(c) Housing and Construction statistics (published quarterly);

(d) Financial Statistics (monthly);

(e) Economic Trends (monthly);

(f) Census of Population;

(g) Census of Production (annual), which has been described as 'one of the most important sources of desk research for industrial marketers' and which provides data about production by firms in each industry in the UK;

(h) Department of Employment Gazette (monthly) giving details of employment in the UK;

(i) British Business, published weekly by the Department of Trade and Industry, giving data on industrial and commercial trends at home and overseas;

(j) Business Monitors, giving detailed information about various industries.

3.7 *Non-government* sources of information include:

(a) the national press (*Financial Times* etc) and financial and professional magazines and journals;

(b) companies and other organisations specialising in the provision of economic and financial data (eg the Financial Times Business Information Service, the Data Research Institute, Reuters and the Extel Group) and research organisations who analyse certain markets and publish and sell the results (eg Mintel, Euromonitor);

(c) directories and yearbooks;

(d) professional institutions (eg Chartered Institute of Marketing, Industrial Marketing Research Association, British Institute of Management, Institute of Practitioners in Advertising);

(e) specialist libraries, such as the City Business Library in London, which collects published information from a wide variety of sources;

(f) trade sources such as the Association of British Insurers (ABI) market share data on the life insurance industry; the Society of Motor Manufacturers and Trades (SMMT) data on the registration of new vehicles by brand. The trade press is also important.

---

**Exercise 3**

Make a list of all the secondary data sources you would use to research the industry/company you work in.

---

## 4 MARKETING RESEARCH PROCEDURE: PRIMARY DATA

*Examined 6/97, 12/96, 6/95*

4.1 The collection of primary data is sometimes known as *field research*. Techniques include:

(a) experimentation;
(b) observation;
(c) sampling;
(d) interviewing;
(e) questionnaires;
(f) consumer panels;
(g) trade audits, such as retail audits;
(h) pre-tests;
(i) post-tests;
(j) attitude scales and methods of analysis.

4.2 *Experimentation* involves the systematic manipulation of a given variable in order to examine its effect on the performance of a subject or system. Measurements are taken before and after the variable is manipulated, and comparisons made with a suitably matched *control* case in order to make inferences about the effects of the variable. This may take place in a laboratory (for example, sensory testing of foods) or in the field (varying exposure to advertising in two matched TV regions).

---

**Exercise 4**

Most people have seen this process - the collection of research data by physical observation - in action. Can you recall an example of it?

**Solution**

It is common to see researchers logging details of traffic passing along a particular road at certain times of day. This enables local authorities to improve services (by introducing traffic lights, constructing roundabouts or whatever). Users of public transport will often see researchers counting the number of passengers passing through, say a railway station at a particular time, again with a view to assessing and possibly improving service levels.

---

4.3 *Observation* may involve machines or fieldworkers. It may involve simply recording behaviour, or require the fieldworker to interpret behaviour, or even interact ('participant observation').

4.4 (a) *Direct observation* involves the examination by an observer of how people behave in particular situations (customers' reactions to product displays and promotions).

(b) Recording devices can be used to monitor the responses of individuals:

(i) an *eye camera* is sometimes used to test response to advertisements;

(ii) a *psychogalvanometer*, which records changes in electrical resistance, and hence emotional reaction, is also used in advertising testing;

(iii) a *tachitoscope* exposes material for a brief moment, and measures the visual impact or legibility of an advertisement.

## Sampling

4.5 In marketing research for consumer goods, surveys of the large total number of consumers will necessarily involve the selection of an appropriate *sample* from the total population, for reasons of practicality and cost effectiveness. Surveying a *total* population is only feasible when the numbers are small, as in the case of industrial markets.

4.6 Samples must be *representative* of the populations from which they are chosen. Representativeness is a statistical concept, which rests on the theory of probability. Broadly, representativeness is achieved by seeking to ensure that samples are chosen at *random*, in a manner which gives all members of a population an *equal chance of being chosen* and in *numbers* sufficient to minimalise the influence of small numbers of individuals from one section of the population on the data which is gathered.

4.7 A *sample frame* is constructed to include all the members of a population (eg 'real ale' drinkers, car drivers). Population here does *not* mean 'everyone in the electoral roll' or 'everyone living in town Y'.

4.8 A complete sampling frame is difficult to obtain in practice because data is often inaccurate, but in any case a comprehensive sampling frame is not justified if the benefits from greater confidence in the accuracy of sample estimates are less than the *cost* of obtaining or maintaining the sampling frame.

### Exercise 5

Suppose you are developing a new product: a piece of computer software designed to simplify the completion of an income tax return. You wish to assess demand for the product by sampling potential users. How would you go about obtaining a sampling frame?

### Solution

Potential users might conceivably include individuals daunted by their own tax returns, but a sampling frame for all such individuals would be almost impossible to obtain. It would be better to reflect that most people with complicated tax affairs use the services of an accountant. Targeting firms of accountants is much easier: they are all registered with a professional body, and the membership lists of these bodies provide a convenient sampling frame.

Another group to target would be people who have retired in, say, the last two years, who no longer have an employer to take care of the Inland Revenue's hunger for information about their finances, and often find their new status confusing.

4.9 Various techniques of sampling (methods of sample design) have been developed so that samples which are 'nearly' random ('quasi-random') can be obtained.

*Random sampling*

4.10 A *random sample* is one selected in such a way that every item in the population has an equal chance of being included.

The use of random number tables, or computer generated random numbers, seeks to eliminate conscious or unconscious bias.

### *Non-random sampling*

4.11 In many situation it is either not possible or else undesirable to use a random sample. The main methods of *non-random sampling* are:

(a) systematic sampling;
(b) stratified sampling;
(c) multistage sampling;
(d) quota sampling;
(e) cluster sampling.

Some of these methods try to approximate the random sampling technique, and are 'quasi-random' sampling methods.

4.12 *Systematic sampling* involves selecting every nth item after a random start. For example, if it was decided to select a sample of 20 from a population of 800, then every 40th (800 ÷ 20) item after a random start in the first 40 should be selected. If (say) 23 was chosen, then the sample would include the following items.

23rd, 63rd, 103rd, 143rd ..........783rd

The gap of 40 is known as the *sampling interval*.

4.13 *Stratified sampling* divides the population into strata, which may conform to a consumer characteristics or a market segment.

For example, a manufacturer of machine equipment may know that 40% of its sales come from one industry A, 30% from another industry B, 10% from industry C and so on. A stratified sample would aim to obtain 40% of its respondents from industry A, 30% from group B, and 10% from C. If all potential customers in each industry are known, the sample within each group could then be selected by random sampling methods using a sampling frame.

4.14 *Multistage sampling* divides the country into a number of areas and a small sample of these is selected at random. Each of the areas selected is subdivided into smaller units and again, a small number of these is selected at random. This process is repeated as many times as necessary and finally, a random sample of the relevant people living in each of the smallest units is made. A fair approximation to a random sample can be obtained.

4.15 In *quota sampling*, investigators are told to interview certain numbers of people in different categories. These may be:

(a) age groups (16-25; 26-35 etc);
(b) gender groups (male; female);
(c) product user groups (light users; medium users; heavy users; non-users).

4.16 These are called 'quota controls'. Out of a quota of, say 50, an interviewer may be required to find at least twenty men and at least twenty women. Ten may be either. The same interviewer may be asked to find ten aged 16-25, ten aged 26-35, ten over 35 and twenty who may be any age. This gives the interviewer greater flexibility, and it is easy to administer, although there is still some risk of bias.

4.17 Using *cluster sampling*, investigators are told to examine every item in the small areas which fit the required definition. Cluster sampling has the advantage of low cost and ease of administration in the same way as multistage sampling, but suffers from a risk of unrepresentativeness because of the restricted group chosen.

*Potential faults in a sampling exercise*

4.18 There are several faults or weaknesses which might occur in the design or collection of sample data.

(a) *Bias*: unless random sampling is used, there will be a likelihood that some 'units' (individuals or households) will have a poor, or even zero chance of being selected. Where this occurs, samples are said to be *biased*.

A biased sample may occur when:

(i) the sampling frame is out of date, and consequently excludes a number of individuals or 'units' new to the population; or

(ii) some individuals selected for the sample decline to respond.

(b) *Insufficient data*: the sample may be too small to be reliable as a source of information about an entire population.

(c) *Unrepresentative data*: data collected might be unrepresentative of normal conditions or affected by actually being collected. This is called the 'Hawthorne Effect' after a study in the 1920s in which the workers involved performed better than usual simply because they were being studied.

(d) *Omission of an important factor*: data might be incomplete because an important item has been omitted in the design of the 'questions'.

(e) *Carelessness*: data might be provided without any due care and attention. An investigator might also be careless in the way he gathers data.

(f) *Confusion between 'cause' and 'correlation'*: it may be tempting to assume that if two variables appear to be related, one variable is the *cause* of the other. Variables may be associated but it is not necessarily true that one causes the other. For example, in a period of hot weather both sales of swimwear and ice creams are likely to rise (a positive correlation). However, one is not causing the other; they are both 'caused' by the hot weather.

(g) Where questions call for something more than simple 'one word' replies, there may be difficulty in interpreting the results correctly. This is especially true of 'depth interviews' which try to determine the reasons for human behaviour (*motivation research*).

## Questionnaires

4.19 Questionnaires may be administered by personal interview, telephone or post.

4.20 Postal surveys tend to attract a relatively low response rate and unrepresentative respondents, with unsolicited questionnaires often obtaining only a 2% or 3% return. Under these circumstances great care should be taken when extrapolating from such results. Follow up letters may improve responses. These are also better in specialist populations (eg enthusiasts) and when inducements are offered.

### Exercise 6

Think of some simple techniques which might improve the response rate to a postal survey.

### Solution

Measures could include sending to named individuals and taking care that information such as job titles is up to date. (This can be difficult if the sample is being drawn from a trade directory. It takes up to one year to update such directories, and the current year's edition will be on average six months old when reference is made.) It also helps to send a covering letter and to stress confidentiality and anonymity for the respondent. Finally, the inclusion of a stamped and addressed envelope for the reply helps, particularly if a stamp rather than a prepaid envelope is used: there is a sort of moral pressure here!

*Questionnaire design*

4.21 There are two main considerations in designing questionnaires.

(a) Questions should generate valid and reliable information on the matter being surveyed. Respondents must therefore find the questions comprehensible. Questions that are likely to produce biased answers should also be avoided.

(b) The questionnaire should be designed with the subsequent data analysis in mind.

4.22 The following guidelines should therefore be adopted.

(a) Leading questions should be avoided.

(b) Questions should be short and unambiguous wherever possible.

(c) Questions should fall in a logical sequence.

(d) The working language of the target group should be used.

(e) *Funnelling*, a technique of moving from general to restricted questions more directly related to the research objectives, can be applied. This technique is sometimes reversed to check limited responses.

(f) Personal questions on potentially sensitive issues such as sex, politics, religion and personal habits should only be asked in exceptional circumstances. Before attempting such questions interviewers need to have established goodwill.

4.23 *Pilot testing* is *essential* to questionnaire design. It involves testing a proposed questionnaire to avoid confusing, ambiguous, silly or unnecessary questions.

It also permits the methods of analysis to be given a trial run.

4.24 *Classification of respondents* is important, since this will be used to analyse responses to find if there are variations between attitudes and behaviour of different types of people. These questions are usually asked at the end of an interview, since some (eg age) may be sensitive.

4.25 Questionnaires can be administered by the following means.

(a) *Telephone interviews*: these offer a speedy response and can cover a wide geographical area fairly cheaply. The drawback is that interviews must be fairly short and cannot use visual methods.

(b) *Personal interviews*: the best, but slowest and most expensive method.

(c) *Replies by mail*: fairly cheap, and avoids interviewer interference, but there is no control over the completion of the questionnaire. Low response (say 10-30%) might make the sample data unrepresentative.

(d) *Self-completion*, perhaps at the place of purchase. The disadvantage of this form of survey is that respondents may not understand questions properly (as with mail surveys). The questionnaire will also need to be short to optimise completion.

## Consumer panels

4.26 Consumer panels consist of a representative cross-section of consumers who have agreed to give information about their attitudes or buying habits (through personal visits or mail questionnaires or data transferred from a home recording computer by modem) at regular intervals of time. Consumer panels with personal visits are called *home audit panels* and panels which send data by post or by computer are called *diary panels*. Panels might be established for either the long term or the short term.

4.27 Consumer panels provide continuous information over time from willing guinea pigs, but recruitment and representativeness are big problems.

Willing participants may be atypical and probably represent only a limited section of the population in question.

### Trade audits or retail audits

4.28 Trade audits are carried out among panels of wholesalers and retailers, and the term 'retail audits' refers to panels of retailers only. A research firm sends auditors to selected outlets at regular intervals to count stock and deliveries, thus enabling an estimate of throughput to be made. This details:

(a) retail sales for selected products and brands, sales by different type of retail outlet, market shares and brand shares;

(b) retail stocks of products and brands (enabling a firm subscribing to the audit to compare stocks of its own goods with those of competitors);

(c) selling prices in retail outlets, including information about discounts.

---

### Exercise 7

How can the data from a retail audit be of any value to a manufacturer who is not making retail sales?

### Solution

Because they provide continuous monitoring of retail activity, retail audits may be of value to such a firm for the following reasons.

(a) Problems in retail sales provide an early warning of problems the manufacturer may soon have to expect in ex-factory sales.

(b) They indicate long-term trends in the market place, thus providing helpful information for strategic marketing planning.

(c) In the shorter term, they may indicate the need for changes in pricing policy, sales promotion or advertising, distribution policy, package design or product design.

---

4.29 A well-known example of a retail audit is the Inventory Audit of Retail Sales, also called the Nielsen Index (after its originator) which has operated since 1939. This monitors sales and stock levels for three product groups: food, drugs and pharmaceuticals. The Nielsen Food Index audits about 800 grocers bi-monthly and reports on each brand, size, flavour etc specified by the client, together with an 'all other' category, showing:

(a) consumer sales in units and £;

(b) retailer purchases in units;

(c) the source of delivery (co-operatives, multiple stores depot, independent wholesalers);

(d) retailers' stocks and stock cover (in days/weeks);

(e) prices;

(f) details of out of stock items;

(g) press, magazine and TV expenditure.

The report is subdivided into shop types (all grocers, co-operatives, multiples, major multiples and independents) and television regions.

### Pre-testing and post-testing

4.30 Marketing research may be carried out before, during and after marketing decisions are implemented. Not all areas of marketing can be investigated easily. While the effects of sales promotions (coupons, three for the price of two and the like) are directly measurable in terms of sales, the effectiveness of advertising often needs to be inferred, and is difficult to distinguish from other factors.

4.31 Other powerful influences in the market place, such as price cuts and sales promotions by competitors can mask the true effect. Much research therefore focuses on the effectiveness of the campaign in communicating with its target audience.

Measurement of the *communication effect* is more reliable than attempts to measure the sales effect attributable to a particular advertising campaign.

*Pre-testing*

4.32 (a) *Motivational research* is carried out to pre-test advertising copy. Subjects are invited to watch a film show which includes new TV advertising, and a measure of the shift in their brand awareness is taken after the show. *Copy research* might involve showing members of the public a number of press advertisements and then asking questions about them (in order to measure the impact of different slogans or headlines).

(b) *Laboratory tests* recording the physiological reactions of people watching advertisements (eg heart beat, blood pressure, dilation of the pupil of the eye, perspiration) measure the arousal or attention-drawing power of an advertisement.

(c) *Ratings tests* involve asking a panel of target consumers to look at alternative advertisements and to give them ratings (marks out of ten) for attention-drawing power, clarity, emotional appeal and stimulus to buy.

---

**Case example**

In 1979, when Ford launched the Fiesta, their advertising agency, Ogilvy Benson Mather, abandoned their first creative idea after motivational research. The proposed copy for the advertisement focused on the theme of Ford's 'new baby'. An expectant father was seen pacing up and down outside his garage. Suddenly, from inside the garage came the sounds of a new born baby crying. The garage door was opened to reveal a proud wife with the new Fiesta. Women reacted very unfavourably to the advertisement which was shown in its pre-production animatic form (drawings with soundtrack). They expressed uncomfortable feelings and anxiety at the thought of a baby being locked up in a garage. Wisely the advertisement was reformulated to a high technology theme.

---

4.33 *Test marketing* aims to obtain information about how consumers react to the product - will they buy it, how frequently, etc? Total market demand for the product can then be estimated.

4.34 A test market involves testing a new consumer product in selected areas which are thought to be 'representative' of the total market. This avoids the costs of a full-scale launch while permitting the collection of market data. The firm will distribute the product through the same types of sales outlets it plans to use in the full market launch, and use the promotion plans it intends to use in the full market. This enables the company to 'test the water' before launching the product nationally. It helps to make sales forecasts, and can also be used to identify flaws in the product or promotional plans.

4.35 Other forms of product testing include the following.

(a) *Simulated store technique* (or laboratory test markets) involves a group of shoppers watching a selection of advertisements for a number of products, including an advertisement for the new product. They are then given some money and invited to spend it in a supermarket or shopping area. Their purchases are recorded and they are asked to explain their purchase decisions (and non-purchase decisions). Some weeks later they are contacted again and asked about their product attitudes and repurchase intentions. These tests provide a quick, simple way to assess advertising effectiveness and forecast sales volumes.

(b) *Controlled test marketing*. A panel of stores carries the new product for a given length of time. Shelf locations, point-of-sale displays and pricing etc are varied; the sales results are then monitored. This test (also known as 'minimarket testing') helps to provide an assessment of 'in-store' factors in achieving sales as well as to forecast sales volumes.

*Post-testing*

4.36 Post-testing concentrates on the communication effect of advertisements. It uses:

(a) *recall tests*, which ask the interviewee to remember, unaided, advertisements which have been seen before the interview; and

(b) *recognition tests*, which involve giving the interviewee some reminder of an advertisement, and testing his/her recognition of it.

*EPOS*

4.37 The recording and use of *electronic point of sales* (EPOS) data has become widespread and offers a real opportunity to measure directly the effect of, say, local radio advertising on the immediate sales of a brand in the media's catchment area. The use of such disaggregated tactical data overcomes the problems of external effects distorting aggregated sales figures.

EPOS enables major retailers, such as the supermarkets, to measure directly the performance of competitive brands. Hitherto, this information has had to be inferred from the use of consumer purchasing audits conducted by organisations like Audits of Great Britain (AGB).

This tracking of sales in this way is increasingly allowing managers to carry out monitoring and analysis of market data using *decision support systems*.

## Recording data about attitudes

4.38 Attitudes are measured by means of attitude scales, and there are two common types used in marketing research.

(a) *Likert scales* consist of statements, about product qualities, consumer attitudes or behaviour and so on. Respondents are asked to state the level of agreement or disagreement which they have towards the statement. Responses are selected from a 5, 7, 9 or 11 point scale marking these levels (from eg 'very strongly agree' to 'very strongly disagree').

(b) *Semantic differential scales* consist of bipolar adjectives (strong-weak, good-bad, masculine-feminine) with intervening gradations. Respondents are typically asked to rate or place a product on these scales.

## Evaluating data

4.39 The evaluation of data collected in a survey will be carried out using statistical techniques. Some forms of analysis are as follows.

(a) *Multiple regression analysis*. This might be used, for example, to analyse the effect on sales of changes in a variety of other variables such as price and advertising.

(b) *Discriminant analysis*. This might be used when the researcher wants to know what consumer traits (for example socio-economic groupings, lifestyle, age and sex) are associated with frequent, or infrequent purchase of a particular product or brand.

(c) *Tests of statistical significance*, for example chi-squared tests and calculation of standard errors.

## The reliability of sample data

4.40 A sample is intended to provide a measure of the attitudes or behaviour of a population as a whole. Whether it does this is usually checked by making statistical tests of significance. Computer packages for statistical analysis will often carry out tests for the significance of data variation automatically.

4.41 Sampling can be used to identify consumer attitudes and behaviour, but also to identify potential market segments.

### The value of research information

4.42 Information is only worth having if the benefits derived from it exceed the costs of its collection. The greater the accuracy of information provided, the more it will cost. At high levels of accuracy the marginal costs of collection will probably exceed the marginal benefits of the extra accuracy obtained.

It is also worth noting that it is only worth paying for market research that provides additional information. Marketing research that merely confirms information that is already widely known has little real value.

---

**Exam focus point**

Marketing research is also covered in *Understanding Customers* and will surface again later in your studies for the CIM qualification.

It featured in the June 1997 exam (Q92 *Christmas gems* of our Practice & Revision Kit) in which you had to research the needs of the retailers of a new product and also the final publishers. Clearly, in both instances you had to collect both primary and secondary data – but the sales force is probably the best way of collecting primary data from retailers whereas surveys and focus groups are probably more appropriate for consumers.

---

### Interpretation of results

4.43 Interpretation of results takes great care. There is some controversy as to how much interpretation market researchers should offer clients. One school of thought suggests presentation of the facts only, leaving the client to draw conclusions. A contrasting approach is for the researcher to interpret results and suggest conclusions or interpretations based on evidence in the findings. The guiding principle should be the brief given to the researcher at the outset of the project.

## 5 MARKETING INFORMATION SYSTEMS

*Examined 12/96*

5.1 Marketing information systems (MKIS) represent a systematic attempt to supply continuous, useful, usable marketing information within an organisation to decision makers, often in the form of a database.

5.2 The design of an MKIS should start with the information needs of decision-makers rather than with technical considerations of the database. It has three components which need to be planned.

(a) *System inputs*

The sources of information which can form an input to an MKIS are, in principle, the same as those discussed above that is, internal and external sources and primary research. The starting point is very likely to be existing customer account records. These sources can be used to identify the types of service which each type of customer is buying along with trend data. These records can be amended as necessary over time and can be augmented by specific market research projects so as to provide a complete picture.

(b) *Data manipulation*

Once collected, the data needs to be manipulated into a suitable form for use by decision-makers. Again, the principles of this manipulation are those noted in the earlier part of this chapter in that the mass of information needs to be summarised so that trends and major features can be identified.

(c) *System outputs*

Once manipulated into a form in which the information can be used by decision makers, outputs from the system can be determined. Information can be applied to the whole range of marketing decisions.

### Case example

Savacentre, the hypermarket chain of J Sainsbury, turned to data warehousing in order to rationalise the management of its information systems concerning home and leisure goods and customer information. These were originally separate systems, but Bob Jones, Systems Development Manager, realised that they overlapped significantly, and decided on a merging of the data. Initial attempts to put it onto a single computer met with frustration and failure - the mainframe could not deliver information to managers quickly enough. Marketing staff had not had a computer system and had previously relied on external agencies to process information for them, which was hideously slow.

The new data warehouse has been a spectacular success; queries which used to take days can now be answered in a few seconds, although Bob Jones is concerned at the rate of growth of the database; 20 gigabytes at the beginning of 1997 is expected to grow into 300 gigabytes within 12 months!

Initial use - mail shots derived from data gathered from loyalty cards - have enabled the company to target customers with children advising them of 'back to school' clothing offers, and when a new store was opened by a competitor close to one of their own, they were able to mail shot customers to persuade them not to go over to that store. Targeting is improving all the time, and as marketing staff get used to the new facility, they have quickly begun to develop their own, new ways of using it. Other staff are now asking to be allowed to use the facility, so that internal barriers within the store are breaking down.

*(Adapted from the Financial Times, February 1997)*

### Case example

'Question: how do you increase sales of canned beer? Answer: display it next to the disposable nappies. Bizarre though it sounds, supermarkets around the US are finding that the beer-and-nappies combination works a treat. Once you think about it, the explanation is simple: men are asked to pick up some nappies on their way home from work, and while they're in the supermarket, decide to pick up some liquid refreshment for the evening too. Spotting these and other quirky sales-boosting combinations is the new challenge for retailers - and the clever ones are meeting it by using information technology to mine the information resources in their sales data. (*Marketing Business, April 1996*)

### Exam focus point

A December 1996 question (Q25 *Systematic research* of our Practice & Revision Kit) asked to develop a formal marketing research and information gathering system. And identify key tasks and responsibilities. This chapter should have given you plenty of ideas as to how to tackle the question.

## Chapter roundup

- *Marketing research* has been a growing source of organisation expenditure in recent years. Very few organisations can afford a large full-time staff of marketing research workers. It is quite probable, therefore, that the organisation will have a small full-time marketing research department, and that it will use the services of external marketing research consultants for specific projects. In addition to market research agencies, there are market research departments in many of the large UK advertising agencies.
- An *external agency* can supply expertise in marketing research not available *in-house* and can bring together its general knowledge of a particular market for all clients or subscribers.
- Marketing research enables companies to gain information on the market and marketing mix *variables* and therefore to make decisions in the light of this information.

## Test your knowledge

1 Differentiate between market research and marketing research. (see Introduction)

2 What is involved in (i) price research and (ii) distribution research? (1.1)

3 What is a market forecast? (1.9)

4 What are the advantages of having an in-house marketing research department? (2.6)

5 Secondary data is collected directly by the user. True or false? (3.3)

6 What is field research? (4.1)

7 Explain how systematic sampling is used. (4.12)

8 What are the major advantage and disadvantage of quota sampling? (4.16)

9 List the potential faults which may occur in sampling. (4.18)

10 What is a diary panel? (4.26)

11 What details are provided by trade and retail panels? (4.28)

12 How can EPOS data be used in market research? (4.37)

**Now try illustrative questions 7 and 8 at the end of the Study Text**

# Chapter 5

# PRODUCT

## This chapter covers the following topics.



| | | *Syllabus reference* |
|---|---|---|
| 1 | Market segmentation | 2.4 |
| 2 | The product life cycle | 2.4 |
| 3 | Product portfolio planning | 2.3 |
| 4 | New product development | 2.5 |
| 5 | Services | 2.3, 2.4 |
| 6 | Brands and packaging | 2.3 |



## Introduction

The best introduction to this topic is to look at the product/service portfolio.

In order to grow, an organisation can decide to use particular combinations of product and market decisions. Ansoff expressed these options in terms of a matrix.

| | *Existing Products* | *New Products* |
|---|---|---|
| *Existing Markets* | Market Penetration | Product Development |
| *New Markets* | Market Development | Diversification |

Market penetration involves trying to increase the share for existing products or services in existing markets. This could be achieved by better market segmentation (see below), that is by tailoring products more closely to the needs of target groups of customers within the existing market. The danger with this strategy is of putting all the organisation's eggs in one basket.

Product development involves formulating new products for the existing market. Existing knowledge of customers and the existing distribution network permit extension of the product range. A danger is cannibalisation: that is, sales of new products may be achieved at the expense of existing products. This strategy may work if the new products make a greater contribution per unit to profit or if there is a danger that, without the new product, customers would switch from the existing product anyway, but to competitors' products.

Market development involves marketing existing products into new markets. Market research is required to ensure products meet the needs of the new market.

The highest risk strategy is to enter new markets with new products, ie diversification. Extensive market research and intensive product development work are likely to be necessary.

This examination of the product/service portfolio sets the stage for examining the product in detail.

Once you have finished this chapter you should understand the following.

(a) The product/service portfolio should offer a mix of functional, physical and symbolic benefits.

(b) Products generally have a life cycle which follows a known model (although this does not apply to all products) and the life cycle of each product will vary from that of another.

(c) New product development is extremely important, but modification of the product life cycle can also extend a product offering.

(d) Brands and packaging have a significant role in the product aspect of the marketing mix.

## 1 MARKET SEGMENTATION

1.1 Market segmentation is an attempt to take different customer characteristics and variations in taste, usage, and so on into account. An homogenous mass market is subdivided into subsets of customers. Within each subset, customers have similar needs which are distinct from those in other subsets.

1.2 By using different marketing approaches for each segment, it should be possible to increase profit contribution for each segment. The marketing approach used for each segment should reflect the particular needs of customers and potential customers in that segment. It is akin to using a rifle (to aim at specific targets) rather than a shotgun (to aim at all targets at the same time).

## Requirements for effective market segmentation

1.3 Clearly there are many possible characteristics of buyers which could be used as a basis for segmenting markets and there are criteria to be used to identify the most effective characteristics for use in market segmentation decisions.

(a) *Measurability*

The degree to which information exists or is obtainable cost effectively in respect of the particular buyer characteristic. Bookshops may be able to obtain information on sales relatively easily, but it is more difficult for them to obtain information about the personality traits of buyers.

(b) *Accessibility*

The degree to which the organisation can focus effectively on the chosen segments using marketing methods. Educational establishments in a bookshop's area can be identified easily and approached using direct mail or telemarketing, while individuals with income over £30,000 per annum in the same area might be more difficult to isolate effectively.

(c) *Substantiality*

The degree to which the segments are large enough to be worth considering as separate markets. Mounting marketing campaigns is expensive, and so a minimum size for a segment is based on likely profitability. Thus, whilst a large number of people in social group DE aged over 65 could be identified, their potential profitability for a bookshop is likely to be less in the long term than a smaller number of 17-18 year old students.

## Benefits of market segmentation

1.4 Apart from improved contribution to profits, other benefits from successful market segmentation include the following.

(a) The organisation will be in a better position to identify new marketing opportunities. This benefit should flow from a better understanding of customer needs in each segment, and the possibility of spotting further sub groups.

(b) Specialists can be used for each of the organisation's major segments. Thus, small business counsellors can be employed by banks to deal effectively with this market segment, and a computer consultancy can have specialist sales staff for, say, shops, manufacturers, service industries and local authorities. This builds competencies and establishes effective marketing systems.

(c) The total marketing budget can be allocated to take into account the needs of each segment and the likely return from each segment. This optimises return on investment.

(d) The organisation can make fine adjustments to the product and service offerings and to the marketing appeals used for each segment. This again promotes efficient resource utilisation.

(e) The organisation can try to dominate particular segments, thus gaining competitive advantage. Advantages accrued function *synergistically* to promote improved competitive ability.

(f) The product range can more closely reflect differences in customer needs. All modern marketing relies on responsiveness to the consumer. When this is improved, benefits flow.

## Bases for market segmentation

1.5 A number of bases are possible and these are discussed in the following paragraphs.

*Geographic segmentation*

1.6 Here, the basis for segmentation is location. A national chain of supermarkets will use geographic segmentation because it interacts closely with the chain's outlet strategy. Each branch or group of retail outlets could be given mutually exclusive areas to service and so the method enables the supermarket chain to make more effective use of target marketing and cover the market available. The obvious advantage to customers is convenience of access, which is a primary motivation to retailers when considering ways of segmenting the grocery shopping market. Of course this customer benefit needs to be considered against the cost of provision of retail branches. Research has shown that one of the major reasons why customers choose particular stores in which to shop is convenience of access.

*Demographic segmentation*

1.7 Here the market is divided on the basis of age, gender, socio-economic group, housing, family characteristics or family life cycle stage. These factors may be used in combination.

1.8 Segmentation by age is the basis of the attempt by the High Street banks to attract 18 year olds as customers, especially new students in the higher education sector. Customers are unlikely to switch accounts between competing suppliers, so banks expect long-term relationships (and profit) to result from success in this target marketing effort, in a highly competitive market.

1.9 Products targeted by gender include cosmetics, clothing, alcohol, cars and even financial services.

1.10 The JICNARS scale is used by the UK market research industry to provide standardised social groupings. These are based entirely on occupation of the head of the household.

*Socio-economic groups in the UK*

| *Social grade* | *Description of occupations* | *Example* |
|---|---|---|
| A | Higher managerial and professional | Company director |
| B | Lower managerial and supervisory | Middle manager |
| C1 | Non-manual | Bank clerk |
| C2 | Skilled manual | Electrician |
| D | Semi-skilled and unskilled manual | Labourer |
| E | Those receiving no income from employment/casual workers | Unemployed |

1.11 Other scales (such as the Registrar General's Classification, and the Hall-Jones Scale) are used elsewhere. This classification is very commonly used in marketing and market research in the UK, yet it is simplistic to make easy assumptions about the implications of classification for consumption. For example, in terms of disposable income (the take-home pay of workers) C2 members often have more money than do Cl, which obviously affects buying capability. Also there is class mobility in that individuals and their families can move between groups, although their underlying influences may remain as they were or change only slowly.

1.12 Socio-economic groups are a useful way of segmenting markets for the following reasons:

(a) with some exceptions we can make many reliable inferences about the relationship between occupation and income;

(b) they can be used to infer differences in purchase and consumption patterns even where the total disposable income between two groups may be similar;

(c) the categories are stable and enduring, and can be compared across time;

(d) each group tends to have identifiable attitudinal and behavioural patterns. For instance, ABCI groups tend to be more 'future orientated' than do C2DE groups which are more 'present orientated'. Such attitudes are clearly highly significant for the marketing of endowment policies or private education, for example.

1.13 Because of criticisms of the JICNARS classification, more sophisticated measures of socio-economic and group membership have been devised. Housing type and ownership are particularly important methods of segmentation for many types of good. The use of this method is made much easier by the major categorisation scheme for all housing types in the UK, known as ACORN (A Categorisation Of Residential Neighbourhoods), which enables precise target marketing based on housing type to be conducted by suppliers. It is based on the Census data gathered by the government every ten years which records details of residential households and their occupants, and also other data collected by HM Statistical Service on employment, consumption and so on.

1.14 This system introduces house type into the classification and every UK household has been classified in ACORN groups. Other work has cross-referenced ACORN with postcodes for every address in the UK making specific identification of customer types more flexible. The 1995 ACORN groups (projected from the 1991 Census) are shown on as follows.

**THE ACORN TARGETING CLASSIFICATION: FULL LIST**

| | | | |
|---|---|---|---|
| **A** | **Thriving (19.7% of population)** | | |
| | *A1* | *Wealthy Achievers, Suburban Areas (15.0%)* | % of population |
| | 1.1 | Wealthy Suburbs, Large Detached Houses | 2.5 |
| | 1.2 | Villages with Wealthy Commuters | 3.2 |
| | 1.3 | Mature Affluent Home Owning Areas | 2.7 |
| | 1.4 | Affluent Suburbs, Older Families | 3.7 |
| | 1.5 | Mature, Well-Off Suburbs | 3.0 |
| | *A2* | *Affluent Greys, Rural Communities (2.3%)* | |
| | 2.6 | Agricultural Villages, Home Based Workers | 1.6 |
| | 2.7 | Holiday Retreats, Older People, Home Based Workers | 0.7 |
| | *A3* | *Prosperous Pensioners, Retirement Areas (2.4%)* | |
| | 3.8 | Home Owning Areas, Well-Off Older Residents | 1.4 |
| | 3.9 | Private Flats, Elderly People | 0.9 |
| **B** | **Expanding (11.6% of population)** | | |
| | *B4* | *Affluent Executives, Family Areas (3.8%)* | |
| | 4.10 | Affluent Working Families with Mortgages | 2.1 |
| | 4.11 | Affluent Working Couples with Mortgages, New Homes | 1.3 |
| | 4.12 | Transient Workforces, Living at their Place of Work | 0.4 |
| | *B5* | *Well-Off Workers, Family Areas (7.8%)* | |
| | 5.13 | Home Owning Family Areas | 2.6 |
| | 5.14 | Home Owning Family Areas, Older Children | 3.0 |
| | 5.15 | Families with Mortgages, Younger Children | 2.2 |

| | | | % of population |
|---|---|---|---|
| **C** | **Rising (7.8% of population)** | | |
| | *C6* | *Affluent Urbanites, Town and City Areas (2.3%)* | |
| | 6.16 | Well-Off Town and City Areas | 1.1 |
| | 6.17 | Flats & Mortgages, Singles and Young Working Couples | 0.7 |
| | 6.18 | Furnished Flats & Bedsits, Younger Single People | 0.4 |
| | *C7* | *Prosperous Professionals, Metropolitan Areas (2.1%)* | |
| | 7.19 | Apartments, Young Professional Singles and Couples | 1.1 |
| | 7.20 | Gentrified Multi-Ethnic Areas | 1.0 |
| | *C8* | *Better-Off Executives, Inner City Areas (3.4%)* | |
| | 8.21 | Prosperous Enclaves, Highly Qualified Executives | 0.7 |
| | 8.22 | Academic Centres, Students and Young Professionals | 0.7 |
| | 8.23 | Affluent City Centre Areas, Tenements and Flats | 0.4 |
| | 8.24 | Partially Gentrified Multi-Ethnic Areas | 0.7 |
| | 8.25 | Converted Flats and Bedsits, Single People | 0.9 |
| **D** | **Settling (24.1% of population)** | | |
| | *D9* | *Comfortable Middle Agers, Mature Home Owning Areas (13.4%)* | |
| | 9.26 | Mature Established Home Owning Areas | 3.3 |
| | 9.27 | Rural Areas, Mixed Occupations | 3.4 |
| | 9.28 | Established Home Owning Areas | 4.0 |
| | 9.29 | Home Owning Areas, Council Tenants, Retired People | 2.6 |
| | *D10* | *Skilled Workers, Home Owning Areas (10.7%)* | |
| | 10.30 | Established Home Owning Areas, Skilled Workers | 4.5 |
| | 10.31 | Home Owners in Older Properties, Younger Workers | 3.1 |
| | 10.32 | Home Owning Areas with Skilled Workers | 3.1 |
| **E** | **Aspiring (13.7% of population)** | | |
| | *E11* | *New Home Owners, Mature Communities (9.7%)* | |
| | 11.33 | Council Areas, Some New Home Owners | 3.8 |
| | 11.34 | Mature Home Owning Areas, Skilled Workers | 3.1 |
| | 11.35 | Low Rise Estates, Older Workers, New Home Owners | 2.8 |
| | *E12* | *White Collar Workers, Better-Off Multi-Ethnic Areas (4.0%)* | |
| | 12.36 | Home Owning Multi-Ethnic Areas, Young Families | 1.1 |
| | 12.37 | Multi-Occupied Town Centres, Mixed Occupations | 1.8 |
| | 12.38 | Multi-Ethnic areas, White Collar Workers | 1.1 |
| **F** | **Striving (22.7% of population)** | | |
| | *F13* | *Older People, Less Prosperous Areas (3.6%)* | |
| | 13.39 | Home Owners, Small Council Flats, Single Pensioners | 1.9 |
| | 13.40 | Council Areas, Older People, Health Problems | 1.7 |
| | *F14* | *Council Estate Residents, Better-Off Homes (11.5%)* | |
| | 14.41 | Better-Off Council Areas, New Home Owners | 2.4 |
| | 14.42 | Council Areas, Young Families, Some New Home Owners | 3.0 |
| | 14.43 | Council Areas, Young Families, Many Lone Parents | 1.6 |
| | 14.44 | Multi-Occupied Terraces, Multi-Ethnic Areas | 0.9 |
| | 14.45 | Low Rise Council Housing, Less Well-Off Families | 1.8 |
| | 14.46 | Council Areas, Residents with Health Problems | 1.9 |
| | *F15* | *Council Estate Residents, High Unemployment (2.7%)* | |
| | 15.47 | Estates with High Unemployment | 1.1 |
| | 15.48 | Council Flats, Elderly People, Health Problems | 0.7 |
| | 15.49 | Council Flats, Very High Unemployment, Singles | 0.9 |
| | *F16* | *Council Estate Residents, Greatest Hardship (2.8%)* | |
| | 16.50 | Council Areas, High Unemployment, Lone Parents | 1.9 |
| | 16.51 | Council Flats, Greatest Hardship, Many Lone Parents | 0.9 |
| | *F17* | *People in Multi-Ethnic, Low-Income Areas (2.1%)* | |
| | 17.52 | Multi-Ethnic, Large Families, Overcrowding | 0.6 |
| | 17.53 | Multi-Ethnic, Severe Unemployment, Lone Parents | 1.0 |
| | 17.54 | Multi-Ethnic, High Unemployment, Overcrowding | 0.5 |

1.15 Another method of segmentation is based on the family type: the size and constitution of the family unit. There have been changes in the characteristics of the family unit in the last few decades; this is shown in the table below. Again, this depends on Census Statistics.

*Households: by type of household and family*

| | *1961* | *1971* | *1981* | *1991* | *1993* |
|---|---|---|---|---|---|
| *One person households* | | | | | |
| Under pensionable age | 4 | 6 | 8 | 11 | 11 |
| Over pensionable age | 7 | 12 | 14 | 16 | 16 |
| *Two or more unrelated adults* | 5 | 4 | 5 | 3 | 3 |
| *One family households* | | | | | |
| Married couple with: | | | | | |
| No children | 16 | 27 | 26 | 28 | 28 |
| 1-2 dependent children | 30 | 26 | 25 | 20 | 20 |
| 3 or more dependent children | 8 | 9 | 6 | 5 | 5 |
| Non-dependent children only | 10 | 8 | 8 | 8 | 7 |
| Lone parent with: | | | | | |
| Dependent children | 2 | 3 | 5 | 6 | 7 |
| Non-dependent children only | 4 | 4 | 4 | 4 | 3 |
| *Two or more families* | 3 | 1 | 1 | 1 | 1 |
| *Number of households (= 100%)(million)* | 16.2 | 18.2 | 19.5 | 21.9 | 22.9 |

1.16 This tells us important market characteristics of family households. An increase in the divorce rate is one of the factors which has led to an increase in single parent families and a decline in the 'traditional' family of working husband, housewife and dependent children. The increase in unemployment in the early 1980s was weighted towards males in traditional industries and the subsequent increase in employment in the late 1980s was weighted towards females in service-orientated industries, often involving part-time rather than full-time work. Thus one would now expect to find more households in which the sole or main breadwinner is female rather than male.

1.17 These household structural changes have been accompanied by other important social trends:

(a) later marriage and delayed childbearing;

(b) house price rises have meant that newly formed households contain partners who both work;

(c) the 'enterprise economy' has encouraged a greater interest in career development;

(d) greater financial independence for women caused by recent economic and social changes;

(e) products aimed at the increased number of 'single person of pensionable age' households are also likely to increase.

1.18 The implication for marketing is that new niche markets are likely to grow whilst traditional markets may be declining. The use of customer databases to direct more specific target marketing may be one solution, as may product proliferation. For the first time in the UK, advertising has begun to make explicit references to divorce and separated families. This has come to be an acceptable subject for certain advertising (for example, Volkswagen's very successful 'just divorced' campaign).

1.19 The *family life cycle* (FLC) is a summary demographic variable; that is, it combines the effects of age, marital status, career status (income) and the presence or absence of children. Herein lies its appeal, for it is able to identify the various stages through which households progress. The table on the next page shows features of the family at various stages of its life cycle. It is clear that particular products and services can be target-marketed at specific stages in the life cycle of families.

*The family life cycle*

| I | II | III | IV | V | VI | VII | VIII | IX |
|---|---|---|---|---|---|---|---|---|
| *Bachelor Stage.*<br>Young single people not living at home | *Newly married couples*<br>Young, no children | *Full nest I*<br>Youngest child under six | *Full nest II*<br>Youngest child six or over | *Full nest III*<br>Older married couples with dependent children | *Empty nest I*<br>Older married couples, no children living with them, head of family still in labour force | *Empty nest II*<br>Older married couples, no children living at home head of family retired | *Solitary survivor in labour force* | *Solitary survivor(s) retired* |
| Few financial burdens.<br>Fashion/ opinion leader led.<br>Recreation orientated.<br>Buy basic kitchen equipment, basic furniture, cars, equipment for the mating game, holidays.<br>Experiment with patterns of personal financial management and control. | Better off financially than they will be in the near future.<br>High levels of purchase of homes and consumer durable goods.<br>Buy cars, fridges, cookers, life assurance, durable furniture, holidays.<br>Establish patterns of personal financial management and control. | Home purchasing at peak.<br>Liquid assets/ savings low.<br>Dissatisfied with financial position and amount of money saved.<br>Reliance on credit finance, credit cards, overdrafts etc.<br>Child dominated household.<br>Buy necessities washers, dryers, baby food and clothes, vitamins, toys, books etc. | Financial position better.<br>Some wives return to work.<br>Child dominated household.<br>Buy necessities foods, cleaning material, clothes, bicycles, sports gear, music lessons, pianos, holidays etc. | Financial position still better.<br>More wives work.<br>School and examination dominated household.<br>Some children get first jobs; others in further / higher education.<br>Expenditure to support children's further / higher education.<br>Buy new, more tasteful furniture, non-necessary appliances, boats etc holidays. | Home ownership at peak.<br>More satisfied with financial position and money saved.<br>Interested in travel, recreation, self-education.<br>Make financial gifts and contributions.<br>Children gain qualifications; move to Stage I.<br>Buy luxuries, home improvements eg fitted kitchens etc. | Significant cut in income.<br>Keep home.<br>Buy medical appliances or medical care, products which aid health, sleep and digestion.<br>Assist children. Concern with level of savings and pension. Some expenditure on hobbies and pastimes. | Income still adequate but likely to sell family home and purchase smaller accommodation.<br>Concern with level of savings and pension.<br>Some expenditure on hobbies and pastimes.<br>Worries about security and dependence. | Significant cut in income.<br>Additional medical requirements. Special need for attention, affection and security.<br>May seek sheltered accommodation.<br>Possible dependence on others for personal financial management and control. |

## Life-style categories

| McCann-Erikson Men | McCann-Erikson Women | Taylor Nelson |
|---|---|---|
| *Avant Guardians*. Concerned with change and well-being of others, rather than possessions. Well educated, prone to self righteousness. | *Avant Guardians*. 'Liberal left' opinions, trendy attitudes. But out-going, active, sociable. | *Self-explorers*. Motivated by self-expression and self-realisation. Less materialistic than other groups, and showing high tolerance levels. |
| *Pontificators*. Strongly held, traditional opinions. Very British, and concerned about keeping others on the right path. | *Lady Righteous*. Traditional, 'right-minded' opinions. Happy, complacent, with strong family orientation. | *Social resisters*. The caring group, concerned with fairness and social values, but often appearing intolerant and moralistic. |
| *Chameleons*. Want to be contemporary to win approval. Act like barometers of social change, but copiers not leaders. | *Hopeful seekers*. Need to be liked, want to do 'right'. Like new things, want to be trendy. | *Experimentalists*. Highly individualistic, motivated by fast-moving enjoyment. They are materialistic, pro-technology but anti-traditional authority. |
| *Self-admirers*. At the young end of the spectrum. Intolerant of others and strongly motivated by success. Concerned about self-image. | *Lively ladies*. Younger than above, sensual, materialistic, ambitious and competitive. | *Conspicuous consumers*. They are materialistic and pushy, motivated by acquisition, competition, and getting ahead. Pro-authority, law and order. |
| *Self-exploiters*. The 'doers' and 'self-starters', competitive but always under pressure and often pessimistic. Possessions are important. | *New unromantics*. Generally young and single, adopting a hard-headed and unsentimental approach to life. Independent, self-centred. | *Belongers*. What they seek is a quiet, undisturbed family life. They are conservative, conventional rule followers. |
| *Token triers*. Always willing to try new things to 'improve their luck', but apparently on a permanent try-and-fail cycle. Includes an above average proportion of unemployed. | *Lack-a-daisy*. Unassertive and easy-going. Try to cope but often fail. Not very interested in the new. | *Survivors*. Strongly class-conscious, and community spirited, their motivation is to 'get by'. |
| *Sleepwalkers*. Contented under-achievers. Do not care about most things, and actively opt out. Traditional macho views. | *Blinkered*. Negative, do not want to be disturbed. Uninterested in conventional success - in fact, few interests except TV and radio. | *Aimless*. Comprises two groups, (a) the young unemployed, who are often anti-authority, and (b) the old, whose motivation is day-to-day existence. |
| *Passive endurers*. Biased towards the elderly, they are often economically and socially disfranchised. Expect little of life, and give little. | *Down-trodden*. This group is shy, introverted, but put upon. Would like to do better. Often unhappy and pressurised in personal relationships. | |

1.20 Demographic segmentation methods are powerful tools to specify target market segments. They are even more effective when each of the bases is used in combination with other factors, since it is clear that bases for demographic segmentation are interdependent. Age and family life cycle stage are strongly linked, as are housing type and socio-economic classification. By using bases in combination target markets can be very precisely defined.

---

**Case example**

Although car marque and model choice have expanded dramatically over the past 15 years, tangible product differences have become fewer, leading automotive marketers increasingly to seek to segment the market around the relationships that customers have with the brands of car. One of the main factors influencing these changes is the different role and influence of women in society. This involves:

(a) more women at work;
(b) later births;
(c) more women in management;
(d) more mixed lifestyles including working mothers;
(e) more women drivers;
(f) more mileage per week;
(g) one in three company car drivers is female;
(h) women are main drivers for 30% of new cars.

Old segmentation strategies, it was felt, were failing to take account of the ways in which women now related to the cars they used. Research confirmed that the old categories did not do justice to the differences between women and their lifestyles

Three types of woman driver were identified by research.

*Independent women*

20-30; single, cohabiting or married; any children have to fit into their lives rather than the other way round. Career important: ambitious, confident, style-conscious, they are independent and optimistic, want more from their life than their parents. Cars for this group are not just functional but symbols of success, independence and personal possessions. Cars put them in control. It needs to reflect their self perception, be stylish but also feminine, and be nippy and controllable rather than very high performance.

*Busy Bees*

Almost certainly married with children. Mothers first and foremost, with exceptionally full and exhausting lives; many work part time, but the children and the tasks associated with them take up most of their time. Maternal and practical, they sometimes need to escape from their exhausting and demanding lives. Much less intense relations with the car; look for reassurance and reliability, at the right price. More rationally driven in their car buying essentially practical; space, reliability and safety are paramount. A car, for them, is to make life easier.

*Rejuvenated women*

Typically in their mid thirties, with children now at secondary school. They may be re-married, separated or divorced; recently back into full time work. They have a strong sense of a 'new start' - rediscovering themselves as women, not just mothers, a sense of independence, of their own wants and needs. They feel better about themselves for the first time in years, and want to treat and enjoy themselves. This goes for the car they use too. They want it to signal that they are more than a mother - it needs to be smarter, the brand is important. They want comfort, style, extras, performance, things which will contribute to their enjoyment of driving. The car is helping them to enjoy themselves again.

Advertising was developed which took account of how these differences would affect the kinds of cars appropriate for women within these groups.

(*Adapted from Admap, September 1995*)

---

*Psychographic segmentation*

1.21 Psychographics or *lifestyle segmentation* seeks to classify people according to their values, opinions, personality characteristics and interests. In today's competitive world where innovation is the key to improved organisational performance, lifestyle segmentation deals with the person as opposed to the product and attempts to discover the particular unique lifestyle patterns of customers. This offers a richer insight into their preferences for various products and services. Lifestyle refers to 'distinctive ways of living adopted by particular communities or subsections of society'. Lifestyle involves combining a number of behavioural factors, such as motivation, personality and culture. Effective use in marketing depends on accurate description, and the numbers of people following a particular lifestyle must be quantified. Then marketers can assign and target products and promotion at particular target lifestyle groups. Lifestyle is a controversial issue, and a full analysis of the arguments is beyond the scope of this text. Its implications for marketing, and the problems of definition involved, can perhaps best be illustrated by some examples.

*Database marketing*, which is becoming much more important in identifying and targeting market segments for direct selling, relies heavily on the theories underlying psychographic segmentation.

1.22 One simple example generalises lifestyle in terms of four categories, as follows.

(a) *Upwardly mobile, ambitious*: seeking a better and more affluent lifestyle, principally through better paid and more interesting work, and a higher material standard of living. A customer with such a lifestyle will be prepared to try new products.

(b) *Traditional and sociable*: compliance and conformity to group norms bring social approval and reassurance to the individual. Purchasing patterns will therefore be 'conformist'.

(c) *Security and status seeking*: stressing 'safety' and 'ego-defensive' needs. This lifestyle links status, income and security. It encourages the purchase of strong and well known products and brands, and emphasises those products and services which confer status and make life as secure and predictable as possible. These would include insurance, membership of the AA or RAC etc. Products that are well established and familiar inspire more confidence than new products, which will be resisted.

(d) *Hedonistic preference*: placing emphasis on 'enjoying life now' and the immediate satisfaction of wants and needs. Little thought is given to the future.

1.23 Two more complex lifestyle analyses are shown in the table on the Page 108. These sets of analysis are based on empirical attitude research, and the agencies that have constructed them use them to advise their clients on how best to design and position existing and new products at target segments made up of people who have similar lifestyle patterns.

1.24 It is possible to gain further insights into lifestyle behaviour by cross-referring demographic variables to observed behaviour which indicates lifestyle types. The table below gives one example relating to leisure, social and travel facilities.

*Profiles by sex, age and social grade, of users of various leisure, social and travel facilities.*

| | All adults | Travel by air (in past 3 years) | Use London under-ground | Visit cinemas | Visit pubs | Visit licensed clubs | Visit rest-aurants (day) | Visit rest-aurants (evening) | Used Yellow pages in last 4 weeks | Listen to Radio Luxembourg |
|---|---|---|---|---|---|---|---|---|---|---|
| Population (in 000's) | 44,150 | 15,333 | 13,397 | 15,749 | 30,300 | 16,411 | 17,590 | 22,881 | 16,990 | 4,417 |
| | % | % | % | % | % | % | % | % | % | % |
| All adults | 100.0 | 100.0 | 100.0 | 100.0 | 100.0 | 100.0 | 100.0 | 100.0 | 100.0 | 100.0 |
| Men | 47.9 | 49.1 | 52.9 | 50.2 | 52.6 | 54.1 | 43.3 | 49.6 | 51.7 | 53.6 |
| Women | 52.1 | 50.9 | 47.1 | 49.8 | 47.4 | 45.9 | 56.7 | 50.4 | 48.3 | 46.4 |
| 15-24 | 20.0 | 20.8 | 22.2 | 35.6 | 24.5 | 28.7 | 16.0 | 22.2 | 21.0 | 42.7 |
| 25-34 | 17.0 | 19.1 | 18.6 | 23.6 | 21.6 | 19.4 | 15.8 | 22.4 | 21.6 | 20.8 |
| 35-44 | 16.3 | 16.5 | 18.6 | 19.2 | 19.0 | 17.0 | 17.9 | 20.2 | 19.6 | 12.9 |
| 45-54 | 13.8 | 15.2 | 15.2 | 10.9 | 13.7 | 13.0 | 15.0 | 15.7 | 14.3 | 8.2 |
| 55-64 | 14.5 | 14.9 | 13.3 | 7.0 | 11.4 | 11.8 | 15.5 | 11.5 | 12.1 | 6.7 |
| 65 or over | 18.4 | 13.5 | 12.1 | 3.8 | 9.8 | 10.0 | 19.7 | 8.0 | 11.4 | 8.7 |
| AB | 16.7 | 26.5 | 28.9 | 23.9 | 18.3 | 13.1 | 24.1 | 23.6 | 23.1 | 10.9 |
| C1 | 22.1 | 27.6 | 27.9 | 26.3 | 24.6 | 23.0 | 26.8 | 26.6 | 24.9 | 20.8 |
| C2 | 28.8 | 26.7 | 24.8 | 28.4 | 30.1 | 33.1 | 25.5 | 29.6 | 29.0 | 33.7 |
| D | 18.1 | 12.3 | 11.4 | 14.2 | 17.1 | 19.6 | 13.4 | 13.6 | 14.4 | 20.1 |
| E | 14.3 | 7.0 | 7.1 | 7.3 | 10.0 | 11.2 | 10.2 | 6.6 | 8.5 | 14.4 |

Clearly, the power of data handling and analysis provided by computer systems will only increase the value and ubiquity of this method of segmentation.

### *Geo-demographic segmentation*

1.25 Geo-demographics is a segmentation technique which was introduced in the early 1980s, but came into its own in the late 1980s and early 1990s. Basically, it classifies people according to where they live. It rests on a similar idea to the ACORN scheme - that households within a particular neighbourhood exhibit similar purchasing behaviour, outlook and so on.

1.26 The central themes of geo-demographics was outlined by one leading market research expert as:

> '... that two people who live in the same neighbourhood, such as a Census Enumeration District, are more likely to have similar characteristics than are two people chosen at random. The second is that neighbourhoods can be categorised in terms of the characteristics of the population which they contain, and that two neighbourhoods can be placed in the same category, that is they can contain similar types of people, even though they are widely separated.'

1.27 Geo-demographics is thus able to target customers in particular areas who exhibit similar behaviour patterns. This system allows organisations to profile the users or potential users of a product or service and then proceed to target customers who match these profiles. This of course should increase the profitability and take-up of the offered product/service.

Modern techniques also allow for data to be combined and projected so that knowledge about neighbourhood and age will also permit projections about attitudes and behaviour with strong statistical reliability. One such system can make useful inferences about consumers based only on their first names.

## Customer database

1.28 It should be clear from the above discussion of segmentation methods that for large scale usage of the more sophisticated methods to be effective, computerised systems have to be adopted. These systems can often be used by organisations which actually hold detailed data on customers, such as banks, building societies and insurance companies. The systems are based on the array of data held about each customer in a relational database. In other words, a sub sample of customers could be formed by the use of any one specifying variable (or combination of variables). Thus all customers aged 18-24 could be identified, for the development of long-term relations, as discussed above, as could all customers aged 25-34 with incomes over £20,000 pa and who live in ACORN type B6 housing.

This data has become more important as POS (point of sale) information is routinely gathered, and personal computer systems have become cheaper, more widely available and more 'user-friendly'.

### Direct mailing

1.29 Such customer database systems allow highly specific target marketing. The most obvious marketing use is by direct mail methods, the particular advantage of which is the capability for exact monitoring of results using the computer system. The costs of each mailshot can be related to the increase in business which results and the types of customers who do buy can be used to refine the target marketing further.

---

**Exercise 1**

C2 met C1 and fell in love. They moved to FLCII and lived in a D10. He was a belonger and she was lady righteous: it would not be long before they reached stage III of the FLC!

What are we talking about?

---

## 2 THE PRODUCT LIFE CYCLE

### The product

2.1 Those unfamiliar with marketing probably think of a 'product' as a physical object. However, in marketing the term must be understood in a broader sense. A product is something that satisfies a set of wants that customers have. When you buy a set of wine glasses, for example, you are buying them because you want to drink wine and you prefer not to do so straight from the bottle. You may also want to impress your dinner guests with your taste, and choose to do so by possessing a particularly fine set of wine glasses.

2.2 A product may be said to satisfy needs by possessing the following attributes.

(a) *Tangible attributes*

- (i) Availability and delivery
- (ii) Performance
- (iii) Price
- (iv) Design

(b) *Intangible attributes*

- (i) Image
- (ii) Perceived value

2.3 These features are interlinked. A product has a tangible *price*, for example (you hand over your hard earned money), but for your money you obtain the *value* that you perceive the product to have. You may get satisfaction from paying a very high price for your wine glasses, because this says something about your status in life: the glasses become part of your self-image.

*Product classification: consumer goods*

2.4 You have probably heard the term consumer goods often. It is used to distinguish goods that are sold directly to the person who will ultimately use them from goods that are sold to people that want them to make other products. The latter are known as industrial goods.

2.5 Consumer goods may be classified as follows.

(a) *Convenience goods*. The weekly groceries are a typical example. There is a further distinction between staple goods like bread and potatoes, and impulse buys, like the unexpected bar of chocolate that you find at the supermarket checkout. For marketing purposes, brand awareness is extremely important in this sector. Advertising tries to make sure that when people put 'beans' on their list they have in mind *Heinz* beans.

(b) *Shopping goods*. These are the more durable items that you buy, like furniture or washing machines. This sort of purchase is usually only made after a good deal of advance planning and shopping around

(c) *Speciality goods*. These are items like jewellery or the more expensive items of clothing.

(d) *Unsought goods*. These are goods that you did not realise you needed! Typical examples would be the sort of items that are found in catalogues that arrive in the post.

### Exercise 2

Think of three products that you have bought recently, one low-priced, one medium priced, and one expensive item. Identify the product attributes that made you buy each of these items and categorise them according to the classifications shown above.

2.6 Industrial goods may be classified as follows.

(a) *Installations*, for example major items of plant and machinery like a factory assembly line

(b) *Accessories*, such as PCs

(c) *Raw materials*: plastic, metal, wood, foodstuffs chemicals and so on

(d) *Components*, for example the Lucas headlights in Ford cars or the Intel microchip in most PCs

(e) *Supplies*: office stationery, cleaning materials and the like

2.7 There are very few pure *products or services*. Most products have some service attributes and many services are in some way attached to products. However, we shall consider some of the features that characterise service marketing later on in this chapter.

### Product life cycle

2.8 This concept has an almost 'biological' basis. It asserts that products are born (or introduced), grow to reach maturity and then enter old age and decline.

2.9 Despite criticisms, the product life cycle has proved to be a useful control device for monitoring the progress of new products after introduction. As Professor Robin Wensley of Warwick University puts it:

> 'The value of the product life cycle depends on its use, ie it has greater value as one goes down the scale from a predictive or forecasting tool, through a planning tool to a control tool.'

2.10 The profitability and sales position of a product can be expected to change over time. The 'product life cycle' is an attempt to recognise distinct stages in a product's sales history. Here is the classic representation of the product life cycle.

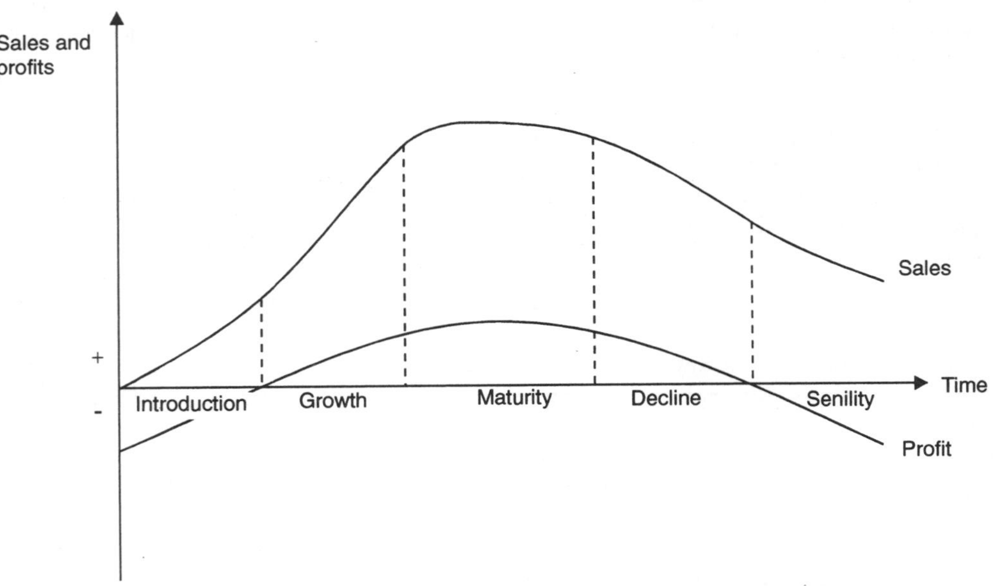


(a) *Introduction*. A new product takes time to find acceptance by would-be purchasers and there is a slow growth in sales. Only a few firms sell the product; unit costs are high because of low output; there may be early teething troubles with production technology and prices may be high to cover production costs and sales promotion expenditure as much as possible. For example, pocket calculators, video cassette recorders and mobile telephones were all very expensive when launched. The product, for the time being, is a loss maker.

(b) *Growth*. If the new product gains market acceptance, sales will eventually rise more sharply and the product will start to make profits. New customers buy the product and as production rises, unit costs fall. Since demand is strong, prices tend to remain fairly static for a time. However, the prospect of cheap mass production and a strong market will attract competitors so that the number of producers is increasing. With the increase of competition, manufacturers must spend a lot of money on product improvement, sales promotion and distribution to obtain a dominant or strong position in the market.

(c) *Maturity*. The rate of sales growth slows down and the product reaches a period of maturity which is probably the longest period of a successful product's life. Most products on the market will be at the mature stage of their life. Eventually sales will begin to decline so that there is overcapacity of production in the industry. Severe competition occurs, profits fall and some producers leave the market. The remaining producers seek means of prolonging the product life by modifying it and searching for new market segments.

(d) *Decline*. Most products reach a stage of decline which may be slow or fast. Many producers are reluctant to leave the market, although some inevitably do because of falling profits. If a product remains on the market too long, it will become unprofitable and the decline stage in its life cycle then gives way to a 'senility' stage.

---

### Exercise 3

Can you think of any products that have disappeared in your lifetime or are currently in decline?

### Solution

Some ideas to start you off are manual typewriters and vinyl records. Also, almost anything subject to fads or fashions.

---

## Buying participants through PLC stages

2.11 The introductory stage represents the highest risk in terms of purchasing a new, as yet untested product. Buyers reflect this: they typically consist of the relatively wealthy, to whom the risk of a loss is relatively small, and the young, who are more likely to make risky purchases.

2.12 In the growth and mature stages the mass market needs to be attracted. By the time decline sets in the product is well tested with all its faults 'ironed' out. At this stage enter the most risk-averse buyers, termed *laggards*. These are the mirror image of those who participated in the introductory stage, being the poorer and older sections of the community.

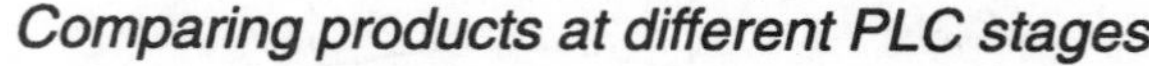

*Comparing products at different PLC stages*

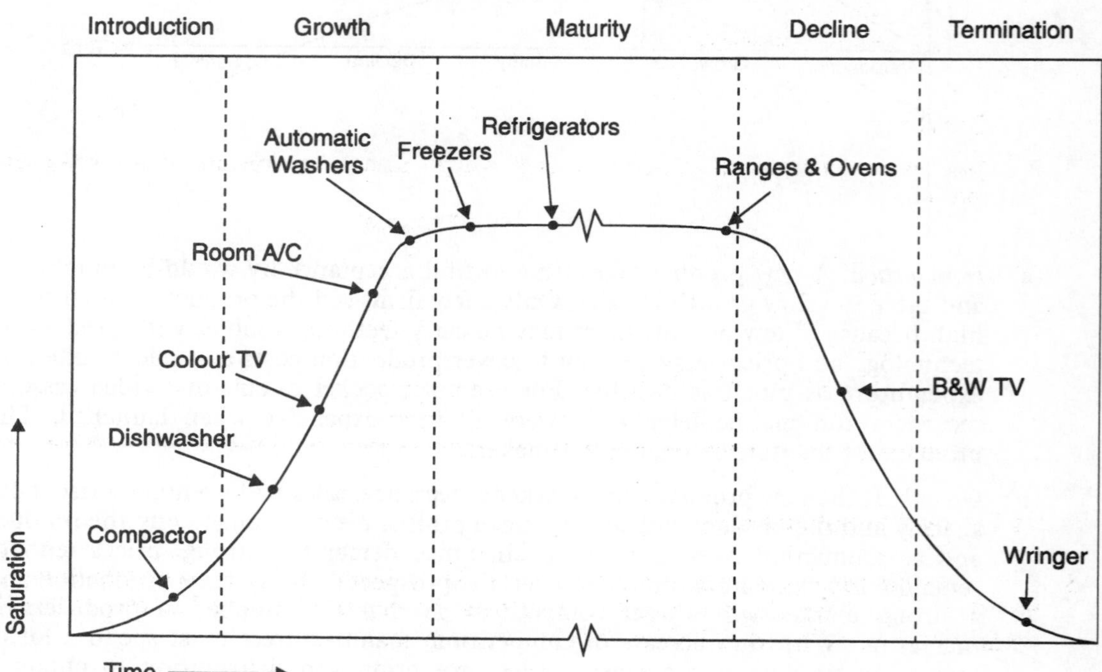


2.13 The above display of products at various stages through the PLC represents the USA in the late 1960s and early 1970s. Studies were conducted to establish whether or not there were significant differences in the purchasers of refrigerators in the mature stage and compacters (waste disposal units) in the introductory stage.

Refrigerators, 1965 -1969

| Income \ Age | 14-24 | 25-34 | 35-44 | 45-54 | 55-64 | 65+ | Total |
|---|---|---|---|---|---|---|---|
| Under $5,000 | 6 | 6 | 5 | 7 | 7 | 19 | 50 |
| $5,000 - 7,000 | 10 | 15 | 10 | 8 | 8 | 5 | 56 |
| $7,000 - 10,000 | 12 | 32 | 27 | 24 | 13 | 6 | 114 |
| $10,000 - 15,000 | 4 | 19 | 24 | 23 | 10 | 2 | 82 |
| $15,000 - 25,000 | 1 | 6 | 11 | 12 | 5 | 1 | 36 |
| $25,000 + | | | 3 | 3 | 2 | | 8 |
| Total | 33 | 78 | 89 | 77 | 45 | 33 | |

346 dots - each dot represents 10,000 refrigerators

Compactors, 1970 - 1971

| Income \ Age | 14-24 | 25-34 | 35-44 | 45-54 | 55-64 | 65+ | Total |
|---|---|---|---|---|---|---|---|
| Under $5,000 | | | | | | | |
| $5,000 - 7,000 | | | 1 | 1 | | | 3 |
| $7,000 - 10,000 | 1 | 2 | 2 | 2 | 2 | 1 | 10 |
| $10,000 - 15,000 | 1 | 7 | 9 | 9 | 3 | 1 | 30 |
| $15,000 - 25,000 | 1 | 10 | 16 | 14 | 5 | 1 | 47 |
| $25,000 + | 1 | 10 | 23 | 18 | 8 | 3 | 63 |
| Total | 4 | 30 | 51 | 44 | 18 | 6 | |

153 dots - each dot represents 1,000 compactors

2.14 The above matrices show income on the vertical axis and age on the horizontal axis. It can be noted that the high income group with a family income of $10,000 or more make up some 90% of those purchasing compacters. There is also a noticeable lack of 65+ year olds. In contrast, the mature refrigerator market appears to reflect the complete population range.

---

### Exercise 4

What proportion of the total market for a new product would you guess that each of Rogers' categories constitutes?

| | *Proportion* |
|---|---|
| Innovators | |
| Early adopters | |
| Early majority | |
| Late majority | |
| Late adopters and laggards | |
| | 100% |

### Solution

The figures produced by Rogers himself, though somewhat arbitrary, make interesting reading.

| | *Proportion* |
|---|---|
| Innovators | 2.5 |
| Early adopters | 12.5 |
| Early majority | 34.0 |
| Late majority | 34.0 |
| Late adopters and laggards | 17.0 |
| | 100.0% |

---

## How are life cycles assessed?

2.15 It is plausible to suggest that products have a life cycle, but it is not so easy to sort out how far through its life a product is, and what its expected future life might be. To identify these stages, the following should be carried out.

(a) There ought to be a regular review of existing products, as a part of marketing management responsibilities.

(b) Information should be obtained about the likely future of each product and sources of such information might be:

(i) an analysis of past trends;
(ii) the history of other products;
(iii) market research;
(iv) if possible, an analysis of competitors.

The future of each product should be estimated in terms of both sales revenue and profits.

(c) Estimates of future life and profitability should be discussed with any experts available to give advice, for example R & D staff about product life, management accountants about costs and marketing staff about prices and demand.

2.16 Once the assessments have been made, decisions must be taken about what to do with each product. The choices are:

(a) to continue selling the product, with no foreseeable intention of stopping production;

(b) to initiate action to prolong a product's life, perhaps by advertising more, by trying to cut costs or raise prices, by improving distribution, or packaging or sales promotion methods, or by putting in more direct selling effort and so on;

(c) to plan to stop producing the product and either to replace it with new ones in the same line or to diversify into new product-market areas.

2.17 Costs might be cut by improving productivity of the workforce, or by redesigning the product slightly, perhaps as a result of a value analysis study.

Strategic and marketing mix decisions are considered in Part C of this Study Text.

### Exercise 5

Where do you consider the following products or services to be in their product life cycle?

(a) Mobile telephones
(b) Baked beans
(c) Satellite television
(d) Cigarettes
(e) Carbon paper
(f) Mortgages
(g) Writing implements
(h) Car alarms
(i) Organically grown fruit and vegetables

### Solution

You could perhaps pin down some of these items, but most are open to discussion, especially if you take an international perspective. For many you may consider that the PLC is not valid, and you will not be alone: see the following paragraphs.

## Criticisms of the product life cycle

2.18 Although it is widely used, the PLC remains controversial. There have been contradictory papers directed at establishing or refuting the validity of the product life cycle by empirical tests. Polli and Cook tested 140 categories of non-durable consumer products. They tested whether the sequence that a product has passed through conformed to a PLC pattern. For instance, if a product was judged to be in a mature phase, they tested whether this was preceded by growth or maturity and followed by maturity or decline. If this test were positive then any sequence of these either/ors would be consistent with the PLC concept.

| *May be preceded by:* | *Period* | *May be followed by:* |
|---|---|---|
| Introduction, growth | Growth | Growth, maturity, decline |
| Growth, maturity | Maturity | Maturity, decline |
| Growth, maturity, decline | Decline | Decline |

(*Note.* The model was further subdivided into 'sustained maturity', 'maturity' and 'decaying maturity'.)

*The results*

| | *Number of product* | *% sequences significantly different from chance at:* | |
|---|---|---|---|
| *Non-durable product class* | *categories* | *5% confidence* | *1% confidence* |
| Health and personal care | 51 | 60.8 | 31.3 |
| Food | 56 | 19.6 | 7.1 |
| Cigarettes | 33 | 60.6 | 51.5 |
| ALL PRODUCTS | 140 | 44.0 | 34.0 |

*Source: The validity of the Product Life Cycle, Polli & Cook, Journal of Business, October 1969*

2.19 Polli and Cook tested whether the results were significantly different from random events. They concluded that 44% of the total of all products were significantly different from chance at the 95% level of significance and 34% at the 99% level. Within the sample there was a considerable range of results when classified into non-durable product groups. 61% of 'cigarettes' and 'health and personal care' product groups were significantly different from chance at the 95% confidence level. This contrasts with only 20% of 'food'.

2.20 Polli and Cook concluded that the PLC is most likely to be relevant for products where consumer demand is high. From these results Polli and Cook concluded that 'for given categories of goods the product life cycle can be a useful model for marketing planning'.

2.21 Dhalla and Yuspeh attempt to expose what they term the myth of the PLC. They point out that:

> 'in the absence of the technological breakthroughs many product classes appear to be almost impervious to normal life cycle pressures, provided they satisfy some basic need, be it transportation, entertainment, health, nourishment or the desire to be attractive.'

2.22 Whilst accepting the possibility of the existence of a *product* life cycle, the paper denies the existence of *brand* life cycles. The authors assert that any underlying PLC is a dependent variable which is determined by marketing actions; rather than an independent variable to which companies should adapt. In other words, if a brand appears to be in decline, this is not happening as a result of market changes, but because of either reduced or inappropriate marketing by the producer, or better marketing by competitors.

---

**Case example**

Dhalla and Yuspeh consider that this notion of the PLC as a binding constraint has led to many marketing errors. They cite the example of Ipana, an American toothpaste, that was marketed by a leading packaged goods company until 1968 when it was abandoned after entering 'decline'. Two Minnesota businessmen who acquired the brand name, with hardly any promotion, generated 250,000 dollars sales in the first seven months of operations. Intelligent marketing, they point out, has kept such brands as Budweiser Beer, Colgate toothpaste and Maxwell House around long after competitive brands have disappeared.

---

2.23 Dhalla and Yuspeh also cite conclusions reached by the Marketing Science Institute who examined over 100 product categories using Polli and Cook's test.

> 'After completing the initial test of the life cycle expressed as a verifiable model of sales behaviour, we must register strong reservations about its general validity, even stated in its weakest, most flexible form. In our tests of the model against real sales data, it has not performed equally well at different levels of product sales aggregation .... Our results suggest strongly that the life cycle concept, when used without careful formulation and testing as an explicit model, is more likely to be misleading than useful.'

2.24 Dhalla and Yuspeh come to the general conclusion that managers adhering to the sequences of marketing strategies recommended for succeeding stages of the cycle are likely to do more harm than good. In particular they cite the potential neglect of existing brands and wasteful expenditures on replacement 'me-too' products.

### Criticisms of the practical value of the PLC

2.25 These criticisms can be summarised as follows.

(a) Stages cannot easily be defined.
(b) The traditional S-shaped curve of a product life cycle is shown here.

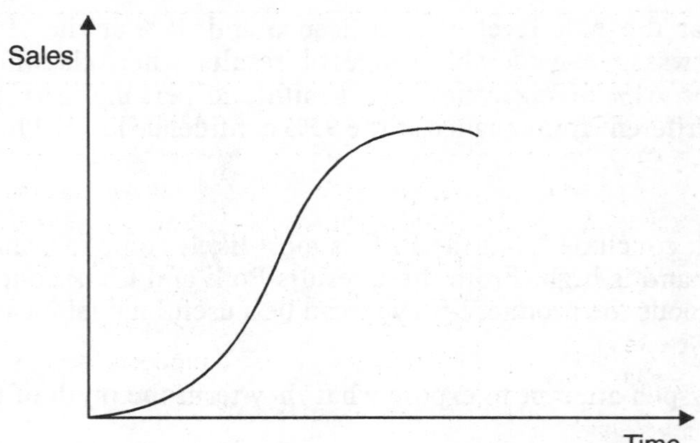


This does not always occur in practice, however. Some products have no maturity phase, and go straight from growth to decline. Others have a second growth period after an initial decline. Some have virtually no introductory period and go straight into a rapid growth phase.

(c) Strategic decisions can change a product's life cycle: for example, by repositioning a product in the market, its life can be extended. If strategic planners 'decide' what a product's life is going to be, opportunities to extend the life cycle might be ignored. For the impact of mix decisions, see Part C of this Study Text.

(d) Competition varies in different industries, and the strategic implications of the product life cycle will vary according to the nature of the competition. The 'traditional' life cycle presupposes increasing competition and falling prices during the growth phase of the market and also the gradual elimination of competitors in the decline phase. Strategic planning may well not be based on these presuppositions. This pattern of events is not always found in financial markets, where there is a tendency for competitors to follow-my-leader very quickly. Competition may build up well ahead of demand. The rapid development of various banking services is an example of this: for example, with bank cash dispenser cards, when one bank developed the product all the other major banks followed immediately.

**Exercise 6**

There must be many products that have been around for as long as you can remember. Companies like Cadbury's have argued that they spend so much on brand maintenance that they should be able to show a value for their brands as an asset in their accounts (though accountants find this hard to swallow).

Think of some examples of products that go on and on from your own experience and try to identify what it is about them that makes them so enduring.

## The strategic implications of the product life cycle

2.26 Having made these reservations about product life cycle planning, the strategic implications of the product life cycle might be as follows.

| | *Phase* | | | |
|---|---|---|---|---|
| | *Introduction* | *Growth* | *Maturity* | *Decline* |
| *Product* | Initially, poor quality<br>Product design and development are a key to success<br>No standard product and frequent design changes (eg microcomputers in the early 1980s) | Competitor's products have marked quality differences and technical differences<br>Quality improves<br>Product reliability may be important | Products become more standardised and differences between competing products less distinct | Products even less differentiated. Quality becomes more variable |
| *Customers* | Initial customers willing to pay high prices<br>Customers need to be convinced about buying | Customers increase in number | Mass market<br>Market saturation<br>Repeat-buying<br>Markets become segmented | Customers are sophisticated buyers of a product they understand well |
| *Marketing issues* | High advertising and sales promotion costs<br>High prices possible<br>Distribution problematic | High advertising costs still, but as a % of sales, costs are falling<br>Prices falling<br>More distributors | Segment specific<br>Choose best distribution<br>Brand image | Less money spent on advertising and sales promotion |
| *Competition* | Few or no competitors | More competitors enter the market<br>Barriers to entry can be important | Competition at its keenest: on prices, branding servicing customers packaging etc | Competitors gradually exit from the market<br>Exit barriers can be important |
| *Profit margins* | High prices but losses due to high fixed costs | High prices. High contribution margins, and increasing profit margins<br>High P/E ratios for quoted companies in the growth market | Falling prices but good profit margins due to high sales volume<br>High prices in some market segments | Still low prices but falling profits as sales volume falls, since total contribution falls towards the level of fixed costs<br>Some increases in prices may occur in the late decline stage |

| | Phase | | | |
|---|---|---|---|---|
| | *Introduction* | *Growth* | *Maturity* | *Decline* |
| *Manufacturing and distribution* | Overcapacity<br>High production costs<br>Few distribution channels<br>High labour skill content in manufacture | Undercapacity<br>Move towards mass production and less reliance on skilled labour<br>Distribution channels flourish and getting adequate distribution is a key to marketing success | Optimum capacity<br>Low labour skills<br>Distribution channels fully developed, but less successful channels might be cut | Overcapacity because mass production techniques still used<br>Distribution channels dwindling |

2.27 In the section on the marketing mix, we consider how the PLC influences decisions on product, distribution, price and promotion.

## 3 PRODUCT PORTFOLIO PLANNING

*Examined 6/95, 12/95*

3.1 Firstly, look at the following table.

| *Product mix* | *Characteristics of company's product line* |
|---|---|
| Width | Number of product lines |
| Depth | Average number of items per product line |
| Consistency | Closeness of relationships in product range eg end users, production, distribution |

3.2 A company's product mix (or product assortment or portfolio) is all the product lines and items that the company offers for sale.

(a) *Width* is the number of product lines that the company carries.

(b) *Depth* is calculated by dividing the total number of items carried by the number of product lines.

(c) *Consistency* is the closeness of items in the range in terms of marketing or production characteristics.

3.3 The product mix can be extended in a number of ways:

(a) by introducing variations in models or style;

(b) by changing the quality of products offered at different price levels;

(c) by developing associated items, eg a paint manufacturer introducing paint brushes;

(d) by developing new products that have little technical or marketing relationships to the existing range.

3.4 *Managing the product portfolio* involves more than the simple extension or reduction of a company's product range. It also raises broad issues such as what role should a product play in the portfolio, how should resources be allocated between products and what should be expected from each product. Maintaining balance between well-established and new products, between cash-generative and cash-using products and between growing and declining products is very important. Managing the product portfolio is thus a key component of marketing. If products are not suitable for the market or not profitable, then corporate objectives will be jeopardised and the marketing function will fall short of its stated goals. Equally, if potentially profitable products are ignored or not given sufficient support then crucial marketing opportunities will be lost.

3.5 It follows that there are benefits to be gained from using a *systematic approach* to the management of the product range. Marketing is not an exact science and there is no definitive approach or technique which can determine which products should remain, which should be pruned and how resources should be shared across the current product range. There are, however, techniques which can aid decision making. Ultimately the burden of the decision is a management responsibility and requires judgement, but analytical tools such as product-market matrices and the product life cycle can illuminate the decision process and provide a useful framework to evaluate the product range.

---

**Case example**

Unilever and Procter & Gamble have cut their sprawling product portfolios. In Unilever's case, this bold move was apparently prompted by the company recognising that its long tail - representing over 20% of its brands and £2 billion of sales - apparently contributes more effort than profit.

---

## Product-market matrices

---

**Exam focus point**

A June 1997 question (Q29 *Life cycle hindrance* in our Practice & Revision Kit) asked you to comment critically on the product life cycle. Many of the points made in section 2 could have contributed usefully to your answer.

---

3.6 The product-market matrix is a simple technique used to classify a product or even a business according to the features of the market and the features of the product. It is often used at the level of corporate strategy to determine the relative positions of businesses and select strategies for resource allocation between them. Thus, for example, a bank might apply such a technique to evaluate the relative position and profitability of its corporate division and its personal division, its international division, its merchant banking division and so on. The same techniques are equally valuable when considering products and the management of the product portfolio. The two most widely used approaches are the *Boston Consulting Group (BCG) growth-share matrix* and the *General Electric (GE) Business Screen.*

### *The BCG matrix*

3.7 The BCG matrix, illustrated below, classifies products (or businesses) on the basis of their market share relative to that of their competitors and according to the rate of growth in the market as a whole. The split on the horizontal axis is based on a market share identical to that of the firm's nearest competitor, while the precise location of the split on the vertical axis will depend on the rate of growth in the market. Products are positioned in the matrix as circles with a diameter proportional to their sales revenue. The underlying assumption in the growth-share matrix is that a larger market share will enable the business to benefit from economies of scale, lower per unit costs and thus higher margins.

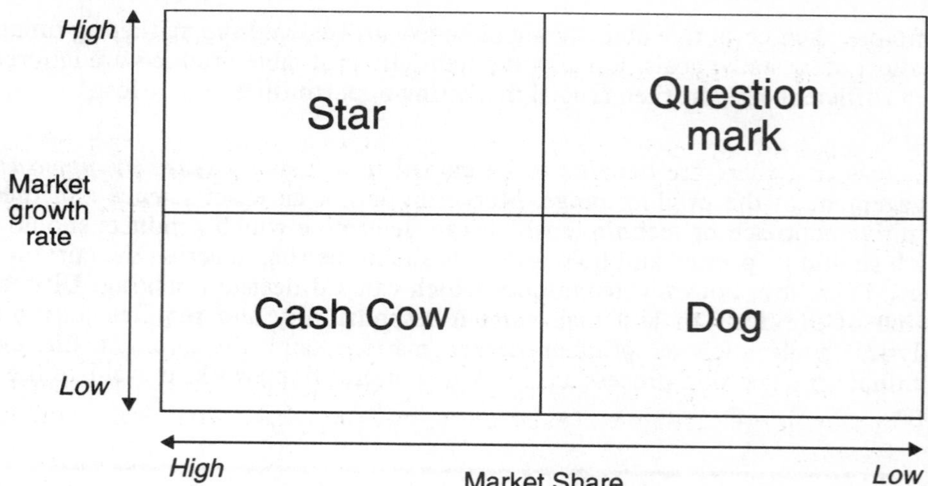


3.8 On the basis of this classification, each product or 'strategic business unit' will then fall into one of four broad categories.

(a) *Problem Child* (or question mark): a small market share but in a high growth industry. The generic product is clearly popular, but customer support for the company brand is limited. A small market share implies that competitors are in a strong position and that if the product is to be successful it will require substantial funds, and a new marketing mix. If the market looks good and the product is viable, then the company should consider a *build* strategy to increase market share. This would essentially involve increasing the resources available for that product to permit more active marketing. If the future looks less promising then the company should consider the possibility of withdrawing the product. What strategy is decided will depend on the strength of competitors, availability of funding and so on.

(b) *The Star*: this is a product with a high market share in a high growth industry. By implication, the star has potential for generating significant earnings currently and in the future. However, at this stage it may still require substantial marketing expenditures to 'maintain' this position, but would probably be regarded as a good investment for the future.

(c) *The Cash Cow*: a high market share but in a mature slow growth market. Typically, a well established product with a high degree of consumer loyalty. Product development costs are typically low and the marketing campaign is well established. The cash cow will normally make a substantial contribution to overall profitability. The appropriate strategy will vary according to the precise position of the cash cow. If market growth is reasonably strong then a 'holding' strategy will be appropriate, but if growth and/or share are weakening, then a *harvesting* strategy may be more sensible: cut back on marketing expenditure and maximise short-term cash flow.

(d) *The Dog*: a product characterised by low market share and low growth. Again, typically a well established product, but one which is apparently losing consumer support and may have cost disadvantages. The usual strategy would be to consider divestment unless cash flow position is strong, in which case the product would be harvested in the short term prior to deletion from the product range.

3.9 Implicit in the matrix is the notion that markets are dynamic. The typical new product is likely to appear in the 'problem child' category to begin with; if it looks promising and with effective marketing it might be expected to become a 'star', then, as markets mature, a 'cash cow' and finally a 'dog'. The suggestion that most products will move through these stages does not weaken the role played by marketing. On the contrary, it strengthens it, since poor marketing may mean that a product moves from being a problem child to a dog without making any substantial contribution to the profitability. Equally, of course, good marketing may enable the firm to prolong the 'star' and 'cash cow' phases, thus maximising cash flow from the product.

The matrix also places great emphasis on the strategic significance of growth, and behind this is the strong reliance on the lifecycle concept.

3.10 The framework provided by the matrix can offer guidance in terms of developing appropriate strategies for products and in maintaining a balanced product portfolio, ensuring that there are enough cash-generating products to match the cash-using products.

3.11 However, there are a number of criticisms.

(a) The BCG matrix oversimplifies product analysis. It concentrates only on two dimensions of product markets, size and market share, and therefore may encourage marketing management to pay too little attention to other market features.

(b) It is not always clear what is meant by the terms 'relative market share' and 'rate of market growth'. Not all companies or products will be designed for market leadership, in which case describing performance in terms of relative market share may be of limited relevance. Many firms undertaking this approach have found that all their products were technically 'dogs' and yet were still very profitable, so saw no need to divest. Firms following a nicheing strategy will commonly find their markets are (intentionally) small.

(c) The matrix assumes a relationship between profitability and market share. There is empirical evidence for this in many but not all industries, particularly where there is demand for more customised products. Some commentators, such as Tom Peters. have argued that this is a very strong trend in modern markets.

(d) The basic approach may oversimplify the nature of products in large diversified firms with many divisions. In these cases, each division may contain products which fit into several of the categories.

Despite these criticisms, the BCG matrix can offer guidance in achieving a balanced portfolio. However, given the difficulty of generalising such an approach to deal with all product and market situations, its recommendations should be interpreted with care.

## The General Electric Business Screen

3.12 The basic approach of the GE Business Screen is similar to that of the BCG matrix but it tries to avoid the criticism levelled against that technique of using a highly restrictive classification system by including a broader range of company and market factors in assessing the position of a particular product or product group. A typical example of the GE matrix is provided below. This matrix classifies products (or businesses) according to industry attractiveness and company strengths. Obviously, there is no single number which can be used to measure industry attractiveness or company (product) strength; instead, the approach aims to consider a variety of factors which contribute to both these variables and sectionalise the matrix on the basis of simple ordinal measures, into high, medium and low. Typical examples of the factors which determine industry attractiveness and company strength are the following.

(a) *Industry attractiveness*: market size, market growth, competitive climate, stability of demand, ease of market entry, industry capacity, levels of investment, nature of regulation, profitability.

(b) *Company strengths*: relative market share, company image, production capacity, production costs, financial strengths, product quality, distribution systems, control over prices/margins, benefits of patent protection.

3.13 Although a broader range of factors are used in the classification of products, this is a highly subjective assessment. Products are positioned on the grid with circles representing market size and segments representing market shares. The strategy for an individual product is then suggested on the basis of that position. It is interesting to note the apparent similarity in recommendations between the BCG matrix and the GE matrix; the basic difference arises from the method of classification.

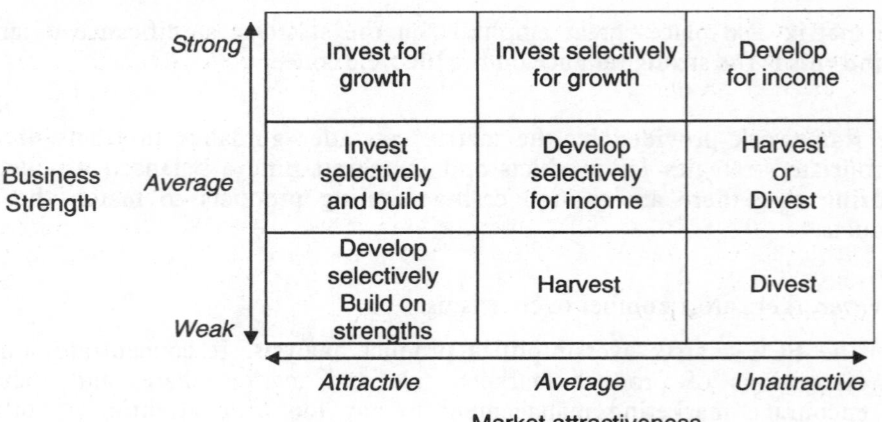

Strong
Average
Weak
Business Strength
Invest for growth
Invest selectively for growth
Develop for income
Invest selectively and build
Develop selectively for income
Harvest or Divest
Develop selectively Build on strengths
Harvest
Divest
Attractive
Average
Unattractive
Market attractiveness


3.14 The broader approach of the GE matrix emphasises the attempt to match distinctive competences within the company to conditions within the market place. Difficulties associated with measurement and classification mean that again the results of such an exercise must be interpreted with great care and not seen as a prescription for strategic decisions.

### 'New' and 'old' products

3.15 The energy and effort placed into adding new products and brands to the portfolio (which we discuss below) is seldom mirrored by a similar effort in identifying and weeding out the weak or declining. One of the benefits of effective marketing strategy is to ensure the organisation's resources are directed to the most suitable market segments; this can easily be thrown away by a proliferation of products.

---

#### Case examples

At one time, Procter & Gamble was selling 35 variations of Crest toothpaste and different nappies for girls and boys. The average supermarket in America devotes 20 ft of shelving to medicine for coughs and colds. Most of this choice is trumpery. New York-based Market Intelligence Service found that only 7% of the 25,500 new packaged products launched in America in 1996 really offered new or added benefits.

In fact, more choice does not translate into more sales. Ravi Dhar, of Yale University, examined how students decided what to buy, based on the number of versions of each product-category on offer. As the choice increased, so did the likelihood that students would not buy anything at all. John Gourville at Harvard Business School believes that some types of choice are more trouble than others. His – as yet incomplete – research suggests that consumers like to be offered choices in a single dimension: different sizes of cereal packet, say. If they are asked to make many trade-offs, such as whether to buy a computer with a modem or speakers, consumers start to feel anxious or even irritated.

*(Adapted from The Economist, 14/3/98)*

---

## 4 NEW PRODUCT DEVELOPMENT

*Examined 12/94, 6/95, 12/96, 12/97*

---

#### Exam focus point

Q35 *New product types* in our Practice & Revision Kit comes from the December 1996 exam. You are asked to give the pros and cons of genuinely innovative products, replacement products (eg much as the Ford Focus is to replace the Ford Escort) or imitative products (ie products which copy competitors). You should consider the risks in innovating in each way (eg taking on a competitor, or investing a lot of money in NPD).

---

4.1 Innovation is the life blood of a successful organisation and the management of innovation is central to this success.

(a) New products may be developed as a result of a technical breakthrough, or as a consequence of changes in society; or simply to copy and capitalise on the success of existing products.

(b) Management, however, can adopt a proactive response to product development by establishing research and development departments to look into ideas for new products, although they do not have to come through this formal departmentalised system. Management, sales people, customers and competitors can all generate new product ideas. One of the tasks of marketing management is to 'tap' these ideas and select some for further development. Later in this section new product development will be discussed in more detail.

4.2 *What is a new product?*

(a) One that opens up an entirely new market.
(b) One that replaces an existing product.
(c) One that broadens significantly the market for an existing product.

*An old product can be new if:*

(a) it is introduced to a new market;
(b) it is packaged in a different way (qualified);
(c) a different marketing approach is used (qualified);
(d) a mix variable is changed (qualified).

Any new product must be perceived in terms of customer needs and wants.

---

### Exercise 7

Can you think of examples of new products and 'new' old products to fit into each of the above categories?

### Solution

You should try to think of your own examples, but these suggestions may help.

*New product*

| | |
|---|---|
| Entirely new market | Web 'browsers', National Lottery |
| Replacing an existing product | Faster PCs |
| Broadening the market | Cable for satellite, TV and telephones |

*'New' old product*

| | |
|---|---|
| In a new market | German confectionery (in the UK) |
| New packaging | Anything |
| New marketing | French wine competing with Australian wine |

---

4.3 There are several degrees of newness.

(a) *The unquestionably new product*, such as the electronic pocket calculator. Marks of such a new product: technical innovation - high price - performance problems - patchy distribution.

(b) *The partially new product*, such as the cassette tape recorder. Marks of such a product: it performs better than the old ones did.

(c) *Major product change*, such as the transistor radio. Marks of such a product: radical technological change altering the accepted concept of the order of things.

(d) *Minor product change*, such as styling changes. Marks of such a product: extras which give a boost to a product.

4.4 Sources for new products include the following.

(a) Licensing (eg Formica, Monopoly)

(b) Acquisition ( buy the organisation making it)

(c) Internal product development (your own Research and Development team)

(d) Customers (listen to and observe them, analyse and research - this is how the Walkman developed)

(e) External inventors (Kodak and IBM rejected Xerox)

(f) Competition (Kodak instant cameras, following the Polaroid concept of the 'hand' camera)

(g) Patent agents

(h) Academic institutions (for example the pharmaceutical industry funds higher education department research)

---

### Case example

Already afraid of piracy, the record and CD producers do not relish squirting their wares into cyberspace. With faster transmission and more storage capacity, it will become easier to transmit entire records over the internet. Much later, customers should possess the technology to be able to download these records and copy them to their CD player, thus enjoying the gratification deferred by mail order.

Given these mouth-watering spectaculations, it is not surprising that several experiments in digital delivery are already under way. Some are "digital jukeboxes" run by pirates, mainly in America, who dodge the efforts of the Recording Industry Association to prosecute them for breach of copyright. Legitimate efforts so far involve only small independent labels, or else limited numbers of customers who have agreed to abide by copyright terms.

Deutsche Telekom is about to start a trial to sell records from main labels to 300 homes in Germany, and hopes to launch the scheme commercially throughout the country next year. In France, a cable-television system owned by Lyonnaise des Eaux is also testing digital-music delivery. So far it is working only with independent labels, but is in talks with EMI, one of the big five. These, however, are still "audio-on-demand" schemes: the music stays on a central computer, and buyers need to be on-line to hear their purchase. This is amazing if it works, but hardly as convenient as slipping a CD player into your car's player, or ambling off to your local record store.

*The Economist*, 16 August 1997

---

### Screening new product ideas

4.5 The mortality rate of new products is very high.

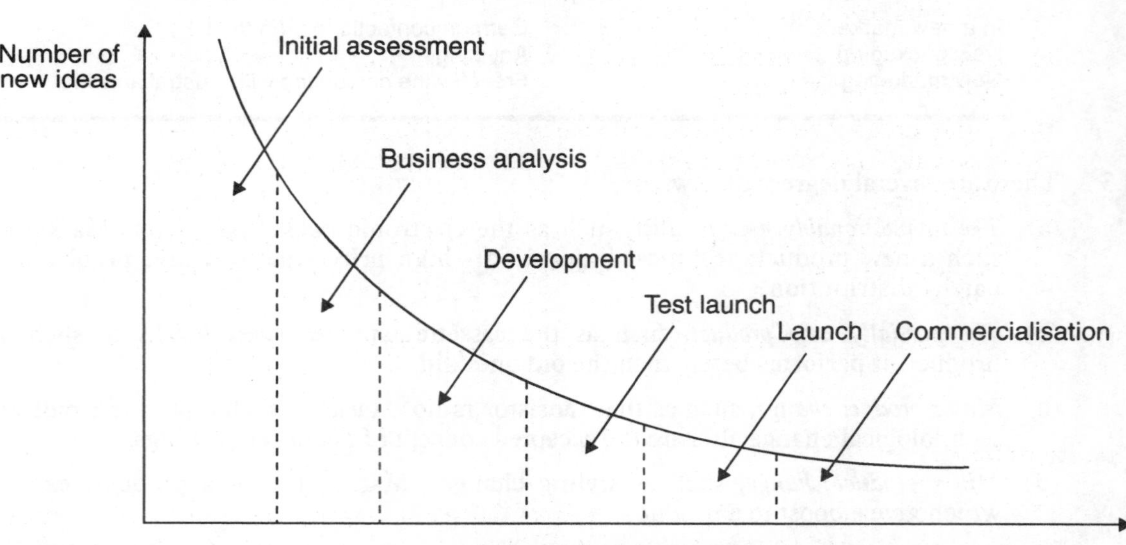


4.6 To reduce the risk of failure new product ideas should always be screened. There is some evidence that the product screening process is becoming more effective. A study by Booz, Allen and Hamilton in 1968 concluded that it took fifty-eight ideas to yield one successful product that achieved commercial success. A repeat study by Booz, Allen and Hamilton in 1981 showed a dramatic improvement. This study of 700 companies in the USA found that on average only seven ideas were needed for every successful product.

## New product development plan

4.7 New products should only be taken to advanced development if there is evidence of:

(a) adequate demand;
(b) compatibility with existing marketing ability;
(c) compatibility with existing production ability.

## Initial concept testing

4.8 At a preliminary stage the concept for the new product should be tested on potential customers to obtain their reactions. It is common to use the company staff as guinea pigs for a new product idea although their reaction is unlikely to be typical. But it is difficult to get sensible reactions from customers. Consider the following examples.

(a) *New designs for wallpaper.* When innovative new designs are tested on potential customers it is often found that they are conditioned by traditional designs and are dismissive of new design ideas.

(b) *New ideas for chocolate confectionery* have the opposite problem. Potential customers typically say they like the new concept (because everyone likes chocolate bars) but when the new product is launched it is not successful because people continue to buy old favourites.

Nevertheless, the concept testing may also permit useful refinements to be made to the concept, if it is not totally rejected.

## Product testing

4.9 A working prototype of the product, which can be tried by customers, is constructed. This stage is also very useful for making preliminary explorations of production costs and practical problems. We need to have some idea of whether the product could be produced in sufficient quantities at the right price were it to be launched. The form the product test takes will depend very much on the type of product concerned. The best advice seems to be that to get realistic responses the test should replicate reality as clearly as possible. Thus, for example:

(a) if the product is used in the home, a sample of respondents should be given the product to use at home;

(b) if the product is chosen from amongst competitors in a retail outlet (as with chocolate bars) then the product test needs to rate response against competitive products;

(c) if inherent product quality is an important attribute of the product then a 'blind' test could be used in which customers are not told who is producing the new product;

(d) an industrial product could be used for a trial period by a customer in a realistic setting.

## Quality policy

4.10 This is an important policy consideration. Different market segments will require products of different price and quality. When a market is dominated by established brand names, one entry strategy is to tap potential demand for a (cheaper) lower quality 'me-too' item.

4.11 Customers often judge the quality of an article by its price. Quality policy may well involve fixing a price and then manufacturing a product to the best quality standard that can be achieved within these constraints, rather than making a product of a certain quality and then deciding what its price should be.

4.12 Quality should also be determined by the expected physical, technological and social life of the product for the following reasons.

(a) There is no value in making one part of a product good enough to have a physical life of five years, when the rest of the product will wear out and be irreplaceable within two years (unless the part with the longer life has an emotional or symbolic appeal to customers; for example, a leather covering may be preferred to plastic).

(b) If technological advances are likely to make a product obsolescent within a certain number of years, it is wasteful and uneconomic to produce an article which will last for a longer time.

(c) If fashion determines the life of a product, the quality required need only be sufficient to cover the period of demand; the quality of fashion clothes, for example, is usually governed by their fashion life. Fashion items are only intended to be worn a relatively small number of times, while non-fashion items are more durable.

4.13 Quality policy must be carefully integrated with sales promotion. If a product is branded and advertised as having a certain quality, when customers then find this is not true, the product will fail. The quality of a product (involving its design, production standards, quality control and after-sales service) must be established and maintained before a promotion campaign can use it as a selling feature.

### Test marketing

4.14 The purpose of test marketing is to obtain information about how consumers react to the product in selected areas thought to be 'representative' of the total market. This avoids a blind commitment to the costs of a full scale launch while permitting the collection of market data. The firm will use the sales outlets it plans to use in the full market launch, and the same advertising and promotion plans it will use in the full market. This can be expensive, but it enables the company to 'test the water' before launching the product nationally. It helps to forecast sales, and can also be used to identify flaws in the product or promotional plans which can be dealt with before the national launch.

4.15 In short, then, the stages of new product development are as follows.

CONCEPTION OF IDEAS
↓
SCREENING OF IDEAS
↓
ANALYSE (IN BUSINESS SENSE)
↓
TESTING - Concept and Use
↓
PRODUCT DEVELOPMENT
↓
MARKETING MIX ISSUES
↓
MARKET TESTING
↓
PRODUCT LAUNCH

### The diffusion of innovation

4.16 The 'diffusion' of the new product refers to the spread of information about the product in the market place. Adoption is the process by which consumers incorporate the product into their buying patterns. The diffusion process is assumed to follow a similar shape to the PLC curve. Adoption is also thought usually to follow a 'normal' bell shaped curve. The classification of adopters is shown below.

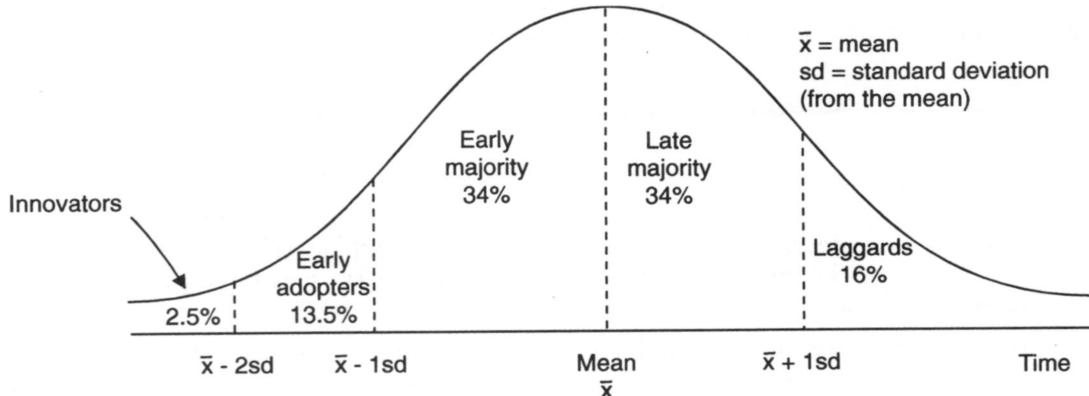


4.17 Early adopters and innovators are thought to operate as 'opinion leaders' and are therefore targeted by companies in order to influence the adoption of a product by their friends.

4.18 The main problem with this model is that the categories appear to add up to 100% of the target market. This does not reflect marketers' experience. Some potential consumers do not adopt/purchase at all. It has consequently been suggested that an additional category is needed: *nonadopters*, or nonconsumers.

4.19 Some researchers prefer a two or three category scheme, comparing innovators/early triers with later triers and/or non-triers. This enables then to generalise the characteristics of the important innovator/early trier segments, which has practical significance for marketing.

### Case example

The marketing *orthodoxy*, backed up by *some* research studies, has suggested that 'first movers' are more likely to become market leaders and dominate the market. Research by Prahalad and Hamel argues this position. First movers, they argue, can reap benefits in lots of ways.

(a) By establishing a monopoly if only for a short time (Sony and the Walkman)
(b) By setting standards (Microsoft and DOS)
(c) By dictating the rules of the game (Wal-mart and the hypermarkets)

Tellis and Golder, in a recent paper, have argued the converse. Previous research, they say, has surveyed surviving companies, and so excludes innovators who have failed. This enables some companies to look like pioneers when actually they are not.

Tellis and Golder have studied 50 different markets using product categories familiar to consumers, and carefully avoided using hindsight to identify pioneers. This revealed a very different picture.

(a) The failure rate for pioneers turned out to be very, high; almost half did not survive.
(b) In only 11% of the markets surveyed were todays leaders true pioneers.
(c) The average market share of survivors is only 10%.

The real success goes to *early leaders* - firms that entered the market an average of 13 years after the pioneers, and now have a market share three times the size of the pioneers. The reasons for this success are pioneers often fail to conjure up a mass market. Quality is often low, prices high and applications limited at this stage.

Examples of this would include the personal computer and the video recorder. The VCR market was pioneered by Ampex in 1956, when it charged $50,000 for its early models and sold only a few, making little effort to cut costs and expand the market. Sony, JVC and Matsushita, in contrast, saw the potential for mass market sales and set out to make a video recorder that would cost $500 - which took them 20 years to achieve.

Many first movers, such as Ampex, were content to have pioneered the technology, believing the breakthrough was enough to bring market leadership. Micro Instrumentation and Telemetry Systems invented the PC in the mid-1970s but ceded market leadership to latecomers (such as Apple Computers and IBM) that invested heavily to turn the PC into a mass-market product. Other examples include *alcopops*: Two Dogs was first in the market but was beaten by Hoopers' Hooch, which was more extensively marketed.

*(Adapted from The Economist, 16/3/96)*

## 5 SERVICES

5.1 'Products' is a generic term and can, in many case, include 'services' for the practical purpose of marketing. However, there are some very specific aspects of service marketing which present particular marketing problems.

(a) *Intangibility*: services cannot be seen, touched, felt or tasted until after purchase
(b) *Inseparability*: services are sold then produced
(c) *Variability*: the standard of service varies from day to day
(d) *Perishability*: services cannot be stored

These are considered in more detail in Part C of this Study Text. It is worth noting, however, that there are very few pure products or services. Most products have some service attributes and many services are in some way attached to products.

5.2 Service quality can be seen to fit into a number of dimensions, some of which are more easily measured than others. Factors which need to be considered include the following.

(a) Tangibles
(b) Reliability
(c) Responsiveness
(d) Communication
(e) Credibility
(f) Security
(g) Competence
(h) Courtesy
(i) Understanding the customer's needs
(j) Access

Discussions of service quality have been particularly influential in the dissemination of ideas about, on the one hand, achieving *total* quality, and on the other, raising standards of customer care. This is discussed in Parts C and D of this Study Text.

5.3 It is worth noting, however, that emphasis on these aspects of service quality leads to a programme which aims to focus on:

(a) customer satisfaction;
(b) putting the customer first;
(c) anticipating customer needs or problems;
(d) tailoring products to customer needs;
(e) establishing lasting customer relationships.

5.4 Service staff must be well trained if the organisation is to provide service which is:

(a) high quality;
(b) personal - applying the right product to the specific customer situation;
(c) friendly, caring and polite;
(d) personalised; and
(e) quick, efficient and accurate.

A programme to achieve these objectives is discussed in Part C of this Study Text.

5.5 In summary, it is easy for the management of an organisation to pay lip service to the need for better customer care. In reality, higher service quality can only be achieved by careful planning specification of objectives and the implementation of operating systems which can be monitored to ensure that they meet set performance standards. Cultural change is much easier to write about than it is to achieve. In practice, it involves the following actions.

(a) *Breaking down barriers.* An essential element, in large, rigid, stable organisations particularly, can involve breaking down the typically traditional, autocratic, paternalistic and hierarchical culture and structure. To achieve this aim we may try:

   (i) mixing staff from widely different levels of the hierarchy at training sessions;
   (ii) promoting the use of first names between management and staff;
   (iii) sharing facilities, including single status restaurants and meeting rooms;
   (iv) reducing the number of tiers of management.

(b) *Improving internal communication.* Communicating to staff their role in the organisation is very important.

(c) *Overcoming inflexible attitudes* and behaviour by staff who do not accept the need for change.

## 6 BRANDS AND PACKAGING

Examined 12/97

6.1 A manufacturer might produce goods under his own brand name and at the same time (or perhaps exclusively) supply large retailers with goods under their own brand name, 'own label' brands or dealer brands. The major examples are the own brands of supermarkets and major chain stores (eg Tesco, Sainsburys, St Michael for Marks & Spencer and Winfield for Woolworths). The advantages of dealer brands to a manufacturer are as follows.

(a) A high level of sales may be necessary to cover fixed costs of production and supplying dealer branded goods to a large retail organisation may be a necessary way of achieving a profitable sales level. New market segments can be covered profitably at less risk and outlay to the producer.

(b) Large retailers with a high sales turnover and considerable control over the retail trade may insist on having their own brand, and supplying dealer branded goods may be essential to retain their business.

(c) It may be a well established and common practice in the industry.

(d) A manufacturer may wish to concentrate on production only, leaving the problem of design, quality and distribution to a multiple retailer.

6.2 The attraction of dealer brands to dealers are:

(a) the use of a brand helps to create customer loyalty to the store;

(b) the buying in price is lower and cost of sales promotion (if any) negligible; therefore the price of dealer branded goods to customers can be lower (price consciousness is a notable feature of dealer brands);

(c) 'Me-too' products may benefit from the generic promotion effect of the market leader's success, but enjoy a price advantage.

### Packaging

6.3 Packaging has five functions:

(a) protection of contents;

(b) distribution, helping to transfer products from the manufacturer to the customer;

(c) selling, as the design and labelling serve promotional objectives of providing information and conveying an image;

(d) user convenience, as an aid to storage and carrying, such as aerosol cans and handy packs;

(e) to conform to government regulations (for example by providing a list of ingredients and contents by weight, as in food packaging).

Remember that goods are usually packaged in more than one *layer*. Consumer goods might be packaged for sale to individual customers, but delivered to resellers in cartons or some similar bulk package.

### Case example

HelpAd combines raising money for a good cause with innovation in packaging practice. The company, which is owned by the Red Cross, persuades makers of consumer goods to leave room for an advertisement on the outside of their packaging, and then sells this advertising space to another manufacturer, who makes something which goes well with the first product. Hovis, one of the first customers, has produced loaves carrying ads for Anchor butter; Tabasco pepper sauce has bought space on the side of bottles of Del Monte tomato juice. The ads all include a little 'HelpAd' logo explaining that the money from selling the space all goes to the Red Cross. Commercially competitive rates are charged for the space sold, and the aim is to secure a sustainable source of income for the charity.

Companies have shown a healthy interest, although there may be problems, for example, where rival products from within a company's portfolio are advertised. Clearly the advantages for the companies are considerable too; value is added to the image of the product through association with a well established and respected international good cause, while there may well be fruitful synergy between the brands involved. It is also intended to extend this idea. Plans are afoot to extend the scheme to another seven European countries and South Africa. The idea originated with Robert Doyle. He has now developed a scheme to encourage sports stars to 'give their right arms to the Red Cross' by using the sleeve of their playing shirts as a location for a HelpAd. HelpAd may also, in the future, function as a broker for charities other than the Red Cross, offering its services for a small percentage of the money paid for the advertisement. *(Adapted from The Economist, 28/9/96)*

## The qualities required of a pack

6.4 The qualities required of a pack are as follows.

(a) The range of size and variety should be minimised in order to keep down purchasing, production and distribution costs, but it should succeed in making the product attractive and distinctive to the target consumer.

(b) In industries where distribution is a large part of total costs, packaging is an important issue.

- (i) Packs should protect, preserve and convey the product to its destination in the desired condition.
- (ii) Packs should use vehicle space cost effectively.
- (iii) Packs should fit into the practices of mechanised handling and storage systems.
- (iv) Packs should be space efficient, but also attractive display items.
- (v) Packs should convey product information to shoppers effectively.
- (vi) Packs should preserve the products' condition.

(c) Packaging is an important aid to selling. Where a product cannot be differentiated by design techniques, the pack takes over the design selling function. This is crucial where there are no real product differences between rival brands, or in the case of commodities such as flour, which are basic goods.

- (i) A pack should help to promote the advertising/brand image. In addition, a logo should be clearly identifiable on the package, to use customer brand loyalty to a range of products.
- (ii) Shape, colour and size should relate to customer motivation (for 'value' or 'quantity').
- (iii) It should be the appropriate size for the expected user of the product (for example, family size packets of food).
- (iv) Some may be designed to promote impulse buying (for example, new FMCG products, snack foods and so on).

(v) A convenience pack (tubes, aerosols) should be provided where this is an important attribute.

(vi) Packaging should maintain product quality standards.

(vii) It should attract attention of potential customers, where appropriate.

6.5 Packaging must appeal not only to consumers, but also to resellers. A reseller wants a package design that will help to sell the product, but also one which minimises the likelihood of breakage, or which extends the product's shelf life, or makes more economic use of shelf space.

6.6 The packaging of industrial goods is primarily a matter of maintaining good condition to the point of use. In itself this is a selling aid in future dealings with the customer. Large, expensive and/or fragile pieces of equipment *must* be well packaged.

### Case example

Packaging is increasingly being used by producers to inform and educate consumers. Information is a way of targeting consumers and meeting their needs more precisely. Supermarkets such as Sainsbury, for example, see packaging information as a way of gaining a larger share of the market for apples. Sainsbury announced that they have developed a new 'flavour gauge' which helps customers choose the variety which best suits their palate.

The gauge identifies five different taste levels - sharp, such as Bramley; fairly sharp; sharp and sweet, such as Cox; fairly sweet; and sweet such as Gala. Prepacks will now carry a label and loose fruit will be identified by shelf tickets.

This promotion coincided very closely with 'National Cox Day' sponsored by the marketing organisation English Apples and Pears. To go along with this, Sainsbury will be stocking up to 40 different varieties of English apple, including 15 that are less well known. Asda has also announced that it is presently promoting English apples, particularly the smaller Cox varieties which are under 55 mm. These are being marketed as particularly suitable for children.

*(Adapted from The Grocer, 29/9/96)*

## Chapter roundup

- In this chapter we have outlined the main aspects of product policy and new product development.
- You should learn the Ansoff table for combinations of products and markets. Make sure you can describe the terms market penetration, product development, market development and diversification.
- You should be able to discuss the benefits of market segmentation, as well as the various methods of segmenting markets.
- The product life cycle can be demonstrated best by reference to the standard diagram, showing the PLC 'curve'. Remember the criticisms of the use of PLC.
- Remember the different terms used in product portfolio planning when classifying products: Problem Child, Star, Cash Cow, Dog.
- You should be able to discuss the major aspects of new product development, service industries and brands and packaging.

## Test your knowledge

1 What is Ansoff's product/market matrix? (see Introduction)

2 What are the requirements for effective market segmentation? (1.3)

3 What are the advantages and disadvantages of using socio-economic groups as a basis for market segmentation? (1.11, 1.12)

4 Outline the changing social trends in UK households of which marketers should be aware. (1.15 - 1.17)

5 Describe the stages in the product life cycle. (2.10)

6 Describe and explain the major criticisms of the PLC. (2.18 - 2.24)

7 A cash cow is a product with a high market share in a growth market. True or false? (3.8)

8 Using the GE Business Screen, what should be done with a strong product in an unattractive market? (3.13)

9 List sources of new products. (4.4)

10 Why might one aspect of quality policy in NPD be to fix a price before fixing a quality standard? (4.11)

11 How can an organisation promote cultural change within itself? (5.5)

12 Why should a manufacturer produce a dealer brand? (6.1)

13 What qualities are required of a pack? (6.4)

**Now try illustrative questions 9 to 11 at the end of the Study Text**

# Chapter 6

# PRICE

**This chapter covers the following topics.** *Syllabus reference*



| | | Syllabus reference |
|---|---|---|
| 1 | The importance of price | 2.6 |
| 2 | Methods of price determination | 2.6 |
| 3 | Pricing policy | 2.7 |
| 4 | Price setting strategies | 2.7 |
| 5 | Price elasticity of demand | 2.6 |
| 6 | Absorption and marginal costing, and breakeven analysis | 2.6 |



## Introduction

We looked at product policy in the last chapter and we now move on to pricing policies and decisions.

All profit organisations and many non-profit organisations face the task of setting a price on their products or services. Price can go by many names: fares, tuitions, rent, assessments and so on. Historically, price was the single most important decision made by the sales department, but the importance of the interrelated elements of the marketing mix has been realised in modern approaches. Price, whilst important, is not necessarily the predominant factor nowadays. Marketing managers may now respond to competition by trying to interpret and satisfy consumer wants and needs by modifying existing products or introducing new products to the range. The typical reaction in production-oriented times was to cut prices in order to sell the firm's product.

It is sometimes suggested that marketing aims to make price relatively unimportant to the consumers' decision making process. There is certainly some truth in this view. The other elements of the marketing mix are ultimately concerned with adding value to the product and tailoring it to the consumers' needs, to ensure that the choice between two products is not simply based on their different prices. This underestimates the role of pricing within the marketing mix.

Once you have finished this chapter you should understand the following.

(a) Price and its determinants represent an extremely important part of the marketing mix.

(b) There are a variety of models which can be used to aid pricing decisions, based on cost, competition and demand; including breakeven analysis, marginal costing and price elasticity.

## 1 THE IMPORTANCE OF PRICE

*Examined 12/94*

### Exam focus point

Price has been examined in one form or another in every exam since this syllabus was introduced in December 1994.

1.1 Price can be defined as a measure of the value exchanged by the buyer for the value offered by the seller. It might be expected, therefore, that the price would reflect the costs to the seller of producing the product and the benefit to the buyer of consuming it.

1.2 Pricing is the only element of the mix which generates revenue rather than creating costs. It also has an important role as a competitive tool to *differentiate* a product and an organisation and thereby exploit market opportunities. Pricing must also be *consistent* with other elements of the marketing mix since it contributes to the overall image created for the product. No organisation can hope to offer an exclusive high quality product to the market with a low price - the price must be consistent with the overall *product offer*.

### Exercise 1

In what circumstances would you expect price to be the main factor influencing a consumer's choice?

### Solution

You might have identified a number of different factors here. Perhaps the most important general point to make is that price is particularly important if the other elements in the marketing mix are relatively similar across a range of competing products. For example, there is a very wide variety of toothpastes on the market, most of them not much differentiated from the others. The price of a particular toothpaste may be a crucial factor in its sales success.

1.3 Although pricing can be thought of as fulfilling a number of roles, in overall terms a price aims to produce the desired level of sales in order to meet the objectives of the business strategy. Pricing must be systematic and at the same time take into account the internal needs and the external constraints of the organisation.

1.4 The ultimate objective of pricing, as with other elements of the marketing mix, is to produce the required level of sales so that the organisation can achieve its specified objectives. Two broad categories of objectives may be specified for pricing decisions; not mutually exclusive, but different nonetheless.

(a) *Maximising profits* is concerned with maximising the returns on assets or investments. This may be realised even with a comparatively small market share depending on the patterns of cost and demand.

(b) *Maintaining or increasing market share* involves increasing or maintaining the customer base which may require a different, more competitive approach to pricing, while the company with the largest market share may not necessarily earn the best profits.

1.5 Either approach may be used in specifying pricing objectives, and they may appear in some combination, based on a specified rate of return and a specified market share. It is important that stated objectives are consistent with overall corporate objectives and corporate strategies.

### Case example

The air market in Europe is currently being deregulated. In response to this, a number of low-cost no-frills carriers have set up in business. A good example is *easyJet*. This airline flies from Luton and Liverpool as opposed to London. Another example is *Virgin Express*, operating from Brussels.

BA is keen to protect its market from this low-cost no-frills approach and has launched its own low-cost no-frills airline to compete in precisely this segment. Virgin and easyJet were concerned that BA would subsidise its low cost service *from profits elsewhere*.

*(Adapted from The Economist, 10/2/96)*

## 2 METHODS OF PRICE DETERMINATION

*Examined 12/97, 6/97*

### Price setting in theory

2.1 In classical economic theory, price is the major determinant of demand and brings together supply and demand to form an *equilibrium market price*. More recently, emphasis has been placed, especially in marketing, on the importance of non-profit factors in demand. Thus the significance of product quality, promotion, personal selling and distribution and, in overall terms, brands, has grown. A competitor may easily copy a price cut, at least in the short term, but it is much more difficult to duplicate a successful brand image based on a *unique selling proposition*. Successful branding can even imply premium pricing.

2.2 Economic theory can only determine the optimal price structure under the two extreme market conditions.

(a) *Perfect competition*: many buyers, many sellers all dealing in an identical product. Neither producer nor user has any market power and both must accept the prevailing market price.

(b) *Monopoly*: one seller who dominates many buyers. The monopolist can use his market power to set a profit maximising price.

2.3 However, in practice most of British industry can be described as an *oligopoly*: relatively small numbers of competitive companies dominate the market. Whilst each large firm has the ability to influence market prices, the unpredictable reaction from the other giants makes the final industry price indeterminate. Economists in the field of oligopoly pricing think that price competition is dangerous, given that there are no clear market forces to support a given price level in this situation.

2.4 It is difficult in economic theory terms to identify precisely what is market power. Many small producers enjoy some market power producing distinctly different products and enjoy a degree of local monopoly.

2.5 Whilst economic theory gives an insight into price decisions, it may be of little practical help.

2.6 However, the concept of *price elasticity* is important. Price elasticity is measured as:

$$\frac{\text{\% change in sales demand}}{\text{\% change in sales price}}$$

(a) When elasticity is greater than 1 (*elastic*), a change in price will lead to a change in total revenue so that, if the price is:

(i) lowered, total sales revenue would rise, because of the large increase in demand;

(ii) raised, total sales revenue would fall, because of the large fall in demand.

(b) When elasticity is less than 1 (*inelastic*), if the price is:

(i) lowered, total sales revenue would fall, because the increase in sales volume would be too small to compensate for the price reductions;

(ii) raised, total sales revenue would go up in spite of the small drop in sales quantities.

We will look at elasticity in more detail in Section 5.

2.7 Marketing management needs to be able to estimate the likely effects of price changes on total revenue and profits.

> 'Price elasticity of demand gives precision to the question of whether the firm's price is too high or too low. From the point of view of maximising revenue, price is too high if demand is elastic and too low if demand is inelastic. Whether this is also true for maximising profits depends on the behaviour of costs.' (Kotler)

In some cases, however, other factors may influence price elasticity, so that previous responses to price changes no longer produce the same consumer responses. Products do not stay the same forever.

### Exercise 2

What are the limitations of price elasticity as a factor in determining prices?

### Solution

The main problem is that, unless very detailed research has been carried out, the price elasticity of a particular product or service is likely to be unknown. As a theoretical concept, it is useful in gaining an understanding of the *effects* of price changes; but it is of little use as a practical tool in *determining* prices.

## Price setting in practice

2.8 There are three main types of influence on price setting in practice: costs, competition and demand.

*Costs*

2.9 In practice cost is the most important influence on price. Many firms base price on simple cost-plus rules: in other words, costs are estimated and then a profit margin is added in order to set the price. A study by Lanzilotti gave a number of reasons for the predominance of this method:

(a) planning and use of scarce capital resources are easier;

(b) easier assessment of divisional performance;

(c) emulation of successful large companies;

(d) belief by management in a 'fair return' policy;

(e) fear of government action against 'excessive' profits;

(f) tradition of production orientation rather than marketing orientation in many organisations;

(g) tacit collusion in industry to avoid competition;

(h) adequate profits for shareholders are already made, giving no incentive to maximise profits;

(i) easier administration of cost-based pricing strategies based on internal data;

(j) stability of pricing, production and employment produced by cost-based pricing over time;

(k) social equability.

Cost-based pricing is in the main an accountants' method.

2.10 There are two types of cost-based pricing: full cost pricing and cost-plus pricing.

2.11 *Full cost pricing* takes account of the full average cost of production of a brand, including an allocation for overheads. A conventional profit margin is then added to determine the selling price. This method is often used for non-routine jobs which are difficult to cost in advance, such as the work of solicitors and accountants where the price is often determined after the work has been performed.

2.12 Although the full cost pricing method is basically straightforward in principle, the allocation or apportionment of overheads between brands in a multibrand company can be difficult, especially when joint or by-products are involved.

2.13 Superficially, it would appear that demand factors are ignored in this analysis; in practice, however, especially in the longer term, demand can be reflected through the level of the profit margin which is added (the margin is not going to be high if demand is being squeezed). The profit margin is also likely to reflect the level of actual or potential competition from firms already in the industry or capable of entering it.

2.14 Using *cost-plus pricing* only the more easily measurable direct cost components such as labour and raw material inputs are calculated in the unit cost, whilst an additional margin incorporates an overhead charge and a residual profit element. This method is used where overhead allocation to unit costs is too complex or too time consuming to be worthwhile.

2.15 A common example occurs with the use of *mark-up* pricing. This is used by retailers and involves a fixed margin being added to the buying-in price of goods for resale. This *fixed margin* tends to be conventional within product classes. In the UK, for example, fast moving items such as cigarettes carry a low 5-8% margin (also because of tax factors), fast moving but perishable items such as newspapers carry a 25% margin, while slow moving items which involve retailers in high stockholding costs such as furniture or books carry 33%, 50% or even higher mark up margins.

2.16 While the percentage margin may vary to reflect changes in demand or competition, the cost basis for calculations may be actual costs, expected costs or standard costs. If all the firms in the industry use the same pricing basis, prices will reflect efficiency; the lowest price firm will be the most efficient.

---

### Exercise 3

Cost-based pricing is quite common in practice, even though it is not necessarily a profit-maximising policy. What do you think are the reasons for its popularity?

### Solution

See Paragraph 2.9.

---

2.17 The problems with cost-plus pricing arise out of difficulties in defining direct costs and allocating overheads, and with over- or underestimation of attainable production levels (particularly where standard costs are used). In addition, price adjustments may cause high administrative costs because of the cost-based price-setting process used.

2.18 However, because the cost-plus approach leads to price stability, with price changing only to reflect cost changes, it can lead to a marketing strategy which is *reactive* rather then *proactive*.

2.19 In addition, there is very limited consideration of *demand* in cost-based pricing strategies. From a marketing perspective, cost-based pricing may reflect missed opportunities as little or no account is taken, particularly in the short run, of the price consumers are *willing* to pay for the brand, which may actually be higher than the cost-based price.

2.20 But the approach does provide a comprehensible, practical and popular solution to the pricing problem, whereas the traditional imperfect competition model in economic theory is of limited practical value for a number of reasons:

(a) it assumes that the demand curve can be identified with certainty;

(b) it ignores the market research costs associated with acquiring knowledge of demand;

(c) it assumes the firm has no productive constraint which could mean that the equilibrium point between supply and demand cannot be reached;

(d) it is a static analysis (concerned with only one point in time).

2.21 Particular problems may be caused by the use of cost-based pricing for a new brand as initial low production levels in the introduction stage may lead to a very high average unit cost and consequently a high price. A longer term perspective may thus be necessary, accepting short-term losses until full production levels are attained. Finally, if the firm is using a product line promotion strategy then there is likely to be added complexity in the pricing process.

---

### Exercise 4

Look at the following advertisement for SWATCH.

**FROM PLASTIC TO PLATINUM**

**WORLDWIDE INDIVIDUALLY NUMBERED LIMITED EDITION OF 12,999**

**£1,000 INC VAT**

- **Most exclusive Swatch ever produced.**
- **950 Platinum case and crown.**
- **Stainless steel presentation case with acrylic glass inlay.**
- **Interchangeable royal blue leather and padded plastic straps.**
- **Limited availability in the UK.**

Suggest how Swatch might have chosen the price of £1,000.

### Solution

We don't know the answer, but a suggestion is that the cost of the product was established (to make sure of breaking even), VAT added since it makes a significant difference for the customer, and comparisons were made with items of similar quality and rarity on the market. A range of possible prices, based on this data, might then have been presented to potential customers to see how they reacted to them. Data may also have been collected about the results of similar exercises by other watchmakers (or the like) in the past.

If you cheated and just read this solution without thinking for yourself, ask yourself how Swatch made the decision to produce no more than 12,999 watches. At what stage would the decision to go ahead and manufacture the watches be made?

---

*Competition*

2.22 Prices may be set on the basis of what *competitors are charging* rather than on the basis of cost or demand. A theoretical justification of the phenomenon was presented by Sweezy as the kinked demand curve theory, shown below.

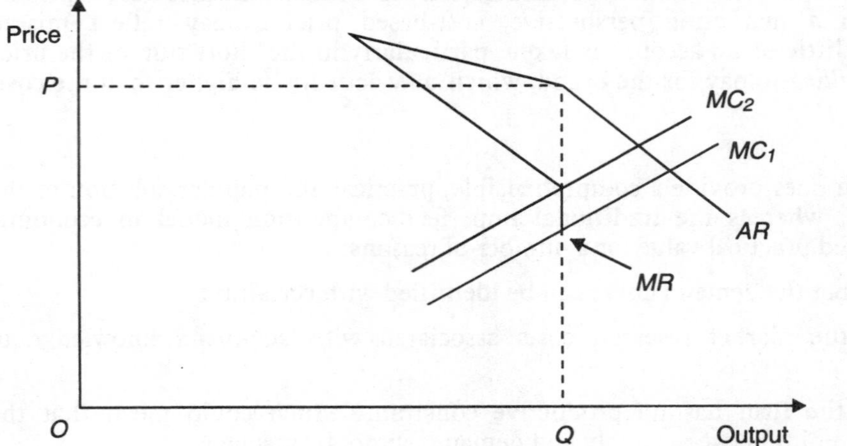


2.23 It is argued that price remains at OP even if marginal costs increase from $MC_1$, to $MC_2$. This is justified by the argument that that firms assume that competitors will all follow a price decrease but that none will follow a price increase. Thus they assume that demand is *elastic* for a price rise, but is *inelastic* for a price fall. In each case a price change would *reduce* sales revenue. But note that this approach does not explain how the price is arrived at in the first place!

2.24 In reality, the kinked demand curve theory would produce *going rate pricing* in which some form of average level of price becomes the norm, perhaps, in the case of a high level of branding in the market, including standard price differentials between brands.

2.25 In some market structures price competition may be avoided by tacit agreement leading to concentration on non-price competition; the markets for cigarettes and petrol are examples of this. Price-setting here is influenced by the need to avoid retaliatory responses by competitors resulting in a breakdown of the tacit agreement and so to price competition. Price changes based on real cost changes are led in many instances by a 'representative' firm in the industry and followed by other firms. From time to time tacit agreements break down leading to a period of price competition. This may then be followed by a resumption of the tacit agreement. Often such actions are the result of external factors at work on the industry. Industry level agreements do not necessarily preclude short-term price competition for specific brands, especially where sales promotion devices, such as special offers, are used (these are discussed later in this Study Text).

### Exercise 5

There is at least one service industry in which this practice is the norm and which is regularly reported in the headlines. Can you think of it?

### Solution

The industry referred to is the financial services industry. When economic factors cause alterations in interest rates (one of the main 'costs' borne by building societies and banks, because of their interest payments to investors), the societies reduce or increase their lending rates (the 'price' of their mortgage products). It is usual to see one of the larger societies leading the way, after which the others fall into line.

2.26 *Competitive bidding* is a special case of competition-based pricing. Many supply contracts, especially concerning local and national government purchases, involve would be suppliers submitting a *sealed bid tender*. In this case, the firm's submitted price needs to take account of expected competitor bid prices. Often the firms involved will not even know the identity of their rivals but successful past bids are often published by purchasers and, if this is so, it is possible to use this data to formulate a current bid price.

2.27 If the firm has the particular problem of bidding for a number of contracts before the result of any one bid is known, the production (or supply) capacity may be important. The firm may need only to win *some* contracts: not too few nor too many.

2.28 If past bid data is not published, then there is very little data on which to base bid price setting. The firm may have to rely on trade gossip, on conjecture or on an estimate of likely competitors' cost and profit requirements in price-setting.

2.29 If the contract is not awarded purely on price (that is, if the lowest bid is not automatically accepted) the problem is more acute. In the case of the supply of branded goods, the relative value of each brand must be considered on a 'value for money' basis by the purchaser. The bidder may have to rely on subjective 'feel of the market' analysis in arriving at bid prices. There are, of course, numerous instances where cases of actual and attempted bribery of officials have been uncovered as firms employ underhand means in the attempt to win contracts.

*Demand*

2.30 Rather than cost or competition as the prime determinants of price, a firm may base pricing strategy on the intensity of demand. Cost and competition factors, of course, remain influences or constraints on its freedom to set price.

2.31 A strong demand may lead to a high price, and a weak demand to a low price: much depends on the ability of the firm to segment the market price in terms of elasticity.

2.32 The diagram below shows a simple downward sloping demand curve in which there is one price ($P_0$) and the total quantity demanded is $Q_0$. The shaded area A represents *consumer surplus*, that is an area of extra benefit to the consumer. For example, a consumer may be willing to pay $P_1$ but only pays $P_0$ the market price, gaining a consumer surplus of $P_1 - P_0$. If the firm can increase prices to those willing to pay more then this area of consumer surplus could be reduced while the consumer may well continue to buy.

*Consumer surplus and price setting*

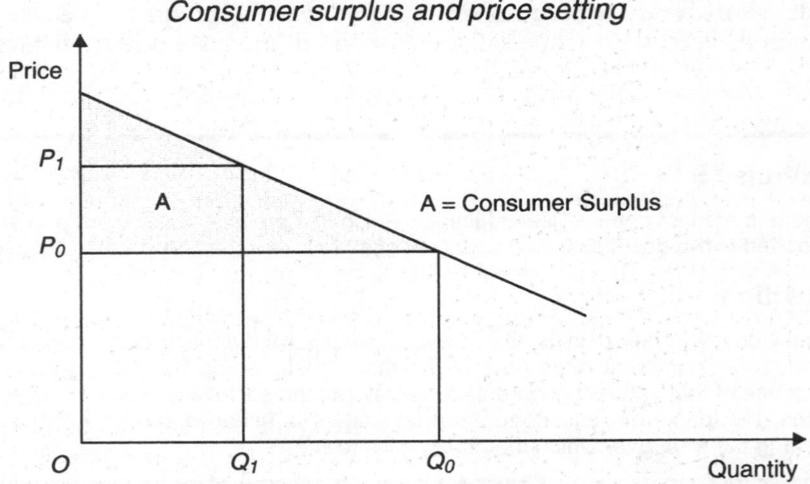


2.33 Identifying a consumer surplus and addressing it is difficult in practice as customers are unlikely to admit to a willingness to pay a higher price! However, if a firm can successfully identify consumer surpluses and charge higher prices for the same product to people who are willing to pay more there is said to be *price discrimination*, or *differential pricing*.

2.34 In practice, measurement of price elasticity and hence implementing differential pricing can be very difficult. There are a number of bases on which discriminating prices can be set.

(a) *By market segment*

A cross-channel ferry company would market its services at different prices in England, Belgium and France, for example. Services such as cinemas and hairdressers are often available at lower prices to old age pensioners and/or juveniles.

(b) *By product version*

Many car models have 'add on' extras which enable one brand to appeal to a wider cross-section of customers. Final price need not reflect the cost price of the add on extras directly: usually the top of the range model would carry a price much in excess of the cost of provision of the extras, as a prestige appeal.

(c) *By place*

Theatre seats are usually sold according to their location so that patrons pay different prices for the same performance according to the seat type they occupy.

(d) *By time*

Perhaps the most popular type of price discrimination. Off-peak travel bargains, hotel prices, telephone and electricity charges are all attempts to increase sales revenue by covering variable but not necessarily average cost of provision. British Rail is a successful price discriminator, charging more to rush hour rail commuters whose demand is inelastic at certain times of the day.

2.35 In each of these cases, some customers pay more than others for essentially the same product or service, reflecting different intensities of demand. There is an ethical dimension to this practice and firms need to consider their objectives carefully before using this approach. For instance, by taking advantage of a short-term shortage of a product and increasing price, a firm may harm long-term profit prospects because customers resent what they interpret as exploitation. This is particularly the case as *consumerism* develops, since vociferous groups of consumers can create damaging publicity for the product supplier in the short and/or longer term.

2.36 Price discrimination can only be effective if a number of conditions hold.

(a) The market must be segmentable in price terms, and different sectors must show different intensities of demand. Each of the sectors must be identifiable, distinct and separate from the others, and be accessible to the firm's marketing communications.

(b) There must be little or no chance of a black market developing so that those in the lower priced segment can resell to those in the higher priced segment.

(c) There must be little chance that competitors can and will undercut the firm's prices in the higher priced (and/or most profitable) market segments.

(d) The cost of segmenting and administering the arrangements should not exceed the extra revenue derived from the price discrimination strategy.

2.37 The firm could use a *market test* to estimate the effect on demand of a price change. This would involve a change of price in one region and a comparison of demand for the brand with past sales in that region and with sales in similar regions at the old prices. This is a high risk strategy: special circumstances (confounding factors) may affect the test area (such as a competitor's advertising campaign) which could affect the results. Also customers may switch from the test brand if a price rise is being considered and become loyal to a competitive brand; they may not switch back even if the price is subsequently lowered.

2.38 Alternately, a *direct attitude survey* may be used with respondents. *Pricing research* is notoriously difficult, especially if respondents try to appear rational to the interviewer or do not wish to offend him or her. Usually there is a lack of realism in such research; the respondent is not in an actual 'choice' situation faced with having to pay out hard earned income and therefore may give a hypothetical answer which is not going to be translated into actual purchasing behaviour. Nevertheless, pricing research is increasingly common as firms struggle to assess the perceived value customers attribute to a brand to provide an input to their pricing decisions.

**Exam focus point**

A number of questions have asked you to brief the finance department or justify your price strategy to them. Many accountants would be happy to base price on costs perhaps, but you have to base it onmarket demand. Indeed in June 1997 (Q44 *Responsibility for pricing* of our Practice & Revision Kit) the question concerned giving responsibility for pricing to the marketing department. You were asked to recommend alternatives to the cost plus approach. This chapter should give plenty of ideas.

## 3 PRICING POLICY

*Examined 12/96*

3.1 Price sensitivity will vary amongst purchasers. Those who can pass on the cost of purchases will be least sensitive and will respond more to other elements of the marketing mix.

(a) Provided that it fits the corporate budget, the business traveller will be more concerned about the level of service and quality of food in looking for an hotel than price. In contrast, a family on holiday are likely to be very price sensitive when choosing an overnight stay.

(b) In petrol retailing, the largest take up of trading stamps and other promotional offerings has been from the company representative, obtaining perks whilst charging relatively expensive petrol to the company.

(c) In industrial marketing the purchasing manager is likely to be more price sensitive than the engineer who might be the actual user of new equipment that is being sourced. The engineer and purchasing manager are using different criteria in making the choice. The engineer places product characteristics as first priority, the purchasing manager is more price oriented.

### Finding out about price sensitivity

3.2 Research on price sensitivity of customers has shown that:

(a) customers have a good concept of a 'just price' - a feel for what is about the right price to pay for a commodity;

(b) unless a regular purchase is involved, customers search for price information before buying, becoming price aware when wanting to buy but forgetting soon afterwards;

(c) customers will buy at what they consider to be a bargain price without full regard for need and actual price;

(d) for consumer durables it is the *down payment* and *instalment price* rather than total price which is important to the buyer;

(e) in times of rising prices the price image tends to lag behind the current price, which indicates a resentment of the price increase.

---

#### Case example

The luxury end of the hi-fi market caters for an elite band prepared to pay huge prices for audio systems. It accounts for $1 billion in sales, compared to $70 billion for US consumer electronics alone. But this market often pioneers features and products which later become standard in the mass market, for example noise reduction systems and CDs. The latest craze, however, is raising some eyebrows, because it threatens to turn the clock back - it is for valve (vacuum tube) powered amplifiers, which were assumed to have died out when they were replaced by transistors in the 50s and 60s.

Why should this be happening? Transistors are smaller, cheaper and more reliable. By 1990, the sales of valve amplifiers had fallen to almost zero. But enthusiasts maintain that the tubes reproduce musical notes more accurately, that the sound is better. By 1996, half of all up-market hi-fi amplifiers in the US were powered by valves.

Further, the most sought after amplifiers use the most antediluvian technology, single end amplifiers using a single 'triode', the design which in 1906 first made amplification possible. Since they produce only a few watts of power, they must be used with ancient but efficient 'horn' loudspeakers - which are consequently, also making a comeback.

This is the equivalent of going back to the Ford Model T when modern cars are on the market. Manufacturers are being tempted in by the lure of fat margins: Audio Note, a pioneer of the single ended market in Japan, sells amplifiers that range from $1,700 to $252,500 for the Gaku-On. Speakers cost around $40,000 per pair. Philips subsidiary Marantz, a mass market organisation, has just launched a tube amplifier for $50,000 while also reissuing a tube amplifier it last made in the 1950s for $8,400. Westrex, a small Atlanta firm, has resumed production of the 300B Triode, and hopes to sell 30,000 per year, giving it 40% of a market currently dominated by the Chinese and East European tube makers.

What effect will this have on the mass market? No-one really knows, but it seems likely that this will become an important segment within the audio market, although no-one can predict the potential size or profitability. *(Adapted from The Economist, 4/5/96)*

## Finding out about price perception

3.3 Price perception is important in the ways customers react to prices. The economist's downward sloping demand curve may not in fact hold, at least in the short term. For example, customers may react to a price increase by buying more because:

(a) they expect further price increases to follow (they are 'stocking up');
(b) they assume the quality has increased;
(c) the brand takes on a 'snob appeal' because of the high price.

3.4 Several factors complicate the pricing decisions which an organisation has to make.

## Intermediaries' objectives

3.5 If an organisation distributes products or services to the market through independent intermediaries, the objectives of these intermediaries have an effect on the pricing decision. Such intermediaries are likely to deal with a range of suppliers and their aims concern their own profits rather than those of suppliers. Also, the intermediary will take into account the needs of its customers. Thus conflict over price can arise between suppliers and intermediaries which may be difficult to resolve.

3.6 Many industries have traditional margins for intermediaries; to deviate from these might well cause problems for suppliers. In some industries, notably grocery retailing (as we have seen), the power of intermediaries allows them to dictate terms to suppliers. The relationship between intermediaries and suppliers is therefore complex, and price and the price discount structure is an important element.

## Competitors' actions and reactions

3.7 An organisation, in setting prices, sends out signals to rivals. These rivals are likely to react in some way. In some industries (such as petrol retailing) pricing moves in unison; in others, price changes by one supplier may initiate a price war, with each supplier undercutting the others.

## Suppliers

3.8 If an organisation's suppliers notice that the prices for an organisation's products are rising, they may seek a rise in the price for their supplies to the organisation, arguing that it is now more able to pay a higher price. This argument is especially likely to be used by the trade unions in the organisation when negotiating the 'price' for the supply for labour.

## Inflation

3.9 In periods of inflation the organisation's prices may need to change in order to reflect increases in the prices of supplies, labour, rent and so on. Such changes may be needed to keep relative (real) prices unchanged (this is the process of prices being adjusted for the rate of inflation).

## Quality connotations

3.10 In the absence of other information, customers tend to judge quality by price. Thus a price change may send signals to customers concerning the quality of the product. A rise may be taken to indicate improvements, a reduction may signal reduced quality, for example through the use of inferior components or a poorer quality of raw material. Thus any change in price needs to take such factors into account.

### New product pricing

3.11 Most pricing decisions for existing products relate to price changes. Such changes have a *reference point* from which to move (the existing price). But when a new product is introduced for the first time there may be no such reference points; pricing decisions are most difficult to make in such circumstances. It may be possible to seek alternative reference points, such as the price in another market where the new product has already been launched, or the price set by a competitor.

### Income effects

3.12 In times of rising incomes, price may become a less important marketing variable than, for instance, product quality or convenience of access (distribution). When income levels are falling and/or unemployment levels rising, price will become a much more important marketing variable.

---

#### Case example

In the recession of the early 1990s, the major grocery multiples such as Tesco, Sainsbury, Safeway and Waitrose, who steadily moved up-market in the 1980s with great success leaving the 'pile it high, sell it cheap' philosophy behind, suddenly found bargain stores such as 'Foodgiant' and 'Netto' a more serious threat.

This led the supermarkets to set up 'own label' product ranges which undercut prices for branded products.

---

### Multiple products

3.13 Most organisations market not just one product but a range of products. These products are commonly interrelated, perhaps being complements or substitutes. The management of the pricing function is likely to focus on the profit from the whole range rather than that on each single product. Take, for example, the use of *loss leaders*: a very low price for one product is intended to make consumers buy other products in the range which carry higher profit margins. Another example is selling razors at very low prices whilst selling the blades for them at a higher profit margin. People will buy many of the high profit items but only one of the low profit items - yet they are 'locked in' to the former by the latter. Loss leaders also attract customers into retail stores where they will usually buy normally priced products as well as the loss leaders.

### Sensitivity

3.14 Price decisions are often seen as highly sensitive and as such may involve top management more clearly than other marketing decisions. As already noted, price has a very obvious and direct relationship with profit. Ethical considerations are a further factor; whether or not to exploit short-term shortages through higher prices: illustrative of this dilemma is the outcry surrounding the series of petrol price rises following the outbreak of the Gulf Crisis in 1990.

## 4 PRICE SETTING STRATEGIES

*Examined 6/95, 12/95, 12/96*

4.1 The next few paragraphs look at different price-setting strategies and then later in the section we look at some complications in price-setting.

4.2 *Market penetration objective*: here the organisation sets a relatively low price for the product or service in order to stimulate growth of the market and/or to obtain a large share of it. This strategy was used by Japanese motor cycle manufacturers to enter the UK market. It worked famously: UK productive capacity was virtually eliminated and the imported Japanese machines could then be sold at a much higher price and still dominate the market.

4.3 Sales maximising objectives are favoured when:

(a) unit costs will fall with increased output (economies of scale);
(b) the market is price sensitive and relatively low prices will attract additional sales;
(c) low prices will discourage any new competitors.

4.4 *Market skimming objective*: in many ways an opposite objective to market penetration. Skimming involves setting a high initial price for a new product in order to take advantage of those buyers who are ready to pay a much higher price for a product. A typical strategy would be initially to command a premium price and then gradually to reduce the price to attract more price sensitive segments of the market. This strategy is really an example of price discrimination over time.

4.5 This strategy is favoured when:

(a) there is insufficient market capacity and competitors cannot increase capacity;
(b) buyers are relatively insensitive to price increases;
(c) high price perceived as high quality (interaction in marketing mix); *but*
(d) there is the danger of encouraging firms to enter market.

4.6 *Early cash recovery objective*: an alternative pricing objective is to recover the investment in a new product or service as quickly as possible, to achieve a minimum payback period. The price is set so as to facilitate this objective. This objective would tend to be used in conditions where:

(a) the business is high risk;
(b) rapid changes in fashion or technology are expected;
(c) the innovator is short of cash.

4.7 *Product line promotion objective*: here, management of the pricing function is likely to focus on profit from the range of products which the organisation produces rather than to treat each product as a separate entity. The product line promotion objective will take account of the constitution of the whole range in terms of:

(a) the interaction of the marketing mix;
(b) monitoring returns to ensure that net contribution is worthwhile.

4.8 *Intermediate customers*: some companies set a price to distributors and allow them to set whatever final price they wish. A variant involves publishing an inflated *recommended retail price* so that retailers can offer large promotional discounts.

4.9 *Cost-plus pricing*: a firm may set its initial price by marking up its unit costs by a certain percentage or fixed amount, as already discussed.

(a) This conforms to internal company rules for 'satisfactory' return on investment.

(b) This takes no account of risk. In fact, riskier product lines should make higher returns.

(c) This cannot ultimately avoid market pressures: if 'overpriced', stocks will build up or if 'underpriced', excess demand will be created exceeding the firm's capacity and encourages market entrants.

4.10 *Target pricing*: a variant on cost-plus where the company tries to determine the price that gives a specified rate of return for a given output. This is widely used by large American manufacturers, such as General Motors and Boeing.

4.11 *Price discrimination (or differential pricing)*: offering different prices to different classes of buyer. The danger is that price cuts to one buyer may be used as a negotiating lever by another buyer. To avoid such leverage:

(a) buyers must be in clearly defined segments, such as overseas and home (Rover cars are cheaper in the USA), or students' concessionary fares;

(b) own branding where packaging is changed for that of a supermarket is a variation on this;

(c) bulk buying discounts and aggregated rebate schemes can favour large buyers.

4.12 *Going rate pricing*: try to keep in line with industry norm for prices. Don't 'rock the boat' if everybody is charging relatively high near-monopolistic prices.

(a) This is typical behaviour of a mature oligopoly, akin to a cartel.

(b) Suppliers engage in less damaging competition than price cutting, such as advertising campaigns and post-sales service.

(c) This is often technically illegal but this does not stop individual firms accepting the role of price leaders in an industry.

4.13 *Quantum price*: in retail selling the concept of a 'quantum point' is often referred to. When the price of an item is increased from, say, £9.65 to £9.95, sales may not be affected because the consumers do not notice the price change. However, if the price is increased from £9.95 to £10.05 a major fall in sales may occur, £10 acting as a *quantum point* which can be approached but not passed if the price is not to deter would be purchasers.

4.14 *Odd number pricing*: sometimes referred to as 'psychological pricing', in fact the odd number pricing syndrome (pricing at £1.99, £2.99 etc rather than £2, £3 etc) is said to have originated not as a marketing concept but in department stores in order to ensure the honesty of sales assistants. The customer has to wait for change from £1.95 when, as is usual, they offer, say, £2 in payment, so the assistant has to use the till. If the price was £2 and the customer need not wait for the change, there was thought to be a greater temptation to shop assistants to pocket the money and not to enter it into the till!

4.15 *One coin purchase*: confectionery firms have used another psychologically based concept of a 'one coin purchase' in pricing tactics. Rather than change price to reflect cost changes, such firms often alter the quantity in the unit of the product and keep the same price. This is a case of 'price-minus' pricing. The firm determines what the market will bear and works backwards, planning to produce and market a brand which will be profitable to them, selling at the nominated retail price.

4.16 *Gift purchases*: gift purchasing is often founded on the idea of price which is taken to reflect quality. Thus if a gift is to be purchased in an unfamiliar product category, a price level is often fixed by the buyer and a choice made from the brands available at that price. Cosmetics are often priced at £4.99 and £9.99 to appeal to gift purchasers at the £5 and £10 price level. Importantly, packaging is a major part of the appeal and must reflect a quality brand image, an important part of the psychology of gift choice.

## Product line pricing

4.17 When a firm sells a range of related products, or a product line, its theoretical pricing policy should be to set prices for each product in order to maximise the profitability of the line as a whole. A firm may therefore have a pricing policy for an entire product line.

(a) There may be a *brand name* which the manufacturer wishes to associate with high quality and high price, or reasonable quality and low price and so forth. All items in the line will be priced accordingly. For example, all major supermarket chains have an 'own brand' label which is used to sell goods at a slightly lower price than the major named brands.

(b) If two or more products in the line are *complementary*, one may be priced as a *loss leader* in order to attract more demand for all of the related products.

(c) If two or more products in the line share joint production costs (*joint products*), prices of the products will be considered as a single decision. For example, if a common production process makes one unit of joint product A for each one unit of joint product B, a price for A which achieves a demand of, say, 17,000 units, will be inappropriate if associated with a price for product B which would only sell, say, 10,000 units. 7,000 units of B would be unsold and wasted.

### Price changes caused by cost changes in the firm

4.18 During the prolonged period of inflation dating back to the 1970s, price increases generated by increased costs to the manufacturer were a common experience. The effect of inflation on price decisions was very noticeable and different organisations reacted in different ways.

(a) Some firms raised their prices regularly.

(b) Other firms gave advance warning of price rises, especially in an industrial market. Customers might then be persuaded to buy early in order to avoid paying the higher price at a later date.

(c) A firm which did not raise its prices was in effect reducing its prices in real terms.

### Competitive pricing

4.19 It is in the field of competition that price is the most potent element in the marketing mix. Professor Corey of the Harvard Business School summarised the role of price in competitive gameplaying.

> 'The struggle for market share focuses critically on price. Pricing strategies of competing firms are highly interdependent. The price one competitor sets is a function not only of what the market will pay but also of what other firms charge. Prices set by individual firms respond to those of competitors; they also are intended often to influence competitors' pricing behaviour. Pricing is an art, a game played for high stakes; and for marketing strategists it is the 'moment of truth'. All of marketing comes to focus in the pricing decision.'

### Competitive price changes

4.20 A firm may lower its prices to try to increase its market share; on the other hand, a firm may raise its prices in the hope that competitors will quickly do the same (that is, in the expectation of tacit price collusion). The purpose of such competitive initiatives will presumably be to raise either profits or the firm's market share. In established industries dominated by a few major firms, however, it is generally accepted that a price initiative by one firm will be countered by a price reaction by competitors. Here, prices tend to be fairly stable, unless pushed upwards by inflation or strong growth in demand. Consequently, in industries such as breakfast cereals (dominated in Britain by Kelloggs, Nabisco and Quaker) or canned soups (Heinz, Crosse & Blackwell and Campbells) a certain price stability might be expected without too many competitive price initiatives, except when cost inflation pushes up the price of one firm's products with other firms soon following.

4.21 In the event that a rival cuts prices expecting to increase market share, a firm has several options.

(a) It will *maintain its existing prices* if the expectation is that only a small market share would be lost, so that it is more profitable to keep prices at their existing level. Eventually, the rival firm may drop out of the market or be forced to raise its prices.

(b) It may *maintain its prices* but respond with a *non-price counter-attack*. This is a more positive response, because the firm will be securing or justifying its current prices with a product change, advertising, or better back-up services etc.

(c) It may *reduce its prices*. This should protect the firm's market share. The main beneficiary from the price reduction will be the consumer.

(d) It may *raise its prices* and respond with a *non-price counter-attack*. The extra revenue from the higher prices might be used to finance promotion on product changes. A price increase would be based on a campaign to emphasise the quality difference between the firm's own product and the rival's product.

### Price leadership

4.22 Given that price competition can have disastrous consequences in conditions of oligopoly, it is not unusual to find that large corporations emerge as price leaders. Price leadership here brings about relative price stability in otherwise unstable price dynamic oligopolies.

4.23 A price leader will dominate price levels for a class of products; increases or decreases by the price leader provide a direction to market price patterns. The price dominant firm may lead without moving at all. This would be the case if other firms sought to raise prices and the leader did not follow, then the upward move in prices will be halted. The price leader generally has a large, if not necessarily largest, market share. The company will usually be an efficient low-cost producer that has a reputation for technical competence.

4.24 The role of price leader is based on a track record of having initiated price moves that have been accepted by both competitors and customers. Often, this is associated with a mature well established management group.

4.25 Any dramatic changes in industry competition, (a new entrant, or changes in the board room) may endanger the price leadership role.

---

**Exam focus point**

Q42 *Pricing new products* in our Practice & Revision Kit covers innovative software products. Similarly, Q90 *Setag Industries* covered pricing for a new product. To find the appropriate strategy you had to consider the nature of the product – was it exposed to competition or could a premium price strategy be justified by the niche nature of the product and the prospect of enthusiastic early adopters? (*Financial Times, 16 February 1996*)

---

## 5 PRICE ELASTICITY OF DEMAND

5.1 We have already looked at price elasticity of demand, but only briefly. In this section we will expand on the topic to give you a fuller understanding and then go on to discuss costing and breakeven analysis in more detail. These topics are mentioned specifically in your syllabus.

### The price elasticity of demand

5.2 If prices went up by 10% would the quantity demanded fall by 5%, 20%, 50% or what? Price elasticity of demand is a measure of the extent of change in market demand for a good in response to a change in its price. It is measured as:

$$\frac{\text{The change in quantity demanded, as a \% of demand}}{\text{The change in price, as a \% of the price}}$$

Since the demand goes up when the price falls, and goes down when the price rises, the elasticity has a negative value, but it is usual to ignore the minus sign.

### Example: price elasticity of demand

5.3 The price of a product is £1.20 per unit and annual demand is 800,000 units. Market research indicates that an increase in price of 10 pence per unit will result in a fall in annual demand of 75,000 units. What is the price elasticity of demand?

### Solution

5.4 Annual demand at £1.20 per unit is 800,000 units.

Annual demand at £1.30 per unit is 725,000 units.

% change in demand $\frac{75{,}000}{800{,}000} \times 100\% = 9.375\%$

% change in price $\frac{10\text{p}}{120\text{p}} \times 100\% = 8.333\%$

Price elasticity of demand $= \frac{-9.375}{8.333} = -1.125$

Ignoring the minus sign, price elasticity is 1.125.

The demand for this product, at a price of £1.20 per unit, would be referred to as *elastic* because the price elasticity of demand is greater than 1. Now try the following exercise yourself.

---

### Exercise 6

If the price per unit of X rises from £1.40 to £1.60, it is expected that monthly demand will fall from 220,000 units to 200,000 units.

What is the price elasticity of demand?

### Solution

Monthly demand at £1.40 per unit = 220,000 units.

Monthly demand at £1.60 per unit = 200,000 units.

% change in demand $\frac{20{,}000}{220{,}000} \times 100\% = 9.09\%$

% change in price $\frac{20}{140} \times 100\% = 14.29\%$

Price elasticity of demand $= \frac{-9.09}{14.29} = -0.64$

Demand is inelastic at a price of £1.40 per unit, because the price elasticity of demand (ignoring the minus sign) is less than 1.

---

### Elastic and inelastic demand

5.5 The value of demand elasticity may be anything from zero to infinity. As we have seen, demand is referred to as:

(a) *inelastic* if the absolute value is less than 1; and
(b) *elastic* if the absolute value is greater than 1.

5.6 Think about what this means. Where demand is inelastic, the quantity demanded falls by a smaller percentage than price, and where demand is elastic, demand falls by a larger percentage than the percentage rise in price.

### Price elasticity and the slope of the demand curve

5.7 Generally, demand curves slope downwards. Consumers are willing to buy more at lower prices than at higher prices. Except in certain special cases (which we look at below), elasticity will *vary* in value along the length of a demand curve.

5.8 At higher prices on a straight line demand curve (the top of the demand curve), small percentage price reductions can bring large percentage increases in quantity demanded. This means that demand is elastic over these ranges, and price reductions bring increases in total expenditure by consumers on the commodity in question.

5.9 At lower prices on a straight line demand curve (the bottom of the demand curve), large percentage price reductions can bring small percentage increases in quantity. This means that demand is *inelastic* over these price ranges, and price increases result in increases in total expenditure.

5.10 There are three special values of price elasticity of demand; 0, 1 and infinity.

(a) *Demand is perfectly inelastic.* There is no change in quantity demanded, regardless of the change in price. The demand curve is a vertical straight line.

(b) *Perfectly elastic demand* (infinitely elastic). Consumers will want to buy an infinite amount, but only up to a particular price level. Any price increase above this level will reduce demand to zero. The demand curve is a horizontal straight line.

(c) *Unit elasticity of demand.* Total revenue for supplies (which is the same as total spending on the product by households) is the same whatever the price.

### The significance of price elasticity

5.11 The price elasticity of demand is relevant to *total spending* on a good or service. Total expenditure is a matter of interest to both suppliers, to whom sales revenue accrues, and to government, who may receive a proportion of total expenditure in the form of taxation.

5.12 When demand is elastic, an increase in price will result in a fall in the quantity demanded, and total expenditure will fall.

5.13 When demand is inelastic, an increase in price will still result in a fall in quantity demanded, but total expenditure will rise.

5.14 Information on price elasticity of demand indicates how consumers can be expected to respond to different prices. Business people can make use of information on how consumers will react to pricing decisions as it is possible to trace the effect of different prices on total revenue and profits. Information on price elasticities of demand will be useful to a business which needs to know the price decrease necessary to clear a surplus (excess supply) or the price increase necessary to eliminate a shortage (excess demand).

### Factors influencing price elasticity of demand for a good

5.15 Factors that determine price elasticity of demand are similar to the factors other than price that affect the volume of demand. Elasticity is really a measure of the strength of these other influences on demand. The main factors affecting price elasticity of demand are as follows.

(a) *The availability of close substitutes.* The more substitute goods there are, especially close substitutes, the more elastic will be the price elasticity of demand for a good. For example, in a greengrocer's shop, a rise in the price of one vegetable such as carrots or cucumbers is likely to result in a switch of customer demand to other vegetables, many vegetables being fairly close substitutes for each other. Again the elasticity of demand for a particular brand of breakfast cereals is much greater than the elasticity of demand for breakfast cereals as a whole, because the former have much closer substitutes. This factor is probably the most important influence on price elasticity of demand.

(b) *The time period*. Over time, consumers' demand patterns are likely to change, and so if the price of a good is increased, the initial response might be very little change in demand (inelastic demand) but then as consumers adjust their buying habits in response to the price increase, demand might fall substantially. The time horizon influences elasticity largely because the longer the period of time which we consider, the greater the knowledge of substitution possibilities by consumers and the provision of substitutes by producers.

(c) *Competitors' pricing*. If the response of competitors to a price increase by one firm is to keep their prices unchanged, the firm raising its prices is likely to face elastic demand for its goods at higher prices. If the response of competitors to a reduction in price by one firm is to match the price reduction themselves, the firm is likely to face inelastic demand at lower prices. This is a situation which probably faces many large firms with one or two major competitors (ie oligopolies).

## 6 ABSORPTION AND MARGINAL COSTING, AND BREAKEVEN ANALYSIS

6.1 The objective of absorption costing is to include in the total cost of a product (unit, job, process and so on) an appropriate share of the organisation's total overhead, which reflects the amount of time and effort that has gone into producing a unit or completing a job.

### Is absorption costing necessary?

6.2 Before describing the procedures by which overhead costs are shared out among products, it may be useful to consider the justifications for using absorption costing.

6.3 Suppose that a company makes and sells 100 units of a product each week. The prime cost per unit is £6 and the unit sales price is £10. Production overhead costs £200 per week and administration, selling and distribution overhead costs £150 per week. The weekly profit could be calculated as follows.

| | £ | £ |
|---|---|---|
| Sales (100 units × £10) | | 1,000 |
| Prime cost (100 × £6) | 600 | |
| Production overheads | 200 | |
| Administration, selling and distribution costs | 150 | |
| | | 950 |
| Profit | | 50 |

6.4 In absorption costing, overhead costs will be added to each unit of product manufactured and sold.

| | *£ per unit* |
|---|---|
| Prime cost per unit | 6 |
| Production overhead (£200 per week for 100 units) | 2 |
| Full factory cost | 8 |

The weekly profit would be calculated as follows.

| | £ |
|---|---|
| Sales | 1,000 |
| Less factory cost of sales | 800 |
| Gross profit | 200 |
| Less administration, selling and distribution costs | 150 |
| Net profit | 50 |

6.5 Sometimes, but not always, the overhead costs of administration, selling and distribution are also added to unit costs, to obtain a full cost of sales.

| | *£ per unit* |
|---|---|
| Prime cost per unit | 6.00 |
| Factory overhead cost per unit | 2.00 |
| Administration etc costs per unit | 1.50 |
| Full cost of sales | 9.50 |

The weekly profit would be calculated as follows.

| | £ |
|---|---|
| Sales | 1,000 |
| Less full cost of sales | 950 |
| Profit | 50 |

6.6 It may already be apparent that the weekly profit is £50 no matter how the figures have been presented. This being so, how does absorption costing serve any useful purpose in accounting? Is it necessary?

6.7 The *theoretical* justification for using absorption costing is that all production overheads are incurred in the production of the organisation's output and so each unit of the product receives some benefit from these costs. Each unit of output should therefore be charged with some of the overhead costs.

6.8 The *practical* reasons for using absorption costing have traditionally been identified as follows.

(a) *Stock valuations* for profit calculations.

(b) *Pricing decisions*. Many companies attempt to fix selling prices by calculating the full cost of production or sales of each product, and then adding a margin for profit. In our example, the company might have fixed a gross profit margin at 25% on factory cost, or 20% of the sales price, in order to establish the unit sales price of £10. 'Full cost plus pricing' can be particularly useful for companies which do jobbing or contract work, where each job or contract is different, so that a standard unit sales price cannot be fixed. Without using absorption costing, a full cost is difficult to ascertain.

(c) *Establishing the profitability of different products*. This argument in favour of absorption costing is more contentious, but is worthy of mention here. If a company sells more than one product, it will be difficult to judge how profitable each individual product is, unless overhead costs are shared on a fair basis and charged to the cost of sales of each product.

## Marginal cost and marginal costing

6.9 Marginal costing is an alternative method of costing to absorption costing. In marginal costing, we identify the marginal costs of production and sales, which consist of:

(a) the variable cost of production, consisting of direct material cost, direct labour cost (usually), and variable production overhead; and

(b) the variable cost of administration, sales and distribution.

## Definition of marginal cost

6.10 The marginal production cost per unit of an item usually consists of the following.

(a) Direct materials
(b) Direct labour
(c) Variable production overheads

6.11 Variable costs depend on the volume of production, whereas fixed costs do not. For example:

(a) if you produce 1,000 cars you need 1,000 × the amount of metal you need for one car (ie a variable cost);

(b) if you produce 10 cars or 10,000, you will still pay the existing factory rent.

6.12 *Contribution* is the difference between sales value and the marginal cost of sales. It is of fundamental importance in marginal costing, and the term 'contribution' is really short for 'contribution towards covering fixed overheads and making a profit'.

6.13 Contribution is defined by the CIMA as 'sales value less variable cost of sales'. It is a central term in marginal costing, when the contribution per unit is expressed as the difference between its selling price and its marginal cost.

6.14 The principles of marginal costing are set out below.

(a) Since period *fixed costs* are the same, no matter what the volume of sales and production (provided that the level of activity is within the 'relevant range') it follows that by selling an extra item of product or service the following will happen.

   (i) Revenue will increase by the sales value of the item sold.

   (ii) Costs will increase only by the variable cost per unit.

   (iii) The increase in profit will therefore equal the sales value minus variable costs, that is, the amount of contribution earned from the item.

(b) Similarly, if the volume of sales falls by one item, the profit will fall by the amount of contribution earned from the item.

(c) Profit measurement should therefore be based on an analysis of total contribution. Since fixed costs relate to a period of time, and do not change with increases or decreases in sales volume, it is misleading to charge units of sale with a share of fixed costs. Absorption costing is therefore misleading, and it is more appropriate to deduct fixed costs from total contribution for the period to derive a profit figure.

(d) When a unit of product is made, the extra costs incurred in its manufacture are the variable production costs. Fixed costs are unaffected, and no extra fixed costs are incurred when output is increased. It is therefore argued that the valuation of closing stocks should be at variable production cost (direct materials, direct labour, direct expenses (if any) and variable production overhead) because these are the only costs properly attributable to the product.

## The contribution/sales ratio

6.15 Since the contribution per unit is the same at all sales volumes, given no change in the unit sales price, there must be a consistent relationship between contribution and sales; in other words the contribution earned per £1 of sales revenue must be constant. The contribution/sales (C/S) ratio (sometimes called the profit/volume or P/V ratio or even the contribution margin ratio) can be important in marginal costing calculations for this reason.

## Marginal costing and absorption costing compared

6.16 Marginal costing as a cost accounting system is significantly different from absorption costing. It is an *alternative* method of accounting for costs and profit, which rejects the principles of absorbing fixed overheads into unit costs.

(a) *In marginal costing*

   (i) Closing stocks are valued at marginal production cost.

   (ii) Fixed costs are charged in full against the profit of the period in which they are incurred.

(b) *In absorption costing* (sometimes referred to as *full costing*)

   (i) Closing stocks are valued at full production cost, and include a share of fixed production costs.

(ii) This means that the cost of sales in a period will include some fixed overhead incurred in a previous period (in opening stock values) and will exclude some fixed overhead incurred in the current period but carried forward in closing stock values as a charge to a subsequent accounting period.

6.17 In marginal costing, it is necessary to identify variable costs, contribution and fixed costs. In absorption costing variable costs and fixed costs are not distinguished.

Its relevance to pricing is as follows. To break even, sales revenue must generate enough to cover fixed costs (such as factory rent). Marginal costing can identify in simple terms how much revenue is needed. If this can be related to the volume of goods sold it is easy to find a quantity of goods to be sold at a given price.

## Breakeven analysis and breakeven point

6.18 Breakeven analysis is an application of marginal costing techniques and is sometimes called cost-volume-profit (CVP) analysis. By using marginal costing techniques, it is possible to ascertain the contribution per unit. The total contribution from all sales during a period is then compared with the fixed costs for that period; any excess or deficiency of contribution over fixed costs represents the profit or loss respectively for the period.

6.19 The management of an organisation usually wishes to know not only the profit likely to be made if the aimed-for production and sales for the year are achieved, but also: 'The level of activity at which there is neither profit nor loss' (the *breakeven point* as defined in CIMA *Official Terminology*) and the amount by which actual sales can fall below anticipated sales without a loss being incurred.

6.20 The breakeven point (BEP) can be calculated arithmetically. The number of *units* needed to be sold in order to break even will be the total fixed costs divided by the contribution per unit. This is because the contribution required to break even must be an amount which exactly equals the amount of fixed costs.

$$\text{Breakeven point} = \frac{\text{Total fixed costs}}{\text{Contribution per unit}} = \frac{\text{Contribution required to break even}}{\text{Contribution per unit}}$$

$$= \text{Number of units of sale required to break even.}$$

## Example: breakeven point

6.21 Expected sales 10,000 units at £8 = £80,000
Variable cost £5 per unit
Fixed costs £21,000

*Required*

Compute the breakeven point.

## Solution

6.22
| | | |
|---|---|---|
| The contribution per unit is £(8 – 5) | = | £3 |
| Contribution required to break even | = | fixed costs = £21,000 |
| Breakeven point (BEP) | = | 21,000 ÷ 3 = 7,000 units |
| In revenue, BEP | = | (7,000 × £8) = £56,000 |

Sales above £56,000 will result in profit of £3 per unit of additional sales and sales below £56,000 will mean a loss of £3 per unit for each unit by which sales fall short of 7,000 units. In other words, profit will improve or worsen by the amount of contribution per unit.

| | 7,000 units | | 7,001 units |
|---|---|---|---|
| | £ | | £ |
| Revenue | 56,000 | | 56,008 |
| Less variable costs | 35,000 | | 35,005 |
| Contribution | 21,000 | | 21,003 |
| Less fixed costs | 21,000 | | 21,000 |
| Profit | 0 | (= breakeven) | 3 |

6.23 An alternative way of calculating the breakeven point to give an answer in terms of sales revenue is as follows.

$$\frac{\text{Required contribution} = \text{Fixed costs}}{\text{C / S ratio}} = \text{Sales revenue at breakeven point}$$

6.24 In the example in Paragraph 6.20 the C/S ratio is $\frac{£3}{£8} = 37.5\%$

Breakeven is where sales revenue = $\frac{£21{,}000}{37.5\%} = £56{,}000$

At a price of £8 per unit, this represents 7,000 units of sales.

The contribution/sales ratio is a measure of how much contribution is earned from each £1 of sales. The C/S ratio of 37.5% in the above example means that for every £1 of sales, a contribution of 37.5p is earned. Thus, in order to earn a total contribution of £21,000 and if contribution increases by 37.5p per £1 of sales, sales must be:

$$\frac{£1}{37.5\text{p}} \times £21{,}000 = £56{,}000$$

---

## Case example

Before you get too worried about or carried away with the pricing methods and their technicalities described in this chapter, you should read the following extracts from an article by Vanessa Holder in the *Financial Times* (29 April 1996).

*'"Pricing is guesswork. It is usually assumed that marketers use scientific methods to determine the price of their products. Nothing could be further from the truth."*

*David Ogilvy*
*Ogilvy on Advertising*

This view of pricing is widely held. "There is very little we know about pricing and pricing research," admitted one international company renowned for its premium pricing recently.

"Pricing is managers' biggest marketing headache," noted Robert Dolan of the Harvard Business School in last September's Harvard Business Review. "It's where they feel the most pressure to perform and the least certain that they are doing a good job."

Yet managers are only too aware of the rewards of a better pricing strategy. It offers the seductive promise of an immediate - and possibly substantial - increase in profits, without heavy upfront costs. It is an attractive lever for companies that want to put a renewed emphasis on expanding revenues after years of cost cutting.

Yet the problem is not usually a lack of familiarity with pricing options, according to Kalchas. Rather, the problem is the under-exploitation of these options as a result of roadblocks within the organisation. Many companies have a poor mechanism for setting prices; in addition, they make insufficient use of available data.'

The article goes on to look at how this problem can be tackled, and indeed how some companies are already dealing with it. This is an article which is well worth reading in full (it is too long to reproduce here), so see if you can find it (perhaps in a good technical library).

---

## Chapter roundup

- *Pricing decisions* are important to the firm as they are the basis of the profits.
- *Pricing* is the only element of the marketing mix which generates revenue rather than creating costs.
- You should appreciate the concept of *price elasticity:* make sure you can describe it.
- Setting prices in practice may be based on *costs* (cost-plus pricing, full cost pricing), *competition* (price elasticity, tenders) or *demand* (price discrimination).
- *Pricing policy* will depend on price sensitivity, price perception and a variety of other factors.
- Companies may undertake any of a variety of *pricing strategies*, depending on their motives, the industry they operate in and so on.
- *Demand* for a good depends largely on price, household income and the relative price of substitutes or complementary goods. Changes in any of these will cause either a movement along the demand curve or a shift in the demand curve. We have seen that elasticity of demand measures how much of a movement or a shift there will be. Price elasticity of demand indicates the responsiveness of total expenditure in a market for a good to price changes.
- Note that the price elasticity of demand mainly reflects the availability of *substitute goods* and the relative importance of the good in the consumer's budget.
- Product costs are built up using *absorption costing* by a process of allocation, apportionment and absorption.
- In absorption costing, it is usual to add overheads into product costs by applying a predetermined overhead absorption rate. The predetermined rate is set annually, in the *budget*.
- Absorption costing is most often used for routine *profit reporting* and must be used for financial accounting purposes. Marginal costing provides better management information for *planning and decision making*.
- *Marginal cost* is the variable cost of one unit of product or service.
- *Contribution* is an important measure in marginal costing, and it is calculated as the difference between sales value and marginal or variable cost.
- The *contribution/sales ratio* is constant at all levels of output and sales, if there are no changes in the sales price or the variable cost per unit.
- The use of either marginal costing or absorption costing for management reporting purposes depends on the particular circumstances.
- Marginal costing is used for *short-term decision making*.
- *Breakeven analysis* has a number of purposes: to provide information to management about cost behaviour for routine planning and 'one-off' decision making; to determine what volume of sales is needed at any given budgeted sales price in order to break even; to identify the 'risk' in the budget by measuring the margin of safety; to calculate the effects on profit of changes in variable costs, C/S ratios, sales price and volume, product mix, and so on.

## Test your knowledge

1 Why do economists believe that price competition in an oligopoly market is dangerous? (see para 2.3)

2 Define price elasticity. (2.6)

3 Why is cost plus pricing popular? (2.9)

4 In determining price by looking at consumer demand, what is a consumer surplus? (2.32)

5 List four bases for price discrimination. (2.34)

6 Why might a price rise lead to a temporary increase in sales? (3.3)

7 When are sales maximising objectives favoured? (4.3)

8 What is a quantum point? (4.13)

9 Why are gift packaged items often sold at £4.99 or £9.99? (4.16)

10 What are the options available to a firm when a competitor cuts its prices? (4.21)

11 What is meant by the price elasticity of demand for a commodity? (5.2)

12 What is the significance of this concept to a manufacturer? (5.14)

13 What are the factors influencing price elasticity of demand? (5.15)

14 What are the reasons for using absorption costing? (6.8)

15 What is marginal costing? (6.9)

16 Define contribution. (6.11, 6.12)

17 What is the main difference between marginal costing and absorption costing? (6.15)

18 What is the formula for calculating the breakeven point in terms of the number of units required to break even? (6.19)

19 Give the formula which uses the C/S ratio to calculate the breakeven point. (6.22)

**Now try illustrative questions 12 and 13 at the end of the Study Text**

# Chapter 7

# PLACE

## This chapter covers the following topics.


| | | Syllabus reference |
|---|---|---|
| 1 | What are distribution channels? | 2.8 |
| 2 | Types of distribution channel | 2.8 |
| 3 | Channel dynamics | 2.8 |
| 4 | International channels | 2.8 |
| 5 | Logistics management | 2.9 |
| 6 | Just in Time | 2.9 |


## Introduction

This component of the marketing mix is essentially concerned with the processes by which the product is made available to the consumer in a particular *place*. Other more commonly used terms for 'place' include distribution, delivery systems and marketing channels. The terms are often used interchangeably since all are related to making products available to the market. Although place is normally the last element in the list of marketing mix variables, its importance should not be underestimated, especially in provision of services. Marketing effort will be futile if the product is not actually in the right place at the right time so that a purchase can be made. Furthermore, effective and efficient distribution can be a crucial source of competitive advantage.

Distribution is often seen as the Cinderella of the marketing mix. In companies where distribution involves the physical transport of goods and stores, a lack of co-ordination in the marketing executive often results in inadequate control over the distribution function. However, the choice of a particular distribution policy, such as whether or not to use wholesalers, may result in the company delegating to intermediaries much of its marketing function, such as selling to the end user.

A profound influence on distribution in recent years has been the introduction of Just-in-Time (JIT) production and purchasing (this is linked to Total Quality Management.) We shall consider the impact of JIT in the final section of this chapter.

Once you finished this chapter, you should understand the following.

(a) Distribution channels are used in different ways depending on the approach adopted: a choice must often be made between the cost involved and the amount of control the organisation retains over distribution.

(b) Availability of products can be used as a competitive edge and systems such as Just in Time capitalise on this.

## 1 WHAT ARE DISTRIBUTION CHANNELS?

1.1 Independently owned and operated distributors may well have their own objectives, strategies and plans. In their decision making processes, these are likely to take precedence over those of the manufacturer or supplier with whom they are dealing. This can lead to conflict. Suppliers may solve the problem by buying their own distribution route or by distributing direct to their customers. Direct distribution is common for many industrial and/or customised systems suppliers. In some consumer markets direct distribution is also common, for instance for service industries such as insurance ('the man from the Pru'), double glazing and Avon cosmetics.

1.2 In order for a product to be distributed a number of basic functions usually need to be fulfilled.

(a) *Transport*

This function may be provided by the supplier, the distributor or may be sub-contracted to a specialist. For some products, such as perishable goods, transport planning is vital. The 'rent or buy' decision on transport is important and has both financial and operational consequences.

(b) *Stock holding and storage*

For production planning purposes an uninterrupted flow of production is often essential, so stocks of raw materials and components accumulate and need to be stored, incurring significant costs and risks.

For consumer goods, holding stock at the point of sale is very costly; the overheads for city centre retail locations is prohibitive. A good stock control system is essential, designed to avoid stockouts whilst keeping stockholding costs low.

(c) *Local knowledge*

As production has tended to become centralised in pursuit of economies of scale, the need to understand local markets has grown, particularly when international marketing takes place. The intricacies and idiosyncrasies of local markets represents key marketing information. Whilst it is possible to buy specialist market research help, the local distributor with day to day customer contact also has a vital role.

(d) *Promotion*

Whilst major promotional campaigns for national products are likely to be carried out by the supplier, the translation of the campaign to local level is usually the responsibility of the local distributor, often as a joint venture. Hence the advertising agency of the supplier will produce local advertising material which leaves space for the local distributor's name to be added. National press campaigns can feature lists of local stockists.

(e) *Display*

Presentation of the product at the local level is often a function of the local distributor. Again, specialist help from merchandisers can be bought in but decisions on layout and display need to be taken by local distributors, often following patterns produced centrally.

---

## Exercise 1

For many type of goods, producers invariably use retailers as middlemen in getting the product to the customer. Try to think of some of the disadvantages of doing this, from the producer's point of view

## Solution

Your answers might include some of the following points.

(a) The middleman of course has to take his 'cut', reducing the revenue available to the producer.

(b) The producer needs an infrastructure for looking after the retailers - keeping them informed, keeping them well stocked - which might not be necessary in, say, a mail order business.

(c) The producer loses some part of his control over the marketing of his product. The power of some retailers (for example W H Smith in the world of book publishing) is so great that they are able to dictate marketing policy to their suppliers.

---

## Exam focus point

The December 1997 exam (the Test Paper in our Practice & Revision Kit) featured a general question on distribution. It suggested that distribution is more than just physical delivery and that it is a component part of marketing. You were asked to show how delivery could improve customer service. Key issues are the customer's perspective, managing the whole supply chain, levels of service and competitive advantage.

---

## Points in the chain of distribution

1.3 Distributors include the following.

(a) *Retailers*. These are traders operating outlets which sell directly to households. They may be classified by:

(i) type of goods sold (eg hardware, furniture);

(ii) type of service (self-service, counter service);

(iii) size;

(iv) location (rural, city-centre, suburban shopping mall, out-of-town shopping centre).

Another classification, overlapping with the first, is:

(i) *independent retailers* (including the local corner shop, although independents are not always as small as this);

(ii) *multiple chains,* some of which are associated with one class of product; others are 'variety' chains, holding a wide range of different stocks;

(iii) still others are *voluntary groups* of independents, usually grocers.

(b) *Wholesalers*. These are intermediaries who stock a range of products from competing manufacturers to sell on to other organisations such as retailers. Many wholesalers specialise in particular products. Most deal in consumer goods, but some specialise in industrial goods (eg steel stockholders and builders' merchants).

(c) *Distributors* and *dealers*. These are organisations which contract to buy a manufacturer's goods and sell them to customers. Their function is similar to that of wholesalers, but they usually offer a narrower product range, sometimes (as in the case of most car dealers) the products of a single manufacturer. In addition to selling on the manufacturer's product, distributors often promote the products and provide after-sales service.

(d) *Agents*. Agents differ from distributors in the following ways.

(i) Distributors buy the manufacturer's goods and re-sell them at a profit.

(ii) Agents do not purchase the manufacturer's goods, but earn a commission on whatever sales they make.

(e) *Franchisees*. These are independent organisations which in exchange for an initial fee and (usually) a share of sales revenue are allowed to trade under the name of a parent organisation. For example few of the Kall Kwik chain of High Street print shops are actually owned by Kall Kwik - most are run by franchisees.

(f) *Multiple stores* (eg *supermarkets*) which buy goods for retailing direct from the producer, many of them under their 'own label' brand name.

(g) *Direct selling*. This can take place by various means:

(i) mail order;

(ii) telephone selling;

(iii) door-to-door selling;

(iv) personal selling in the sale of industrial goods;

(v) a vertically-integrated organisation which includes both manufacturing and retail outlets;

(vi) computer-shopping or TV shopping. General principles in the choice of distribution channel.

### Case example

Safeway has introduced a satellite tracking system in order to improve its distribution system. The company is to employ the system to track the movements of 600 trucks around the country and computers to check on drivers' techniques. It hopes to save at least £1m per year in fuel costs as well as improving the efficiency of its distribution system serving 420 supermarkets. The system could be used to tell, for example, whether a driver was overrevving in third gear, and using more fuel as a consequence; drivers could also be routed around traffic congestion, and stores warned of late deliveries. Safeway expect to recoup the costs (£1.5m installation and £350,000 per year operational) within the first year. Satellite tracking has already cut 10% off the full costs of one of the groups largest distribution depots at Warrington, and the savings could potentially be far greater in delay reduction and reduced labour costs. Streamlining the system is felt to be an essential element in improving service to customers. According to a spokesman: 'By changing the warehouse process, we can add one days life to fresh produce'.

The computer software involved will be integrated with Safeways bar coding system for products coming into and leaving the depots, allowing managers to track the whereabouts of individual items as they move from depot to store. This control is felt to be essential in developing an effective marketing system. *(Adapted from the Financial Times, 24/2/97)*

## 2 TYPES OF DISTRIBUTION CHANNEL

Examined 12/94

2.1 Choosing distribution channels is important for any organisation, because once a set of channels has been established, subsequent changes are likely to be costly and slow to implement. Distribution channels fall into one of two categories: *direct* and *indirect channels*.

2.2 *Direct distribution* means the product going directly from producer to consumer without the use of a specific intermediary. These methods are often described as *active* since they typically involve the *supplier* making the first approach to a potential customer. Direct distribution methods generally fall into two categories: those using *media* such as the press, leaflets and telephones to invite response and purchase by the consumer and those using a *sales force* to contact consumers face to face.

2.3 *Indirect distribution* refers to systems of distribution, common among manufactured goods, which make use of an intermediary; a wholesaler, retailer or perhaps both. In contrast to direct distribution, these methods are often thought of as being *passive* in the sense that they rely on consumers to make the first approach by entering the relevant retail outlet.

### Exercise 2

One factor influencing the choice between direct and indirect methods is the average order size for a product. State what you think the relationship might be between average order size and the occurrence (or non-occurrence) of direct distribution.

### Solution

Other things being equal, if the order pattern is a small number of high-value orders, then direct distribution is more likely to occur. If there are numerous low-value orders, then the cost of fulfilling them promptly will be high and the use of intermediaries is likely.

### Case example

The importance of place in marketing was borne out by the success of Thorntons in gaining a 13% rise in like for like sales, lifting interim profits by 30%. Roger Paffard newly appointed chief executive has seen his strategy of paying attention to the stores in which the company sells its chocolates pay off handsomely - in refitted stores, like for like sales were up by 22.5% he claimed. Pre-tax profits increased from £7.63m to £9.94m in the 28 weeks to January 11. Christmas sales were up by 25%.

Paffard sees this as the result of a programme of refitting and resiting its shops, and of course, opening new stores when it can. All 300 outlets would be upgraded in this way within three years, he maintained, and along with expected gains from new products - chocolate heads of the Labour and Conservative party leaders who are about to contest the UK parliamentary elections are selling well - profits are expected to show real growth for some years to come. *(Adapted from the Financial Times, 3/4/97)*

## General principles

2.4 Marketing involves certain basic processes.

(a) Bringing buyers and sellers into contact
(b) Offering a sufficient choice of goods to meet the needs of buyers
(c) Persuading customers to develop a favourable opinion of a particular product
(d) Distributing goods from the manufacturing point to retail outlets
(e) Maintaining an adequate level of sales
(f) Providing appropriate services (eg credit, after-sales service)
(g) Maintaining an acceptable price

The choice of channels of distribution will depend on how far a manufacturing company wishes to carry out these processes itself, and how far it decides to delegate them to other organisations, ie there is a range of choice between direct selling and selling through independent outlets.

2.5 In building up efficient channels of distribution, a manufacturer must consider several factors.

(a) How many intermediate stages should be used? There could be zero, one, two or three intermediate stages of selling. In addition, it will be necessary to decide how many dealers at each stage should be used - ie how many agents should be used, or how many wholesalers should be asked to sell the manufacturer's products, and even then 'what should the size of the direct sales force be?'

(b) The support that the manufacturer should give to the dealers. It may be necessary to provide an efficient after-sales and repair service, or to agree to an immediate exchange of faulty products returned by a retailer's customers, and to regularly weekly, bi-weekly or monthly visits to retailers' stores. To help selling, the manufacturer might need to consider advertising or sales promotion support, including merchandising.

(c) The extent to which the manufacturer wishes to 'dominate' a channel of distribution. A market leader, for example, might wish to ensure that its market share of sales is maintained, so that it might, for example, wish to offer exclusive distribution contracts to major retailers.

(d) The extent to which the manufacturer wishes to integrate its marketing effort up to the point of sale with the consumer. Combined promotions with retailers, for example, would only be possible if the manufacturer dealt directly with the retailer (and did not sell to the retailer through a wholesaler).

## Channel design decisions

2.6 In setting up a channel of distribution, the supplier has to take into account:

(a) customers;
(b) product characteristics;
(c) distributor characteristics;
(d) the channel chosen by competitors; and
(e) the supplier's own characteristics.

### *Customers*

2.7 The number of potential customers, their buying habits and their geographical locations are key influences. The use of mail order for those with limited mobility (rural location, illness) is an example of the influence of customers on channel design. Marketing industrial components to the car industry needs to take account of location of the car industry in the UK. Selling to supermarket chains in the UK is now very difficult as the concentration of grocery retailing into a few large chains has increased the power of the buyers: specialist centralised buyers can extract highly favourable terms from suppliers. Unless the supplier is successful in selling to the big chains, the product will only be available to small numbers of shoppers each week.

*Product characteristics*

2.8 Some product characteristics have an important effect on design of the channel of distribution.

(a) *Perishability*

Fresh fruit and newspapers must be distributed very quickly or they become worthless. Speed of delivery is therefore a key factor in the design of the distribution system for such products.

(b) *Customisation*

Customised products tend to be distributed direct. When a wide range of options is available, sales may be made using demonstration units, with customised delivery to follow.

(c) *After sales service/technical advice*

Extent and cost must be carefully considered, staff training given and quality control systems set up. Training programmes are often provided for distributors by suppliers. Exclusive area franchises giving guaranteed custom can be allocated, to ensure distributor co-operation; the disadvantage of this is that a poor distributor may cost a supplier dearly in a particular area.

(d) *Franchising*

Franchising has become an increasingly popular means of growth both for suppliers like the Body Shop and for franchisees who carry the set-up costs and licence fees. The supplier gains more outlets more quickly and exerts more control than is usual in distribution.

*Distributor characteristics*

2.9 The capability of the distributor to take on the distributive functions already discussed above is obviously an important influence on the supplier's choice.

*Competitors' channel choice*

2.10 For many consumer goods, a supplier's brand will sit alongside its competitors' products and there is little the supplier can do about it. For other products, distributors may stock one name brand only (for example, in car distribution) and in return be given an exclusive area. In this case new suppliers may face difficulties in breaking into a market if all the best distribution outlets have been taken up.

*Supplier characteristics*

2.11 A strong financial base gives the supplier the option of buying and operating their own distribution channel: Boots the Chemist is a prime example. The market position of the supplier is also important: distributors are keen to be associated with the market leader but the third, fourth or fifth brand in a market is likely to find more distribution problems.

## Making the channel decision

2.12 Producers have to decide the following.

(a) What types of distributor are to be used (wholesalers, retailers, agents)?

(b) How many of each type will be used? The answer to this depends on what degree of market exposure will be sought:

(i) intensive - blanket coverage;
(ii) exclusive - appointed agents for exclusive areas;
(iii) selective - some but not all in each area;

(c) Who will carry out specific marketing tasks such as:

(i) credit provision;
(ii) delivery;
(iii) after sales service;
(iv) training (sales and product);
(v) display?

(d) How will performance of distributors be evaluated?

(i) In terms of cost?
(ii) In terms of sales levels?
(iii) According to the degree of control achieved?
(iv) By the amount of conflict that arises?

2.13 To sum up, to develop an integrated system of distribution, the supplier must consider all the factors influencing distribution combined with a knowledge of the relative merits of the different types of channel available.

### Factors favouring the use of direct selling

2.14 These are as follows.

(a) The need for an expert sales force to demonstrate products, explain product characteristics and provide after sales service. Publishers, for example, use sales reps to keep booksellers up to date with new titles, to arrange for the return of unsold books and so on.

(b) Intermediaries may be unwilling or unable to sell the product. For example, the ill-fated Sinclair C5 eventually had to be sold by direct mail.

(c) Existing channels may be linked to other producers, reluctant to carry new product lines.

(d) The intermediaries willing to sell the product may be too costly, or they may not be maximising potential sales. This problem caused Nissan to terminate its contract with its sole UK distributor in 1991: Nissan believed that the distributor's pricing strategy was inappropriate.

(e) If specialised transport requirements are involved, intermediaries may not be able to deliver goods to the final customer.

(f) Where potential buyers are geographically concentrated the supplier's own sales force can easily reach them (typically an industrial market). One example is the financial services market centred on the City of London.

### Factors favouring the use of intermediaries

2.15 These are as follows.

(a) Insufficient resources to finance a large sales force.

(b) A policy decision to invest in increased productive capacity rather than extra marketing effort.

(c) The supplier may have insufficient in-house marketing 'know-how' in selling to retail stores.

(d) The assortment of products may be insufficient for a sales force to carry. A wholesaler can complement a limited range and make more efficient use of his sales force.

(e) Intermediaries can market small lots as part of a range of goods. The supplier would incur a heavy sales overhead if its own sales force took 'small' individual orders.

(f) Large numbers of potential buyers spread over a wide geographical area (typically consumer markets).

### Case example

Nine out of ten women in the USA have bought products made by Avon, and the company is still immensely profitable ($257m profit in 1996). Yet it seems to be aging and its marketing seems to belong to a previous age.

(a) The direct marketing force of 445,000 in the US looks misplaced. Many customers and potential salespeople are now working in full time jobs.

(b) Younger customer prefer 'hipper' products such as Body Shop, L'Oreal and Estee Lauder which can be found in stores.

(c) The image of the product is aging.

Avon is trying to improve its marketing in the developed world as sales begin to fall, but this seems likely to be slow and difficult. The real profits, however, are to be made in what CEO James Preston refers to as 'Avon Heaven', the developing countries which in 1995 accounted for 38% of total sales and 49% of pre-tax profit. This has been an area of dramatic growth in the 1990s, with Avon going into 14 new markets. The main advantages for the company are:

(a) underdeveloped retailing structure, which makes the traditional 'direct selling' method ideal;

(b) local products which are generally of poor quality and offer little competition;

(c) women in underdeveloped countries who are eager to work in order to supplement the family income, and make an extremely effective and active sales force, calling on three or four times as many clients as western counterparts; and

(d) minimal investment generates huge profits. For less than $500,000 investment in the Russian market, 16,000 representatives have sold $30 million of products in 1996, from zero in 1993. Avon will obtain an operating profit margin of 30%.

Because Avon's representative is often the only shop in town, the firm has been able to introduce a secondary catalogue, including the products of around 30 other companies, which account for 15% of sales in some of these markets.

In trying to tie these brands together, Avon's strategy is to focus on a number of global brands it can sell worldwide. Six lines were launched in 1996. By 2000 the company expects sales from these markets to constitute 60% of cosmetics, toiletries and fragrance revenues (from 27% in 1996).

The consolidation of these brands has enabled Avon to improve quality and reduce the number of suppliers, cutting costs by 35%. Clearly the use of this old fashioned 'human distribution system' is presently more successful in developing markets, but no-one is really sure how it will develop in the traditional markets of the developed world.

*(Adapted from The Economist, 13/7/96)*

## Multi-channel decisions

2.16 A producer serving both industrial and consumer markets may decide to use intermediaries for his consumer division and direct selling for his industrial division. For example, a detergent manufacturer might employ salesmen to sell to wholesalers and large retail groups in their consumer division. It would not be efficient for the sales force to approach small retailers directly.

The distribution channels appropriate for industrial markets may not be suitable for consumer markets.

## Industrial and consumer distribution channels

2.17 *Industrial markets* may be characterised as having fewer, larger customers purchasing expensive products which may be custom built. It is due to these characteristics that industrial distribution channels tend to be more direct and shorter than for consumer markets. It has to be remembered, however, that the most appropriate distribution channels will depend specifically on the objectives of the company regarding market exposure. There are specialist distributors in the industrial sector, which may be used as well as, or instead of, selling directly to the companies within this sector.

2.18 There are fewer direct distribution channels, from the manufacturer to the consumer in the *consumer market*. Examples may be found in small 'cottage' industries or mail order companies. It is more usual for companies in consumer markets to use wholesalers and retailers to move their product to the final consumer.

(a) *Wholesalers* break down the bulk from manufacturers and pass products on to retailers. They take on some of the supplier's risks by funding stock. Recently in the UK there has been a reduction in importance of this type of intermediary.

(b) *Retailers* sell to the final consumers. They may give consumers added benefits by providing services such as credit, delivery and a wide variety of goods. In the UK, retailers have increased in power whilst wholesalers have declined. Retailing has also become more concentrated with increased dominance of large multiples.

### Distribution strategy

2.19 There are three main strategies.

(a) *Intensive distribution* involves concentrating on a segment of the total market, such as choosing limited geographical distribution rather than national distribution.

(b) Using *selective distribution*, the producer selects a group of retail outlets from amongst all retail outlets on grounds of the brand image ('quality' outlets), or related to the retailers' capacity to provide after sales service. Rolls Royce's image is safe in the hands of H R Owen but would be damaged if sold by an 'Arthur Daley'.

(c) *Exclusive distribution* is an extension of selective distribution. Particular outlets are granted exclusive handling rights within a prescribed geographical area. Sometimes exclusive distribution or franchise rights are coupled with making special financial arrangements for land, buildings or equipment, such as petrol station agreements.

## 3 CHANNEL DYNAMICS

3.1 Channels are subject to conflicts between members. This need not be destructive as long as it remains manageable. Manufacturers may have little influence on how their product is presented to the public. Conflicts are usually resolved by arbitration rather than judicial means.

(a) A distribution system with a central core organising marketing throughout the channel is termed a *vertical marketing system*. Vertical marketing systems provide channel role specification and co-ordination between members.

(b) In *corporate marketing systems* the stages in production and distribution are owned by a single corporation. This common ownership permits close integration and therefore the corporation controls activities along the distribution chain. For example, Laura Ashley shops sell goods produced in Laura Ashley factories.

(c) *Contractual marketing systems* involve agreement over aspects of distribution marketing. One example of a contractual marketing system that has become popular over the last decade is franchising.

(d) If a plan is drawn up between channel members to help reduce conflict this is often termed an *administered marketing system*.

3.2 Channel leadership gives power to the member of the channel with whom it lies. We considered earlier in this section the changing power relationship between manufacturers and retailers in consumer goods markets. In industrial markets where channel lengths are generally shorter (more direct) then power often lies with manufacturers of products rather than 'middlemen'.

---

### Exercise 3

One of the fastest growing forms of selling in the US over the past decade has been the *factory outlet centres.* Discount factory shops, often situated on factory premises, from which manufacturers sell of overmakes, slight seconds, or retailers' returns are already well-established in the UK, but in the US developers have grouped such outlets together in purpose-built malls.

What would you suggest are the advantages of this method of distribution for customers and manufacturers?

## Solution

Prices are up to 50% below conventional retail outlets and shoppers can choose from a wide range of branded goods, that they otherwise might not be able to afford. They can also turn a shopping trip into a day out, as factory outlet centres are designed as 'destination' shopping venues, offering facilities such as playgrounds and restaurants.

Manufacturers enjoy the ability to sell surplus stock at a profit in a controlled way that does not damage the brand image. They have also turned the shops into a powerful marketing tool for test-marketing products before their high street launch, and selling avant-garde designs that have not caught on in the main retail market.

---

## Case example

The supply chain is often a crucial element in the success or failure of a product. In the case of Over the Counter (OTC) medicines, because of the unique features of the product , the situation and the constraints on marketers, the supply chain plays a key role in consumer choice making.

Medicines satisfy a powerful and basic need - relief from pain. As a consequence, products tend to be evaluated in terms of their strict efficacy, and the functions of branding or advertising are far less prominent than usual. According to Mellors Reay and Partners, who work on the marketing of OTC medicines, this is compounded by regulations and restrictions on the advertising and retail promotion of products. These include:

(a) strict regulation of claims and impact of advertising;

(b) non-display of items on retailers shelves;

(c) restrictions on merchandising, discounting, the use of personality endorsement, loyalty schemes, cross promotions and free trials;

(d) huge price rises when products transfer from prescription to OTC;

(e) similarity between brand names because of reference to ingredients (for instance paracetomol based analgesics include Panadeine, Panadol, Panaleve, Panerel, Paracets, and so on); and

(f) the influence of the pharmacist who can overcome or counter any promotional effect.

The role of the pharmacist is crucial, and is becoming more ambivalent, as the old semi-medical professional role is combined with one as an employee of commercial and market oriented enterprises. The increasing availability of OTC medicines previously only available on prescription only increases this power. Marketing OTC medicines directly to consumers must involve, to some extent, countering the respect and trust of consumers for pharmacists.

Yet brands can become established in spite of these problems. Nurofen, for example, an ibuprofen based analgesic, has established a powerful presence by building a brand which is distinctive by using advertising which suggests both power and empathy, and also by visualising and emphasising in an imaginative way the experience and relief of pain.

Another brand which succeeded in overcoming the problems of this supply chain is Nicotinell, the smoking cessation patch launched as an OTC in 1992. Its main obstacles were:

(a) price increase from £4.99 to £15.99;
(b) no facings in many outlets;
(c) no promotional activity or discounting;
(d) the emergence of similar brand names, ie Nicorette, Nicabate, Nicobrevin, Niconil;
(e) the homogeneity of competitive product benefits;
(f) the powerful influence of pharmacist's recommendations; and
(g) an anxious isolated consumer.

The success of this brand rested on research which yielded a superior understanding of consumers and their complex psyche during the process of giving up smoking. This revealed the importance of, and reliance on willpower during this process and thereby the essential value of NOT representing Nicotinell as a 'miracle cure'. Because consumers believed they had insufficient willpower, this had to be counterbalanced by genuine empathy and demonstration of what it must be like when people considered giving up smoking.

Within six months of launch, the market for nicotine patch products grew by 400%, and Nicotinell held onto 60% of that. Research showed that this was due to effective promotion and marketing which took into account the nature of the supply chain involved.

*(Adapted from Admap, November 1996)*

## 4 INTERNATIONAL CHANNELS

4.1 As markets open to international trade, channel decisions become more complex. A company can export using host country middlemen or domestic middlemen. These may or may not take title of the goods. Implications of channel management in the case of exporters include a loss of control over the product (price, image, packaging, service etc). A producer may undertake a joint venture or licensing agreement or even manufacture abroad. All will have implications for the power structure and control over the product.

## 5 LOGISTICS MANAGEMENT

Examined 12/94

5.1 Logistics management involves physical distribution and materials management encompassing the inflow of raw materials and goods and the outflow of finished products. Logistics management has developed because of an increased awareness of:

(a) customer benefits that can be incorporated into the overall product offering because of efficient logistics management;

(b) the cost savings that can be made when a logistics approach is undertaken;

(c) trends in industrial purchasing that necessarily mean closer links between buyers and sellers, for example Just in Time purchasing and computerised purchasing.

5.2 Logistics managers organise inventories, warehouses, purchasing and packaging to produce an efficient and effective overall system. There are benefits to consumers of products that are produced by companies with good logistic management. There is less likelihood of goods being out of stock, delivery should be efficient and overall service quality should be higher.

### Exam focus point

Cost control of logistics featured in December 1994 (see Q49 *Logistics cost control* of our Practice & Revision Kit). Our answer takes a broad-brush look at the problem. The aim of controlling costs is to preserve profit. Our answer suggests that the logistics system can, if properly planned, add value. Specify the objectives of the system by analysing customer needs. Customers might pay for a premium service. The extra revenue can justify the costs of providing it.

### Case example

Distribution is now a critical factor in Europe's paper industry. Logistics is seen as a means of reducing costs and increasing efficiency, to counteract declining demand and 'dumping' of cut-price products from overseas. The *buyer* dominates the market and manufacturers therefore expect their distribution specialists to develop supply systems that result in zero damage and allow customers to minimise stockholding costs. One of the leading UK producers of paper for packaging has customers in the Benelux countries and northern France who expect orders to be delivered within 24 hours. The supplier is therefore having to set up warehouses to hold stock closer to the customers and speed up the delivery reaction time.

### Exercise 4

Consider the following extract adapted from an article in the *Financial Times*.

'UK Steel is aware of the stiff competition it faces in its planned assault on European mainland markets. Physical distribution is an important plank in its campaign and the costs and efficiency of the service will help determine the success or failure of the venture.

High on the agenda for discussion is the setting up of regional distribution centres closer to customers and the development of world class information technology (IT) links between production plants, distribution operators and customers.

Meanwhile, the company spends some £375m a year on shipping products to mainland Europe and tends to deal direct with transport operators and suppliers rather than go through forwarding agents.

Its sales in Europe represent about 2.5 per cent of the total European market and the objective is to achieve significant increases.

Its main European destinations are Italy, Germany and Spain, followed by France, Greece and the Netherlands.'

If you were the marketing manager of a small business contemplating the opportunities of the Single European Market would you be encouraged or discouraged by this article?

### Solution

Initially you might be discouraged. It is more difficult to identify target markets in a foreign culture and there are language barriers, and problems of control to be overcome. The cost of overseas representation (people/offices or both) may be prohibitive.

On the other hand most of these barriers are psychological rather than real. A relationship with an agent could be established. Costly investment in high tech systems may be unnecessary for the smaller business, especially if products are specialised, high value items. The potential for obtaining a share of the total European market as opposed to restricting operations to the domestic market must be a temptation.

## 6 JUST IN TIME

*Examined 12/95, 6/96*

### Creative use of availability as a source of competitive advantage

6.1 That availability is a critical factor in the formulation of the marketing mix cannot be seriously doubted. Increasingly, logistics management has been recognised for the advantages in terms of customer benefits which such an approach brings, along with saving in costs, and improved company image. A more profound impact has been proposed, however, with the use of more creative and sophisticated systems bringing in, not just new possibilities of improved delivery systems, but also higher quality and increased profitability and efficiency.

6.2 Distribution is a key issue for the paper industry in Europe. Logistics here are viewed as a way of reducing costs and increasing efficiency, since there is a great problem from declining demand and the market penetration of low cost, low quality product from overseas competitors. Here, the buyer dominates the market and manufacturers are looking to their distribution specialists in order to implement supply systems which protect the product, and deliver in a form which involves minimum waste and keeps stockholding costs at ground level. Customers often require delivery of orders within 24 hours, and to accomplish this suppliers are establishing warehouses which are adjacent to the markets they are seeking to supply, in order to satisfy these time constraints. Margins are becoming squeezed and there are new techniques available to cope with these pressures, but also to provide creative means to accomplish new market opportunities.

### The challenges of the new market

6.3 Lancaster (1993) has argued that a 'new marketing' is emerging as a consequence of changing market conditions, but particularly the possibilities afforded by the new technologies for handling information. This is needed because, not only is technology affecting production processes, it is:

> '... transforming choice, and choice is transforming the marketplace. As a result, we are witnessing the emergence of a new marketing paradigm - not a "do more" marketing that simply turns up the volume on the sales trend of the past, but a knowledge and experience based marketing that represents the once-and-for-all death of the salesman.' (McKenna)

6.4 Customers are, increasingly, faced with a plethora of companies striving to satisfy their needs. As a consequence, they have become more discriminating and competition has hotted up. Product differentiation and the identification and satisfaction of the precise needs of clearly targeted market segments means that companies must not only be aware of their customer needs but place them at the heart of their corporate thinking.

6.5 These needs can, and increasingly do, change very rapidly. Tom Peters has referred to this complex mix of factors as the 'chaos' of the modern marketplace, and the consequent acceleration of the pace of change as the 'nanosecond nineties'. To compete in this marketplace, a company must be aware not just of its customers but of competitors' strategies, the pace and scope of the market, and the technology available within it.

6.6 This cannot be accomplished by traditional marketing, which is bound by outmoded assumptions and formulated around a time-frame which makes it too slow to respond to change. Corporate structure, and the strategies which they evolve, are too rigid and hierarchical and find themselves unable to respond to market opportunities and changes in the tastes and behaviour of existing customers.

### Exam focus point

JIT has featured twice so far (in June 1995 and June 1996, see Q52 *JIT tender* and Q53 *JIT quick* in our Practice & Revision Kit). Both of these questions described manufacturing settings, so you had to consider some of the issues involved in dealing with *business* customers.

### Just in Time: a creative competitive tool

6.7 Just In Time (JIT) is a system of inventory control invented by the Japanese. The benefit is that it allows 'pull' in the market, in contrast to the traditional system of 'just in case'. JIT is:

> 'an inventory control system which delivers input to its production or distribution site only at the rate and time it is needed. Thus it reduces inventories whether it is used within the firm or as a mechanism regulating the flow of products between adjacent firms in the distribution system channel. It is a pull system which replaces buffer inventories with channel member co-operation.'

JIT aims to:

> 'produce *instantaneously*, with perfect quality and minimum waste.'

Graham argues that JIT:

> 'completely tailors a manufacturing strategy to the needs of a market and produces mixes of products in exactly the order required.'

*Traditional vs 'new' thinking*

| *Issue* | *Just in Case* | *Just in Time* |
|---|---|---|
| Official goal | Maximum efficiency | Maximum efficiency |
| Stocks | Integral part of system - a necessary 'evil' | Wasteful - to be eliminated |
| Lead times | Taken as given and built into production planning routines | Reduced to render small batches economical |
| Batch sizes | Taken as given and economic order quantity is calculated | Lot size of *one* is the target - because of flexible system |
| Production planning and control | Variety of means - MRP models existing system and optimises within it. Information 'pull' for hot orders | Centralised forecasts in conjunction with local pull control |
| Trigger to production | Algorithmically derived schedules. Hot lists. Maintenance of sub-unit efficiencies | Imminent needs of downstream unit via Kanban cards |
| Quality | Acceptable quality level. Emphasis on error detection | Zero defects. Error prevention |
| Performance focus | Sub-unit efficiency | System/organisation efficiency |
| Organisational design | Input-based. Functional | Output based. Product |
| Suppliers | Multiple; distant; independent | Single or dual sourcing. Supplier as extension |

(N Oliver, *JIT: Issues and Items for the Research Agenda*, 1991)

6.8 Oliver's model (shown below) of the kind of JIT system which might be involved in channels from a raw material supplier to consumer illustrates the nature of the processes involved and the typical elements in such a system.

6.9 *Synchronisation* is an essential component of such systems. A successful channel will require precise synchronisation between suppliers, through the production units to retailers and finally suppliers. This depends crucially on *information* being freely passed back and forth between channel members; suppliers need to be informed about raw material deliveries, and also the components delivered to manufacturers. For their part, manufactures must be confident that their deliveries will arrive on time.

6.10 In the Japanese system, this exchange of information can be supplied throughout the production process by 'Kanban'. This is a very simple 'pull' system which operates at the local level, and is very effective for avoiding stockpiles.

6.11 Customers need to be treated in a new way; loyalty is no longer to be taken for granted. Indeed, as consumers more and more realise the power they wield, and become more sophisticated in the criteria they apply when evaluating and choosing products, manufacturers find that they must become responsive to these needs and also be able to adjust themselves rapidly in order to satisfy them. The keyword of the modern marketplace is *flexibility*, and this is coupled with *profitability*.

6.12 This flexibility is now the key element in:

(a) the company meeting customer requirements;
(b) the production process;
(c) the company's organisation.

*Oliver's model of a JIT system: from raw material to consumer*

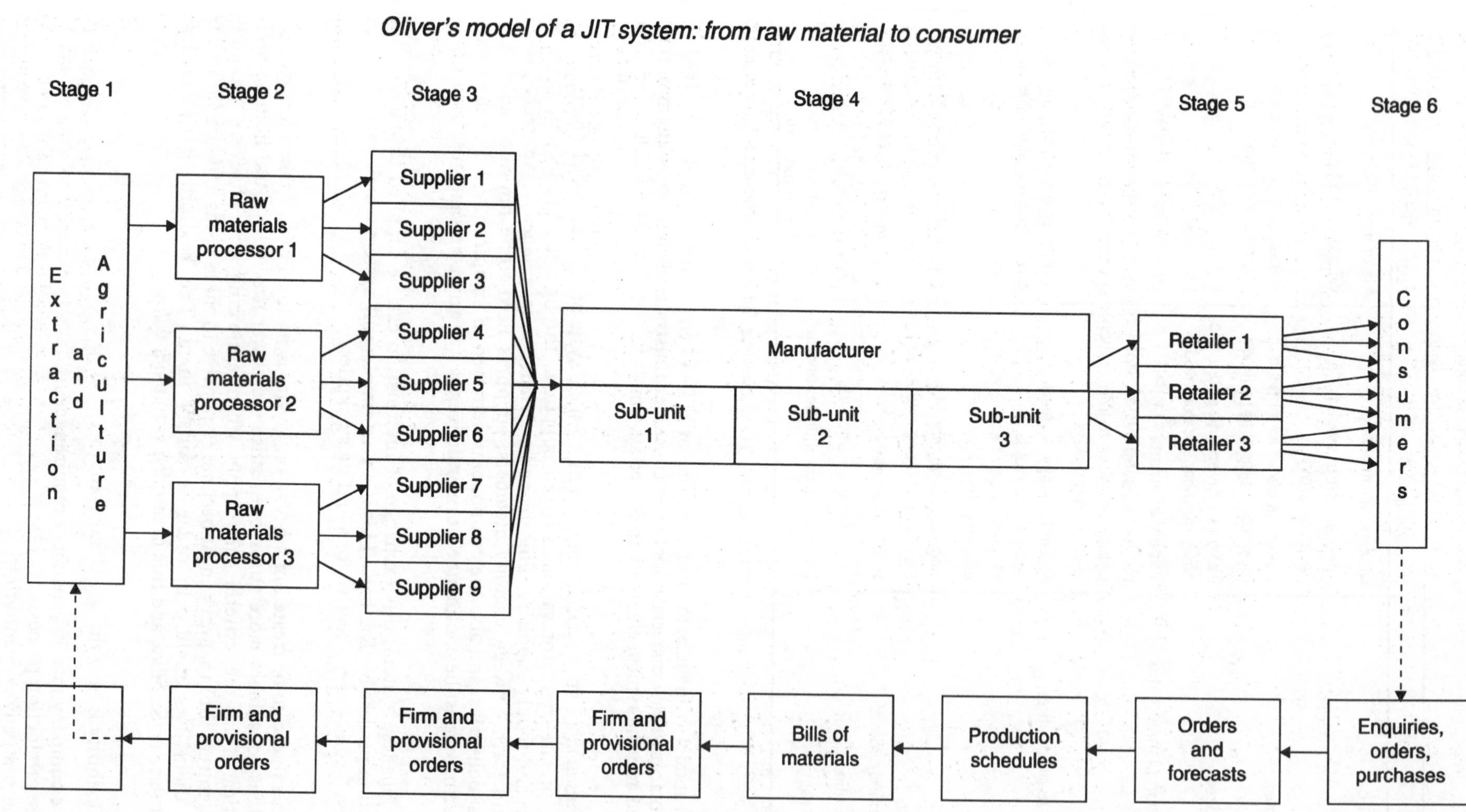


(Adapted, Oliver: *JIT: Issues and items for the Research Agenda*, 1991)

6.13 Manufacturing and marketing systems need to be programmable, above all else. Manufacturing and marketing must be able to re-tool and re-formulate systems rapidly so that new requirements can be identified, formulated into new products, and those products constructed and made available when they are needed.

6.14 New production processes which aim to meet these requirements have been called 'lean production', and combine efficiency, quality and flexibility with a capacity to innovate.

6.15 The 'lean' firm is involved in producing products which are:

(a) *profitable* - with an emphasis on productivity and cost effectiveness;

(b) *high quality* - deriving from the need to compete not just on price, but standards;

(c) *matched to market needs* - which requires the firm to employ production processes which are flexible, involving teams of multiskilled workers producing small batches of varied, diversified products;

(d) *responsive to change* - the firm must be customer-orientated, and able to produce products which match rapidly changing and highly individual customer requirements.

6.16 Time lags are critical in these processes. Reducing times taken for the product to get from the design stage to the market place is critical for success. This is one of the crucial differences between the Japanese and European or American car manufacturers. Japanese manufactures can get a concept into the marketplace in about 46 months - at least 13 months quicker than the Europeans and 14 months quicker than the Americans.

6.17 Japanese companies are often using flexible production processes, organised around flexible 'cells' of workers and fluid working arrangements, which enable them to respond to changes quickly.

6.18 Marketing, and the need to be aware of customer needs and respond to them, have now been recognised as the difference between success and survival, and failure, and as a consequence have been propagated throughout the modern organisation. One of the key areas in to which this philosophy has reached is the distribution process. Success nowadays, some commentators have argued, depends on the ability of the company to perform *simultaneously* rather than *sequentially* in the processes involved in product development through to product release.

6.19 Lower investment in goods within this process and faster response to customer needs means reduced costs, better value for customers, and increased benefits for other channel members within the distributive process, enabling everyone within the channel to compete more effectively.

---

### Exercise 5

A system called ShopperTrak has been developed that tracks people entering and leaving stores, where they go when inside, and the average amount of time spent there. It can distinguish adults from children. The system uses infra-red sensors at strategic points linked to the retailer's tills or electronic point of sales systems.

What might be the uses of such a system?

### Solution

The main idea is to cut down long waits in check-out queues and weary searches by customers for staff. The system enables managers to adjust staffing to demand and so increase purchases per visit, encourage return visits and to lift 'conversion rates' – the percentage of people entering the stores who actually buy something. The system also provides information to improve the quality and style of service and enables stores to be designed and laid out more effectively.

---

6.20 Organisational resources, then, form a pool which can be used to counter the challenges of change in competitive markets. Every aspect of the company policy is therefore critical in this effort to maximise competitive capability. At the heart of this is the system by which product and service is made available to the customer.

6.21 Information about consumer demand is supplied by retailers, in the form of 'firm' and 'tentative' orders. The effectiveness of this for providing control on distribution costs is demonstrated in the volume car market in Japan. Nearly all cars are made to order and consequently, 'lead times' can be as short as ten days!

6.22 If this synchronisation is effectively organised, a JIT system can meet consumer demand while at the same time profits may be maintained or enhanced, because stockpiles and inventory levels - and consequently, the costs of capital tied up unproductively in materials or products which are not being used - are cut dramatically.

6.23 The supplier/manufacturer interface is, however, crucial to the success of these changes, and a close relationship must be built up. The changes mean that increasing numbers of component parts will be bought from outside the organisation, rather than being manufactured internally.

6.24 When this system is instituted suppliers become important to the planning process in manufacturing and may well be brought into production forecasts, schedules and even the design stage. When decisions related to these are being made, the capacities and constraints faced by suppliers is obviously critical. In fact, liaison becomes an important function; their salespersons may well spend less time selling and become intermediaries, conveying information and mediating between buyer, engineering and their own production management. Finding new customers becomes less important than sustaining and improving relations with existing patrons.

6.25 JIT, it can be argued, even improves product quality. If suppliers are being provided with minimum resources and required to focus on using it to maximum effect, then it becomes even more important to get it 'right first time', since there is very little leeway in the amounts available to do it again. Right first time and just in time go together very well indeed!

6.26 However, problems with JIT have been identified, according to some commentators. These include the following.

(a) *Conflicts over customers.* Suppliers will often, of course, have commitments to other customers, and this may well cause expensive and disruptive delays.

(b) *Conflicts with the workforce.* Excellent industrial relations are vital to the success of this system, as are flexible, sometimes multiskilled workforces with a willingness to accept flexible work routines and hours, so that management can vary manning arrangements. Single union deals, famously, are a *sine qua non* when Japanese companies establish UK operations, and this is a major reason.

(c) *Problems over timescales.* These systems take a very long time to develop. Toyota took twenty years to develop theirs!

6.27 JIT, then, is expanding as lean production becomes more important. Focusing as it does on consumer choice, company profit and strong company-supplier relations, this concept fits comfortably alongside other managerial developments such as TQM and accelerating change in product markets.

---

**Exercise 6**

A large company has just installed a JIT system. One of its suppliers has had a history of poor labour relations. What consequences does this have for the company?

### Solution

If there is a strike at the suppliers', the company's operations will come to a halt quickly as it has no stock. JIT, therefore, requires good industrial relations.

## The future of JIT: institutional creativity?

6.28 Marketing cannot ignore the challenges which are springing up to confront it. Technology is transforming both the kinds of products consumers are demanding and the ways in which marketing channels are responding to these needs. The defining characteristics of this new 'technological imperative' is 'programmability' according to McKenna.

6.29 Consumers are now being offered more and more choices, but this degree of choice produces more competition which in turn ferments new ideas and motivates the market to produce both new products and new strategies to bring them to the marketplace. Proliferation, diversification and more extended product ranges bring new customers for new products, as what were previously relatively homogeneous markets become increasingly segmented.

6.30 In response, companies seek to develop even more highly organised, flexible and consumer-responsive practices. JIT is very much part of this revolution. Quick response to customer needs, through flexible, skilled workforces and finely-tuned organisations, must be accompanied by speedy availability, and the capability of providing the product that the customer wants, when he wants it. But this must be at a profit! With competition comes shrinking margins and the need to attend to the details of the system - to make every process as cost-effective as possible.

6.31 In the organisation of the future, JIT will sit alongside TQM, but also TQC (Total Quality Control), FA (Factory Automation) and TPM (Total Product Maintenance). To institute these, companies will have to institute cultural changes to involve every employee and every manager in a new conception of what business itself is, and what is necessary for survival in the modern business world.

6.32 If the aim is flexibility, then there is also a tendency for the system to bring new relationship. JIT, with its aim of low stockholding, a low inventory and quick response to changes in consumer tastes, fits perfectly into this system, but the closer links between purchaser and supplier have another side. To make improvements necessary to meet the demands of such a new relationship, the supplier may well need to invest; most, consequently, would require a long-term contract to provide the necessary reassurance and security in order to make this worthwhile. A partnership between different channel members is the logical consequence, in which both parties would in principle gain.

6.33 Often, of course, supplier and manufacturer exert very different degrees of market power. If long-term relationships are to develop, to foster co-operation and collaboration, the larger, more powerful partner (almost always the manufacturer) may well seek to drive prices down, or use JIT as a way of 'shedding risk' or moving inventory back along the supply chain.

### Case example

This is very similar to what happened within the agro-food industry more than twenty years ago, when food manufacturers such as Birds Eye began to exert strong influence over suppliers. Needing to ensure high and consistent quality in the products which they were supplying to the increasingly powerful supermarket chains, they found themselves having to be able to make very firm guarantees in order to compete in cut-throat conditions. Consequently, farms and market gardeners found that they had less and less control over what they produced in their fields, or where and when, as their customers exerted their closer together. In the UK, at least, the pressure is exerted by supermarkets which demand absolute consistency in terms of shape and quality.

6.34 The logic of this process may result in manufacturers demanding that their partners meet quality standards such as ISO9000, or 'green' environmental standards such as BS7750 or operating a 'vendor rating' system.

6.35 Of course, the time perspective of the decision-makers involved is circular. In the long term, it is important that a co-operative and mutually supportive relationship be fostered, for the benefit of both sides. JIT cannot succeed, as we emphasised earlier, without trust, commitment and a free flow of information on both sides of the relationship and indeed between all the members of the marketing channel.

6.36 This will promote flexibility and responsiveness, and make creativity possible - creativity which is essential to business success. But this depends on the quality of the managers involved, as well as the existence of a JIT system. This is not a recipe for success but a system which permits good practice to flourish and promotes its development.

6.37 As computer programmers have it, however, 'rubbish in, rubbish out' - the input, in terms of technological and human resources, must be right in order to produce success.

## Chapter roundup

- Without an *efficient distribution system* goods may not reach the target customers. The options open to companies are vast, and are complicated if the company decides to export goods.
- Each way in which goods are distributed has advantages and disadvantages, although often this comes down to *'control' aspects*. The longer the length of the distribution chain, the greater the loss of control over how the product is delivered.
- You should be able to define different types of *distribution channel*; channel design decisions and channel dynamics.
- *Just in Time (JIT)* is based on Japanese methods. Oliver's model provides a useful summary of the system, which you should learn.

## Test your knowledge

1. Give examples of direct distribution in consumer markets. (see para 1.1)
2. What effect do product characteristics have on channel design? (2.6)
3. Why use direct selling? (2.12)
4. List the factors favouring the use of intermediaries. (2.13)
5. Distinguish between intensive, selective and exclusive distribution. (2.17)
6. What is a vertical marketing system? (3.1)
7. To which type of marketing system does franchising belong? (3.1)
8. Why has logistics management developed? (5.1)
9. Define Just in Time (JIT). (6.7)
10. What problems have been identified with JIT? (6.26)

**Now try illustrative questions 14 to 17 at the end of the Study Text**

# Chapter 8

# PROMOTION

| **This chapter covers the following topics.** | | *Syllabus reference* |
|---|---|---|
| 1 | Promotion and communicating with customers | 2.10 |
| 2 | Personal selling | 2.10 |
| 3 | Advertising | 2.10 |
| 4 | Planning a promotion campaign | 2.10 |
| 5 | Successful advertising | 2.10 |
| 6 | Branding | 2.10 |
| 7 | Sales promotion | 2.10 |
| 8 | Publicity | 2.10 |

## Introduction

'Promotion' is concerned with *communication* between the seller and the buyer and is controlled by the seller who seeks to promote his products. It includes:

(a) advertising;
(b) sales promotion activities, also known as *below-the-line* activities;
(c) publicity or public relations;
(d) the activities of the sales force.

You may find these activities referred to as the *communications mix.*

Firms will use a combination of these promotion methods and the optimal communications mix will depend on the nature of the product, the market and the customer. A manufacturer of industrial goods may rely more heavily on direct selling and sales literature, whereas a consumer goods manufacturer will use advertising and sales promotion.

Once you have finished this chapter, you should understand the following.

(a) The communication process is vital: the selling message must reach the customer intact via the sales team, advertising etc.

(b) The promotional mix has a variety of elements, the individual combination of which will vary depending on the product and its target market.

## 1 PROMOTION AND COMMUNICATING WITH CUSTOMERS

*Examined 12/94, 6/95, 12/95, 6/96*

### Communicating with customers: the selling function

1.1

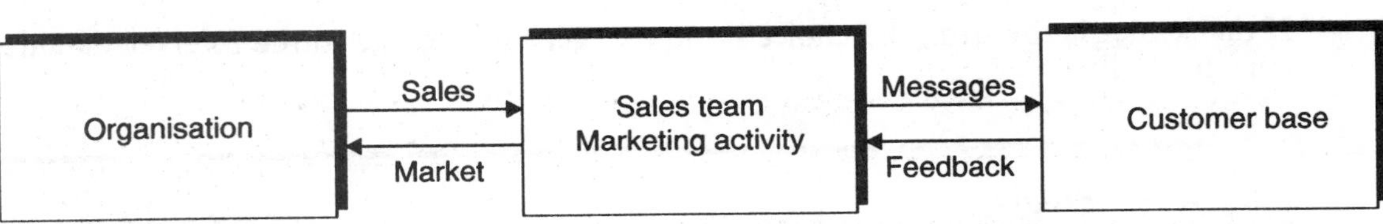


Communication with customers involves many aspects of the marketing mix, but *promotion* is paramount.

1.2 Personal selling is not of course the only communication medium available to the organisation. In firms with a co-ordinated promotional strategy the activity of the sales team will be supported and supplemented by a combination of other communication tools. This combination is referred to as the *promotional mix*.

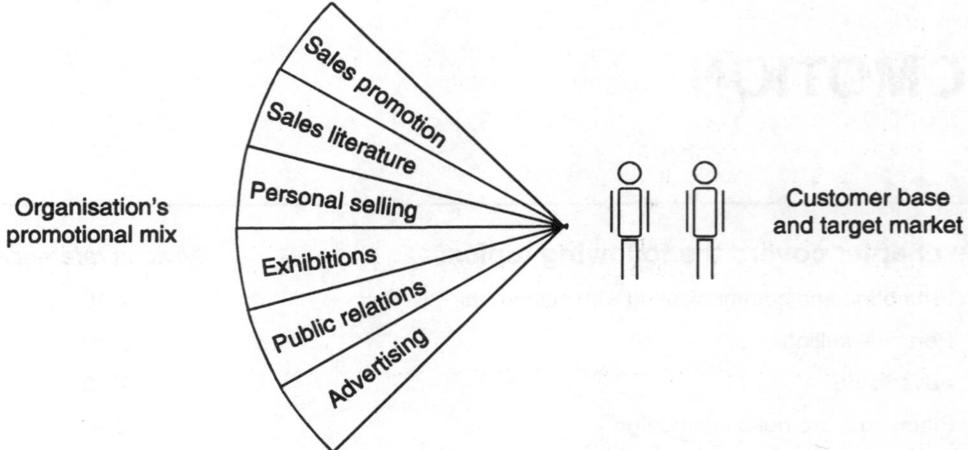


1.3 These other communication tools are used to increase the efficiency and effectiveness of the sales effort. In combination, it represents the entire external communications activity of the organisation.

1.4 It is possible to use the same model of the communication process to describe one-to-one communication between friends, or a major multinational organisation communicating with its market place.

1.5 Effective communication requires several elements.

(a) A sender
(b) A receiver
(c) A message
(d) A communication channel or medium
(e) A feedback mechanism

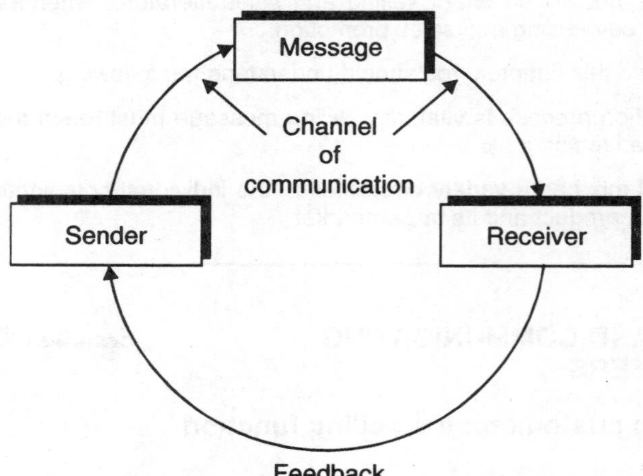


If the sender is the firm, the choice of how to get the message to the receiver includes personal selling.

### Case example

Holiday company Going Places is courting controversy by tying up with schools in a scheme to use holidaymakers' money to fund schools' sports equipment.

The National Consumer Council (NCC) says such tie-ups should have educational value and curriculum relevancy. It also stipulates that sales and promotional materials should not include explicit encouragement to buy branded or own-branded products or services.

The NCC issued guidelines last year following an investigation which found a "worrying number of flaws" in educational teaching packs and activities. All schools should have copies of the guidelines.

The NCC says it has not discussed the scheme with Going Places, while Going Places refuses to comment on the detail of its arrangements with schools.

The travel agent, owned by tour operator Airtours, is the UK's second largest. The scheme involves using a proportion of holidaymakers' deposits to buy sports equipment for schools. The move is thought to be the first time a holiday company has become involved in a "collector" scheme with schools.

There have been other sponsorship schemes to raise money for school sports equipment. Boots was forced to make a U-turn on its voucher scheme in 1993 after criticism that too many vouchers were needed to buy the most basic equipment.

(*Marketing Week* 11 September 1997)

---

## Combining promotional techniques

1.6 Advertising, sales promotion and the sales force are all methods of effecting marketing communication with potential and existing consumers.

1.7 Marketing theory stresses that a range of tactics is more successful than 'putting all your eggs in one basket'. It would seem more feasible to have advertising, sales promotion *and* the sales force working in unison with each other to produce more effective marketing. Some of the following may explain how advertising and sales promotion actually help the sales force.

1.8 We must recognise some objectives of advertising and sales promotion and then consider whether they enhance the sales force's position.

(a) Advertising's fundamental objectives are:

- (i) to influence attitudes;
- (ii) to create awareness of products/services;
- (iii) to increase knowledge;
- (iv) to act as a reminder;
- (v) to motivate enquiries; and
- (vi) to provide leads for the sales force.

(b) Sales promotion objectives are:

- (i) to encourage product trial;
- (ii) to encourage greater use;
- (iii) to attract non-users;
- (iv) to stimulate larger orders; and
- (v) to encourage brand switching.

1.9 From the above list, the sales force will recognise objectives that apply to them as well. The sales force aims:

- (a) to inform about new products;
- (b) to demonstrate products;
- (c) to provide after sales service;
- (d) to effectively display products; and
- (e) to provide training for use of the product.

Much of the above objectives rely on earlier awareness from advertising and sales promotion.

1.10 Advertising and sales promotion can actually assist the sales force with their job performance. If the sales force were expected to start with introducing the product and raising awareness before being able to concentrate on achieving their objectives, there would need to be considerably more sellers. Starting with cold calling is a much more difficult position to be in and proportions of sales to customers visited would be much lower.

If the sales force were to work independently, there would be a large amount of time wasted on potential customers who are not interested in buying the product at all. If the advertising and sales promotion could raise initial awareness of genuinely interested parties then the job of the sales force will be considerably more effective.

1.11 Advertising is effective at building an image for the sales force to promote. Sales promotion can provide physical incentives for consumers which the sales force can then introduce, explain and promote to the potential consumers. In this situation, elements of communication are likely to boost the sales forces' capabilities.

1.12 Advertising and sales promotion can also benefit the sales force through confirming the product's image and capabilities. The marketing mix will support the sales force's selling process and again help to maximise profits - the overall objective of all elements of the marketing mix.

1.13 All the points we have noted confirm that money spent on advertising and sales promotion would *not* be better spent on the sales force. It can be seen that communication elements actually complement each other and work towards a more effective marketing mix.

Advertising and sales promotion fundamentally raise awareness and knowledge, and remind and provide leads for the sales force to turn into measurable sales. Their job would be less effective without the synergetic ability that the communication elements have when they work in conjunction with each other.

---

### Exam focus point

A June 1997 exam question (Q55 *Communication job* of our Practice & Revision Kit) covered the job description of a communications manager. You were asked to summarise the duties involved in the post so that the personnel department could write a job description. These duties range from dealing with publicity to implementing a communications strategy for a brand. This was similar to a question asked in June 1995 (Q62 *Job specification for a promotions manager* of our Practice & Revision Kit).

---

## 2 PERSONAL SELLING

*Examined 12/95*

2.1 Unlike advertising, selling is not able to deliver the message to a large number of receivers simultaneously, but it *is* able to modify the message to ensure it is both received by the correct audience and understood, and it is also able to provide feedback to the firm. These characteristics of selling make it a special and valuable tool of communication.

2.2 This simple model of communication can also be used to show where failures in the process can cause communication to be less effective. In this diagram we have looked at the model as though the sender was the salesperson.

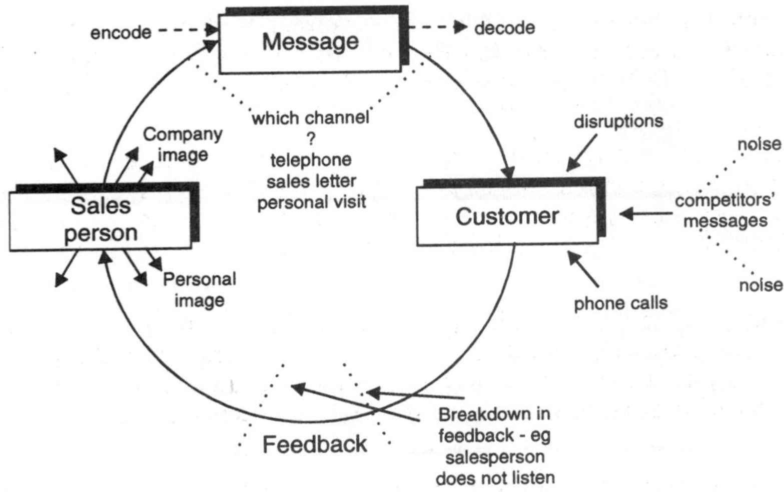


2.3 The following table expands on the above diagram.

| *Element in process* | *How it can go wrong in personal selling* |
|---|---|
| Sender | The salesperson transmits a personal and personified company image. The dress, the language used, and the car they drive creates that image. If it is inconsistent with the sales message or the customer's perceptions, communication can be adversely effected. |
| Message | The message has to be encoded and accurately decoded if it is to be effective. The words and pictures used can help or hinder this process. Using technical jargon to a non-specialist customer, or not having visual support aids and leaflets are examples of hindrances. |
| Channel | Choosing the wrong channel to transmit the sales message: an intrusive personal visit, instead of a phone call, or a phone call instead of a more effective personal visit. |
| Receiver | Much sales time and effort can be wasted talking to the wrong person. Ensuring the market has been correctly targeted and the decision making unit (DMU) identified, is essential to the selling process. Even when face to face with the decision maker, there will be distractions, or noise. This can include disruptions to a sales presentation like phone calls, or the impact of competitors' sales messages. |
| Feedback | The strength of personal selling lies in its ability to modify the message in response to customer feedback. If the feedback mechanism fails to work, selling loses its distinct advantage as a communication tool A sales person who fails to 'listen' to the customer and does not pick up body language cues will be not an effective salesperson. |

2.4 The salesperson has to be aware that as a communicator it is not just 'what is said' which has an impact. 'How it is said', also 'speaks volumes'. How something is said directly communicates the salesperson's attitude to customers and reflects the degree to which customer care is meant.

## Body language

2.5 The 'how' of external communication is transmitted not by the spoken word, but through the unspoken signals of body language and the physical clues which we broadcast to those we meet.

2.6 The salesperson is a professional communicator, and so his or her functional expertise is as dependent on skilled use of body language as it is on skill with the spoken word. As body language is a culturally based form of communication, those selling in international markets have to pay particular attention to the unspoken words to ensure cues received are not misinterpreted and those sent are not inadvertently causing offence. Some simple harmless gestures in one culture can be unpardonable obscenities in another, or to take an even more basic example, nodding the head means *yes* in the UK, but *no* in Bulgaria.

---

### Exercise 1

We are all instinctive body language communicators. You can develop your own skills through observing others. 'People watching' is a fascinating pastime and well publicised by authors like Desmond Morris. Watch people at social gatherings, parties and pubs. You will soon identify friends from relative strangers by the physical distance between them and the amount of physical contact. Couples and would be couples give themselves away with eye contact and body movements (they tend to lean towards each other).

---

2.7 Whilst controlling and positively using body language takes practice, some aspects of unspoken communication are much easier to control and just as important.

### The salesperson's image

2.8 The salesperson is, from the customer's perspective, a personification of the company. The quality of their appearance, the company car they drive, their social confidence, and organisational competence all reflect directly on the company. These aspects therefore need to be recognised and considered by sales management and the sales person.

2.9 The role of training is also critical if the company is to feel confident in the sales force's command of both the what and the how of communication. Customer care training is fundamental for anyone in direct contact with the external customer.

### Liaison and feedback

2.10 The salesperson must think of his or her role as being that of the spokesperson for the rest of the organisation, with a clear responsibility to provide feedback to the company.

2.11 The salesforce can make an important contribution to the management information system. Feedback and market intelligence gathered by the sales team are a valuable by-product of the sales process.

2.12 Management must provide systems and opportunities to encourage this information. The members of the sales team on their part need to recognise their contribution in providing such market knowledge and take a positive and proactive approach to it. A proactive approach involves not only taking positive steps to bring information to management's attention, but also actively to look out for changes and developments in the market place.

2.13 Management are likely to be particularly interested in customer feedback covering a number of key areas.

(a) The product/service
(b) Promotional activities
(c) Pricing and credit
(d) Delivery and service queries
(e) The sales activity

---

### Case example

Creating a corporate image has become a familiar business: developing a logo, a corporate style, decor, matching notepaper, brochures and even staff uniforms have all become part of normal business practice. In order to stand out from the crowd, however, companies are now moving into another perceptual dimension, and developing the idea of a corporate aroma.

One of the first companies to move into this area is BOC gases. Although companies such as Body Shop already have a recognisable concoction of smells because of the products they deal in, many others have a subliminal odour that goes unnoticed for most of the time, arising from the products, or the production process, or the premises. This may already be part of the 'image' of the company. Technology which can replicate and diffuse smells has existed for some time, and has been used by companies like Superdrug to install smells like musk and baby oil in its stores. The company also experimented with the use of a chocolate smell on Valentines Day. Other smells used include:

(a) line dried linen for a chain of men's shops;
(b) pineapple and mulled wine for Woolworths.

BOC gases business development manager Chris McGolpin thinks that companies are only one step away from incorporating distinctive smells into their reception areas as part of their image. The company has developed a system called Aromagas, adopted by Superdrug, which allows for the control and variation of smells for different occasions. It has also been found that various smells have measurable effects on employee performance and output, and it is in this area that the idea may find difficulties. Some employees, in a survey to test its acceptability, felt that it suggested unacceptable methods of employer control.

*(Adapted from The Financial Times, 27/2/97)*

---

### Communicating with the sales team

2.14 The role of management in maintaining not just routine communication, but informative, supportive, persuasive and effective communication, is key to successful sales operations.

2.15 It is fair to say that ideally all management need to be equally rigorous in their communications with any staff. The sales job is peculiar: it is often isolated and difficult, yet performance can be measured and monitored by the success or not of yesterday's sales calls.

2.16 The communication task facing the sales manager is made more difficult by another characteristic of the sales team. They are trained communicators and so likely to see through any insincere messages.

### Sales manuals and bulletins

2.17 Sales manuals can be useful reference documents for the sales team, providing detailed information about products and procedures. However, these should be used to support other forms of staff briefing and training.

2.18 Sales bulletins can be seen as more immediate communication, useful when staff are not in regular contact with managers. They provide a means of keeping staff up to date on relevant issues between sales meetings. Information on product availability, promotional activity or price changes can all be communicated quickly in this way.

2.19 Written communications should be used in support of other kinds of communications. They should be kept factual and functional.

### Sales meetings or sales conferences

2.20 Using face to face communication, these approaches have the advantage of offering two-way communication opportunities. Feedback allows managers to assess attitude and monitor responses from their teams.

2.21 Effective meetings are those which are called for a specific reason; they have a clear objective. There can be many reasons or objectives for a sales meeting ranging from motivating to informing, from planning and training to discussing and reporting. Important general points are as follows.

(a) Venues, times and frequency of meetings need careful consideration to minimise disruption to other sales activities and to ensure maximum support.

(b) Objectives need to be translated into a clear agenda, with plenty of opportunity for participation from all those attending.

(c) Results and outcomes need to be reviewed and analysed. Training inputs may need to be repeated and messages reinforced in other ways.

### Remuneration strategies

2.22 In order to maintain an effective sales force, businesses must make sure that members of the sales team are properly remunerated to promote efficiency and effectiveness and to keep staff motivated. There is a huge range of remuneration packages which could be used and each business must tailor a package to suit its requirements. For example, the choice might be between using employees on a salary plus a modest annual bonus, or appointed agents working on a commission only basis.

2.23 A number of issues arise through the selection of a particular compensation scheme, in particular the ability of the company to achieve its specific objectives. The compensation scheme will influence the level of motivation of the sales force, could possibly affect profitability and will influence the direction of the salesperson's effort. It is also important to recognise that all of the sales team will not be motivated in the same way and that moving from a salary-with-bonus scheme to a commission-only scheme may have serious implications for staff morale, retention of staff and sales performance.

2.24 Considering the advantages and disadvantages of the options above, the following points can be made.

*Agents on commission-only scheme*

| *Advantages* | *Disadvantages* |
|---|---|
| Earnings based performance | Little financial security |
| Personnel motivated by monetary rewards | Monetary reward not the only motivating factor |
| Higher earnings potential | Smaller accounts may receive less attention |
| Less cost incurred for less effective sales personnel (relative to salaried employee) | Higher cost incurred for most successful sales personnel |
| Commission can be varied by product, to direct sales force effort | Representatives will only sell high commission products |
| Operate as 'own boss', with self employed status | Danger of 'hard sell' with possible detriment to company image |
| | Loss of management control over sales activity |
| | Possibly less sense of responsibility and commitment as agent rather than as 'part of the company' |

*Salaried employees on salary-with-bonus*

| *Advantages* | *Disadvantages* |
|---|---|
| Consider more than just the quick sell | Requires closer management control |
| Recognises other motivating factors | Limited incentive to sell |
| Allows team selling | High sales 'overhead' cost |
| Recognises profit not just volume | Not linked to performance |

| More job security/guaranteed income | Lower average earnings for successful sales person |
|---|---|

## 'Push' and 'pull' effects

*Examined 12/95*

2.25 The promotional mix is often described in terms of 'push' and 'pull' effects.

(a) A 'pull' effect is when customers ask for the brand by name, inducing retailers or distributors to stock up with the company's goods.

(b) A 'push' effect is targeted on getting the company's goods into the distribution network. This could be a special discount on volume to ensure that wholesalers stock up with products that the company is promoting.

2.26 For example, many industries have to communicate with the final consumer, the public, retailers *and* wholesalers effectively.

2.27 'Push' promotional techniques aim to encourage the distribution and/or retail outlets to stock and sell the product. Essentially the product is being pushed through the distribution channel. 'Pull' techniques communicate directly with consumers, to arouse their interest in the product, which can be communicated to the retailer by making enquiries, and their desire to purchase it.

2.28 Pull techniques include such things as television and media advertising, sales promotions and direct marketing. Push techniques include trade advertising, promotions/incentives and selling

2.29 Each technique or effect has advantages and disadvantages.

*Push techniques*

| *Advantages* | *Disadvantages* |
|---|---|
| They gain shelf space | No contact with the consumer |
| They gain distributor support | The cost involved reduces profit margins |
| They educate distributors | The need to differentiate from competitive promotions |
| They build relationships with distributors | The power of distributors to control distribution |
| They offset competitor activity | Their effects are only short term |
| They improve profitability through increased sales volume | |

*Pull techniques*

| *Advantages* | *Disadvantages* |
|---|---|
| Build brand image | High cost of media |
| Develop relationship between brand and consumer | Fragmenting audiences |

| | |
|---|---|
| Create rapid brand awareness | More 'canny' consumers |
| Differentiate product | Power of distributor |
| Maintain loyalty | No trade support |
| Can be used tactically | |

2.30 As can be seen from the above, both push and pull techniques have a range of advantages and disadvantages associated with them. Most businesses will use a combination of both push and pull techniques which, when effectively integrated, meet both consumers' and distributors' needs. In combination, the disadvantages of each technique can to some degree be negated.

---

**Exam focus point**

Sales remuneration featured in the June 1997 exam (Q60 *High pressure selling* of our Practice & Revision Kit). You had to draft a report advising the company of the benefits and dangers of these sales techniques and their effect on the company's reputation and its ability to offer proper customer care. You could have got the bones of your answer from this section.

---

### Definitions of advertising and sales promotion

2.31 *Advertising* is defined by the American Marketing Association as 'any paid form of non-personal presentation and promotion of ideas, goods or services by an identifiable sponsor'.

This definition clearly distinguishes advertising from personal selling and publicity (which is often not paid for, and if it is, the sponsor does not openly present ideas or products).

2.32 Between advertising and publicity lies *sponsorship*. This is now a common feature in sporting competitions and events which bear the name of the sponsor.

2.33 *Sales promotions* are 'those marketing activities other than personal selling, advertising and publicity, that stimulate consumer purchasing and dealer effectiveness, such as displays, shows and exhibitions, demonstrations and various non-recurrent selling efforts not in the ordinary routine'. They are also called 'below-the-line' activities, distinguishing them from advertising, personal selling and publicity, which are 'above-the-line' activities (see Paragraph 3.7).

## 3 ADVERTISING

3.1 Promotion, especially advertising, can be seen as attempting to move consumers along a continuum stretching from complete unawareness of the product to regular usage (brand loyalty). The AIDA model postulated by Strong in 1925 is a simple example of this approach known as the 'hierarchy of effects' model.

Awareness → Interest → Desire → Action

3.2 These models assume that customers formulate a behavioural intention which then leads to actual purchasing behaviour.

### The purpose of advertising

3.3 Advertising is 'purposive communication' to a target market. It assists in selling by drawing attention to the characteristics of a product which will appeal to the buying motives (conscious or subconscious) of customers in the target segment of the market. It does not necessarily instruct or inform about all the characteristics of a product; its function is to identify an exploitable characteristic (that is, one which distinguishes it from other products) and to suggest that this characteristic gives it a special value for potential customers. If the product does not have a distinguishing characteristic, uniqueness is promoted by brand image.

3.4 'The purpose of advertising is to enhance potential buyers' responses to the organisation and its offerings. It seeks to do this by providing information, by trying to channelise desires and by supplying reasons for preferring the particular organisation's offerings.' (Kotler)

3.5 Advertising is often classed under one of three headings.

(a) *Informative advertising*. Conveying information and raising consumer awareness of the product. Common in the early stages of the lifecycle, or after modification.

(b) *Persuasive advertising*. Concerned with creating a desire for the product and stimulating actual purchase. Used for well established products, often in the growth/maturity stages of the product life cycle. The most competitive form of advertising.

(c) *Reminding advertising*. Reminding consumers about the product or organisation, reinforcing the knowledge held by potential consumers and reminding existing consumers of the benefits they are receiving from their purchase.

## Brand vs generic advertising

3.6 It will only be worthwhile for an individual firm to advertise if it can *differentiate* its brands from competitors in the eyes of the consumer. In the absence of *product differentiation* all advertising purchased by an individual firm would be *generic*, benefiting all producers equally at the firm's expense.

## Above-the-line and below-the-line

3.7 The 'line' is one in an advertising agency's accounts *above* which are shown earnings on a commission basis and *below* which are shown earnings on a fee basis.

(a) Above-the-line refers to advertising in media such as the press, radio, TV and cinema.

(b) Below-the-line promotional tools include direct mail, exhibitions, package design, merchandising and so on. This term is sometimes regarded as synonymous with sales promotion.

## The objectives of advertising

3.8 The objectives of advertising may be any of the following:

(a) to ensure a certain exposure for the advertised product or service;

(b) to create awareness of new products, or developments to existing products;

(c) to improve customer attitudes towards the product or the firm;

(d) to increase sales (although it is difficult to relate advertising to sales volumes) and profits. For a non-profit-making organisation, the equivalent purpose will be to increase response to the product or service;

(e) to generate enquiries from potential customers;

(f) to change the attitudes and habits of people.

3.9 Advertising is also a means of protecting the longer-term position of a company, by building a strong, established image.

### Exercise 2

Can you think of adverts that have left a lasting impression on you?

### Solution

Some messages are now part of our everyday language, for example BA's 'fly the flag' or 'clunk-click' for seat belt advertisements.

3.10 The objectives of advertising which were listed above are rather general. The more specific targets of an advertising campaign might be as follows.

(a) To communicate certain information about a product. This is perhaps the most important objective.

(b) To highlight specific features of a product which make it different from the competitors. The concept of the *unique selling proposition* (or USP) is that by emphasising a unique feature which appeals to a customer need, customers will be influenced to buy the product.

(c) To build up a 'brand image' or a 'company image' through *corporate advertising*.

(d) To reinforce customer behaviour.

(e) Influencing dealers and resellers to stock the items (on as much shelf-space as possible).

(f) In the case of government advertising, to achieve a policy objective.

### Exercise 3

Look through a magazine or watch commercial TV for a while (neither task should be terribly demanding!) and see if you can spot examples of each of these types of campaign.

## The role of advertising in industrial marketing

3.11 Looking specifically at advertising aimed at industrial rather than consumer markets, the following are the principal aims of advertising.

(a) *Awareness building*. If the prospect is not aware of the company or product, he may refuse to see the salesman, or the salesman may have to use up a lot of time in introducing himself and his company.

(b) *Comprehension building*. If the product represents a new concept, some of the burden of explaining it can be effectively carried on by advertising.

(c) *Efficient reminding*. If the prospect knows about the product but is not ready to buy, an advertisement reminding him of the product would be much cheaper than a sales call.

(d) *Lead generation*. Advertisements carrying return coupons are an effective way to generate sales leads for salesmen.

(e) *Legitimisation*. Company salesmen can use tear sheets of the company's advertisements to show prospects in order to demonstrate that their company and products are not fly by night but respectable and sufficiently financially sound to run an advertising campaign.

(f) *Reassurance*. Advertising can remind customers how to use the product and reassure them about their purchase.

### Case example

Financial services have always presented something of a paradox. Consumers generally have little if any intrinsic interest in financial services except around the time of purchase, but at the same time consumers know what they want to a greater degree than ever before. Their expectations of service and product performance are higher than ever before - the legislative deregulation and editorial coverage of the financial revolution has produced a new more knowledgeable consumer.

Most of the time, however, they have no involvement with financial markets; most of the time, then, a large number of financial institutions are chasing a small number of active consumers. Advertisers are faced with a dilemma; either they can try to interest a large group of uninvolved consumers who are totally disinterested in their message, or a small group who are likely to be receptive to the message. One way to achieve a solution is to see effective advertising as 'preprogramming choice' to make sure that the brand is present in the consumer's memory in such a way that it exercises the maximum positive effect at the moment that the decision to buy is reached. A good example of this approach was adopted by Scottish Amicable, the financial services and insurance company. They sought to expand their share of existing business rather than trying to accelerate category growth, which might have benefited competitors. Research showed them that using a comparison of consumer awareness and 'willingness to accept' scores, the better known a company, the more likely it is to be accepted by the customer if recommended by a broker

Independent financial advisors were asked to rate companies on a range of attributes (measures of perceived performance and image), which Scottish Amicable then used to cluster companies into six groups. One of the groups accounted for most of the IFAs regular business, and one of the key distinguishing features of this group was 'well known to the public'.

At two key stages in the sales process, then:

(a) when the broker is making a recommendation which the consumer is intended to accept; and

(b) when the consumer is making the decision to accept the broker's recommendation,

being well known to the public had a crucial impact. Making Scottish Amicable famous through advertising will 'pre-programme' potential customers and maximise the likelihood of being recommended. It follows that the target audience must be any potential future customer; the man in the street should feel a sense of ownership of advertising, and advertising competes with other famous campaigns, not just other financial institutions.

The 'Amicable Man' campaign dramatised the idea that 'with Scottish Amicable you can cope with whatever real life throws at you', using real life camcorder footage of things going wrong (before the use of this idea in Jeremy Beadle's 'You've Been Framed' series, incidentally).

The result of the campaign was that consumer awareness, and willingness to accept ratings doubled. Scottish Amicable became the most recalled financial advertiser amongst IFAs; IFA ratings of both 'well known to the public' and 'competitiveness' doubled. One in five IFAs wrote more business with Scottish Amicable and their total income grew by 15% year on year (the only company to grow pensions business and growing life assurance business in a declining market).

Conservatively, Scottish Amicable estimate econometrically that in the first year of the campaign, new advertising generated about £300 million of additional lifetime cover. Their top estimate for the same period is an extra £l billion. This was achieved with a total media spend of £3 million! *(Adapted from ADMAP, 26/4/96)*

## 4 PLANNING A PROMOTION CAMPAIGN

4.1 There are six distinct stages in such a campaign (focusing on advertising as a promotional technique).

*Step 1* Identify the target audience
*Step 2* Specify the promotional message
*Step 3* Select media
*Step 4* Schedule media
*Step 5* Set the promotional budget
*Step 6* Evaluate promotional effectiveness

### Step 1 Identify the target audience

4.2 A list of dimensions which could be of use in identifying the target audience, depending on the type of product, is given below.

4.3 The target audience will be defined in terms of the segmentation variables described in Chapter 7. The *psychographics* approach enables campaigns to be planned which emphasise how the brand has relevance for the style of living of the target audience. Creativity is used to emphasise mood, atmosphere and environment for brand usage, usually relying on non-verbal communication such as background setting for an advertisement (indoor/outdoor, relaxed or tense environment, type of music, style of furniture, use of colour schemes, appearance of models etc).

4.4 These factors are particularly relevant when the aim of the campaign involves persuasion of the audience. Various research projects have been conducted which have attempted to identify relevant correlates of persuasibility. On balance the evidence is not conclusive. However, much advertising aims to accomplish very precise and limited changes in awareness of, or perceptions of, product attributes (*repositioning*).

**Case example**

The Tate Gallery launches a branding campaign this month aimed at widening the gallery's appeal to non-art buffs. The campaign is devised by BDDP.GGT and will run on 16-sheet cross-track posters in the London Underground. Striking ads take everyday objects such as a conker, an apple and a rock, and show how they take on a different appearance after a visit to a gallery. The campaign launches with a poster featuring a photograph of a conker, which at second glance looks like an eye. John Allen, BDDP.GGT deputy chairman says: 'This campaign is a simple, yet charming, way to illustrate the benefits of visiting the Tate for Anyone, regardless of their knowledge of art.'

*Financial Times*, 20 July 1995

4.5 For industrial goods the social and sociopsychological variables are still valid but are perhaps not as important as are economic factors in the audience dimension process. Factors affecting behaviour include:

(a) size of company (turnover, number of employees, profit levels);
(b) production process;
(c) type of business activity;
(d) location;
(e) centralisation of buying;
(f) buying process; and
(g) interdepartmental rivalries.

### Step 2 Specify the promotional message

4.6 People are very specific about the advertisements to which they pay attention. Most of us have the opportunity to see many hundreds of advertisements in many media each day, and cannot give our attention to each and every one.

4.7 The essence of specifying the promotional message lies in identifying the intended function of the campaign. This function could be:

(a) to convey information;
(b) to alter perceptions;
(c) to stimulate desires;
(d) to produce conviction;
(e) to direct action;
(f) to provide reassurance.

Each function can suggest an appropriate form for, and content of, the message. Messages are usually tested before use in 'qualitative' group discussions with potential consumers.

4.8 Much research has been directed at how far the content of the message is likely to be influential in effecting attitude change. In particular, studies have been concerned with the varying effects of persuasive messages, some of which are assumed to have greater influence because they play upon the emotions of an audience, whilst others rely on a rational approach to intelligence and good sense. Both the rational and emotional appeal approaches have strong supporters - people tend to advocate one or the other as being the more potent.

4.9 The conclusion from various studies appears to be that a strong emotional appeal induces considerable anxiety but is unlikely to change attitudes. A restrained appeal may well change attitudes (resulting, for example, in purchase of a new brand of toothpaste) and such attitudes are likely to last longer.

### Step 3 Select media

4.10 'Media advertising' means advertising through the media, which include the following.

(a) National newspapers
(b) Regional newspapers
(c) Magazines and trade press
(d) Television
(e) Commercial radio
(f) Posters and transport advertising
(g) Cinema

Each medium provides access to a certain type of audience.

4.11 The criterion governing the choice of medium for conveying a persuasive message for a potential market is that the medium used should be the one which will contact the optimum number of potential customers most efficiently at the lowest cost. The choice of medium will depend on who the advertiser wishes to reach with the advertising message. If the advertiser wishes to sell to a particular market segment, advertising through a national medium might not be cost effective.

4.12 The choice of medium begins with a study of the target audience's *media habits*. The audience for a particular medium may be analysed and the media which are most used by customers in the potential market will be chosen for advertising.

(a) *Television* is watched by viewers from all social groupings and is an ideal medium for advertising mass consumer goods.

(b) A particular medium may reach audiences with special characteristics, for example:

   (i) the cinema is visited mainly by young couples;

   (ii) many magazines and local newspapers are read predominantly by women;

   (iii) there are magazines for qualified accountants, magazines for student accountants, magazines for data processing managers and so on.

(c) The size of *circulation* or *audience* for a particular medium is important, but there is no value in reaching a wide audience if they are not potential customers for the product being advertised.

(d) It may be too expensive to try and reach an entire potential market with an advertising campaign; too wide a choice of media will probably bring diminishing returns on the money spent.

---

### Exercise 4

Where should the following businesses advertise to reach the right audience?

(a) Expensive camera equipment supplier
(b) High street butcher
(c) Industrial goods

#### Solution

(a) Photography magazines (small, specialist readership)
(b) Locally, for example in local newspapers

(c) Trade magazine

4.13 The advertiser will want reliable information about the audiences for each medium in order to help in the choice of media for an advertising campaign. Research into audiences is provided by the following:

(a) for major newspapers and magazines, the National Readership Survey or JICNARS (the Joint Industry Committee for National Readership Surveys);

(b) for television, BARB (British Audience Research Bureau);

(c) for radio, RAJAR (Radio Joint Audience Research);

(d) for poster audiences, JICPAS;

(e) for the cinema, the Screen Advertisers' Association.

4.14 Another important consideration is *cost*. Advertising costs consist of:

(a) the cost of producing the advertisements;
(b) the cost of exposure in the media.

The costs of exposure are perhaps ten times the cost of production in consumer goods advertising.

4.15 The cost of a medium is measured by the 'cost per thousand' criterion. If a full page advertisement in a national newspaper circulating to 2 million readers is £7,000, the cost per thousand is £3.50.

### Exercise 5

Cost per thousand is a very simple measure, which should be interpreted with caution. Why?

### Solution

(a) There is no value in advertising female fashions to male readers, although males might account for half the readership of a newspaper; in other words, the advertisement might be reaching many people who will not be affected by it.

(b) Not all users of the medium will see the advertisement. Many TV viewers will leave the room during a commercial break; magazine and newspaper readers will not look at every advertisement.

## Step 4 Schedule media

4.16 An advertiser will not restrict his campaign to one advertisement in a single newspaper or one appearance of an advertisement on television.

(a) An advertisement must be repeated because many of the target audiences will miss it the first time it appears.

(b) It has been found that a larger target audience is reached by advertising in several newspapers instead of just one, and in several media instead of just one.

### *The theoretical optimal level of advertising*

4.17 It is generally undisputed that it is necessary to advertise. The problem facing management is just how much advertising maximises profits. This cannot be based on relations between advertising expenditure and sales figures because exogenous influences such as the marketing activities of competitors mask any underlying relationship between advertising spend and profits.

### Step 5 Set the promotional budget

4.18 In an ideal world the budget for a campaign should be determined by a consideration of the four steps discussed so far. The budget needed is that which meets the objectives using the chosen media to convey the required message. In reality the constraint of what the organisation can afford is commonly paramount.

4.19 The promotional budget is often linked to sales using:

(a) a percentage of last period sales;
(b) a percentage of expected (target) sales;
(c) a percentage of past (or target) profit.

### Step 6 Evaluate promotional effectiveness

4.20 An advertising campaign can only be termed successful if it generates profit for the company. However, it is almost impossible to measure the effect on sales and profits by any direct means. The problem is that advertising never takes place in a vacuum and other events in the market place, such as competitors' actions, changing attitudes and relative price changes, swamp the advertising effect. It is therefore necessary to observe changes earlier on in the buying process. The assumption being that favourable changes in awareness and attitude will result in higher sales and profits.

4.21 There is a paradox involved in trying to measure the effectiveness of advertising. The early stages in the process by which advertising generates sales are easy to measure (for example exposure by readership and/or viewer surveys) but are of little direct importance. The real effect that is of interest is obviously the net increase in sales. However, the sales effect can at best be inferred.

This diagram indicates some measures of effectiveness.

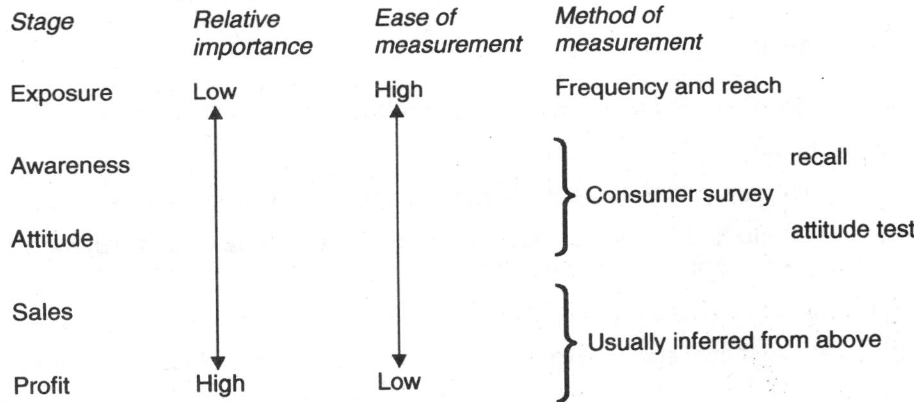


## 5 SUCCESSFUL ADVERTISING

5.1 The *content* of an advertisement is determined largely by the objective of the advertising and the motivation of the potential customer. An advertisement should present information which leads to a greater awareness of the product; using non-economic emotions (fear, humour) should be an attention-getter, but inciting these feelings should not be allowed to be the only effect of the advertisement.

5.2 Advertising will be most successful if the following conditions apply.

(a) The product should have characteristics which lend themselves to advertising.

(i) It should be distinctive and identifiable (if it is not, a distinctive brand may be created).

(ii) It should stimulate emotional buying (emotive products such as medicine, insurance and cosmetics and products which can be made to arouse social instincts, such as cars, alcohol, cigarettes and household appliances, can be advertised with great effectiveness).

(iii) If at the point of sale a customer can refute an advertising claim simply by inspecting the product, advertising will achieve no sales at all.

(b) There should be consistency throughout the sales operation. Advertising, the activities of salesmen and dealers, branding, packaging and pricing should all promote the same product image.

(c) There should be co-operation between advertising staff and all other activities in the company. Product design, production, distribution, selling and financial operations should all combine to achieve customer orientation and maximum selling efficiency.

## Advertising agencies

5.3 Most large scale advertising involves not just an advertiser and the media owners, but also an advertising agency. An advertising agency advises its client on the planning of a campaign and buys advertising 'space' in various media on behalf of its client.

5.4 An advertising agency is appointed by clients to conduct an advertising campaign on their behalf. In the UK they receive a commission (of 10% or 15%) from the owners of the media with whom they place the advertisements.

5.5 Large or medium-sized agencies may be creative agencies (specialising in originating creative ideas, which are necessary for, say, TV advertising) or media buyers (whose specialist skills are in buying media space and air time). Advertising of industrial goods is usually handled by smaller 'industrial agencies' which have the accounts of chemical, transportation and engineering firms. Most of their work is in the sphere of sales promotions, such as direct mail, exhibitions and public relations.

### *Advantages of agencies*

5.6 The advantages of advertising agencies are as follows.

(a) From the media owner's point of view:

(i) they reduce the number of organisations with whom they have to deal;

(ii) agencies are bound to conform to the British Code of Advertising Practice in order to obtain their commission.

(b) From the advertiser's point of view:

(i) an agency's specialised services are likely to be cheaper than an internal advertising department;

(ii) an agency will have broader contacts with ancillary services such as printers and photographers;

(iii) the advertiser receives expert advice (for example from the agency's account executive) free of charge;

(iv) agency employees have a broad experience in the field of advertising.

### *The advertiser and the agency*

5.7 To take full advantage of the agency's services, the advertisement manager of the advertising company must:

(a) have a working knowledge of advertising;

(b) be able to negotiate with the agency so that the proposed campaign appears to achieve the marketing aims of the organisation;

(c) transmit whatever information is necessary to the agency which may be of value in furthering the advertising campaign in the best interests of the organisation (for example the annual report and accounts, copies of all the news releases and house journals, changes in products, packaging or distribution methods and news about R & D).

5.8 Before looking at other promotional activities we will discuss the role of 'branding' in the communications mix and product design.

---

**Exercise 6**

The trade journal of the advertising industry is Campaign. This is targeted at people working in ad agencies, but, although a lot of the gossip about individuals will go over your head, reading Campaign will give you a very strong flavour of the industry and some fascinating insights into what goes on behind the scenes. You will also become familiar with the industry's jargon and find articles that are directly relevant to your studies.

Your task, then, is to buy (and read) a copy of Campaign from time to time.

---

## 6 BRANDING

6.1 Expenditure on promotion gives rise to brands. A 'brand' is a name, term, sign, symbol or design intended to identify the product of a seller and to differentiate it from those of competitors.

6.2 Not long ago, and this is still the case in many less developed countries, most products were sold unbranded from barrels and bins etc. Today in developed and even developing countries hardly anything goes unbranded. Even salt, oranges, nuts and screws are often branded. There has however been a limited return recently in some developed countries to 'generics'. These are cheap, unbranded products, packaged plainly and not heavily advertised.

6.3 *Branding* is a very general term covering brand names, designs, trademarks, symbols, jingles and the like. A *brand name* refers strictly to letters, words or groups of words which can be spoken. A *brand image* distinguishes a company's product from competing products in the eyes of the user.

6.4 A brand identity may begin with a name, such as 'Kleenex', 'Ariel', but extends to a range of visual features which should assist in stimulating demand for the particular product. The additional features include typography, colour, package design and slogans.

6.5 Often brand names suggest desired product characteristics. For example, 'Fairy' gives impressions of gentleness and hence mildness.

---

**Exercise 7**

What characteristics do the following brand names suggest to you?

Brillo (scouring pads)
Pampers (baby nappies)
Cussons Imperial Leather (soap)
Kerrygold (butter)
Hush Puppies (shoes)

---

6.6 The reasons for branding are as follows.

(a) It is a form of product differentiation, conveying a lot of information very quickly and concisely. This helps customers readily to identify the goods or services and thereby helps to create a customer loyalty to the brand. It is therefore a means of increasing or maintaining sales.

(b) Advertising needs a brand name to sell to customers and advertising and branding are very closely related aspects of promotion; the more similar a product (whether an industrial good or consumer good) is to competing goods, the more branding is necessary to create a separate product identity.

(c) Branding leads to a readier acceptance of a manufacturer's goods by wholesalers and retailers.

(d) It facilitates self-selection of goods in self-service stores and also makes it easier for a manufacturer to obtain display space in shops and stores.

(e) It reduces the importance of price differentials between goods.

(f) Brand loyalty in customers gives a manufacturer more control over marketing strategy and his choice of channels of distribution.

(g) Other products can be introduced into brand range to 'piggy back' on the articles already known to the customer (but ill-will as well as goodwill for one product in a branded range will be transferred to all other products in the range). Adding products to an existing brand range is known as *brand extension strategy*.

(h) It eases the task of personal selling (face-to-face selling by sales representatives).

(i) Branding makes market segmentation easier. Different brands of similar products may be developed to meet specific needs of categories of users.

6.7 The relevance of branding does not apply equally to all products. The cost of intensive brand advertising to project a brand image nationally may be prohibitively high. Goods which are sold in large numbers, on the other hand, promote a brand name by their existence and circulation.

6.8 Where a brand image promotes an idea of quality, a customer will be disappointed if his experience of a product fails to live up to his expectations. Quality control is therefore an important element in branding policy. It is especially a problem for service industries such as hotels, airlines and retail stores, where there is less possibility than in a manufacturing industry of detecting and rejecting the work of an operator before it reaches the customer. Bad behaviour by an employee in a face-to-face encounter with a customer will reflect on the entire company and possibly deter the customer from using any of the company's services again.

6.9 The decision as to whether a brand name should be given to a range of products or whether products should be branded individually depends on quality factors.

(a) If the brand name is associated with quality, all goods in the range must be of that standard. An example of a successful promotion of a brand name to a wide product range is the St Michael brand of Marks & Spencer; and Kelloggs use their family brand name to promote their (quality) cereal products.

(b) If a company produces different quality (and price) goods for different market segments, it would be unwise to give the same brand name to the higher and the lower quality goods because this would deter buyers in the high quality/price market segment.

## Branding strategies

6.10

| *Branding strategy* | *Description* | *Implies* |
|---|---|---|
| Family branding | The power of the family name to help products | Image of family brand applicable across a range of goods |
| Brand extension | New flavours, sizes etc | High consumer loyalty to existing brand |
| Multi-branding | Different names for similar goods serving similar consumer tastes | Consumers make random purchases across brands |

6.11 *Brand extension* denotes the introduction of new flavours, sizes etc. New additions to the product range are beneficial for two main reasons.

(a) They require a lower level of marketing investment (part of the 'image' already being known).

(b) The extension of the brand presents less risk to consumers who might be worried about trying something new. (Particularly important in consumer durables with relatively large 'investment' in a car, stereo system or the like.) Recent examples include the introduction of Persil washing up liquid and Mars ice cream.

6.12 *Multi-branding*: the introduction of a number of brands that all satisfy very similar product characteristics.

(a) This can be used where little or no brand loyalty is noted, the rationale being to run a large number of brands to pick up buyers who are constantly changing brands.

(b) The best example is washing detergents. The two majors, Lever Brothers and Proctor & Gamble, have created a barrier to fresh competition as a new company would have to launch several brands at once in order to compete.

6.13 *Family branding*: the power of the 'family' name to assist all products is being used more and more by large companies, such as Heinz. In part this is a response to retailers own-label goods. It is also an attempt to consolidate highly expensive television advertising behind just one message rather than fragmenting it across the promotion of numerous individual items. Individual lines can be promoted more cheaply and effectively by other means such as direct marketing and sales promotions.

### Case example

The success of the Pacific Rim economies is fuelling an accelerating demand for the lifestyles associated with middle class affluence amongst the population there, and a big part of that lifestyle is the designer brand. Until recently, virtually all of the most desirable brands, outside of the area of high tech products, have been European or American. It is predicted that by the end of the decade, however, Asian sales will make up half of the world's luxury goods markets. But the locals are beginning to get into this area too.

Local entrepreneurs have been engaged in buying up top brands. Ong Beng Seng, the Singapore businessman, for example, owns significant interests in the Planet Hollywood restaurant chain and a controlling interest, it is said, in DKNY, the Donna Karan fashion house. 'Brand Barons' in other parts of the area own controlling stakes in some of the most important brands of watches, luxury clothing, accessories and fashion items. Brand names, it is said, are being damaged through being overworked in this area - DKNY initials appear on everything from coffee cups to inflatable swimming rings - but entrepreneurs are also trying to create their own, local brands.

Can they do it? The Japanese have done so for some technologically based items, such as cars, cameras and televisions, and Kenzo is one Japanese fashion brand to make an impact on the world stage (although now French owned!). It appears more difficult than simply making good products. To make a global brand involves a certain geographical caricature - good clothes come from France, the best leather is Italian, the top watches Swiss. Western brands coveted in Asia rely for their appeal on a host of nebulous qualities, including the lifestyle they represent. It is the combination that counts, rather than simply one aspect. Brand barons in Asia are moving towards building local brands, but it may be a long term business, and no-one is able to predict how it will turn out in the long run.

*(Adapted from Economist, March 1996)*

## Trademarks

6.14 A trademark is a legal term covering words and symbols. A legally protected mark can be a very valuable asset because:

(a) the legal protection can continue after patent protection runs out;

(b) competitors will be prevented from using a market leader's branding as a generic term for a class of products (as has happened with aspirin and cellophane).

6.15 The Trademarks Act 1994 has expanded the range of items that can be registered to include smells, musical sounds and the shape of goods or their packaging, in addition to the existing list of: devices (eg the Mercedes three-pointed star), names, words (eg Kodak), letters (eg BP) and numerals (eg '4711')

### Case example

It used to be called the Chinese gooseberry, but only older people will recall that now. The kiwi fruit was born out of the marketing efforts of a group of farmers who formed the New Zealand Kiwi Fruit Marketing Board in 1988 in order to promote the erstwhile Chinese gooseberry under the cuddlier name thought up a few years earlier by some patriotic New Zealand horticulturists.

The promotion was spectacularly successful, and the market grew rapidly until markets throughout the world couldn't get enough of the fruit. Rather than becoming an exclusively New Zealand brand, however, the kiwi turned into a generic name by which the fruit was known. The farmers had not 'branded' the product, but simply given it a new, more acceptable name which anyone could, and did, use. Connections with New Zealand, and the flightless national bird have been forgotten. The incompetent marketers were so successful that American consumers are now unaware of any other meaning for a 'kiwi' than the fruit.

Farmers in other countries - many closer to the high consumption areas such as Germany - simply moved into the market. Orchards planted in the early 80s by farmers in Italy, France and Chile who had seen the growth of New Zealand kiwi exports by 40-70% per year, matured in the late part of the decade. Todays market is about 800,000 tonnes; New Zealand has only a quarter of that.

In a desperate attempt to win something back, New Zealand farmers have done what they should have done in the first place - think of a new name, but this time, register it as a trademark which only they can use. Only time will tell if the kiwi fruit will go the way of the Chinese goose berry, to be supplanted by the 'Zespri'.

*(Adapted from The Economist, August 1996)*

### Exercise 8

Even with trademark protection the impact of a market leader's branding may be weakened by consumers who perceive the brand name as a generic term. Can you think of some examples?

### Solution

(a) How may people 'hoover' with an Electrolux machine?
(b) Have you ever 'xeroxed' on a photocopier not made by Rank?
(c) Hence the message 'It's the real thing' from Coca Cola.

## 7 SALES PROMOTION

7.1 *Sales promotions* are 'those marketing activities other than personal selling, advertising and publicity, that stimulate consumer purchasing and dealer effectiveness, such as displays, shows and exhibitions, demonstrations and various non-recurrent selling efforts not in the ordinary routine'. As we have seen, they are also called 'below-the-line' activities, distinguishing them from advertising, personal selling and publicity, which are 'above-the-line' activities.

7.2 Sales promotions are used extensively, because there is often a direct link between the promotion and short-term sales volume. For example, the offer of a free gift or a reduced price 'bargain' will be made dependent on the purchase of the product. A promotion offer might be a free gift if the consumer sends in three packet tops of the product; or a competition entry form might be printed on the product's packaging.

7.3 Sales promotional techniques have a more direct effect on usage than does advertising. As such sales promotions can be particularly useful in inducing trials by consumers of rival products, the three for the price of two offer being a sufficient inducement to wean the consumer away from purchasing their usual brand.

7.4 Examples of sales promotion activities are as follows.

(a) *Consumer promotions*:

- (i) free samples;
- (ii) coupon offers (money-off offers);
- (iii) price reductions as sales promotions;
- (iv) competitions;
- (v) free gifts (in exchange for, say, packet tops - these are known as 'free sendaway premiums');
- (vi) combination pack offers (two for the price of one);
- (vii) off-price labels;
- (viii) trading stamps;
- (ix) samples;
- (x) exhibitions and demonstrations (eg the Motor Show or Ideal Home Exhibition);
- (xi) catalogues (notably the large mail order catalogues of mail order firms);
- (xii) on-pack offers (ie free gifts which come with the product. This is sometimes used for first editions of new magazines).

(b) *Retailer or middleman promotions as a 'push policy'*:

- (i) extended credit;
- (ii) merchandising facilities;
- (iii) contests for retailers or shop assistants;
- (iv) consumer promotions and advertising act as a 'pull policy' to attract dealer attention by means of consumer demand.

(c) *Sales force promotions*:

- (i) bonuses;
- (ii) contests between salesmen (based on volumes of sale);
- (iii) sales motivators: gifts linked to sales.

(d) *Industrial promotions*:

- (i) sales literature and catalogues;
- (ii) special discounts;
- (iii) exhibitions and trade fairs;

(iv) events, say invitations to customers to visit the Wimbledon Tennis Championships or the Open Golf Championship;

(v) trade-in allowances;

(vi) inducements (such as diaries and calendars).

---

### Case example

Major manufacturers are now trying to understand exactly why shoppers behave as they do by using video cameras to observe people shopping to see if how they buy corresponds to the way they think they buy. This enables the manufacturer to understand more fully the role its products play so that it can position its product and target its marketing activity more accurately.

ID Magasin, a market research and store design company, argues that video data shows that customers do not move around the store in a logical and uniform fashion, and that their movements become more random as they progress. How do we make sense of this?

EPOS data will tell us which products are selling, and how many customers visited on a particular day. The video data tells us:

(a) which product comparisons are taking place;
(b) which products are picked up and then replaced; and
(c) how many products a consumer looks at before making the final decision.

This type of research reveals to a brand manufacturer the role played by the product within the category of which it is part (for instance, Heinz the brand within the category 'tinned baked beans'). The relation between premium brands and other labels is also highlighted, and the consequence of siting one line next to others brought out, as well as the importance of instore and on pack information. This enables stores to develop merchandising and instore promotional techniques to match 'consumer search strategies'.

Research shows that a number of surprising interactions take place. Some brands provide a means by which consumers orient themselves - Heinz labels, for instance, will tell them what they will find in a particular aisle. Poor sales of a product which may serve an important function in 'signposting' consumers may actually result in poorer sales for a particular category.

This suggests that it will be important for the overall sales of a category to ensure that brands play their full part in the merchandising activity taking place within a particular store, and that a degree of cooperation between brands is potentially profitable for all.

*(Adapted from The Grocer, February 1997)*

---

7.5 Sales promotions are essentially short-term sales measures and an advertiser planning a campaign should not be tempted to sacrifice long-term prospects (for example brand image built up through media advertising) in order to spend too much on short-term promotions. Although sales promotion is short-term in its effects, its objectives are broadly similar to those of above-the-line advertising:

(a) to increase sales revenue by generating extra interest;
(b) to attract new customers;
(c) to encourage resellers to stock the item or increase their stocks;
(d) to encourage slow moving lines;
(e) to clear out stocks;
(f) to counter the moves of a competitor;
(g) to launch a new product;
(h) to encourage the sales force to greater effort.

### Merchandising

7.6 A manufacturer of consumer goods usually relies on reseller organisations (rather than direct selling) to bring the goods to the point of sale with the consumer. This dependence on resellers for the sales volume of a product will be unsatisfactory to the manufacturer who may therefore try to take on some of the job of selling to the consumers. Manufacturer involvement in selling to consumers is achieved by advertising, packaging design or sales promotion offers. Another way of extending manufacturer involvement in selling is by means of merchandising.

7.7 Merchandising is a method by which the manufacturer tries to ensure that a retailer sells as many of his products as quickly as possible. The manufacturer therefore gives advice to the retailer, either from the sales force or from full time merchandising specialists.

7.8 Merchandising is concerned with putting the manufacturer's goods in the *right place* at the *right time*.

(a) *In the right place*. The right place means not just the stores and shops with the highest turnover, but also the best locations within the store. In self service stores, some shelves are in 'strategic' positions which attract greater customer attention, and merchandising staff attempt to secure these strategic positions for the manufacturer's products. Due to the costs of merchandising work, these efforts will usually be restricted to the larger, more profitable stores with a high turnover.

(b) *At the right time*. In most stores, there are some days when demand is at a peak. Merchandising staff should try to ensure that if a strategic location is only available for a limited time, then this time should include a period of peak demand. Similarly, it is important to ensure that seasonal goods (Christmas items or Easter eggs) receive prominent display at the right time of year.

7.9 As an aspect of sales promotion activity, merchandising is designed to give a short-term boost to sales. It is essentially short-term in its intended effect and the retailer will later move the product away from prime locations, or give it a reduced amount of shelf space.

7.10 Other items associated with merchandising activities are *point of sale material*. The point of sale is the shop where goods are sold, and point of sale material is used in sales promotion. It includes:

(a) posters (for example holiday posters in travel agents' offices);
(b) showcards (for example dispensers from which customers can take the product);
(c) mobiles (display items suspended from the ceiling of, say, a supermarket);
(d) dump bins or dumpers: a product is dumped into a bin, suggesting a bargain offer;
(e) dummy packs;
(f) metal or plastic stands (to display the birthday cards etc of one manufacturer, say);
(g) plastic shopping bags;
(h) 'crowners' - the price tags or slogans slipped over the neck of a bottle.

---

## Case example

'Show me the money' say the marketing departments of Hollywood's studios, echoing the catchphrase from the hit film 'Jerry Maguire', but a more accurate version would go 'Show me other people's money'. More and more, films represent a coming together of marketing activity involving toy and clothing makers, retailers, pop bottlers and fast food companies. This involves what the trade refers to as an 'event picture'. Hollywood studios typically spend two thirds of the films production costs on promoting its release - but add-on promotion from product licensees adds hugely to this spend. '101 Dalmations' for example, garnered an additional $135m extra from this source including $35m from McDonald's television slots advertising 'Happy Meals' linked to the film. Perhaps more important for the Disney company, the franchise on the dalmation, taken out by Disney in 1961 with the cartoon version, was extended for the foreseeable future, by which time the ungenerous reviews of this particular version will be forgotten.

The relation between the film and the merchandising surrounding it is clearly changing. As relations with merchandising companies grows ever more symbiotic and the industry becomes ever more vertically integrated, is the film still the driving force?

Industry specialists still maintain that, even if a production is not a hit, it still has to make a big enough 'marketing impression'. Today, drawing cinema audiences and stirring enough interest to reap later rewards from home video sales is not enough. 'Event pictures' are a marketing process, and they work only if they succeed in paying back all the money from sponsors and franchisees. which has gone into their production. The 'Jurassic Park' sequel, 'The Lost World' began trailing 1,000 manufacturers and retailers representatives through the studio sets two years before the film was released in May 1997. A book several hundred pages long and costing half a million dollars to produce was issued to lay down the precise delineations of the film logo, colour schemes, dinosaur types and postures. 800 licensees were signed up, including Hasbro and Mercedes Benz (their first entertainment related promotion). Competition surrounding this type of merchandising has become very intense. Retailers are conservative and nervous about taking multi-million dollar buying decisions months before the film comes out, so studios try to co-opt leading brand manufacturers as licensees, to reassure the retailers, while they also put in a significant amount of promotional effort into toys, T-shirts and burger wrappers which 'trail' the upcoming production, and put pressure on cinema operators to open the film on preferred dates such as public holiday weekends.

Event films which lend themselves to sequels are preferred because they can generate an endless stream of merchandising revenue. Batman toys have figured in the top 10 sellers in the US every year since 1989. The brand is now worth $1billion per year to Warners, whether there is a film out or not.

Generating or reviving merchandisable screen properties is now a prime goal at most of Hollywood's leading studios. In the late 1980s, annual retail sales of Bugs Bunny merchandise were $200m a year. By 1997 this has risen to $4billion a year at retail prices.

Is there a danger of saturation? Disney think not. In 1996, while most studios were content to back one full blown event film per year, Disney squeezed in 'The Hunchback of Notre Dame'. 'Toy Story' and '101 Dalmations' into 1996. According to a spokesperson: 'This is a global business for us now. We are coming close to the time when we will be opening these films on the same date around the world.' *(Adapted from The Financial Times, February 1997)*

### Exercise 9

Everything that you have read about advertising, branding and sales promotion will sound very familiar, but would you have examples at your fingertips in an examination? Pick some products that you buy regularly or are interested in and make a point of tracking their advertising and promotion over a period of several months. Note how posters and shop displays back up TV campaigns, and see whether the campaign attracts any 'free' publicity in the form of press coverage, or references by public figures like TV comedians. Is the promotion talked about at work or in the pub? Has the slogan caught on and fallen into general usage?

The more you look, the more you will see.

## Exhibitions and trade fairs

7.11 Britain has been fairly backward in its use of exhibitions and trade fairs and even the new Birmingham centre does not rival the foreign exhibition centres of Hanover or Geneva.

7.12 The advantage of exhibitions to the visitor are that:

(a) the products can be viewed and demonstrated;

(b) a wide range of up to date products can be seen in one place and expert assistance is available for answering queries.

7.13 The advantages of exhibitions to the manufacturer are:

(a) they attract many visitors who are potential customers; prospective customers are met quickly and cheaply;

(b) they are a valuable public relations exercise;

(c) they are useful for launching a new product, or testing a market;

(d) they sell the product.

7.14 Disadvantages of exhibitions are:

(a) they are costly to prepare and operate;

(b) they take salesmen away from normal selling duties because exhibition stands must be permanently staffed.

7.15 Exhibitions are more naturally suited to some products than to others. Where demonstrations are particularly valuable to the prospective customer (for agricultural equipment for example) or at least visual inspection and expert information are required (for example motor cars) exhibitions are a valuable means of sales promotion.

## 8 PUBLICITY

8.1 Publicity is defined as being any form of non-paid, non-personal communication, and like advertising, it involves dealing with a mass audience. Although some components are 'paid for', we can also include *public relations* under this general heading since it is concerned more generally with building and maintaining an understanding between the organisation and the general public.

8.2 Publicity offers a number of benefits to the organisation - so long as it is *good* publicity. It has no major time costs, it provides access to a large audience and the message is considered to have a high degree of credibility. The information is seen as coming from an independent or quasi-independent source as opposed to from the company itself.

8.3 Traditionally, publicity and public relations were seen as being centred around producing regular, informative press releases and building up good contacts with journalists. As a consequence, its importance has often been underestimated. However, with increasing pressure on advertising space, time and costs, the importance of publicity seems likely to increase.

---

### Case example

A PR campaign to bombard the Japanese public with scientific studies detailing the health benefits of eating chocolate led to a 30% increase in chocolate bar production within a year. The westernisation of Japanese food habits meant that there was great potential for increasing cocoa consumption, and in terms of the total market, $4 billion was chocolate, out of a total of $34 billion total confectionery market. Sales rose by 20% year on year, while sugared cocoa production rose by 265%, and milk chocolate production by 30%.

Competition is stiff, and sugar is expensive in Japan, although Japanese do not regard chocolate as an expensive confection. Japanese confections, such as rice crackers and youkan, made from sugar and beans, are fierce competition as the snack of choice at 'o-yatsu' (afternoon tea). The Chocolate and Cocoa Association of Japan responded by assembling an industry task force, and holding a series of symposiums also supported by the Ministries of Agriculture and Health. This task force advertised and gained huge media coverage for the findings of studies which indicated that sugar was not linked to tooth decay and obesity. PR experts also targeted schools and members of the Japanese Nutritionists Society. The result has been a massive increase in the consumption of chocolate by Japanese consumers. *(Adapted from the Financial Times, 11/3/97)*

---

### Sponsorship

8.4 In marketing terms, sponsorship can be seen as a form of marketing communication. It stands alongside media advertising, personal selling, public relations and other forms of sales promotion as a method by which companies can communicate with potential customers.

8.5 It can be argued that the objective of sponsorship should be communication and is therefore seen as one form of marketing communication. There are many other influences on sales, and it is extremely difficult to isolate the effects on them of specific marketing activity. There are, however, several other potential *advantages* of sponsorship, besides awareness creation in a wider audience than could be reached cost-effectively by other forms of advertising and the media coverage generated by the sponsored events.

(a) Distributor and customer relations.

(b) The impact of sponsoring 'worthy' events can have a wide positive effect on the attitude of *potential customers* toward the company's services.

(c) Sponsorship has wider implications in public relations terms. It demonstrates good *corporate citizenship* and it may also have a positive impact on the company's employees.

---

### Case example

A clock to count off the last 1,000 days of the millennium at Greenwich also marked the surprising marketing success of a small, family run British company in the face of massive Swiss and Japanese competition. Accurist has seized pride of place on the meridian which has become the centre of world timekeeping as a brilliant international branding opportunity. MD Andrew Loftus sees it as just the latest coup for a company famous for its marketing. This began in 1983 with the sponsorship of the telephone 'speaking clock', which resulted in 2 billion callers hearing the brand name, and securing the position as official watches for the pilots of the newly launched supersonic airliner Concorde.

The company has since become Britain's biggest watch brand in terms of value, with sales increases of more than 1,000% since the early eighties, with more than 1.5 million units accounting for group turnover of more than £25m. In the lucrative but highly fragmented UK watch market, Accurist is brand leader with more than 40% of sales of watches worth more than £40. The Millennium celebrations presented too good an opportunity to miss; the company saw offering to site the special clock as a way of demonstrating how it was pushing forward its technological developments, as well as being the official centre of the world's millennium celebrations. The arrangement has led to a partnership with Greenwich Millennium 2000, organisers of the big event, and has already produced advertising slogans such as 'Accurist. The standard by which all watches are set' and 'Accurist Mean Time'. More than £5m will be spent over the next two years to maintain the effectiveness of this campaign. The company will seek to extend and exploit the commercial effect with the launch of a range of replica Accurist Millennium Countdown Clocks as corporate and personal gifts and is already selling countdown watches in many foreign countries, including Japan and Switzerland!! *(Adapted from The Independent on Sunday, 30/3/97)*

---

### Case example

This example leads into the next chapter on combining the marketing mix. You will, of course, know all about Pepsi's $500m programme to turn its image from red to blue (mentioned previously). Some interesting points are made by Peter Martin in an article in the *Financial Times* (4 April 1996), from which the following extracts are taken.

'The cola wars, to paraphrase von Clausewitz, are the continuation of price competition by others means.

When PepsiCo launches a $500m (£328m) programme to turn its international image from red to blue as it did this week, or Cola-Cola changes it taste as it did briefly in the 1980s, both companies are reacting to the oligopolist's visceral instinct: anything is better than competing on price.

'Pepsi's more glamorous set of images has given it - at least so its marketers believe - a stronger hold over the most voracious consumers of soft drinks, young men. It has even succeeded in selling them a diet drink, traditionally something they have scorned as a girls' taste. Pepsi Max manages to avoid the metallic after-taste traditionally associated with diet colas; but just as important has been the relentlessly masculine image which Pepsi has attached to it.

So successful has Pepsi Max been that the company is now using some of the same colour and advertising themes for its main brand as it seeks to tackle Coke's international dominance. The new blue Pepsi livery, launched this week at Gatwick airport outside London, will be in 20 countries by the end of the year and in the rest of Pepsi's markets outside North America by the end of 1997.

In making this switch, Pepsi is taking a number of risks. First, red is traditionally regarded as a stronger colour than blue for mass-market products. In many markets, the leading brand has attempted to appropriate red; when IBM, Big Blue itself, set up its own high street shops in the 1980s, it plumped for a red decor in deference to the advice of its retailing advisers. For Pepsi to make a play with blue represents a studiedly unconventional move. Second, by attempting to transfer the values successfully developed for Pepsi Max to the main brand, the company risks weakening the unique attributes of the diet drink without strengthening Pepsi itself.

Such image transplants are always risky. But in making these calculations, Pepsi can comfort itself that it is back on the familiar ground of image manipulation and "psychic benefits". The price competition genie, which Pepsi once summoned up so effectively, is back in its bottle.'

Note the interaction between the different parts of the marketing mix: price, product (particularly packaging) and promotion.

## Chapter roundup

- If the salesperson is to fulfil his or her role as a facilitator of *communication* between the firm and the market, three dimensions of effective communication must exist:
  - between the sales person and the customer;
  - between the sales person and the firm;
  - between the sales management and the salesperson.
- Any effective communication relies on all the *elements* of the process working: the sender; the receiver; the message; the channel of communication; the feedback system.
- The *salesperson* needs to be particularly aware of the silent communication of body language - paying attention not just to what is being said, but how it is said.
- The recognition that the *sales team* will personify the company to the client should be evident in the recruitment, selection and training of the salesforce. The ability of the personal seller to provide feedback and market intelligence to management is an important benefit, which must be encouraged and used.
- *Management* must also recognise their need to keep sales staff informed and inspired.
- *Promotion* comprises advertising, sales promotion, publicity and the sales force's activities. Firms use varying combinations of these activities depending on the nature of their business.
- Promotional activity may have either a *pull effect* (whereby consumers ask distributors for the product) or a *push effect* (whereby distributors decide to stock it) or both.
- The *AIDA model* suggests that promotion moves consumers from awareness to interest to desire to action. Advertising may therefore be informative, persuasive or reminding. It must be able to differentiate the advertised product rather than advertise the generic product.
- The *six steps* in a promotion campaign are:
  - identify the target audience;
  - specify the promotional message;
  - select media;
  - schedule media;
  - set the promotional budget;
  - evaluate promotional effectiveness.

  You should be able to discuss each of these steps, in particular the factors involved in selecting media, the factors affecting the promotional message and the difficulty of determining the optional amount of, and the effect of, advertising.
- *Branding* is used to differentiate products and so build consumer and distributor loyalty. It is most relevant in marketing mass market items in competition with very similar generic products.
- *Sales promotion* activities have a more direct but possibly shorter term effect on sales than does advertising. There are many techniques, which you should be able to list and discuss. Merchandising is a particularly important one. Sales literature, exhibitions and trade fairs are also important, but with a less immediate effect on sales.
- Finally, promotion may include *public relations* exercises, including sponsorship. The purpose of this type of activity is not directly to increase sales but to increase and improve the profile of the firm and its products, particularly in its target market.

## Test your knowledge

1 What communication techniques might you expect to be used as part of the promotional mix? (see para 1.2)

2 In what way could poor encoding of a sales message impair sales performance? (2.3)

3 What attitude to feedback should the salesperson be encouraged to adopt? (2.12)

4 What kind of information might management expect from the sales team? (2.13)

5 Why is management communication so important in the area of sales? (2.15)

6 What is a push effect, in promotional terms? (2.25)

7 Distinguish between advertising and sales promotion. (2.31, 2.33)

8 What is the AIDA effect? (3.1)

9 List three main types of advertising. (3.5)

10 What is the role of advertising in industrial markets? (3.11)

11 What is likely to be the effect of a health promotion campaign which tries to frighten its target audience into changing its behaviour? (4.9)

12 Which organisation measures radio audiences? (4.13)

13 What are 'frequency' and 'reach'? (4.21)

14 List the conditions for successful advertising. (5.2)

15 How can a firm make best use of an advertising agency? (5.7)

16 Why is branding used? (6.6)

17 Give examples of sales promotion activities aimed at (i) the retailer; (ii) the sales force. (7.4)

18 What is merchandising? (7.7)

19 Give examples of point of sale material. (7.10)

20 Give reasons for engaging in sponsorship. (8.5)

**Now try illustrative questions 18 to 22 at the end of the Study Text**

# MARKETING FUNDAMENTALS IN ACTION

*For most parts of each Study Text, we take a look at the subject matter covered in the light of real companies, either to offer more detail, or to give an understanding of the wider corporate context.*

We have looked at various examples of marketing theory in practice covering all the chapters in this part of the Study Text. Here, we can look at some disasters that have occurred in marketing. Although these are very funny (and provide some welcome light relief), there is a serious side to how and why each disaster occurred. What is surely *really* worrying is how easy it is for such debacles to happen!

The following points are based on an article by Rhys Williams in the *Independent* on 1 June 1995. Think about why they happened and how they should have been avoided.

## Great marketing disasters of all time

### *QE2*

Unfinished bathrooms, workmen drilling all hours, equipment strewn around the corridors. And that was first class. The pride of Cunard, the QE2, set sail from Southampton bound for New York and the Caribbean, its £30m refit still incomplete. 'It is like being in an unfinished Spanish hotel except that we are about 900 miles west of Ireland and we can't get off', said one disgruntled passenger, who had paid £7,400 for the privilege of being woken at 8am by a man with a Black and Decker. The dream cruise turned into a public relations nightmare, with passengers in the US now suing Cunard for millions.

### *Hoover*

To quote Leonard Hadley, chairman of Hoover's US parent company Maytag, the UK company's free flights offer was like 'a bad accident and you can't determine what was in the driver's mind'. Hoover offered any customer who spent a minimum of £100 on its products two free flights to Europe and the US. The promotion attracted more than double the anticipated applications, leading to the dismissal of three senior managers and a £19m provision to cover its costs. Apart from failing to take out insurance, Hoover's biggest mistake was to offer too good a bargain. The market in second-hand vacuum cleaners is still recovering from over-supply.

### *Perrier*

'What a fiasceau' - one of the headlines from the avalanche of press coverage that followed Perrier's decision to withdraw its sparkling water from worldwide sale after tiny amounts of the cancer-inducing chemical benzene were picked up by scientists in the US. The problem was traced back to a careless employee at the company's plant in Vergeze who splashed the wrong cleaning fluid on to a bottling machine. Around 140 million bottles were taken off the shelves for two months, costing the company at least £20m.

### *Mercury*

Another in the Hoover vintage. In a bid to transform the mobile phone from the strict preserve of irritating men in restaurants into a mainstream consumer good, operators went into promotional overdrive before Christmas last year. Mercury promised that anyone buying its One-to-One mobile telephones after 8 November would be entitled to unlimited free calls worldwide on Christmas Day. However, massive demand meant its network seized up and many callers were unable to get through. Mercury reported that at least 20 people had spent more than 12 hours on the telephone.

### *Persil*

To the long-time boast that Persil washes whiter, Lever Brothers last year added the more dubious claim 'Persil leaves ruddy great holes in your underpants'. Persil Power was rushed out on to the market to steal a march on Procter & Gamble's Ariel Future. Despite the millions of pounds spent on research and advertising, the product was fatally flawed - the manganese 'accelerator' it contained to shorten washing time also had the unfortunate side effect of damaging clothes. Following a public outcry, the product was withdrawn and reformulated. Lever Brothers maintains the technology is 'first class' and 'well ahead of the market', but it is a lead that competitors have happily lived without.

### *Coca-Cola*

Apart from hiring Michael Jackson and Madonna to provide a wholesome image of Pepsi, the biggest gaffe in the Cola wars was Coca-Cola's decision to reformulate the brown stuff's flavour in 1985. On 23 April, Roberto C Goizueta, the Cuban-born chairman of Coca-Cola, told a flashy New York gathering that the $7.5bn consumer giant was changing the flavour of Brand Coke for the first time in 99 years. 'The best has been made even better,' he said. Problem was, few agreed. An estimated 150 million people in the US and Canada sampled the new, sweeter, Pepsi-tasting Coke, with nearly two-thirds preferring the original. Consumers were enraged, forcing Coca-Cola to relaunch the old Coke as Coke Classic three months later.

### *The Ford Edsel*

*The Motor Industry's Titanic* was the title of Robert Daines's history of the car that represented the nadir in Ford's fortunes. For many, however, the description fails to capture the true horror of this marketing disaster. Launched in 1957, the car was named after Henry Ford's son (just as well he wasn't called Wilbur). It was massively over-hyped prior to launch, making the cover of *Time* magazine, but the product failed to deliver. Literally - there was a near catastrophic hiatus between marketing push and availability in showrooms. The vehicle itself was an ugly beast. Its radiator grille has regularly been likened to female genitalia. Its reliability was abysmal. By the end of 1959, when the car finally died, 80 per cent of dealers were losing money, with Ford forced to buy back stocks.

### *McDonald's*

Sometimes circumstances beyond a company's control drive a bus through the best laid promotional plans. For the 1984 Olympic Games in Los Angeles, McDonald's issued customers with cards carrying the names of various events. If the US won a gold medal in that event, the customer won a prize. The small matter of a games boycott by most of the Eastern bloc, however, meant that the US collected an unusually high tally of golds and McDonald's customers won an unexpectedly high number of prizes.

### *Ratners*

The best company chairmen are the ones who keep their mouths shut, a point Gerald Ratner well demonstrated seven years ago. As head of the company which, through its Ratners, H Samuel and Ernest Jones chains, grew into the world's biggest jewellery retailer, Ratner transformed the market using cheap products, heavy promotions and accessible shops to attract millions of customers intimidated by traditional jewellery stores. Then in April 1991, he told an Institute of Directors conference the secret of his success. He said he sold some earrings for less than a Marks & Spencer prawn sandwich - 'but I have to say the earrings probably won't last as long', while adding that a £4.95 sherry decanter was 'complete crap'. The tabloids loved it, the shareholders didn't. The company plunged close to collapse, culminating in a £122m loss, 330 store closures and 2,500 job losses. Ratner was ousted 19 months later.

### *Cadbury's*

Until Hoover came along, Cadbury's Golden Egg treasure hunt was always the one considered by the industry as the 'promotion from hell'. In the summer of 1984, the company buried a dozen caskets around the country in locations hinted at by a book of clues. Each casket contained a scroll entitled the finder to a golden egg worth £10,000. More than 100,000 people set about excavating the countryside, with one band of eager diggers straying on to a former high-explosives test range. The biggest problem was not the harm people appeared happy to inflict upon themselves, but the untold damage they did to archaeological sites and monuments across the country. The Rollright Stones near the Oxfordshire-Buckinghamshire border had stood straight since before Christ's birth, but are now leaning because rain seeped under them before the gold-diggers' surrounding holes could be filled in. The promotion was halted after the then Environment Secretary Patrick Jenkin informed Sir Adrian Cadbury of the archaeological vandalism for which his company was indirectly responsible.

### And finally ...

Five urban myths: marketing flops that the sales promotion industry swears blind are true.

### Jellyfish

Simple one for the children here - buy a packet of Chivers jelly, get a goldfish free. Sales went mad, of course, as did the children. When they opened the package sent by Chivers it contained a plastic bag in which hung one dead goldfish. They should have sent them First Class.

### Mad turkeys

Six planes took off and unloaded their cargo of live turkeys over a US city to promote Wild Turkey bourbon whiskey. Hundreds were released before it was realised that turkeys cannot fly.

### Naming problems

Apparently McDonald's ran into all sorts of trouble when it tried to sell the Big Mac to the French - its literal translation rendering Le Gros Mac colloquially translates as the 'big pimp'. Similar woes for the nippy Vauxhall Nova on its introduction to Spain, where 'no va' means 'does not go'.

### Twin dilemma

A local petrol station chain in Scotland offered free fuel for people that looked like each other. A safe promotion, the organisers thought, until they discovered that their town was hosting the annual Twins Society convention.

### Competition fun

The winner of a national newspaper's free conservatory competition lived in a second-floor flat.

# Part C
# Combining the marketing mix

# Chapter 9

# COMBINING THE MARKETING MIX

**This chapter covers the following topics.** *Syllabus reference*



| | | |
|---|---|---|
| 1 | The product life cycle revisited | 3.1 |
| 2 | Marketing mix decisions related to the stages of the life cycle | 3.1 |
| 3 | Assumptions and limitations of the product life cycle concept | 3.1 |
| 4 | The mix in different market places and internationally | 3.2 |
| 5 | Service marketing | 3.2 |



## Introduction

As we saw earlier, the concept of the product life cycle rests on the notion that, from the entry of a product onto the market to the withdrawal of the product, involves a cycle of stages. The stages of the cycle, although they do not correspond precisely to the various types of goods in a wide range of market environments, provide a useful analytical framework within which the marketing mix decisions of a strategic plan can be determined.

The stages can also serve as a theoretical framework for prediction and forecasting in the strategic planning process.

There are four stages, or different patterns of demand, in the cycle, according to the original concept.

(a) Introduction
(b) Growth
(c) Maturity
(d) Decline

Once you have finished this chapter, you should understand the following.

(a) The marketing mix for any product will alter during the product life cycle, to meet the needs of different market places.

(b) There are differences between goods and services. There are said to be three additional 'Ps' in service marketing.

## 1 THE PRODUCT LIFE CYCLE REVISITED

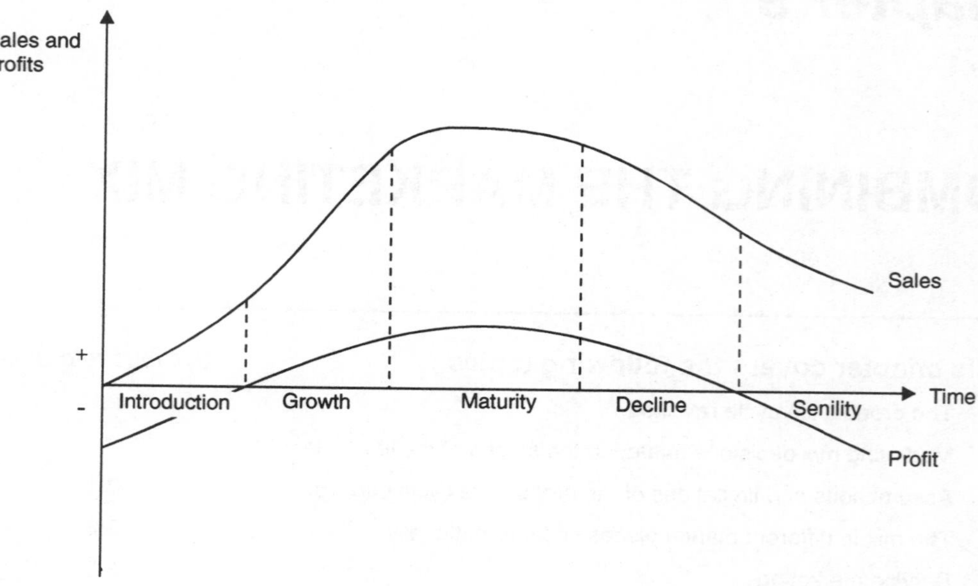


### Stages of the life cycle

1.1 According to the theory of the product life cycle, each of the stages noted in the introduction above involves different market conditions. When the product has been newly introduced, for instance, consumer awareness will be extremely limited, and it will be necessary for promotion to be geared towards *telling an identified target group that the product exists*, and *communicating a selling proposition* to them, involving the needs the product can fulfil and the satisfactions it offers. Prices may need to be adjusted to take account of the unresponsiveness and initial lack of demand within the marketplace; distribution channels may be very limited because there is not yet a proven market for a product, and so on. Later these policies will need to be adjusted as the product becomes first established and, later, hopefully, successful. The marketing mix, then, will have to be varied according to the stage of the life cycle at which the product has arrived.

#### *When do stages begin and end?*

1.2 The points at which these stages begin and end are somewhat vague. The duration of the stages (and consequently the profile of the demand curve which is associated with these stages) is likely to vary a great deal, according to product type and market conditions, since how the 'life' of the product works out can be affected by the consumer world into which it is born, how it is received and how competitive products behave.

1.3 For each product, then, the life cycle is a stylised and generally idealised representation of how such products develop. In reality:

(a) strategic decisions must be taken for each stage;

(b) critical changes (movement from one cycle stage to the next) must be identified; and

(c) the overall trajectory of the lifecycle curve must be calculated;

in order to arrive at the appropriate business decisions.

*The product life cycle concept and its mix implications*

| | *Introduction* | *Growth* | *Maturity* | *Decline* |
|---|---|---|---|---|
| *Product* | Initially poor quality. Product design and development key to success. No standard product and frequent design changes. | Competitors' products have marked quality differences and technical differences. Quality improves. Product reliability may be important. | Products become more standardised and differences between products less distinct. | Products even less differentiated. Quality becomes more variable. |
| *Prices (and profits)* | High advertising and sales promotion costs. High prices possible. | Increasing numbers. | Mass market saturation. Repeat buying becomes significant. Brand image also important. | Customers are sophisticated buyers of a product they know and understand well. |
| *Promotion* | High advertising and sales promotion costs. High prices possible. | High advertising costs still, but as a % of sales these are falling. Prices falling. | Markets become more segmented. Segmentation and extending the maturity of the life cycle can be key strategies. | Less money spent on advertising and sales promotion. |
| *Place* | Few distribution channels. | Expanding distribution channels very important. | Fully developed network, but less successful channels can be cut. | Few distribution channels, dissatisfied intermediaries. |
| *Customers* | Initial customers willing to pay high prices need to be convinced about buying. | Increasing numbers. | Mass market saturation. Repeat buying becomes significant. Brand image also important. | Customers are sophisticated buyers of a product they know and understand well. |

## 2 MARKETING MIX DECISIONS RELATED TO THE STAGES OF THE LIFE CYCLE

*Examined 6/96, 12/96, 12/97*

2.1 At every stage of the lifecycle of the product, each component of the marketing mix, then, involves distinctive problems and necessitates particular kinds of policies, according to the strategic objectives of the company.

### Introduction stage of the product life cycle

2.2 Here, failure risks and actual product failures are high. Although business and initial sales may be slow there is, in many cases of new product introduction, little or no competition, since at least some new products are innovative. Purchasers at this stage are innovators and are a small proportion of the total marketplace, with different tastes and behaviour from the rest of the population. Profit margins may well be small (because of low sales and the need to recover start-up costs). All marketing expenditure, at this stage, will be very heavy. Strategically, companies will be aiming to recover these costs in the medium or long term. All aspects of the mix are involved, however, and a number of factors may necessitate choosing between a number of strategic alternatives.

*Product*

2.3 Quality may be problematic. Production processes and the performance of the product in the field are still naturally discovering flaws and problems which may have been unsuspected during the product development programme. Quality problems may also occur in the process of delivery and in responses to customer problems. A high failure rate is general in almost all product areas. Few competitive products, if any, are around when a product is newly launched. The risk element is still predominant and until there are apparent profits to be made from the concept, competitors will stay off the bandwagon!

*Place*

2.4 Distribution is limited but growing during the introductory stage. For many companies, dealerships and space on shelves has to be fought for, with special deals and intensive personal selling.

*Price*

2.5 The distinctiveness of a product, or 'product differentiation factor' will be a key consideration in the formulation of a pricing policy. Products which have a very strong differentiation from potential competitors, which is likely to be sustained over the medium or long term, will have different pricing options than products which are likely to attract 'me too' competitors very quickly.

2.6 Most products have two options in pricing decisions.

(a) *Skimming* involves asking a high price of a small group of consumers (early adopters) and is used when a product is unusually distinctive (like the Apple Macintosh) and demand is inelastic (that is, unlikely to be strongly affected by price changes). When price reductions occur, they are often related to careful identification and targeting of new groups of consumers.

(b) *Penetration* is used as a pricing strategy when demand is elastic, competition is fierce and product differentiation will not provide a lasting competitive edge. Prices are set low in order to attract the largest number of consumers at an early stage of the lifecycle and acquire market share.

These are not, in either case, strategies aiming at short-term profit maximisation, but are rather looking to short-term survival and development, and the long term and medium-term achievement of profitability and success, building the brand into a profit-making line.

*Promotion*

2.7 Directed at creating product awareness, promotion here may involve relatively high spending and the heavy use of personal selling in order to generate interest and commitment both from end consumers and intermediaries in the distribution process. For consumer goods, advertising expenditure will be very high, relative to other costs and returns.

2.8 Between introduction and growth stages there occurs what marketers refer to as the 'shake-out', when products and even companies disappear from the scene. Which products survive has a strong impact on the ways in which the strategies of other products in the market place are formulated.

**Exercise 1**

Here is a newspaper article about the launch of a new product.

### 'Hewlett-Packard to launch new desk-top range

By Louise Kehoe in San Francisco

Hewlett-Packard will today launch two product lines to expand in the corporate computing market.

HP will announce an enterprise desktop computer combining the high performance of a scientific workstation with the lower cost and software standards of personal computers. The company will introduce a line of network servers, priced to compete with PC servers but offering performance that competes with mini-computers.

The new computers, based on a low-cost version of HP's PA-Risc microprocessor chip, are aggressively priced. The desktop machines, which start at $3,995, will compete with high-end PCs. The new HP servers, which range in price from $7,569 to $14,919, outperform PC servers while undercutting the price of mini-computers, such as the IBM AS/400.

HP's new computers are aimed at companies adopting the client server networked computing model.

"These are the machines needed by companies that are re-engineering their businesses," says Mr Willem Roelants, general manager of HP's computer systems operations. "The fundamental idea of re-engineering is to give employees tools so that one person can complete a job, such as a customer transaction without having to pass it on to several different people in different departments."

Sales of enterprise workstations are rising sharply according to a market report issued last week by Frost and Sullivan, the US market research group. World sales were expected to reach $25bn per year by 1999, the researchers predicted.

HP's challenge in the enterprise workstation market is to displace high-end PCs. To do so, it will offer compatibility with programs designed for the Microsoft Windows environment as well as UNIX applications. HP will introduce multi-media programs for video and voice applications.

HP has designed its new desktop and server computers so that they can run Microsoft's new Windows NT operating system.

Lotus Development, Applix and Clarity have developed programs for the new HP desk-top machines.

The new HP desktop computers will run standard PC programs and UNIX application programs.'

Analyse this *Financial Times* article in terms of the four Ps (and indeed any other aspect of marketing that you are now familiar with).

#### Solution

One point that you may have missed is that the article itself, which appeared in the *Financial Times,* is a fine piece of promotion in the form of public relations: it sounds as if it is taken verbatim from HP's press release. There are numerous other more obvious points to make about products satisfying needs, marketing strategy, pricing and so on.

---

## Growth stage of the life cycle

2.9 Those products which survive the introduction phase will find that during growth competition will increase, and competitive 'copy-cat' or 'me too' products will try to capture part of what has proved to be a viable market. The product will face a struggle to retain distinctiveness and rising sales are linked to increasing profitability. This may well attract the attention of larger and more powerful companies, who may try to take over the company or the product which has proved successful.

### *Product*

2.10 The line becomes established during this phase as important attributes are identified and consolidated, and the product developments and 'tweaking' which was still going on in the introductory stage are left behind. Product quality has improved and reliability is also important to the growing volume of consumers.

*Place*

2.11 Distribution is an important aspect of the fight to establish a particular brand within an increasingly competitive section of the marketplace. Dealership and distribution outlets are the key to many markets which are served by a smaller number of retail chains - as for instance in parts of the UK retail sector, where a small number of supermarket chains account for a very large proportion of grocer sales. Gaining space on the shelves of these outlets is life or death for many types of product, since fast moving consumer goods (FMCGs) are bought by consumers who are spending less time on shopping and visiting smaller numbers of shops than they used to do in the past. To miss out on one supermarket chain will close off a large section of the possible buying public. For makers of certain products gaining shelf space with one particular retailer may be the difference between great success and almost certain failure. In the case of prepared meal products, for instance, Marks & Spencer gained 60% of total sales in the UK market at one stage, although they accounted for only 6% of the total grocery trade. Gaining acceptance on to their shelves was clearly important for any manufacturer.

*Price*

2.12 It is during this phase, probably towards the end, that maximum profitability is achieved by the brand. Brand shares will have achieved their 'ambient' level and become stable, and competitors within the same market have accepted the way in which the market is divided, by and large. As a consequence prices stabilise and some profit taking can happen, while prices may well fall towards the end of this stage, to gather in a few more prospects.

*Promotion*

2.13 As in the preceding stage, advertising and promotion feature heavily here and are a significant part of marketing budgets. Since consumers are now aware of the existence of this product type, however, the messages involved seek to generate awareness and appreciation of a *brand* or trade name. In addition it is now more important for the product to be generating profit, so that expenditures are not allowed to reach the same levels which were found during the introductory phase. When a large company is thinking in terms of a long-term strategy of market dominance, however, gaining very large proportions of the available market and building up consumer loyalty may yet outweigh immediate profit.

2.14 The end of the growth stage, axiomatically, involves the beginning of decline or stagnation.

## Maturity stage of the life cycle

*Examined 6/95*

2.15 At any one time, most markets are dominated and composed for the most part of mature products. The most successful products, as we can see by looking around us, persist, and have been earning large profits for the major companies who control them for many years. Marketing strategy in the maturity stage is a major preoccupation of decision-makers. This stage is longer than any other and it is the stage, according to the theory of the lifecycle, when the bulk of profits are realised. Sales may be continuing to grow, but the rapid increases of the growth stage are left behind; new ways to increase profits are sought.

2.16 Problems of strategy are a product of the success of products. Competition increases and crowds the marketplace, so maintaining competitive edge through differentiation becomes difficult. This is further complicated by 'wearout' effects, as customer needs and preferences may shift, and by environmental changes such as increased costs for raw materials, production processes or new entrants in the market as a consequence of, for example, more open trade policies bringing in low-cost 'me-too' competition.

### Case example

This is what happened to Timex, who dominated the low price end of the US market for watches until the 1970s when imported digital watches, and shifts in consumer tastes towards more fashion-related and prestigious brands, cut swathes through its market share.

2.17 Changes may also provide the opportunity to use the mix as a means to increase profits and open up new markets. Product improvements are a regular consequence of increased competition and market conditions may also provide the opportunity for growth.

### Exercise 2

Gold Blend is a mature product. A recent Nescafé Gold Blend promotion included three mini-packs of After Eight with a jar of coffee.

Why does this represent the producers of Nescafé taking advantage of new opportunities?

### Solution

Because Nestlé, who make Nescafé, had only relatively recently taken over Rowntree, who make After Eight. Both the coffee and the mini-packs were being promoted, of course.

Watch out for other examples of novel ways of marketing products that are very familiar to you.

### Case example

We may be moving towards a McWorld as McDonalds opens more and more outlets - 18,700, serving 33 million people, with 3,200 new restaurants opening in 1996 - but in America, the market is beginning to become saturated. Restaurants outside America now account for more than half its operating profit, compared to one fifth ten years ago. Competition at home has become too keen.

Like for like sales have fallen steadily in McDonalds' US outlets, and it seems to be due to saturation in a mature, slow growing market.

Companies like McDonalds, Burger King and Wendys are caught in a competitive spiral - to boost sales, all are forced to seek a continual expansion of outlet numbers, if only to prevent the others from seizing prime sites. In an effort to fill every possible market niche, McDonalds is packing high streets with tiny McDonald Express 'storefront' restaurants, adding McDonalds to petrol stations and building outlets in Wal-mart stores. 'Happy Meals' for children are even being served on United Airlines flights.

Many franchisees are beginning to complain that this is damaging their existing business, as the company embarks on a domestic strategy of trying to put a McDonalds within four minutes of every American. McDonalds have been paying compensation to franchisees who have lost out.

The firm's quality, cleanliness and service - qualities central to the legendary marketing expertise of Ray Kroc, builder of the modern company - have been seriously affected by the expansion. Franchisees have been chided by the centre for a decline in standards.

But it is price which is most dangerous for the company, and this is a deciding factor with many burger eaters. Burger King has been undercutting McDonalds for many years, and now the margins appear to be shrinking to dangerous levels. McDonalds have responded by cutting their operating costs, which have been rising faster than revenues. By simplifying its restaurants, McDonalds has already reduced the average cost of a new one to $1.2m in the USA, a 25% reduction over six years. Menus have also been simplified.

At the same time, the company has moved up market. The biggest product launch since the Big Mac of 1968, has resulted in the Arch Deluxe, a belated assault on the $5 billion a year US market for burgers that come with bacon, lettuce and tomato. This is clearly a bid to lure more adults into the restaurants. 100 million were sold in the first month but it is not yet clear whether this product will be effective in creating more sales for McDonalds.

Marketing has also been stepped up. McDonalds will sponsor the Olympic Games in 1998 (winter) and 2000 (summer) - this global agreement will shut out its rivals - and the company has also signed a ten year alliance with the Disney organisation, damaging the rise of Burger King, which had seen its sales soar thanks to film promotions linked to Disney films.

How much of this is a matter of obsessiveness and pride? In the growing foreign markets, McDonalds faces no big organised competitors, while their global distribution, purchasing, operational and marketing infrastructure is the most cost effective in the business. Growth is proceeding at 20% per annum. But all may not be plain sailing, and some markets abroad seem likely to be more difficult to exploit than others. One of the main reasons for the continuous push for domination in the home market is the degree to which the lessons learned in that difficult area can be exported, and used to deal with difficulties abroad. The aim internationally is to achieve US levels of patronage - 7% of Americans eat in a McDonalds every day. That may well be a target which can be met, if the US experience is anything to go by. *(Adapted from The Economist, 29/7/96)*

*Products*

2.18 Market shares for the product have typically stabilised during the growth stage, and with market growth fairly limited, products are often modified or used as the basis for extension lines; for example, new colours or styles for a car, new flavours or basic ingredients (vegetable kievs, curried beans) in the case of food products. Differentiation is difficult to achieve at this stage. Since the product is well established and familiar, many consumers may be strongly attached to the product in this form and changing a winning recipe or a familiar appearance can be dangerous!

2.19 A number of ways in which product differentiation can take place relate to the improvement of product and service quality. Market leaders may choose to analyse their market and invest in product development to retain a competitive edge, particularly where active technological development is still going on, and the market looks likely to expand strongly for some time (for instance, information technology markets in the 1990s).

2.20 Defending a market share may best be accomplished by emphasising superior quality or service or by maintaining a low cost or value for money approach.

2.21 Dimensions of differentiation may relate to the following.

| *Product quality differentiators* | *Service quality differentiators* |
|---|---|
| Functional performance, eg speed, economy, comfort, handling for automobiles | Tangibles - appearance of facilities, equipment, personnel, communications materials |
| Durability or safety | Reliability |
| Absence of defects ('conformance') | Responsiveness: willingness to help, speed |
| Variety of features: standard and optional | Assurance: knowledge and courtesy of employees and their ability to convey trust and confidence |
| Reliability: consistency over a number of purchases or continued delivery of promised attributes | Empathy: caring, individualised attention |
| Serviceability: speed of repairing | |
| Fit and finish, reputation of brand name | |

(David A Aaker *Strategic Marketing Management,* 1988 and Zelthaml, Parasuraman and Berry *Delivering Quality Service: Balancing Customer Perceptions and Expectations,* 1990)

Quality is discussed in more detail in Chapter 2 and in Part D of this Study Text.

*Place*

2.22 Distribution here poses its own problems. When the popularity of products falls, it may be difficult to retain their place within retail outlets and there is a fair amount of 'rationalisation' and the replacement of products which cannot compete for their space on the shelf with other, more profitable lines. These 'shakeouts' in the transition from growth to maturity are becoming much more common, as the number of products proliferates within many markets.

2.23 When distribution is a high proportion of the total delivered cost of a product, alternative low cost channels are an effective option. This often involves the limitation, or shifting to the customer, of functions performed by traditional channels to achieve a lower price. For example, in PC hardware and software industries, mail order discounters can offer lower prices because they have fewer fixed costs than retail stores. This means dispensing with customer support services such as technical advice and post-sale service, however.

*Price*

2.24 Prices are beginning to fall, largely as a consequence of battles between established products for market share. This may well involve falling profits too, since the need to promote the product is likely to remain strong. Nevertheless, a low cost position can be an effective strategy at this stage of the lifecycle. This may be achieved by adopting:

(a) a no-frills approach, developing a basic product without the extras;

(b) innovative product design, simplified with standardised components;

(c) cheaper raw materials, compressed fibre rather than 'natural wood' for example;

(d) innovate production processes, such as CAD, CAM, transfer to low labour cost locations;

(e) low cost distribution, such as mail order, direct marketing;

(f) reducing overheads, by downsizing labour and upgrading plant.

*Promotion*

2.25 This can be crucially important for the success of a number of different mature market strategies. Growth extension strategies, for example, rely heavily on effective advertising and promotion. If it is decided to increase penetration, this involves targeting present non-users with a view to converting them into users, and this requires an extensive promotional programme to communicate the benefits of the product to non-user targets. This may include:

(a) advertising through appropriate media;
(b) sales promotions aimed at stimulating trial;
(c) sales effort redirected to new account generation.

2.26 If the strategic objective is to extend use, to increase frequency of usage, or to encourage a wider variety of uses, this will require consumer promotions to offer quantity discounts, multipack purchase, flier programmes and reminder advertising, or the communication of new product uses through information packs, in-store presentations, sales promotions or tie-ins with complementary products.

2.27 A market expansion strategy, in which a product is re-positioned or re-differentiated to focus on untapped or underdeveloped market segments, will often require new advertising, personal selling, packaging and sales promotion campaigns related to the specific interests and concerns of potential customers in these new markets.

### Decline stage of the product life cycle

2.28 Since markets may well remain in the mature stage for decades (although there are some indications that the lifecycle of many product types is becoming shorter), milking or harvesting mature product markets by minimising short run profits makes little sense in the majority of cases. Pursuing this kind of objective usually means substantial cuts in marketing and R&D expenses. That may lead, in turn, to premature losses of volume and market share, and lower profits in the longer term. During the early years of maturity, the main objective should be to maximise the flow of profits over the remaining life of the product market. Critically, this requires that the manager needs to maintain and protect the business's market share. If few new customers buy the product for the first time in a mature market, a business must continue to win its share of repeat purchases from existing customers.

2.29 Even though products are in decline they may still be profitable. Even when, for example, the number of potential customers is declining (for demographic reasons, perhaps), if the company is prepared for the change and adopts appropriate strategies, the market will still remain profitable for years to come.

2.30 Three factors are crucial in determining the attractiveness of declining markets. These are:

(a) conditions of demand;
(b) rivalry determination; and
(c) exit barriers.

2.31 Demand may decline swiftly (as when a product becomes overtaken by superior technology which is rapidly accepted by the markets) or relatively slowly (when new technology does not offer sufficient extra benefit to existing users to make switching cost effective). Slow decline is more likely to promise continuing profit. This is also likely to be associated with 'pockets' of enduring demand, with consumers who are brand loyal (who have invested effort and time into 'learning' about a product, for example) and with stable prices, which do not threaten premiums or actually fail to recover costs.

---

#### Case example

Losses of FFr743million in 1995-6 have forced the Club Mediterranee leisure group to accept that it is entering a new era. The fifty year old company has become one of the symbols of French culture, and one of its most widely copied exports. The idea of 'Sea, Sex and Sun' was central to the new leisure-oriented lifestyle which became accepted in the 1960s and 70s. When France was dominated by rigid social norms, Club Med symbolised escapism and informality, including compulsory use of first names, and tutoiement, the familiar form of personal address 'tu' being de rigeur in the holiday villages. In a country not known for its emphasis on friendly customer services, this organisation achieved unparalleled celebrity for friendliness, with highly trained and helpful staff. Packages included limitless food and innumerable sporting activities in the price, and this format has been endlessly copied by other tour operators. This was coupled with superb locations, and the overall image become an essential part of the spirit of those times, not least in its communal 'hippy-like' lifestyle-shared huts, group activities and large dining tables designed to break down the barriers.

This is a successful formula, but one of the reasons it has kept ahead until recently is the recognition that it needs to adapt to the changing needs of loyal clients as they grow older. The average age of the Club Med client has increased to 37, and many have married and raised children. Bedrooms have been upgraded, telephones installed and dining tables shrunk to take two rather than the mandatory eight.

When first created in the 1950s the Club was non-profit making, offering holidays in 'tent villages'. By 1966 it was quoted on the French Stock Exchange, and profits peaked in 1989-90 at FFr 400m. Consumer tastes have led the way in which the company has developed, however; its latest catalogue still offers holidays in spartan huts in Tunisia reserved for those over the age of 17, but there are also luxury apartments in Bora Bora, Internet sessions and massage sessions for stressed Parisians on short breaks in its French resorts. More than 30 offer creche facilities. As other companies have realised, relationships with customers are essential in the development of long-term business, and a product concept must always seek to identify and meet customer needs. *(Adapted from the Financial Times, 24/3/97)*

---

### Exercise 3

Suppose you have a large number of very good quality black and white television sets. You find that your market has dried up. What can you do with the TVs?

### Solution

The UK market may have dried up but there are plenty of countries less advanced than the UK that would be glad of your TVs. Failing this, perhaps the best option is to break them up and sell or re-use any components that are suitable. Other possibilities are selling them at such a cheap price that they are seen as a bargain spare set, in case the main family set goes wrong; dressing them up in, say, a 1950s casing so that they can be sold as novelty nostalgia items; perhaps marketing them as a package with a series of classic black and white films on video (though you would be pushing your luck, here). You may have had other ideas.

2.32 Exit barriers, representing the ease or trouble involved in weaker competitors leaving a product market, can create very inhospitable conditions within a declining market. If weak competitors find it hard to leave a product market as demand falls (because, for example, their brand generates a large proportion of their profits, or the plant involved in producing the product represents heavy investment) excess capacity develops, and firms engage in aggressive pricing wars or mount promotional efforts aiming to prop up their volume and hold down unit costs. Whether this is likely to create problems within the market can be assessed by looking at needs for reinvestment, excess capacity within the market, the age of assets, their resale value, amounts of shared facilities, the degree of vertical integration and the amount of single product competition.

2.33 The intensity of potential future rivalry is also important. Even if there are large pockets of continuing demand available, if rivalry is likely to be intense, it may not be wise to remain within the market. This is likely to be influenced by the size and bargaining power of remaining customers, their ability to switch to substitute products or alternative suppliers (how safe is their loyalty to this product?) and potential diseconomies of scale which may be involved in pursuing this declining group of consumers.

2.34 Five options are open to the firm in the decline stage of the life cycle. These are as follows.

(a) *Divestment or liquidation*: recovering some of the investment by selling the business in the earliest possible stages of decline.

(b) *Harvesting*: maximising short-term cash flow; maintain or increase margins, even if this generates quicker decline in market share.

(c) *Maintenance*: when the product line is important to the firm, but the future is uncertain. This is a short-term strategy to maintain market share even at the cost of declining margins.

(d) *Profitable survivor*: aims to increase his share of the declining market, with a view to future gains. Usually when weaker competitors are leaving the market.

(e) *Niche*: identify a small number of segments and concentrate activity into those areas. Again, this is a longer-term strategy.

For all the mix variables at the decline stage, policies vary according to the strategy selected. For most, reduction in cost is the major issue. Divestment or liquidation will obviously preclude contemplation of the other options.

*Product*

2.35 (a) *Harvesting*. R&D expenditure is eliminated, along with capital investment related to the product in question. The product is not being developed.

(b) *Maintenance*. Product and process expenditures are maintained, at least for the short term. Product quality may even be improved.

(c) *Profitable survivor.* Product and process expenditures are maintained, as part of a process of pursuing increased market share. Link up with 'private' (own brand) labels.

(d) *Niche.* Continued product and process R&D aiming at product improvements or modifications to appeal to target segments; extend production into private labels.

### Place

2.36 (a) *Harvesting.* Focus on maintaining existing channels, to retain present customers.

(b) *Maintenance.* Trade promotion focuses on maintaining existing channels and distribution coverage.

(c) *Profitable survivor.* Maintaining existing distribution channels. Own label distribution may be considered.

(d) *Niche.* Maintain distribution channels appropriate for reaching the desired target segment. Try to develop unique channel arrangements to reach targeted customers better.

### Price

2.37 (a) *Harvesting.* Across the board cost cutting in all areas. Price may well be raised to maintain margins.

(b) *Maintenance.* Lower prices, if necessary, to maintain market share. Reduced margins are acceptable under this strategy.

(c) *Profitable survivor.* Lower prices as appropriate to increase market share even with much lower margins.

(d) *Niche.* Prices tied to the nature of the segment targeted. Unit costs are critical, and the means of holding them down (through, for instance, expanding production into private labels) may be part of this strategy.

### Promotion

2.38 (a) *Harvesting.* Sales and marketing budgets are slashed under this strategy. Advertising is reduced or eliminated, trade promotions are cut to the minimum level necessary to prevent rapid loss of distribution coverage, and salesforce efforts are concentrated simply on getting repeat orders from existing customers.

(b) *Maintenance.* Maintenance levels of advertising and sales promotion are continued here, while trade promotions are sustained at a level sufficient to prevent any erosion of existing coverage. The sales force is seeking to get repeat purchases from current users.

(c) *Profitable survivor.* This strategy requires that a signal be sent out to competitors that the firm intends to remain in this market, and increase its share of the market. Advertising and promotion are increased or at least maintained, while increased distribution coverage is sought by strong trade promotions. Attempts are made by the sales force to get competitors' customers to switch.

(d) *Niche.* Advertising, sales promotion and personal selling campaigns are all focused on customers in the target segment(s) with appeals carefully identified and targeted precisely at these new customers.

---

**Exam focus point**

The December 1997 exam (the Test Paper in our Practice & Revision Kit) featured a question on the transition of products from one stage of the life cycle to the next, and you had to do a report explaining the different strategies which could be adopted at each stage. Hopefully the paragraphs above will give you some ideas when you tackle this question. Moreover, the December 1997 mini-case asked you to consider one element of the mix, price, at the growth stage of the life cycle.

---

## 3 ASSUMPTIONS AND LIMITATIONS OF THE PRODUCT LIFE CYCLE CONCEPT

3.1 We have already indicated that the PLC concept has a number of problems associated with its use, as well as obvious benefits in the analysis and formulation of marketing mix strategies. These arise partly because the PLC rests on a number of key, and interrelated, assumptions about how product markets develop and what factors are important in their profitability.

3.2 Key assumptions of the PLC concept are as follows.

| *Assumption* | *But... ?* |
|---|---|
| Products have finite life spans. | When is it over? Many seem to go on and on. Many die very early, too. |
| Strategic objectives and marketing strategy should match the market growth rates. | Strategy also influences and generates growth. |
| For most mass-produced products, costs of production are closely matched to experience (volume) - unit costs go down as production volume increases. | Many markets are never going to reap the benefits of 'economies of scale' - the product may require specialised techniques which can only be carried out by a skilled craftsman. Many markets are too small to warrant large production runs. |
| Expenditures are directly related to rates of growth - products in growth markets will use more resources than products in mature markets. | When do the stages begin and end? The most important shortcoming of the concept is the difficulty of saying when 'growth' finishes and 'maturity' begins. |
| Margins and the cash generated are positively related to the share of the market. Products with high relative share of their market will be more profitable than products with a low share. | (a) Leadership is not the only way to profitability.<br>(b) Not every product can be, or wants to be, a market leader! |
| At the maturity stage, products with high market share generate a stream of cash greater than that needed to sustain them in the market. This cash is available for investment in other products or in research and development to create new products. | Whether this is what the company actually does depends on a whole raft of other issues (market conditions, technical change, competitor activity and so on) rather than simply 'lifecycle' stage. Acceptance of 'mature' status denies the possibility of relaunch or reposition which can happen right into the 'decline' stage! |

3.3 The PLC provides a framework for planning and not a rigid predictive device. The span of the curve involved, the onset of stages, progression through stages - all of these are subject to strategic action by managers, and are subject to influences from the environment which may override the 'logic' of lifecycle development; for instance, catastrophic economic recession, or revolutionary technological change (the digital watch, transistorisation and so on).

3.4 Product lives go on and on. Nylon, as Levitt points out, has been endlessly extended because endless new uses have been found for the generic product. New users can be found, or the product can be re-positioned.

### Case example

Hellman's mayonnaise was a mature product, in terms of the lifecycle, until it was re-launched with promotion targeting it at a younger, broader mass market as a 'fun' product. Market share went from around 10% to 50% in a very short time. In some ways, the new image and the new marketing message created a 'new' product. Certainly, if considering the product to be the end result of a value-adding process, including the symbolic values added by promotion (fun, in the case of Hellman's mayonnaise) and the satisfactions which promotion adds to the product concept, then it is a new product.

3.5 The importance of the product life cycle should not be underestimated. It has been extended and incorporated into a number of other tools for strategic analysis and decision making, such as the Boston Consulting Group Portfolio Analysis method, the General Electric Matrix and Barksdale and Harris, all of which highlight additional issues. Barksdale and Harris, for instance, place great emphasis on differentiating products within lifecycle stages, so that pioneering new products, 'infants', may require a distinct strategy, while for products in declining markets, how profitable they are - whether they are warhorses (high market share) or 'dodos' (lowshare) - will determine how decisions are taken. This approach is based on the idea that the introduction and decline stages are also important, whereas, it is claimed, use of the lifecycle alone tends to lead to other stages being emphasised. The Barkdale and Harris approach claims to be:

(a) comprehensive;

(b) relevant to all levels of analysis;

(c) an improved system for classifying and analysing the full range of market situations;

and aims:

(a) to reveal relative competitive position of products;

(b) to indicate the rate of market growth;

(c) to enable the configuration of strategic alternatives in a general sense if not in specific terms.

3.6 Many of the extensions to the lifecycle idea have made similar claims; some have been more careful. In fact, this approach:

(a) does not eliminate problems of definition;
(b) provides only general guidance, not specifics;
(c) is highly dependent on the quality of the data on which it is based; and
(d) is not prescriptive about the quality of that data.

3.7 Like every other attempt to provide a 'recipe' for prediction, then, this approach is inadequate. The range of approaches which have used the lifecycle concept, however, testify to its enduring appeal and relevance in the attempt to understand the way in which the mix changes over time, and the factors which are influencing how products perform.

### Exercise 4

Apply some of your knowledge of the product life cycle to hifi equipment over the past decade.

### Solution

The compact disc player demonstrates the product life cycle. Initial high prices meant that it took a while to be accepted, but its benefits have led to a considerable growth in sales. CD players have come down considerably in price and the market is reaching maturity. Consequently, turntables and vinyl records are in decline. The CD as a product is now being developed in other fields of data storage, games, film etc, ie another growth stage is developing.

3.8 We turn next to a consideration of how the mix is influenced by where products are marketed; how the mix may vary in different settings.

## 4 THE MIX IN DIFFERENT MARKET PLACES AND INTERNATIONALLY

4.1 Marketers may find that, within a single country, mix variables assume different degrees of importance. For instance, the same media may not be appropriate, effective or available in different regions. Radio may be more effective at reaching certain segments of the market in some places than others. For example, ethnic minorities are more important market segments and larger sections of the population in some parts of the UK, France, Germany, Australia and the USA, and media provision varies accordingly. Spanish language TV and radio in parts of the south west of the USA is speaking to a very large market segment. Hindi and Gujarati-speakers are better catered for on the radio stations in the Midlands than they are in, for example, Scotland. Marketers aiming for these segments cannot rely on the same 'reach' in other areas, so that promotion may well have to be varied.

4.2 The other elements of the mix will vary too. Competition, local tastes or differences in levels of disposable income will make price variations necessary. In the UK, for example, many brewers provide 'bands' of prices for the same product within different areas of the same locality, but allow the licensee of the public house to adjust the price up or down to achieve certain kinds of advantage for the premises in question: special low prices at certain times ('happy hour') or special offers on certain products.

4.3 Distribution costs, of course, will vary greatly within the same country, although these are usually absorbed equitably across the different regions, so that the most distant from a manufacturer is not disadvantaged. One of the main exceptions occurs where postal costs are a significant part of the total outlay for the distributor; in many mail order businesses postal charges have to be varied according to the cost to the business.

4.4 Products generally remain very similar within national boundaries, although local variations in taste and tradition (particular local delicacies or specialities incorporated into a range of foodstuffs) or local conditions (the kinds of fuel which can be burned by a stove, or the size of dish required by a satellite TV receiver) may be incorporated into the product portfolio.

4.5 Major variations in the marketing mix are likely to be necessary across national boundaries, however, and we next turn to a consideration of how the mix varies in international marketing.

### The marketing mix within international marketing practice

4.6 Most of the considerations detailed previously within this Study Text are also, of course, relevant in the practice of international marketing. There are some factors, however, which have a special significance.

4.7 In developing an international marketing mix, the key considerations to be borne in mind when we decide which aspects can be standardised and which must be related to local conditions are particularly important.

#### Case example

American fashion designer Donna Karan claims that her new store in London is '.. an experience that's not just about clothes. It's a nurturing, nourishing environment'.

The new store is part of a trend known as 'entertainment shopping'. Stores are no longer just places to sell goods but an integral part of a company's marketing strategy. Shopping has become spectacle.

At the Niketown athletic footwear store in Chicago, displays of sports memorabilia spread the message that famous athletes use Nike. At Borders and Barnes & Noble book chains, store cafes promote an aura of intellectualism.

Gimmicks in flagship stores are intended to promote company products at other locales rather than just increase sales on site. Calvin Klein aims to improve the cachet of his products outside New York by filling his Madison Avenue outlet with art exhibits. 'Entertainment retail' is big business in such tourist centres, and shops can become tourist destinations in themselves.

Even companies outside the retail business are getting in on the act, with the Coca Cola store in New York selling merchandise related to the brand such as T-shirts and toys, selling coke in bottles long discontinued in the US and showing archival videos which tie the product to American history. Both this and the Disney store next door are intended to promote global sales of the product by serving as a marketing vehicle which targets the tourist, and makes an impression on them, rather than simply selling the product.

*(Adapted from the Financial Times, 17/3/97)*

## Product

4.8 The international marketing mix in relation to *product* strategy involves the following possible approaches.

(a) *Marketing the same product to all countries* (*a world product*) is possible when the products are not culture-sensitive and when economies of scale are significant. It assumes that consumer needs are very similar everywhere or that low prices will prove attractive enough to overcome differences.

(b) *Adapting the product to local conditions*. Keeping the physical form essentially the same in working conditions is very attractive, for obvious reasons, but faces certain dangers.

(c) *Developing a country-specific product* may be necessary. The physical form of the product is specifically altered for one of a number of different reasons.

4.9 Products developed and successfully marketed within one country cannot necessarily be moved *tout court* into an alien market without problems. Since a product is composed of *physical dimensions* such as its shape, colour, smell and so on and also *symbolic and psychological* aspects such as the image or personality of the product, the associations and meanings involved, entry often entails a different set of cultural, religious, economic, social and political factors.

4.10 Target marketing and segmentation suggest that the way to maximise sales is to identify specific consumer needs and to tailor *promotional* appeals specifically to those needs (that is, to *adapt* a product for a new foreign market). It is less costly to produce a *standardised* product for a larger market segment.

4.11 Arguments *in favour of product standardisation* include the following.

(a) *Economies of scale* in the following.

(i) *Production*

(1) Plant probably confined to one country rather than duplicated.

(2) Plant expansion may attract 'home' government's grants or other support.

(3) Plant used to maximum capacity offers best return on its costs.

(4) Exporting is easier rather than difficult licensing deals.

(ii) *Research and development*

Product modification, such as that needed to tailor products to specific foreign markets, is costly and time consuming in an area where resources are always jealously husbanded.

(iii) *Marketing*

Promotion which can use the same images and themes in advertising is clearly more cost effective. If distribution systems, salesforce training, aftersales provision and other aspects of the product mix can be standardised, this also saves a great deal of money.

(b) *Consumer mobility*. Often the same people will have come across products in different countries, as a result of holidays, or because of living and working abroad. Differences may not be as great as they appear.

(c) *Technological complexity*. It may not be easy to modify some products to suit the special requirements or conditions found in the foreign marketplace. For example, some computer software may be difficult to programme into certain kinds of languages easily. The costs of developing a special version of a wordprocessor or a spreadsheet for a particular, comparatively small groups of language speakers may be disproportionate to the potential profit involved.

4.12 Arguments *in favour of product adaptation* include the following.

(a) *Greater sales* where this also means greater profitability - which it may not!

(b) *Varied conditions of product use* which may force a company to modify its product. These may include:

(i) climatic variations (corrosion in cars produced for drier climates);

(ii) literacy or skill levels of users (languages which can be used on a computer);

(iii) cultural, social or religious factors (religious or cultural requirements for food products, for example Halal slaughtering of New Zealand lamb for Middle Eastern markets, or dolphin-friendly tuna catching methods for Europe and the USA).

(c) *Variation in market factors*. Consumer needs are in their nature idiosyncratic and there are likely to be distinctive requirements for each group not met by a standard product.

(d) *Governmental or political influence*. Political factors may force a company to produce a local product through:

(i) taxation;
(ii) legislation; or
(iii) pressure of public opinion.

(e) *Local competition* may be particularly effective because of sensitivity to the particular needs of local markets, so that the business is forced to adapt its product to local conditions in order to compete at all.

4.13 Conditions of entry are also particularly important and bear heavily on the mix which is arrived at for local conditions.

## Place

4.14 Distribution channels are a key issue for entrants to foreign markets. Getting the product to the consumer is a major hurdle and presents problems quite different in range and scale from those faced by marketers within a domestic setting. Major alternative methods of entry would divide into the following approaches.

(a) Export goods manufactured outside the target country.

(b) Transfer the technology and skills necessary to produce and market the goods to an organisation in the foreign country through licensing/contractual arrangements.

(c) Transfer manufacturing and marketing resources through direct investment in a foreign country.

4.15 *Major entry modes* are as follows.

| | |
|---|---|
| *Export entry modes* | Indirect<br>Direct agent/distributor |
| *Contractual entry modes* | Licensing<br>Franchising<br>Technical agreements<br>Service contracts<br>Management contracts<br>Turnkey construction contacts<br>Contract manufacture<br>Coproductive agreements |
| *Investment entry modes* | Sole venture: new establishment<br>Sole venture: acquisition<br>Joint venture: new establishment acquisition |

(F R Root *Entry Strategies for International Markets*, 1987)

### *Simple exporting*

4.16 This is often based on the need to dispose of excess production for a domestic market and is the commonest form of export activity. Minimal financial risk is involved and it is often viewed as an 'opportunity' rather than long term project. It may, however, involve an intermediary (a company 'selling on' to export, after purchasing from manufacturer) and it may be direct or indirect.

4.17 Indirect exporting involves less risk, less investment. The firm makes no investment in an overseas sales force and relies on the expertise of domestic international middlemen such as export merchants, export agents and co-operative organisations.

4.18 Direct exporting is used when there are enough business opportunities abroad to warrant investing in marketing activities. This involves using foreign based distributors/agents or setting up operating units in the foreign country in the shape of branches or subsidiaries.

4.19 In general, *exporting* (as opposed to more involved methods of market entry such as overseas manufacture) is suited to:

(a) small firms with limited resources;
(b) markets where there is political risk (eg of civil war, nationalisation);
(c) small overseas markets;
(d) overseas markets where there is no pressure for local manufacture.

---

**Exercise 5**

What would you suggest is the major danger in exporting?

**Solution**

The main problem for most companies is collecting the debts of their foreign customers. There is however a sophisticated system of export credit guarantee insurance that can be purchased, and certainly should be if exporting is to become a regular activity.

---

### *Contractual entry modes*

4.20 Non-equity contractual arrangements involve the transfer of technology and/or human skills to an entity in a foreign market.

4.21 *Licensing* involves a firm offering the right to use its intangible asset (technology, know-how, patents, company name, trade marks) in exchange for royalties or some other form of payment.

This is less flexible than exporting, with less control than when the company is controlling its own manufacturing and then exporting. A small capital outlay is required, however, and it is particularly appropriate when the market is unstable and the licensing firm would have financial and marketing problems in penetrating the foreign market. Favoured by small and medium-sized companies, it is the least profitable method of entry but has the least associated risks. A positive approach to export decision making and planing is required.

4.22 *Franchising* differs from licensing:

(a) motivation is different;
(b) services are rendered; and
(c) duration is specified.

Franchising grants the right to use the company's name, trademarks and technology. Typically the franchisee receives help in setting up. Service firms are particularly appropriate franchisees (for example, fast food businesses).

This is a low cost option which combines local knowledge with entrepreneurial spirit.

4.23 *Contract manufacturing* involves sourcing a product from a manufacturer located in a foreign country for sale there or elsewhere. It is attractive when:

(a) the local market is small;
(b) export entry is blocked;
(c) a quality licensee is not available.

4.24 Various forms exist. *Turnkey construction contracts* require that the contractor makes the project operational before releasing it to the owner, or in some cases providing the services, such as worker training, when the project is completed. High risks are involved. *Management contracts* give a company the right to manage the day-to-day operations of a local company and are used mainly in conjunction with turnkey or joint venture agreements.

### *Investment overseas*

4.25 Investment overseas can take one of two forms:

(a) joint ventures; and
(b) sole ownership.

4.26 *Joint ventures* involve collaboration with one or more foreign firms to produce/market goods in the foreign market. The degree of ownership for the 'home' partner can vary from small to 50%, but this approach is increasing in popularity: it avoids quotas and import taxes and satisfies government demands for local production. The outstanding examples are Japanese companies such as Nissan, Mitsubishi and Toyota, which have established joint venture motor manufacturing in the UK and the USA. Honda operated in a joint venture with Rover in the UK until the latter was taken over by BMW in 1994. Globalisation of certain markets requires alliances because:

(a) costs of technological competition are too high for any but the largest companies;
(b) change from a variable to a fixed cost environment is involved;
(c) increasing numbers of giant multinational competitors are in the market place;
(d) there is a growing convergence of consumer needs.

4.27 This approach is subject to changes in the market position of the partners and suffers from a lack of flexibility. There are reduced economic and political risks, however, and the advantage of a partner's 'ready made' distribution system. Access is the critical factor; this may be the only way to gain entry to particular foreign markets.

4.28 *Sole ownership* involves establishing a manufacturing facility in a host country which then makes its own operating decisions. The parent company provides finance, R&D, product specifications and product technology and retains complete control - there is no shared management. A high level of commitment and high risks are involved. At a macro-economic level, a total country may be affected, while at a micro-economic level only one economic sector may be involved. It is only justified by very heavy demand.

(a) *Advantages*

(i) Lower labour costs
(ii) Avoidance of import taxes
(iii) Lower transport costs

(b) *Disadvantages*

(i) Significant commitment
(ii) Higher involvement levels
(iii) Higher levels of risk

4.29 There is a further, limited method of overseas investment, *management contracts,* which are produced by necessity rather than choice. Countries may only allow contractual arrangements when unable to service an industry with home personnel (eg when an industry has been taken over). Circumstances usually dictate the choice, or the solution is sometimes forced upon a company making a strategic decision about methods of entry.

## Promotion

4.30 Aside from the size and location of the target market, one of the major considerations in the selection of advertising media relates to the logistics of the communication process. Many different factors can lead to decreased profitability or even failure. These include the following.

(a) *Cultural factors*. Language, social systems and religious differences may well cause severe problems in marketing a product for reasons unsuspected by a marketer used to a single, culturally homogeneous market.

(b) *Customs* can also be an important consideration. For instance, it may be important to produce goods which are used by wives but actually bought by (and consequently initially promoted to) husbands.

(c) *Geographical remoteness*. Can the media actually penetrate to the areas in question?

---

### Case example

When Ever Ready were marketing a standard radio across the whole of Africa just before World War II, their research determined that the only colour which would be acceptable across the various cultural boundaries involved was blue.

---

4.31 If possible, international marketers would wish to use essentially the same advertising in as many different countries as possible. There are some factors which encourage this.

(a) The widespread international ownership of TV set
(b) The growing importance of satellite and cable systems

But there are many more tending towards local adaptation.

(a) Very localised tastes (eg food and drink)

(b) Differences in the availability of media

(c) Problems in translating advertising messages (an English ad runs 15% longer in French, 50% longer in German)

The general response is to use broadly the same approach but given a 'twist' which customises the campaign for specific audiences.

### Media problems

4.32 Media problems are likely to relate specifically to the following.

(a) *Availability*. Media may be more important and effective in some countries than in others (for instance, cinema in India, radio in the USA) while there may be a lack of specific media in others.

(i) Newspapers may not be widely available because of low levels of literacy, or even specific policies on the part of the government.

(ii) Magazines, which are so important for specialist products such as industrial machinery, may be very restricted.

(iii) TV commercials are restricted, or even banned, in many countries. For instance, advertising specifically directed at children is banned in some Scandinavian countries. It is also sometimes very difficult to gauge effectiveness because of missing MR data.

(iv) Billboards, direct mail and other forms of promotion may be unfamiliar or ineffective (for example, very limited use of billboards in some formerly Communist countries).

(b) *Financial aspects*. Costs may be very difficult to estimate in many countries, since negotiation and the influence of intermediaries is likely to be much greater. There may also be expectations of gift giving in the negotiation process.

(c) *Coverage of media* (or *'reach' of advertising message*). This relates to the forms of media employed as well as the physical characteristics of the country. Inaccessible areas may rule out the use of direct mail or posters, scarcity of telephones may rule out this form of advertising promotion. It may also be difficult to monitor advertising effectiveness.

(d) *Lack of information on the characteristics of the target markets*. Often there is little information on the differences between groups within the population towards which advertising and promotion is being targeted. This is, of course, critical for decisions about the mix to be employed and decisions such as standardisation/ adaptation.

4.33 As we can see, developing a marketing mix for international markets is a challenging and complex business. Product, promotional and place decisions are, in themselves, radically different from those involved in domestic marketing, with complex environmental and strategic factors at play.

## Price

4.34 Pricing decisions are equally complex, with all the added complications of considerations about exchange rates, fluctuations in the currency markets and rapid economic changes within overseas markets which may make it very difficult to establish appropriate levels of pricing. Famously, in countries suffering from hyperinflation, stores are busiest in the early mornings. Often workers are paid daily and the value of the currency may change several times in the course of a few hours, so that there is a rush to buy goods in the early morning in order to maximise purchasing power!

4.35 Obviously this bears heavily on the calculation about method of entry. At the end of the day, there is probably:

> '... no best strategy for a firm - the optimum choice will depend on the specific product-market-company mix.' (Lancaster and Massingham, *Essentials of Marketing*)

In other words, when decisions are taken, the quality of the manager and his capacity to use these tools for effective decision-making are the difference between good and bad decisions - and not simply the choice of one or other method of describing or analysing the market, or the selection of a strategy.

## 5 SERVICE MARKETING

*Examined 12/96, 6/97*

### The rise of the service economy

5.1 There are a number of reasons why services are more important today than they were in the past. These include the following.

(a) *The growth of service sectors in advanced industrial societies*

In terms of employment, more people now work in the service sector than in all other sectors of the economy. In terms of output, the major contributor to national output are the public and private service sectors. 'Invisible' service earnings from abroad are of increasing significance for Britain's balance of trade.

(b) *Increasingly market-oriented trade within service-providing organisations* (eg 'internal markets', 'market testing' and so on).

The extension of the service sector and the application of 'market principles' across what were previously publicly owned utilities has made a large number of service providers much more marketing conscious.

5.2 The service sector extends, in Britain, across public provision in the legal, medical, educational, military, employment, credit, communications, transportation, leisure and information fields. Some are 'not-for-profit' but increasingly there are profits involved in others. The private sector embraces not for profit areas such as arts, leisure, charities, religious organisations and educational factors, but also, of course, business and professional services involved in travel, finance, insurance, management, the law, building, commerce, entertainment and so on.

### Services: some definitions

5.3 The definitions offered of services are as follows.

> '... those separately identifiable but intangible activities that provide want-satisfaction, and that are not, of necessity, tied to, or inextricable from, the sale of a product or another service. To produce a service may or may not require the use of tangible goods or assets. However, where such use is required, there is no transfer of title (permanent ownership) to these tangible goods.'
>
> (Donald Cowell, *The Marketing of Services)*

> '... any activity of benefit that one party can offer to another that is essentially intangible and does not result in the ownership of anything. Its production may or may not be tied to a physical product.'
>
> (P Kotler, *Social Marketing)*

### Goods and services

5.4 Services marketing differs from the marketing of other goods in a number of crucial ways. Marketing services faces a number of distinct problems and as a consequence the approach adopted must be varied, and particular sorts of marketing practices must be developed. While it is difficult to make a judgement which encompasses the wide variety within service types and situations, there are indeed many service organisations which are highly market oriented (for instance, in retailing, transport hire, cleaning and hotel groups) but there are many which remain relatively unaffected by marketing ideas and practices, or which have only just begun to adopt them (for example, legal and financial services). Marketing ideas are likely to become much more important as competition within the service sector intensifies.

### Marketing characteristics of services

5.5 Characteristics of services which make them distinctive from the marketing of goods have been proposed. There are five major differences.

(a) Intangibility
(b) Inseparability
(c) Heterogeneity

(d) Perishability
(e) Ownership

## Intangibility

5.6 'Intangibility' refers to the lack of substance which is involved with service delivery. Unlike a good, there is no substantial material of or physical aspects to a service: no taste, feel, visible presence and so on. Clearly this creates difficulties and can inhibit the propensity to consume a service, since customers are not sure what they have.

> 'Ultimately the customer may have no prior experience of a service in which he or she is interested, nor any conception of how it would satisfy the requirements of the purchase context for which it was intended.' (Morden, *The Marketing of Services)*

In fact it would be incorrect to make this a 'black or white' phenomenon. Shostack has suggested viewing insubstantiality, not as an 'either/or' issue, but rather as a continuum.

5.7 Shostack has also proposed that marketing entities are combinations of elements which are tangible or intangible. She uses the metaphor of a molecule to represent the 'total market entity'; a molecule (product) is created not only by various atoms (goods or services), but also by the way the atoms (goods and services) are connected (interrelationships) and the relevant dominance of those goods and services, both tangible and intangible. A product then comes to be conceived as a 'gestalt', or blend of various elements which is constituted by combining *material entities* (the aeroplane we are flying in, the airport lounge and so on) with various sorts of processes (the courtesy of the airline staff, the frequency of services and so on).

5.8 Clearly, for each service the number, complexity and balance of the various elements involved will vary a great deal. What is experienced at the end of the process when the service is delivered remains insubstantial, although many parts of the process (the machines, buildings and staff of an airline, for instance), are very substantial but still the actual service itself cannot be owned, only experienced.

5.9 Marketers and consumers need to try to overcome this problem and typically seek to do so in a number of different ways, and of course for different reasons. The consumer needs information to avoid making a mistake, to obtain some grounds for forming a judgement and to cut down risk. The marketer wishes to make the choice of the product 'safer' and make the consumer feel more comfortable about paying for something they do not then own and which has no physical form.

5.10 This may be countered by:

(a) the consumer seeking opinions from other consumers; or
(b) the marketer offering the consumer something tangible to represent the service.

5.11 Intangibility, once again, is a matter of degree varying between:

(a) intangibles making a tangible product available;

(b) intangibles adding value to a tangible product (house decorating, hairdressing, vehicle or plant maintenance and so on); and

(c) complete intangibility (entertainment or leisure services).

*The Service Continuum*

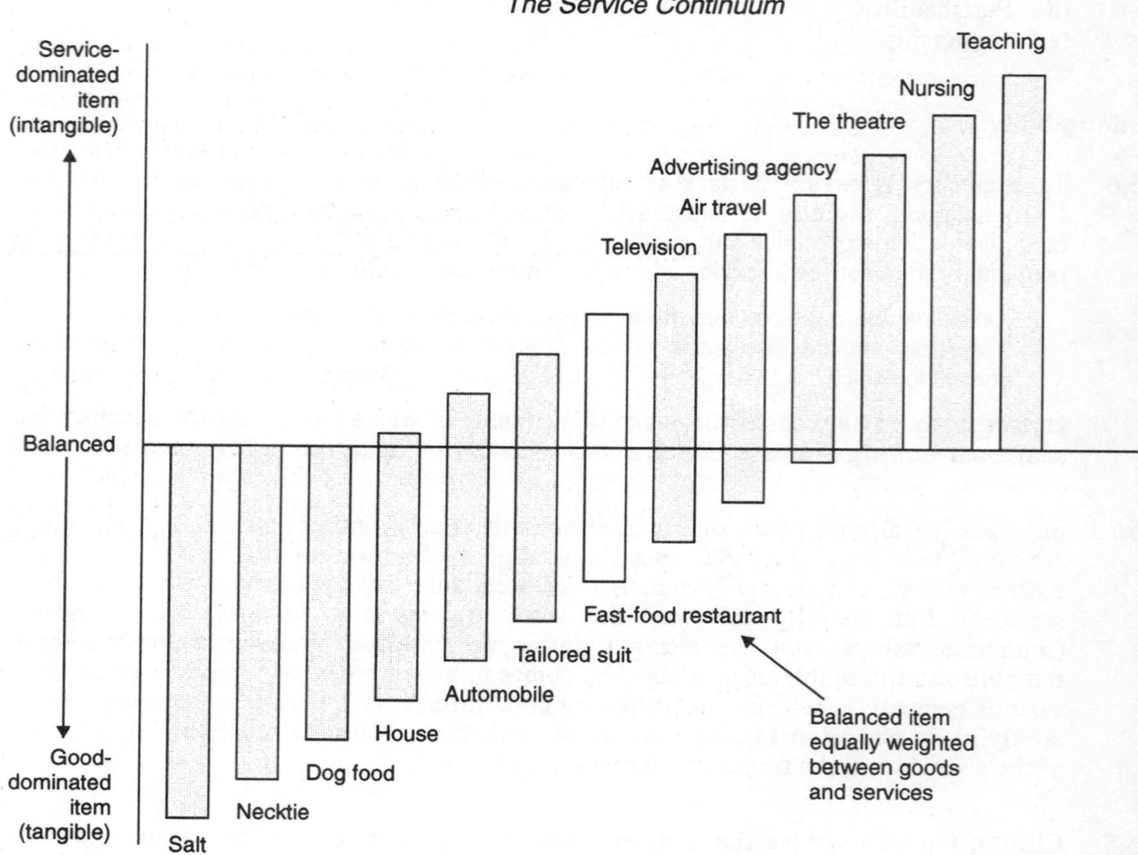


*Marketing implications*

5.12 Dealing with the problems discussed above may involve the following strategies.

(a) *Increasing the level of tangibility.* When dealing with the customer, staff can use physical or conceptual representations/illustrations to make the customer feel more confident as to what it is that the service is delivering.

(b) *Focusing the attention of the customer on the principal benefits of consumption.* This could take the form of communicating the benefits of purchasing the service so that the customer visualises its appropriateness to the usage requirements within which the principal benefit is sought. Promotion and sales material could provide images or records of previous customers' experience.

(c) *Differentiating the service and reputation-building*: enhancing perceptions of customer service and customer value by offering excellence in the delivery of the service and promoting values of quality, service reliability and value for money. These must be attached as values to brands, which must then be managed to secure and enhance their market position.

---

**Exercise 6**

*There may be trouble ahead ...*

Insurance is perhaps the least tangible of all the purchases that people commonly make. Insurance adverts create *fears* and then try to sell peace of mind.

Life assurance company Allied Dunbar's Dennis Potter/Nat King Cole style advertisements are part of a £75m campaign to move the company ahead in the market-led 1990s. Part of the research for the campaign aimed to discover how the company was seen by employees and consumers. The message that came back was that the company was both crusading and manipulative, simultaneously caring and aggressive. The next step was to establish what Allied Dunbar's brand or reputation ought to be.

What do you think was the response of consumers?

### Solution

Consumers wanted to know that the company was large, successful and financially secure; they wanted to be treated as individuals and have individually tailored solutions to their financial needs throughout their life; and they wanted to find the company caring, honest, knowledgeable and experienced. They also wanted unpleasant and difficult issues confronted when investments, life assurance and pensions were discussed, and to have a clear idea what provision was being made for which eventualities.

Watch out for life assurance marketing to see how companies try to meet these needs.

## Inseparability

5.13 Services often cannot be separated off from the provider. The creation, or the performance, of a service often occurs at the same instant a full or partial consumption of it occurs. Goods in the vast majority of cases have to be produced, then sold, then consumed, in that order. Services are only a promise at the time they are sold: most services are sold and then they are produced and consumed simultaneously. Think of having dental treatment or a journey. Neither exists until they are actually being experienced/consumed by the person who has bought them.

5.14 Creation of many services is coterminous with consumption. Services may have to be, at the same time:

(a) made available;
(b) sold;
(c) produced; and
(d) consumed.

### *Marketing implications*

5.15 Provision of the service may not be separable from the person or personality of the seller. Consequently increasing importance is attached to the need to instil values of quality, reliability and to generate a customer service ethic in the personnel employed within an organisation, which can be transferred to the service provision. This points up the need for excellence and customer orientation and the need to invest in high quality people and high quality training for them.

5.16 Major design considerations in *high- and low-contact service systems* are as follows.

| *Decision* | *High-contact system* | *Low-contact system* |
|---|---|---|
| Facility location | Operations must be near the customer | Operations may be placed near supply, transportation or labour |
| Facility layout | Facility should accommodate the customer's physical and psychological needs and expectations | Facility should enhance production |
| Product design | Environment as well as the physical product define the nature of the service | Customer is not in the service environment so the product can be defined by fewer attributes |
| Process design | Stages of production process have a direct immediate effect on the customer | Customer is not involved in majority of processing steps |

| *Decision* | *High-contact system* | *Low-contact system* |
|---|---|---|
| Scheduling | Customer is in the production schedule and must be accommodated | Customer is concerned mainly with completion dates |
| Production planning | Orders cannot be stored, so smoothing production flow results in a loss of business | Both backlogging and smoothing are possible |
| Worker skills | Direct work force comprises a major part of the service | Direct work force need only have technical skills |
| Quality control | Quality standards are often in the eye of the beholder and hence variable | Quality standards are generally measurable and hence fixed |
| Time standards | Service time depends on customer needs, and therefore time standards are inherently loose | Work is performed on customer surrogates (eg forms) and time standards can be tight |
| Wage payment | Variable output requires time-based wage systems | 'Fixable' output permits output-based wage systems |
| Capacity planning | To avoid lost sales, capacity must be set to match peak demand | Storable output permits setting capacity at some average demand level |
| Forecasting | Forecasts are short term, time-oriented | Forecasts are long term, output-oriented |

(Richard B Chase, 'Where does the customer fit into a service operation?', *Harvard Business Review*, November-December 1978)

### Heterogeneity

5.17 Many services face the problem of maintaining consistency in the standard of output. Variability of quality in delivery is inevitable because of the number of factors involved. This may create problems of operation management, for example, it may be difficult or impossible to attain *precise standardisation of the service offered.* The quality of the service may depend heavily on who it is that delivers the service, or exactly when it takes place. Booking a holiday using standard procedures may well be quite different on a quiet winter afternoon and on a hectic spring weekend, and may well vary according to the person dealing with your case.

It may also be impossible to obtain *influence or control over perceptions of what is good or bad customer service.* From the customer's perspective it is, of course, very difficult to obtain an idea of the quality of service in advance of purchase/consumption.

5.18 This points up the need to constantly *monitor* customer reactions. A common way of addressing this problem involves applying a system to deliver a service which may be *franchised* to operators. The problem remains, however, and almost the only way to address it is by constant monitoring and response to problems.

*Marketing implications*

5.19 In terms of marketing policy, this problem illustrates the need to maintain an attitude and organisational culture which emphasises:

(a) consistency of quality control;
(b) consistency of customer service; and
(c) effective staff selection, training and motivation.

5.20 Note also the importance of:

(a) clear and objective quality measures;

(b) standardising as much as possible within the service; and

(c) assuming the Pareto principle (80% of the difficulties arise from 20% of events surrounding the provision of the service). Therefore identify and respond most closely to these potential 'troublespots'.

## Perishability

5.21 Services cannot be stored, of course. They are innately *perishable*. Seats on a bus or the services of a chiropodist consist in their availability for periods of time, and if they are not occupied, the service they offer cannot be used 'later'.

5.22 This presents specific marketing problems. Meeting customer needs in these operations depends on staff being available as and when they are needed. This must be balanced against the need for a firm to minimise unnecessary expenditure on staff wages. Anticipating and responding to levels of demand is, therefore, a key planning priority.

5.23 Risks include:

(a) inadequate level of demand is accompanied by substantial variable and fixed costs; and

(b) excess demand resulting in lost custom through inadequate service provision.

### *Marketing implications*

5.24 Policies must seek to smooth supply/demand relationship by:

(a) price variations which encourage off-peak demand; and
(b) promotions to stimulate off-peak demand.

## Ownership

5.25 Services suffer from a fundamental difference compared to consumer goods: they do not result in the transfer of property. The purchase of a service only confers on the customer access to or a right to use a facility, not ownership. Payment is for the use of, access to or the hire of particular items. Often there are tight constraints on the length of time involved in such usage. In the case of purchasing a product there is transfer of title and control over the use of an item. This may well lessen the perceived customer value of a service and consequently make for unfavourable comparisons with tangible alternatives.

### *Marketing implications*

5.26 (a) *Promote the advantages of non-ownership.* This can be done by emphasising, in promotion, the benefits of paid-for maintenance, and periodic upgrading of the product. Radio Rentals have used this as a major selling proposition with great success.

(b) *Make available a tangible symbol or representation of ownership* (certificate, membership of professional association). This can come to embody the benefits enjoyed.

(c) *Increasing the chances or opportunity of ownership*, for example, time-shares or shares in the organisation for regular customers.

5.27 The issue of how to deal with these problems has occupied many different writers. Some have claimed that the critical factor is the marketing mix which is formulated. Research into the ways in which service quality is evaluated shows that the dimensions of service evaluation are distinctive and quite different criteria are given emphasis when customers are making a judgement.

5.28 Aspects of quality and customer care are demonstrated in the following table.

| *Dimension and definition* | *Examples of specific questions raise by stock brokerage customers* |
|---|---|
| *Tangibles*: Appearance of physical facilities, equipment, personnel and communication materials | Is my stockbroker dressed appropriately? |
| *Reliability*: Ability to perform the promised service dependably and accurately | Does the stockbroker follow exact instructions to buy or sell? |
| *Responsiveness*: Willingness to help customers and provide prompt service | Is my stockbroker willing to answer my questions? |
| *Competence*: Possession of the required skills and knowledge to perform the service | Does my brokerage firm have the research capabilities to accurately track market developments? |
| *Courtesy*: Politeness, respect, consideration and friendliness of contact personnel | Does my broker refrain from acting busy or being rude when I ask questions? |
| *Credibility*: Trustworthiness, believability and honesty of the service provider | Does my broker refrain from pressuring me to buy? |
| *Security*: Freedom from danger, risk or doubt | Does my brokerage firm know where my stock certificate is? |
| *Access*: Approachability and ease of contact | Is it easy to get through to my broker over the telephone? |
| *Communication*: Keeping customers informed in language they can understand, and listening to them | Does my broker avoid using technical jargon? |
| *Understanding the customer*: Making the effort to know customers and their needs | Does my broker try to determine what my specific financial objectives are? |

(Zeithaml, Parasuraman & Berry, *Delivering Quality Service*, 1990)

**Exercise 7**

Apply the dimensions above to two similar services that you use frequently, such as two different supermarkets, two types of public transport or the like. Devise appropriate questions and see how your chosen services measure up against each other.

## The marketing mix for services

5.29 As always, each firm has its own unique formula of people, processes and problems to deal with and, in that sense, arriving at a marketing mix for services is little different from the process involved for goods.

5.30 It has, however, been pointed out that in the marketing of services, four Ps do not adequately describe the importance of mix elements. It has been suggested that an extra three, and perhaps four, Ps should be added to the mix for services.

(a) Personal selling
(b) Place of availability (operations management)
(c) People and customer service
(d) Physical evidence

### *Personal selling*

5.31 Personal selling is more important here because it is harder to sell services than products, for reasons outlined above. Because of greater perceived risk involved and greater uncertainty about quality and reliability, the reputation of the supplier may be of greater importance, and there is a perception on the part of the customer of the need for greater reliance on the honesty, sincerity and so on of the individual sales person. When consumers seek reassurance, personal contact with a competent, effective representative may provide the necessary confidence. In some cases, however, since the quality of the individual salesperson varies, this may not be achieved. Greater contact with the sales person may potentially generate even more anxiety about the quality of the service. This underlines the need to place even more emphasis on the reduction of customer uncertainty, and to develop standard procedures to minimise customer anxiety ('closing techniques').

### *Place of availability*

5.32 Place of availability is really covered by the distribution system, but of course there are special problems for services in the area of *operations management*. The place of availability and the frequency of availability are key service variables, while planning to deal with capacity and making sure that levels of productivity for the assets to be used are optimised, is essential for efficient and profitable operation.

5.33 To the efficient organisation, the level and also the quality of service which is available to the customer is especially sensitive; and in particular, the processes by which services are delivered. Problems with regulating the supply make this a key factor in competitive advantage - a company which gets it right is likely to be clearly differentiated from competitors. Key factors are:

(a) *capacity utilisation*, matching demand sequences to staff utilisation to avoid unprofitable underprovision and problematic understaffing;

(b) *managing customer contact*, to avoid crowding and customer disruption, meet needs as they arise and increase employee control over interactions.

(c) *establishing objectives within the not for profit sector*, for example, standards for teachers or medical staff.

5.34 For marketing service managers, the 'quality control' and 'engineering' of the interactions which take place between customers is a key strategic issue. Customers are often, in the course of service delivery, interacting with other customers to gather information and form views about the nature and quality of the service of which they are contemplating purchase. Minimising exposure to negative feedback and promoting the dissemination of positive images and messages about the value of the service and the quality of customer response to it, are important objectives here.

### *People*

5.35 The personnel of the service deliverer are uniquely important in the service marketing process. In the case of some services, the physical presence of people actually performing the service is a vital aspect of customer satisfaction: think of clerks in a bank, or personnel in catering establishments. The staff involved are performing or producing a service, selling the service and also liaising with the customer to promote the service, gather information and respond to customer needs.

5.36 Thus, another key strategic issue for the service marketing mix is the way in which personnel are involved in implementing the marketing concept, and measures need to be established which will institute a customer orientation in all sectors of organisational activity.

5.37 Customers who lack security and confidence in an intangible service will tend to use cues from the demeanour and behaviour of staff to establish a view about the image and efficiency of the organisation. The higher the level of customer contact involved in the delivery of a service, the more crucial is the staff role in generating customer service and adding value. In many cases the delivery of the service and the physical presence of personnel involved are completely inseparable; technical competence and skill in handling people are of equal importance in effective delivery of a service since, as we have already noted, quality is in the eye of the (consuming) beholder.

5.38 All levels of staff must be involved in customer service; to achieve this end, it is vital for senior management to consciously promulgate values of customer service constantly to create and build a culture of customer service within the company. This means concrete policies and the continuous development of:

(a) policies of selection;
(b) programmes of training;
(c) standard, consistent operational practices ('McDonaldisation');
(d) standardised operational rules;
(e) effective motivational programmes;
(f) managerial appointments;
(g) the attractiveness and appropriateness of the service offer;
(h) effective policies of staff reward and remuneration.

### *Physical evidence*

5.39 Physical evidence, as we have already seen, is an important remedy for the intangibility of the product. This may be *associated with the service itself*, providing cues as to the nature of the service itself (for example, reports of previous work, or credit cards which represent the service available to customers), building up an association with a particular event, person or object, or building up an identification with a specific individual (a 'listening' bank manager).

5.40 Alternatively, the physical evidence may be *incorporated into the design and specification of the service environment* involving the building, location or atmosphere. Design here can:

(a) convey the nature of the service involved;

(b) transmit messages and information;

(c) imply aesthetic qualities, moral values or other socio-cultural aspects of a corporate image;

(d) reinforce an existing image;

(e) reassure;

(f) engender an emotional reaction in the customer, through sensory and symbolic blends.

---

**Exercise 8**

You ask a friend to empty his wallet of receipts and lay them on the table. You find receipts for the following.

| | | |
|---|---|---|
| (a) | A pint of milk | £0.47 |
| (b) | A man's suit | £149.99 |
| (c) | A bottle of wine | £6.50 |
| (d) | A book of 10 first class stamps | £2.50 |
| (e) | A season ticket for London Underground | £650 |

In each case the price tells you something about one or more of the following:

(a) the product/service purchased;
(b) the place where it was purchased;
(c) the circumstances in which it was purchased;
(d) the purpose for which it was purchased;
(e) the person making the purchase.

Explain each of the purchases in these terms.

## Exercise 9

A national charity want to send out a mailshot to attract donations. Describe in detail what you would suggest that receivers should find in the envelope (or if you prefer, create the contents of such a mailshot for a charity of your choice).

## Solution

You may well have received such a mailshot yourself. One received by the editor from the National Society for the Prevention of Cruelty to Children (NSPCC) contained five items in an envelope printed with black and white photo of a sad and bedraggled-looking little girl. The five items were as follows, in no particular order.

(a) An A3 sheet folded to make a four A4 page letter printed in two colours and with more black and white photos of neglected children on paper with a recycled feel. The letter tells the story of Ellie, the child shown on the envelope, in highly emotive language, asks for £15 and describes what good can be done with that money by the NSPCC.

(b) An A5 size donation form printed on both sides. You can tick a box saying '£15' or fill in your own amount. You can give your credit card details. You can opt *not* to receive further mailings. On the other side, Ellie's story and NSPCC action is described again in a sort of brief 'photo-story'.

(c) An envelope addressed to the Director of the NSPCC at a FREEPOST address (but suggesting that if you use a stamp it will save the NSPCC the postage).

(d) A 'Thank You' card with a picture of Ellie smiling on the front, a further plea from the Director of the NSPCC, and a thank you message in a 'hand-written' typeface.

(e) A car sticker saying 'Support the NSPCC'.

## Exam focus point

Services marketing has been a popular exam topic recently. Both the December 1996 and June 1997 exams contained questions on the subject (Q74 *Services marketing* and Q75 *Services and research*). Both of them covered the difference between the 4Ps and the 7Ps.

## Chapter roundup

- We have looked at various aspects of the *product life cycle* earlier in this Study Text. Here, we have brought together the various threads of discussion.
- We have looked at what *marketing mix decisions* are taken in relation to the product life cycle at each stage.
- We have also looked at the *assumptions* underlying the PLC concept, and limitations and criticisms of the concept.
- You should be able to discuss all these matters as well as the marketing mix in *different marketplaces* (as well as internationally).
- Marketing mixes for *services* often place extra emphasis on:
  - personal selling;
  - operations management;
  - people and customer services;
  - physical evidence.
- In the *overall management picture*, this greater emphasis on 'people issues' typically involves the management in tight and closely organised practices within the enterprise, in the ways in which personnel are selected and used. Service marketing involves a 'totalitarian' organisational culture, in the same way that is being advocated for philosophies such as TQM, but for this sector these issues are perhaps even more directly relevant to success.
- As a consequence, rigorous procedures are typically applied in the following areas.
  - Selection and training
  - Internal marketing, promulgating the 'culture' of service within the firm
  - Ensuring 'conformance' in terms of quality procedures, with standards:
    - in behaviour
    - of dress and appearance
    - in procedures
    - in modes of dealing with the public
  - Mechanising procedures where possible
  - Constantly auditing personnel performance and behaviour
  - Extending the conscious promotion of image and tangible representations of the service and its qualities into the design of service environments and the engineering of interactions within and between staff and customers
- If there is one overall message about the essential quality required in successful service marketing, it is that *attention to details*, however small, is the key to success.

## Test your knowledge

1. In the introduction phase of the PLC, describe skimming and penetration as pricing strategies. (see para 2.6)
2. Why is 'place' so important in the growth stage of the life cycle? (2.11)
3. In the maturity stage, how can low costs be used to offset prices falling? (2.24)
4. How do exit barriers affect weaker competitors in the decline stage? (2.32)
5. How does 'harvesting' in the decline stage affect promotion? (2.38)
6. List the key assumptions of the PLC concept. (3.2)
7. What are the possible approaches to product strategy in international marketing mix? (4.8)
8. What are the arguments in favour of product standardisation? (4.11)
9. List the different types of contractual entry modes to foreign markets. (4.15, 4.20)
10. What extra factors affect promotion strategy in foreign markets? (4.30)
11. Define 'services'. (5.3)
12. What are the marketing characteristics of services? (5.5)
13. What are the extra 4 Ps which should be added to the marketing mix for services? (5.30)

**Now try illustrative question 23 at the end of the Study Text**

# MARKETING FUNDAMENTALS IN ACTION

*For most parts of each Study Text, we take a look at the subject matter covered in the light of real companies, either to offer more detail, or to give an understanding of the wider corporate context.*

In this part of the text we have tried to draw together and combine all the strands of the marketing mix. As a final example, let us look at the way some very large companies are changing their attitudes to promotion and advertising.

## *Vernons Pools*

It's official: Vernon's Pools is not for sale. And that is the final word from parent company Ladbroke's press spokesman. Unless, of course, someone offers a high enough price.

Despite seeing its turnover fall by 70 per cent since the launch of the National Lottery in November 1994, Ladbroke insists that Vernons can be built into a profitable core business to sit alongside the other Ladbroke divisions.

Littlewoods Pools, Vernons' giant rival based a few miles away across Liverpool, has shown that it has an interest in taking over Vernons.

Both companies have seen the pools market devastated by the National Lottery, but Vernons and Littlewoods have responded in different ways to the problem.

Littlewoods has maintained the system of collectors who deliver pools coupons and pick up the cash. It has 53,000 self-employed collectors around the country. But Vernons has pulled back from using collectors. It has withdrawn them from most parts of the country, retrenched into urban areas, and is now concentrating on direct sales. The company has built a database of 5 million names, operated by CCN, and markets to 1 million of these "active" names directly to their homes by post or telephone.

But whichever distribution system is used, direct mail or doorstep collections, one thing is clear. The pools are on their way out.

"The pools are a product that is nearing the end of its lifecycle," says Vernons Pools marketing director Peter Ammundsen. "As people stop playing – and many are elderly – they are not being replaced. It is not attracting new, young people."

With the knowledge that the pools operations of Vernons and Littlewoods are on course for a no-score draw, the words "new product development" have an urgency not found in many marketing departments. Ammundsen, and his rival Tony Hillyer, Littlewoods commercial director, have to design some popular new games, or face slow, painful death.

Vernons is now believed to be looking at a National Lottery game, which it would run and whose proceeds would go to the Good Causes. For this to happen, it would need to throw open its books to Camelot and detailed discussions of its finances, under Oflot rules, would be required before they could strike a deal. That would make it more vulnerable to takeover by the Lottery operator, which would gain much-needed financial information.

But not all agree that Vernons is doomed to a profits slide. Paul Heath, leisure analyst at UBS, says: "Vernons is such a small profit centre for Ladbroke, the only way to make headway is to cut costs. The business was stable until the arrival of the Lottery. If it is given sufficient stimulus, it could be a small but viable business."

Vernon's marketing director Peter Ammundsen argues that the company has staunched its profit haemorrhage by investing heavily in direct marketing. In the first half of this year, profits slipped to £3.2 million from £3.4 million in the same period of the previous year. But along with this came a collapse of turnover from £45 million to £33.2 million – a fall of over £12 million. Clearly the policy of radical cost-cutting managed to ensure profitability.

The magnitude of National Lottery sales (at nearly £5 billion a year) suggests there is a demand among the public for soft gaming – gambling where the odds are just too long to predict. But nothing that either Littlewoods or Vernons has come up with has caught the public imagination like the Lottery.

Whatever happens, Vernons and Littlewoods need to come up with new types of games to fight the incursions of the National Lottery. Many eyes are on the UK as a hugely lucrative market. Overseas investors, such as the Malaysians who bought the NHS Loto operation, may see Vernons as an ideal beachhead to enter the UK gaming market.

The more likely scenario of a takeover by Littlewoods depends on one important factor: Ladbroke putting Vernons up for sale.

(Extracts from *Marketing Week*, 25/9/97)

# Part D
## Customer care

# Chapter 10

# CUSTOMER CARE

**This chapter covers the following topics.** *Syllabus reference*


| | | |
|---|---|---|
| 1 | The nature of customer care | 4.1 |
| 2 | The importance of quality | 4.1 |
| 3 | Improving the standard of customer care | 4.2 |
| 4 | Customer care within the marketing process | 4.1, 4.2 |
| 5 | Setting up a customer care programme | 4.2 |


## Introduction

Customer care has become recognised recently as a critical factor in the success of a business, whether concerned with providing services or selling products. Tom Peters, in a series of best-selling books, has acted as an advocate for its importance. Most of the ideas which he puts forward are familiar aspects of the marketing approach.

Customer care is a widely used term, yet definitions of precisely what it involves vary quite a lot. Sometimes the term is used interchangeably with 'customer service', a more familiar term which has never acquired the same cachet. Customer service developed from a focus on 'order-cycle' related activities in to a much more general and all-embracing approach which covers activities at the pre-, during- and post-transaction stages. It is seen as a task, separate from proactive selling, that involves various transactions with customers.

This last chapter provides the focus for the whole text on *the customer.*

Once you have finished this chapter, you should understand the following.

(a) Customer care levels must be assessed and monitored.

(b) Customer care is associated with concepts such as Total Quality Management (TQM).

(c) There is a wide variety of practical approaches to improving the quality of customer care and marketing will have a key role in this area.

## 1 THE NATURE OF CUSTOMER CARE

*Examined 6/95, 12/96*

1.1 Customer care is the preferred term when we are forced to consider activities which are outside the realm of direct contact with the customer. One commentator describes it as '... the ultimate marketing tool', and a critical factor in the process of differentiating products or services, to develop a competitive edge. It involves:

> '... the management and identification of "moments of truth", with the aim of achieving customer satisfaction.' (Thomas, 1986)

1.2 These moments of truth are contacts between companies and customers, where a firm's reputation is at stake. Interaction is still a critical dimension and the focus has moved away from specific activities to examine customer satisfaction in general 'holistic' ways.

1.3 According to Brown (1989) customer care emphasises the importance of attitude and covers every aspect of customer/supplier relationships. Customer care is aiming to close the gap between customers' expectations and their experience.

1.4 Customer care is also, by common assent, a policy and a set of activities. Most analysts distinguish between the *concept* and the *scope* of customer care activities. In a definition which covers both these areas, Clutterbuck describes customer care as:

> '... a fundamental approach to the standards of service quality. It covers every aspect of a company's operations, from the design of a product or service to how it is packaged, delivered and serviced.'

1.5 As can be seen from these statements, it is not clear how customer care can be distinguished from the approaches advocated by 'marketing-oriented' or 'customer-oriented' businesses, while the terms used are also very close to those which form the basis for the practice of total quality management in its various forms. What is highlighted, however, is the degree of organisational commitment required to deliver these objectives successfully. Most commentators see customer care as involving a *culture change* within a business; it is not an addendum or an adjunct to company strategy, but a core value which must form the basis for all policymaking and strategic thinking.

1.6 Various descriptions of customer care agree that *customer-impinging activities in policies or as a guiding concept* is the core element in the implementation of customer care within a company.

1.7 Most practitioners would agree that modern strategic marketing begins and ends with the consumer - yet customer care may well be overlooked in the pursuit of broader, more abstract objectives.

---

**Exercise 1**

Think of a recent major purchase you made of a product or service. What was your experience of customer care?

---

### Does customer care matter?

1.8 In his book *Perfect Customer Care* (1994), Ted Johns suggests that there may be some organisations which do not consider customer care particularly important.

(a) Those which compete with organisations that don't care about their customers either.

(b) Those which may be able to compete on factors other than customer care, like price.

(c) Monopolies, which have no need to compete.

(d) Those 'solitary geniuses' which offer products or services which are in great demand, but which no-one else can yet supply.

1.9 Such organisations, however, are fooling themselves.

(a) What happens if just one of your competitors suddenly decides to compete advantageously by building a reputation for customer service?

(b) Competing solely on price is based on the (incorrect) assumption that cost or price is the dominant or only factor concerning the customer. In fact, in most cases companies which compete on price are not successful; other factors are also relevant to the customer.

(c) Will your monopoly position last forever?

(d) Genius of any one type is normally in demand for only a limited time. Your competitors will catch up.

1.10 Ted Johns goes on to demonstrate the above using some salutary stories, perhaps the most interesting of which are as follows.

**Exam focus point**

Customer care affects consumer and business markets. The December 1996 exam covered the business-to-business market, in that a customer care role was built into the job of maintenance engineer (Q81 *Customer care and maintenance* of our Practice & Revision Kit).

## 2 THE IMPORTANCE OF QUALITY

2.1 *Quality* has been thought of as the critical differentiating factor between British firms and their successful foreign competitors. As a consequence, the pursuit of quality has become a major pre-occupation of British companies. A by-product of the process, which involved in many cases cuts in investment, downsizing, wage cuts and so on, was often poorer service to customers. As many studies showed, perceptions of quality and service in British products were significantly lower. Customer satisfaction levels were also poor and these things together represented a sure recipe for disaster in a situation where foreign competitors were meeting targets for quality improvement.

2.2 One of the reasons for the success of these firms was the ability to create organisations dedicated to the pursuit of total quality; that is, organisations which are focused entirely on the delivery of quality to customers.

### From mass production to the consumption of services

2.3 The consumption of services has become more and more important over the past twenty years. In the service age, competition depends on quality being delivered, whether this is in catering and fast food, leisure provision, hospitality, entertainment or nowadays in medicine and other public services such as education.

2.4 The total quality management (TQM) approach to such businesses uses customer care to deliver better service, or 'to meet customer requirements first time, every time'.

2.5 Customer care and TQM are closely related to each other. Quality programmes cover many topics other than dealing with customers. Customer care programmes focus on gaining deep knowledge of customers and aim to identify their needs and improve care provided for them. Care is the outcome of this process, however, and 'satisfied customers' are the focus of customer care programmes. The challenge is to maintain this emphasis throughout a quality process. While customer care should be the way in which customers experience the delivery of the product or service, it is quality programmes which direct the processes constituting the services or products which the customers are experiencing and to which they are responding.

2.6 How quality programmes affect customer care, what objectives TQM can have and what it can do are clearly important issues for marketers interested in the implementation of customer care programmes.

### Quality management

2.7 The origins, nature and practice of quality management have been discussed at length in Chapter 2 of this Study Text. Briefly, quality management can be defined as combining the satisfaction of customer needs with the achievement of company objectives. That the two are intimately and inextricably connected is an article of faith for all who dissemble on the subject.

2.8 The following areas are connected, within the terms of this analysis, in *systems* aimed at achieving success and profitability by placing the customer at the centre of all enterprise activities by providing the right amount of:

(a) quality;

(b) availability (at launch and afterwards);
(c) service;
(d) support;
(e) reliability;
(f) cost/value for money.

2.9 By common assent such programmes must be *total*, reaching forward to distributors down the chain and back to suppliers in the case of manufactured goods, to assure the quality of raw materials and the condition of the product which reaches the ultimate consumer. The customer-supplier relationship is very important indeed within the TQM philosophy. This relationship is one of a long chain of such customer-supplier relationships, with each customer being a supplier to someone further down the chain, so that it makes no sense to differentiate one role from the other. Rather than pursuing self-interest and creating an adversarial relationship, the aim of TQM is to expand the pie which represents profits to be shared between all the parties involved, rather than simply dividing the existing pie up, as under the traditional view.

2.10 The establishment of such programmes has been the foundation for startling corporate success stories, such as those enjoyed by Jaguar Motors and Ford. Consumer surveys showed large numbers of faults in the components which were bought in from outside suppliers. Quality programmes installed as a consequence used testing systems which were installed with the suppliers, and extensive quality studies and audits were implemented. The improvement in quality and performance within the marketplace as a consequence has been widely admired and analysed.

### Quality and customer care

2.11 As with quality programmes in general, TQM gives central place to the customer. Satisfying the customer is the first principle of TQM since customers are the guarantee of the organisation's continued existence.

2.12 Customer-driven quality is recognised in the US as a core value of the Malcolm Baldridge National Quality Award. The guidelines for its winners state the following.

> 'Quality is judged by the customer. All products and service attributes that contribute value to the customer and lead to customer satisfaction and preference must be the foundation for a company's quality system. Value, satisfaction and preference may be influenced by many factors throughout the customers' overall purchase, ownership and service experiences.'

2.13 Three principles guide customer-supplier relationships under TQM.

(a) Recognition of the strategic importance of customers and suppliers.
(b) Development of win-win relationships between customers and suppliers.
(c) Establishing relationships based on trust.

2.14 These principles are translated into practice by:

(a) constantly collecting information on customer expectations;

(b) disseminating this information widely within the organisation; and

(c) using this information to design, produce and deliver the organisation's product and services.

2.15 TQM programmes require the following conditions to be fulfilled.

(a) *Total involvement from staff*

This is another way of talking about a structural or a cultural change being essential for the achievement of a quality programme. Often these schemes are presented as 'a philosophy of life' or a 'total way of thinking' rather than just another technique for management. It is a peculiar feature of these systems that they have a religious or messianic quality: advocates are spoken of as 'evangelists' or, more commonly, 'gurus'. It is perhaps unsurprising that the generation which toyed with transcendental meditation and flower power in the sixties should focus on gurus of a different kind in the nineties!

For this system to work, however, it is a practical necessity for all members to be involved. Those best placed to make quality work are the people who actually carry out the processes which are involved in delivering products or services. In addition, partial quality improvements will constantly face the problems created by those parts of the system which have not been reformed, when staff are trying to improve the quality of what they deliver to customers.

(b) *A customer orientation*

As suggested above, each internal group in the quality chain is comprised of a customer and/or supplier to other internal groups and in some cases to the market. Although programmes can start at any point in this chain, even if the quality of the goods from a supplier is low, the group should aim to build up its own quality before addressing the shortcomings of its own supplier.

(c) *Defining customer requirements and obligations*

From the viewpoint of an organisation, customers can be thought of as an agglomeration of requirements and obligations. Customers may be external consumers, employees, shareholders, top management, government and so on. Requirements will be fitted to resource constraints and the objectives of the organisation and must be realistic and obtainable. Obligations need to be clearly defined and requirements need to be quantified and accepted by both sides as reasonable. If a customer care programme is to be effective, the relations must be clearly specified on both sides.

(d) *Measurement*

This is extremely important for any quality programme and in relation to customer care measurements must be continual and ubiquitous. Required performance needs to be clearly specified in terms which can be measured and mechanisms must be instituted which provide clear indicators that these have been achieved. These must be in place before programmes are instigated. Customer care programmes will require survey data on internal and external customers, on customer behaviour and on the degree to which customer needs are being satisfied. These should permit the application of techniques such as key ratio and trend analysis, and fit into a cycle of assessment, planning, implementation and monitoring.

(e) *Commitment from the top management*

Top management need to ensure that the programme is delivered and also that it provides the cash payoff from improved quality in customer service.

(f) *Adherence to standard processes and procedures*

Processes and procedures which are developed and specified as an end product of a TQM customer care programme are intended to be followed. Such directions are intended to reproduce proven consistent quality and should specify administered processes, timing, responsibility and areas of expertise, gathering feedback data and so on. When these strictures are adhered to, the output remains consistent, processes are appropriately monitored and the data provides the basis for learning and consistent improvement.

(g) *Paying customer objectives*

The end product of any programme must be to satisfy the needs of the paying customer in order to accomplish particular commercial, financial or strategic objectives. To that end, all analysis within customer care programmes, and the development of any processes and procedures within such programmes, must relate to these objectives. Examples of such objectives would be:

(i) increasing sales and profits;
(ii) lowering prices of service provision;
(iii) improving customer perceptions of service;
(iv) shortening waiting lists and prioritising customer needs.

The mission of the organisation, and the corporate values which underlie it, must always be clearly and directly related to the formulation of such objectives. If they are not, then TQM programmes will not accord with the strategic direction which has been agreed.

## 3 IMPROVING THE STANDARD OF CUSTOMER CARE

*Examined 12/94, 12/96*

3.1 The close relationship between the 'customer orientation' which lies at the heart of marketing and the notion of customer care is readily apparent. Customer care can be seen as a perspective which focuses on working with customers at every stage of the planning and implementation process. It is important in marketing all types of product and service. It is a *service component* and as such shares the *characteristics* of service marketing. It is, for example:

(a) people based;
(b) perishable;
(c) dependent on high customer involvement;
(d) based on perceptions;
(e) sensitive to images;
(f) heavily dependent on consumption context; and
(g) delivered over time.

3.2 While marketing is, as we have seen, fundamentally based on customer orientation, it is possible in the pursuit of marketing objectives to lose sight of the things which will satisfy customer needs.

### Encouraging customers to complain

3.3 Organisations lose customers for various reasons, given below.

| | |
|---|---|
| Customers die | 1% |
| Customers move away | 3% |
| Customers naturally float | 4% |
| Customers change on recommendation | 5% |
| Customers go because they can buy more cheaply elsewhere | 9% |
| Customers are chronic complainers | 19% |
| **Customers go elsewhere because the people they deal with are indifferent to their needs** | **68%** |

Ted Johns, *Perfect Customer Care*, 1994

3.4 In order to find out what is wrong, how often, and how it should be put right, customers should be encouraged to complain. The following guidelines are given by Ted Johns in *Perfect Customer Care* (1994).

(a) Make it easy for people to complain, eg 0800 numbers (which are free), complaint forms (perhaps attached to order forms for reorders).

(b) Ask for complaints, perhaps by selecting and approaching customers at random.

(c) Pretend to be a customer and see things from the sharp end.

(d) Listen to the complaints without becoming defensive: ask questions, ask for suggestions etc.

(e) Act quickly and with goodwill to solve the problem.

(f) Replace defective products immediately, or repeat the service.

(g) Take positive steps to prevent recurrence: any complaint is unlikely to be a one-off.

(h) Use some imagination in finding ways to secure feedback.

(i) Award positive recognition for customer feedback, eg prizes for completed questionnaires.

3.5 Think about ways you have been able (or unable) to complain as a customer.

3.6 Customer satisfaction can be said to be based on four types of variable.

(a) Variables related to the product or service itself
(b) Variables related to sales and promotion
(c) Variables related to after-sales
(d) Variables related to the organisational culture

## Marketing management and customer care

3.7 Following a marketing plan in the delivery of a service can result in customer care shortcomings in the following ways.

(a) *As a result of an unrealistic corporate mission*

Those in charge of the company may make promises which the company cannot possibly deliver. The company may aim to deliver the wrong level of care to the customer, when the company is, for example, turning customers away.

(b) *As a result of poor information about customers and the market*

Ignorance of customer needs, and consequent mismatch of care levels to needs can produce a lack of customer care. This may come about because the information system fails to identify those areas in which customer needs must be given priority, and focuses instead upon general aspects of customer satisfaction. Business priorities - for example, carrying out the processes involved in delivering a service - can be out of line with customer priorities. Tom Peters emphasises this aspect of customer satisfaction constantly: good products or services which are perceived as failing because customers' small but important needs (being able to get coffee in a hotel in the early morning; having a space in an expensive car on which to place food or small items which may be needed quickly) are neglected.

(c) *Poor timing*

When information which has been gathered in the past about what it is that customers want is used for too long, mismatch can occur. Customer priorities are changing and it may be that, for example, selling on price or on functional product attributes becomes inappropriate as products become mature, competition increases and differentiation is more problematic. In addition, good marketing may seek to identify needs of which some customers may not be fully aware; in marketing a product to satisfy those needs, we are adding even more value to a product by raising customer awareness of the needs which it can meet which they do not, initially, anticipate.

(d) *Poor staff communication*

In the delivery of services particularly it is vital that staff should be aware of the needs which customers require them to satisfy. When staff are not fully trained, or perhaps inadequately informed of the aims of a marketing programme, they may well fail to deliver the appropriate levels of service. Local improvisation will cause inconsistencies and variations in the quality of product and service delivered will arise. Often staff will react to problems by falling back on a 'defence' of the systems which they are operating.

(e) *Poor staff motivation*

When staff are not properly informed, trained or involved in delivering customer care, they will be inadequately motivated. This will invariably be communicated to customers.

(f) *Poor control*

Systems of control are essential to the establishment and maintenance of customer care standards throughout an organisation. When such systems are absent or inadequate, levels of quality of customer care will vary. In some cases, such variation may well take the form of very damaging inconsistencies which may well undo the effects of good practice which take place in other parts of an organisation or at other times with the same staff or customers.

(g) *Confused priorities*

When staff are following through the delivery of, for example, specific practical aspects of service delivery (such as progressing an order or carrying out a task for the customer) they may find that there are too many priorities for them to pursue effectively. Attention to marketing tasks, or attendance to customer relations is perceived to be an 'extra' in some organisations, and is strongly at risk of being sacrificed.

(h) *Organisational confusion*

Many structures do not effectively delegate responsibilities for marketing or customer care. In principle, it should be part of everyone's job but, at the same time, it must be expedited and responsibility for the establishment and delivery of the systems which promote these priorities must be clearly defined within the organisation.

(i) *No acceptance of marketing and customer care*

When staff are pressurised into delivering too many difficult practical aspects of their jobs (for example, meeting efficiency or productivity targets, delivering increased levels of output) they may well feel that concerns over meeting customer needs are not something over which they should be greatly concerned.

(j) *Short term emphasis*

The problem in (i) above is exacerbated when the feedback, or the benefits of satisfying such needs, arise in the long rather than the short term. In this case, distortions in the delivery of services or products may arise because only behaviour (satisfaction of needs) which brings short term rewards to the supplier is being reinforced by positive feedback from the customer.

(k) *Power conflict*

Inconsistencies will also occur when there are imbalances between the power which is at the disposal of different functions within an organisation. Here, the level of care which customers are offered varies according to which parts of the organisation are contacted. When customers require the involvement of more than one part of the system they are likely to experience inadequate service levels.

3.8 In order to deliver adequate levels of customer care in the pursuance of marketing objectives it is necessary for an enterprise to carry out the following.

(a) *Produce an adequate definition of the corporate mission*

Sir John Harvey Jones has defined a mission statement as 'Motherhood and apple pie, arrived at by a committee of fifty, cooks all. A vision statement, on the other hand, is an impossible dream of the chairman!'

An effective definition of what the business is about probably falls somewhere between these stools, taking into account economic and social trends, the information which is available about what customers actually want and about the choices they actually make.

(b) *Use up-to-date and reliable information*

Assumptions about what it is that customers want and notions that it is 'obvious' which product attributes are most important to the customers are all too common, and frequent causes of dissatisfaction. Information about customers should come from customers or from those who are closest to them in delivering a product or service. Information about competitor activity, about changes in market conditions and even about the performance and perception of the company itself, should come from sources which are in touch with the recent reality of the situation and not dependent on remote or potentially partial individuals or organisations.

(c) *Use information to inform decisions and planning*

Too much information is gathered ritualistically or simply because it seems like a good or useful thing to do. When information about customer needs is gathered, it must be used to make effective decisions, and placed at the heart of the planning process. If information is being gathered which is not being used in this way, the organisation needs to ask, 'Why is it being gathered at all?'.

(d) *Act quickly*

Information decays quickly. Failing to act on the basis of information that is available now and acting after the information has ceased to be relevant are equally damaging and inappropriate. Customer needs and standards change very quickly in some markets and when action is needed it should be taken as quickly as possible.

(e) *Written plans must be understandable, achievable and provide motivation for staff*

Written plans should aim to meet communicated objectives. If they are written for staff to implement they should aim to provide a basis on which practical actions can be taken, effects can be identified and measured, and staff achievements can be formulated. Plans are counterproductive if those who are required to live by them feel they cannot realistically be met or that meeting them engenders no commitment and offers no reward or sense of achievement of challenges being met.

(f) *Regular progress reports must be produced on the implementation of the marketing plan*

These must be reliable and detailed and not simply reports on results.

(g) *Measurement is central to the process of implementation*

Scores and systems of measurement provide invaluable benchmarks of progress and provide targets which can be seen to be met or not.

(h) *Marketing must be everyone's credo but also someone's job*

If everyone's job involves marketing, trouble can occur if no-one is actually responsible for making it happen. There must be clearly defined responsibilities here, as well as a core commitment to building marketing into the way in which the organisation functions at all levels.

## 4 CUSTOMER CARE WITHIN THE MARKETING PROCESS

4.1 Marketing involves applying a structured approach and applying information about customer needs in order to achieve strategic objectives. Steps, typically, are:

(a) defining corporate mission, corporate objectives and strategies;
(b) analysing the environment;
(c) setting marketing objectives;
(d) developing marketing strategies;
(e) devising action plans;
(f) measuring results; and
(g) reacting to results.

4.2 Within each of these steps, customer care issues arise and must be met. Often consideration of these issues will materially influence the ways in which the overall objectives of the marketing process are pursued.

### *Defining the business, corporate objectives and strategies*

4.3 While definition of what business the enterprise is involved in, who is being served and how this will be accomplished seem incontestably essential questions for anyone involved in business, the simplicity which they propose as the foundation of business activity is difficult to achieve. As the size of an organisation and its tasks increases, so does their complexity and the possibility of being diverted from central issues.

4.4 In defining a market, looking at who our customers are and how we see ourselves as serving their needs, we need to take a large number of factors into account. Initial explorations of what customers want may actually reveal that this cannot be met by what the enterprise has to offer, in which case markets have to be re-defined.

4.5 Corporate objectives and strategies which fail to accommodate the establishment of customer loyalty and the promotion of customer care as primary aims are bound to fail. Likewise, it is essential that objectives and strategy must espouse and promote effective plans to maintain high levels of caring for customers within the operating framework of the enterprise.

*Analysis of the external environment*

4.6 Analysis of the external environment must attempt to identify and define factors within the external environment which promote customer satisfaction and generate loyalty. This typically involves comparisons between different policies, evaluations of the different degrees to which they actually promote customer loyalty and analysis of why differences occur.

*Analysis of the internal environment*

4.7 Audits of the internal environment aim to evaluate the performance of the different factors within the enterprise which promote customer satisfaction. The identification of sources of dissatisfaction should be a major element in the marketing process.

*Action plans for the formulation of the marketing mix*

4.8 Problems, from the point of customer care, arise when such plans focus on short-term objectives, particularly sales and the promotion of improved margins. These very often prove antithetical to the main objectives of customer care based strategies, which aim for the long-term; not just winning custom, but winning customers by promoting good ongoing relationships, and looking for substantial long-term profits by sustaining customer loyalty.

*Action plans to formulate marketing operations*

4.9 Problems arise here when emphasis is placed on the efficacy and efficiency of procedures involved in the marketing process (for example, the cost-effective and efficient delivery of beer to a public house) rather than the perception and response of customers to what is involved in that process (an unfavourable comparison between product delivered in 'natural' old fashioned wooden barrels, and that delivered in modern, cost-effective aluminium kegs and a consequent attribution of many undesirable product characteristics such as chemical taste, additives, poor quality and so on).

*Results*

4.10 When too much emphasis is placed on tracking sales and profit, rather than customer inventory movements, results may not be providing the most effective form of feedback for the organisation to make long-term plans.

## Examples of the effect of inappropriate marketing processes

4.11 The following table provides a useful summary.

| | |
|---|---|
| Corporate strategy and objectives | Omission of objectives for customer loyalty and customer care<br><br>No strategy for caring for customers |
| External environmental analysis | No analysis of what makes customers loyal and how well they respond to different policies aimed at encouraging them to do so |
| Internal environmental analysis | No analysis of suppliers' capabilities in relation to keeping customers |
| Marketing objectives and strategy | Marketing objectives and strategy focus on profit, sales and market share, not on long-term impact on customer loyalty |
| Action plans - marketing operations | Focus on efficiencies of procedures, not effect on customers |
| Results | Track sales and profit not customer inventory movements |

(Stone and Young, *Competitive Customer Care)*

4.12 When this framework is followed attention is effectively focused on the delivery of customer care. What is also required, of course, is a clear idea of what customers want from the organisation. This requires a systematic approach to the gathering and evaluation of information about what may actually be a number of different types of customer, since the product portfolio of many companies extends over different types of market for the same type of product or, of course, different brands and product types.

## 5 SETTING UP A CUSTOMER CARE PROGRAMME

*Examined 12/95*

### Identifying customer needs and perceptions of the company

5.1 'In a competitive environment, customer care is not a luxury but a necessity.'

(Stone & Young, *Customer Care)*

5.2 To use a strategy based on customer care successfully two questions need to be answered.

(a) What policy of customer care is most appropriate for our company?
(b) How far should this policy affect our operations?

5.3 In order to succeed, knowledge of customer needs is vital. What expectations should the company aim to meet? In the real world these expectations will be related to the way in which the company is perceived. There are, for example, limits to the expectations which a reasonable person has and these are related to the realities of what resources a company has at its disposal and how these must sensibly be employed.

5.4 Minimum rights are expected to be respected, independently of such constraints. These are universally expected and are the *sine qua non* of customer care. All customers have the absolute right to:

(a) a basic minimum level of customer care;
(b) common courtesy from staff; and
(c) effective response to complaints.

5.5 Customers' requirements in terms of care are likely to vary according to the significance, as they perceive it, of each transaction with the supplier. When customers perceive a contact with the supplier to be important they have higher expectations of the level of care which they should receive.

5.6 Many products are bought as a package, of which customer care is a greater or smaller part. Among the factors which may be involved are the following.

(a) Time taken

(b) The importance of the service element of the package relative to other elements at different times in the relationship (for example, in the relationship between a car dealer and a customer, service is vital just before and just after purchase, around regular service time and at the time of a breakdown)

(c) How important it is for the customer to be in control

(d) The degree of dependency on the supplier

(e) The importance of the service to the customer

(f) The degree of risk which is felt to attach to the supply of the service

(g) The dependence of the service on staff or equipment

(h) Contact with staff

(i) Degree of control perceived in staff

(j) Contact with other customers

(k) Skill/expertise expected of staff

(l) Degree of routineness involved in encounters

(m) Number and complexity of stages and service encounters involved

(n) Emotions anticipated and experienced by customers at different stages

5.7 The mix of factors involved is also affected by the characteristics and experience of individual customers. As a consequence, different individuals will view the same service in different ways; what is new and potentially stressful for one individual is routine and relaxed to the experienced user of a service or product.

5.8 Given this important element, it appears likely that the role of the customer in the service-production system can be increased according to the experience or number of usage occasions in which the customer is involved.

5.9 Levels of customer care may well be influenced by this phenomenon. While customers invariably have an expectation of the minimum levels of care which they expect, they probably also have a desired level, which is influenced by the degree of experience which they have of the organisation. The greater experience they have, the more likely that they will entertain a realistic perception of the level of care which they should receive.

5.10 These perceived levels contrast with actual levels - that is, the levels which the supplier states are provided in terms of customer care activities.

Perceptions of the levels of care are the strongest influence on satisfaction levels.

5.11 It is extremely important to *define precisely which are the minimum levels of care expected by the customers*. For many aspects, these can be quantified very effectively (for instance, time taken to respond to a request for a repairman). Regular users will have a clear idea of desired and minimum standards, but how these are perceived will obviously vary across a group of customers.

5.12 It is important for the company to *identify minimum and optimum levels*. This would avoid the wastefulness and potential harm created by over-provision of certain aspects of customer care, for example, having staff who are constantly pestering customers with offers of help.

5.13 *Identifying the bands within which customer care levels must be provided* is particularly important. It is known that experience with the company providing the service or product, or with a competitor, provides a benchmark against which expectations are formed and delivery evaluated.

5.14 Identifying and analysing customer requirements involves:

(a) choosing customers;
(b) researching and modelling needs;
(c) determining care levels; and
(d) building in flexibility.

## Practical processes for a customer care programme

5.15 *Establish management processes.* These are clear specifications of how jobs should be done. These should include the following.

(a) Formalised planning and decision-making (regular meetings, formal allocation of tasks, progress review).

(b) Information flows (promoting the gathering and dissemination of information within the company).

(c) People processes (the human resources function, concerned with motivation, management of people, monitoring performance and administering rewards and sanctions).

5.16 *Define tasks according to time factors* (for example, timing of recurrent work, seasonal factors and so on).

This should be accurately and comprehensively catalogued and the programme of customer care must create systems by which the work can be handled according to the objective of satisfying customer needs, and also using resources efficiently and cost effectively.

5.17 *Standards should be specified.* Standards can be drawn from a variety of sources. They can refer to the dimensions of service quality, some of which are more easily measured than others.

(a) Tangibles etc (cleanliness, lighting)
(b) Reliability (customer complaints, number of errors)
(c) Responsiveness (eg how many 'rings' before a telephone is answered)
(d) Communication It is possible to ensure that company documentation is clear
(e) Security and confidentiality
(f) Competence
(g) Courtesy
(h) Understanding customer needs
(i) Access (eg queuing times)

Sometimes these can be measured directly, but customer satisfaction surveys can also be used.

5.18 *Establish process administration systems.* These may be:

(a) self-administered; or
(b) monitored/overseen by managers.

## Successful customer care

5.19 If programmes are to work, the following conditions must be met.

(a) Staff must be:

(i) clear about the programme and their role in it;
(ii) committed to the programme;
(iii) well trained in programme needs;
(iv) sufficiently resourced to carry out their roles;
(v) sufficiently skilled to carry out their roles.

(b) The programme must:

(i) provide clear benefits for the staff;

(ii) be reinforced by top management action, involving:

(1) effective implementation regimes;
(2) setting clear priorities;
(3) sanctions and rewards.

(c) Management must be:

(i) informed about progress and effectiveness of staff performance;
(ii) provided with regular and appropriate information.

(d) The process must support marketing objectives and facilitate the work of staff towards its achievement.

### Exercise 2

To what extent would you say that your organisation was concerned with customer care? Try and discern ten areas where customer care could be improved.

## Chapter roundup

- The concept of *customer care* is fundamental to marketing. It aims to close the 'expectation gap' between customers' expectations and their experience.
- The concepts of *quality* and in particular *total quality management* are important parts of the customer care ethos. TQM programmes concentrate on the customer-supplier relationship, with the orientation firmly on the customer.
- We have looked at some of the *practical issues* of customer care. In particular you should note why there are often shortfalls in the standard of customer care and what practical methods can be employed to avoid such failures.
- Defining strategy and analysing environments are the two main *tools* to aid customer care.
- The important *questions* to ask initially when setting up a customer care programme are:
  - What policy of customer care is most appropriate for our company?
  - How far should this policy affect operations?

  The programme can be developed from the answers to these questions.

## Test your knowledge

1. How has customer care been described as a term? (see paras 1.1 - 1.5)
2. Who might not consider customer care important? (1.8)
3. Why should they consider customer care? (1.9)
4. How is TQM related to customer care? (2.5)
5. Which three principles guide customer-supplier relationships under TQM? (2.13)
6. Briefly list the conditions required by TQM to be fulfilled. (2.15)
7. What characteristics does customer care share with service marketing? (3.1)
8. How can customers be encouraged to complain? (3.4)
9. What four variables can customer care be said to be based on? (3.6)
10. Briefly list the customer care shortcomings which are possible in the delivery of a service. (3.7)
11. What must an organisation do in order to achieve adequate levels of customer care? (3.8)
12. Why is it important to define a corporate strategy? (4.3 - 4.5)
13. Briefly note the main effects of inappropriate marketing processes. (4.11)
14. List the main practical processes for a customer care programme. (5.15 - 5.18)

**Now try illustrative question 24 at the end of the Study Text**

**Now that you have completed the Study Text you should attempt the case study from the specimen paper at the end of the bank of illustrative questions**

## MARKETING FUNDAMENTALS IN ACTION

*For most parts of each Study Text, we take a look at the subject matter covered in the light of real companies, either to offer more detail, or to give an understanding of the wider corporate context.*

Customer care is the focus of marketing. Many companies have only just discovered this, however, and some companies still have no idea about it. The following is based on an article in *Marketing Business* in March 1996 by Beverley Cramp. It demonstrates the problems involved in setting up customer care lines.

### *Coca-Cola & Schweppes Beverages*

Coca-Cola & Schweppes Beverages (CCSB) is the largest manufacturer and distributor in the UK of soft drinks including well known brands such as Coca-Cola, Schweppes and Perrier. CCSB's customer care centre opened in September 1992 because, as David Glynn, human resources manager for CCSB admits, having a big brand name isn't enough.

'CCSB has some of the most famous and recognisable brands in the world but we recognise that consumers want more than just high quality products. They expect and demand individual attention and the responsiveness that comes with it,' says Glynn, who heads up the care centre unit.

As soon as CCSB's carelines started ringing, the first of the centre's problems arrived.

'We had not recognised the difficulties in understanding posed by the dialect differences in our country. A broad Scouse or Glaswegian dialect can be very difficult to cut through,' says Glynn.

But an even more ominous problem emerged.

'We also had our first taste of a problem that was to dog us throughout the time the centre has been in existence. At least half the calls we received were hoax. But most of the calls were harmless enough and our operators became skilled in using their initiative to turn a prank call into a genuine call.'

Predicting the pattern of calls to ensure that the care centre was staffed properly to handle them, was another problem.

'We soon learnt how wildly inaccurate our estimates of call volumes would be. We had predicted between 1,000 and 1,500 calls per week but we were soon getting 2,000 calls a week. During one week in April of 1993, 12,000 people attempted to phone in to us. As you can imagine we did what many people would do in similar circumstances - panicked. We were only able to answer about 2,000 of them. Gradually though we started to understand the pattern of calls. For example, we noticed that 80 per cent of them were made in the afternoon and so our staff was structured to give us more support in the afternoon hours. We also got permission from the board to spend more so that we could do the work. We are now able to answer about 95 per cent of all incoming calls,' claims Glynn.

CCSB's introduction of the careline had the effect of increasing the number of complaints, yet Glynn is happy about this.

'What I believe we are seeing is the result of the fact that we are making it easier for consumers to talk to us and, believe me, we would much rather they talk to us and obtain some satisfaction than look for it from other sources. I come back to the basic premise of the freephone service, which was that we wanted people to ring and talk - and, if we do things wrong, to complain,' he says.

Glynn reckons the care centre has retained customers to the value of £450,000, which, he says, is a conservative estimate.

The care centre continues to evolve and improve so that it now has a marketing focus. CCSB goes beyond just a short phone call. Each complaint that is dealt with is followed up with a questionnaire which asks the consumer to give CCSB a more complete understanding of their satisfaction with the company and its products.

Care centre staff are trained to view their job as a way of improving the service CCSB offers consumers. Regular weekly team meetings review the activities of the previous week and suggestions are aired as to how the service can be enhanced. Staff also have extra training to develop their technical knowledge so that they are better equipped to answer searching questions from consumers.

Not only does CCSB investigate each complaint thoroughly to ensure any mistakes are understood and corrective action is taken, but the careline helps to identify defects that the company is not aware of. An intermittent fault on a can sealer is an example of one such defect.

# *Illustrative questions and suggested solutions*

1 **MARKETING ORIENTATION**

How does marketing orientation differ from product orientation?

2 **THE MARKETING MIX**

What are the elements of the marketing mix? Outline some of the factors to be considered for a company to arrive at an appropriate marketing mix.

3 **SALES TO MARKETING ORIENTATION** **Specimen paper**

Discuss the problems that might arise when a company moves from sales orientation to marketing orientation.

4 **GREEN MARKETING**

Explain what is meant by the term 'green marketing'. Discuss the reasons why such a policy might be followed, and explain the problems involved.

5 **ENVIRONMENTAL FACTORS** **Specimen paper**

In the context of marketing, discuss the influence of environmental factors upon an industry of your choice.

6 **OBJECTIVES, STRATEGIES AND CONTROL**

Using a product of your choice, distinguish between objectives, strategies and control as key elements in the annual marketing plan.

7 **PRIMARY AND SECONDARY RESEARCH**

Using examples, distinguish between primary and secondary research. Explain the limitations of using secondary research in practice.

8 **THE MARKET RESEARCH PLAN**

Outline the structure and content of a market research plan designed to examine the trade opinion of your competitors.

9 **THE PRODUCT LIFE CYCLE**

Describe the stages in the Product Life Cycle.

10 **PACKAGING** **Specimen paper**

In relation to a product range of your choice, prepare a report to management that explains the role of packaging in respect of:

(a) product promotion;
(b) product protection.

11 **SEGMENTATION** **Specimen paper**

Using a consumer *and* an industrial product or service by way of comparison, list and justify sets of segmentation bases for each of these.

12 **PRICING**

Write brief notes on:

(a) cost plus pricing;
(b) market skimming pricing;
(c) marginal cost pricing;
(d) market penetration pricing.

**13 PRICING POLICY** **Specimen paper**

Construct a report to marketing management that explains the factors that should be taken into consideration when pricing for a product line.

**14 DISTRIBUTION**

Distinguish between selective, intensive and exclusive methods of distribution.

**15 MAIL ORDER SELLING**

Describe and account for the growth in mail order selling.

**16 PHYSICAL DISTRIBUTION MANAGEMENT**

What is the role and function of physical distribution management in connecting products to consumers?

**17 WHOLESALER** **Specimen paper**

The principal function of a wholesaler is the breaking down of bulk. As a wholesaler, write a piece of publicity material to your customers informing them of other services that you perform.

**18 SALES PROMOTION**

As promotions manager of a well established UK manufacturer of women's beauty products, explain how you would use sales promotion to support the national launch of 'Chico'. This is a new fragrance targeted at B, C1, 18-45, experimentally minded women who are prepared to try a new perfume.

**19 NOTES ON PROMOTION**

Write brief notes on the following:

(a) unique selling propositions;
(b) the promotional mix;
(c) point of sales display;
(d) publicity.

**20 PUBLIC RELATIONS**

Discuss the statement that public relations can reduce the effects of corporate crisis upon an organisation's publics.

**21 AGENCY/CLIENT RELATIONSHIPS**

The achievement of advertising campaign objectives depends upon effective agency/client relationships. Discuss.

**22 PULL TECHNIQUES** **Specimen paper**

Prepare notes for presentation to general management that describe a range of typical promotional 'pull' techniques that can be employed in order to reach a target audience.

## 23 SERVICES MARKETING

What are the distinctive features of services marketing? Why are they becoming more important for marketing in general?

## 24 CUSTOMER CARE

Describe what you would expect to be the common elements in TQM and customer care programmes. Discuss the relationship between these ideas.

## MINI-CASE

**Specimen paper**

Fine Furnishings Limited is a small chain of distributors of good quality office furniture, carpets, safes and filing cabinets. The company keeps in touch with advances made in the office furniture field world-wide and introduces those products which are in keeping with the needs of the market in terms of design, workmanship, value for money and technical specifications.

It is contended that furniture purchased is a capital investment and a wise decision can help the buyer save on future expenses, because cheaper alternatives have to be replaced more frequently.

Fine Furnishings only trades in good quality furniture which is sturdily constructed. Differences between their products and cheaper, lower quality ones are well known to those who have several years of experience in the business.

An important feature they feel is the availability of a complete list of components of the furniture system. This enables customers to add bits and pieces of matching design and colour in the future. Such components are available for sale separately. Systems are maintained in stock by the company for a number of years and spare parts for chairs and other furniture are always available.

The company has experienced a downturn in trade over the past two years. In addition they had to trim their profit margins. Last year, they barely broke even and this year they are heading for a small loss for the first time in the company's twenty year history.

(a) Advise the company in relation to its product mix. How will your recommendation affect the company's image?

(b) Advise the company in relation to its stockholding policy. How will your recommendations affect customer service?

(c) Suggest ways in which promotional activity might help the company out of the difficulties it now faces.

## 1 MARKETING ORIENTATION

Product orientation as a business philosophy can take two forms, *product orientation* and *sales orientation*.

*Product orientation*

In the last half of the nineteenth and the beginning of the twentieth century business was mainly *production oriented*. Demand for new products was high, due to the mass production methods that reduced prices and increased output. The products that were produced and the prices paid for them depended on the production methods and raw materials that were available. Typical of this ethos is Henry Ford's statement 'you can have any car you like as long as it is black'.

A production orientation looks at what the company can produce rather than what the customer wishes to purchase. Promotion is not considered to be of great importance. Good quality products are supposed to 'sell themselves', and if they do not this is usually blamed on the sales staff or on the customers themselves! Improvements are concentrated on the productive efficiency of the company. Companies that follow a production orientation are often called 'marketing myopic'. Senior management in this type of company often have production backgrounds. If demand is buoyant this approach can be reasonably successful but can be difficult to sustain in the long run. Some firms still are production oriented, for example some high technology industries.

*Sales orientation*

Sales oriented companies are also basically product oriented. In the 1920s and 1930s the downturn in economic activities made firms realise they did not face an insatiable demand for their products and products do not simply sell themselves. Promotional activities came to be of more importance than under a production orientation but the main focus in a sales oriented business is selling the products that have been produced. Again the products and sales figures are important rather than any aspect of customer satisfaction. Companies which are sales oriented are often typified by 'hard sell' tactics. Examples still occur of sales oriented companies, especially in home improvements or insurance sectors. It should be remembered that selling is an important function of the marketing mix. The basic assumption of a selling orientation is that customers will not seek out your products and they actually have to be sold to them, which is closer to a market orientation than a production orientation. However, a selling orientation does not build brand loyalty and is a rather short-term vision of the market place.

*Marketing orientation*

Marketing orientation is often called *customer orientation*. Instead of products and the selling of products being of central importance, the consumer is the focus of the marketing oriented firm. This takes a longer term view of business and profitability. A marketing oriented company sets out to define what the customer actually wants and then produces goods that fill those wants. Companies then make what customers want to buy rather than produce what they are good at or have traditionally supplied.

To be truly marketing oriented the firm should practice consumer orientation at all levels and within all functions of the organisation. This means that from Managing Director to shop floor workers all staff should have the customer in mind. Marketing should not simply be a functional department that organises the promotional aspects of the firm, rather it should be practised as a philosophy by all departments whether they be finance, production or marketing. This will change the objectives of all departments: for example, if the production department is customer oriented it may only produce short runs of certain products, whereas from a purely production point of view, it might prefer longer runs.

*Change to marketing orientation*

The organisational changes necessary for a company to move from being product oriented to marketing oriented are difficult for companies to make because they are not simply bureaucratic but require retraining and reorganisation at all levels. Usually a would be marketing oriented firm has a marketing director high up in the organisation's hierarchy, but this must be more than a token gesture if a true marketing orientation is to be achieved.

Within a customer oriented firm there is a great need for marketing research as this is the main way in which customer needs are identified. These needs may not simply be the obvious need that the product fills, but the less obvious needs that encompass the total product offering. For example, a car fulfils the need for transportation but there are many more personal and social needs that are filled by the particular model of car.

Markets are dynamic: they are constantly changing. Customer orientation means that these changes can be monitored and perhaps acted upon before the competition. Customer orientation also fosters the idea of brand loyalty. If you are satisfying customer needs, and are monitoring those needs for changes, then customers are less likely to go elsewhere for products. A marketing orientation takes a much longer term view of business than a product orientation.

*Societal marketing*

Recently there has been an interest in what has been termed *societal marketing.* What the customer wants may not be in his best interest in the long run (eg smoking) or in society's best interest. Societal marketing aims to move from a simple marketing orientation to one that assesses the environmental and long-term consumer interest. In practice, of course, this is unlikely to make much headway unless backed by government legislation, but in the UK the Body Shop is one example of a company whose marketing orientation has a strong societal bias.

*Conclusion*

A product orientation makes the needs of the producer central, but marketing orientation makes the consumer central. For a company to be truly marketing oriented it should adopt a marketing orientation throughout the whole organisation and not simply treat it as a divisional role.

## 2 THE MARKETING MIX

A company's marketing mix includes all the tools that come under the organisation's control to affect the way products and services are offered to the market. Borden coined the phrase 'the marketing mix' from the idea that business executives were mixers of ingredients. From observing industries and individual firms it can be seen that there are wide ranging applications of the tools of marketing. The elements of the marketing mix are often described as the 'four Ps', Product, Price, Place and Promotion. It includes all the policies and procedures involved in each of these elements. This can be on a strategic level: for instance, whether to adopt a penetration or skimming pricing policy for a new product. It can also be on a more tactical level, for instance special price discounts. Each element is looked into in more detail below.

*Product*

Decisions to be made regarding products include the product lines that are produced, product improvements, new product development and which market(s) to sell them in, including whether to adopt a market segmentation approach.

*Pricing*

Decisions include the appropriate price level to adopt, the specific prices, price strategy for new products and price variations.

*Place*

The 'place' aspect of the four Ps is often also called 'channels of distribution'. This includes the way in which goods are passed from the manufacturer to the final consumer.

*Promotion*

Promotional aspects include personal selling, advertising, publicity and sales promotions. Each of these must be looked into to give an overall consistent message to the public. For example, it is not good to stress service quality in advertising if the actual personal selling of the organisation is not of high calibre. Decisions have to be made on the amount of time and money spent, media selection, desired image and length of campaign.

This is obviously not an exhaustive list. Some elements of the marketing mix do not easily fall exclusively into one category. Packaging, for example, has promotional aspects and product aspects.

There are many factors that come into play when the organisation is considering the most appropriate marketing mix. Some of these are market forces and some are product specific.

Many product areas are dominated by players that excel in one area of the marketing mix. A market may be typified by price competition for example, whereas in another branding may be of importance. This dominance of one aspect of the marketing mix will have an influence on competitors in the industry. This does not mean to say that all firms within the industry successfully differentiate themselves from the competition by focusing on neglected areas of the marketing mix. The stage in the product life cycle also has an influence on the appropriate marketing mix. In the introductory stage any design problems with the actual product should be solved. Price will depend on the costs of developing the product and the strategy regarding required market share. Promotion may concentrate on creating awareness and distribution may be selective. Throughout the other stages in the product life cycle the objectives of the marketing mix may change and the growth and maturity stage product differentiation, image building and quality may be concentrated on; whilst in the decline stage rationalisations may occur.

Other factors that should be taken into account when designing a marketing mix include the following.

*Buyer behaviour*

The behaviour of consumers and the behaviour of intermediaries should be taken into account. The actual number of buyers in a market is important as is the motivation for purchase and their buying processes. It is of no use to provide products by mail order, for example, if there is a strong resistance from buyers to purchasing products in this way. Whether the firm is providing goods or services will have an influence on buyer behaviour, as will whether the purchaser is in the consumer or industrial market. All these aspects will have an influence on marketing mix decisions.

*Competitors*

To a certain degree this has been dealt with above. However, the influence of competitors on marketing mix decisions is far reaching. Companies must analyse competitor strengths and weaknesses and their likely response to any marketing tools used.

*Government*

The government imposes some controls on marketing that would affect decisions made regarding the marketing mix. These include regulations on advertising (eg cigarette ban), product specifications, pricing and competitive practices.

*Company specific*

All the above factors have to be taken into account when designing an appropriate marketing mix. However, it is easy to overlook one important consideration, that is company resources. The amount of money and staffing resources that marketing is allocated will determine to a large extent the elements of the marketing mix that are viable. The efficiency and effectiveness of marketing programmes need to be constantly monitored and built into the marketing planning process for the future.

All these factors, including the size and resources of the organisation, should be taken into account when marketers are designing marketing mix programmes.

## 3 SALES TO MARKETING ORIENTATION

With this question the central factors to be dealt with are:

(a) the nature of a sales orientation to business;
(b) the nature of a market orientation to business.
(c) a discussion of the problems involved from (a) to (b).

(a) *The nature of a sales orientation*

This type of approach prioritises 'making the sale'; the profit motive, rather than customer needs or quality provision dominates corporate organisation. The organisation of information, staff and work activity are all geared towards 'getting more business'.

The business is likely to be very tightly controlled by strict budgets, and the product range limited to accommodate fast turnover of product. Unless the market is highly competitive, customer servicing would not be considered important. Customers are perceived as 'numbers' rather than as a priority.

The organisation is likely to be highly centralised, usually around a founder sales-orientated entrepreneur who does not prioritise any focus on 'marketing', and who may use the occasional marketing concept, but only as it becomes necessary to make a sale. Autocratic management of such businesses is also quite common. Such businesses tend to be resistant to change and operate much on a 'we've always done it this way' approach.

(b) *The nature of a market orientation*

Customer considerations are prioritised and marketing personnel are in the highest executives positions. External market influences are considered, the business's objectives being to match total company resources against marketing opportunities. There is more emphasis given to marketing strategy and business planning. The firm desires and builds a successful corporate image through relationship marketing and active public relations.

There is flexibility in production so as to meet customer needs and made to measure (bespoke) production is possible: the firm only produces that for which it has found a market.

The firm actively seeks to create markets and to develop (though a commitment to on-going research and development) saleable products. Marketing is often seen as a company-wide function or at the very least it has strongly integrated links with other business functions.

There is greater attention to what the customer will pay, to how pricing can be used as a marketing weapon and to how competitors will react. Budgets are based on marketing requirements and funds are allocated on the basis of marketing tasks to be accomplished. There is an active and complex market intelligence system in operation.

Based on market research - suggestions for improved or new products stem from research into customer's needs and close attention is given to adding competitive value through customer servicing.

Motivation and training of the sales organisation is given high priority, the chief sales executive being regarded as part of the senior management team.

Advertising and promotion are considered as of strategic importance and often as a source of competitive differential advantage. There is often a high commitment of financial resources to well-researched promotion plans. There is an active and complex management of the product portfolio and a clearly focused and detailed product/market strategy.

(c) *Problems involved with moving from a sales to a marketing orientation*

(i) *Cultural change.* People need time and training in the new approaches; it cannot happen overnight.

(ii) *No change in top management.* A marketing orientation necessitates executive change at senior level - a true 'marketeer' is needed to lead the change.

(iii) *A superficial approach.* Management only adopt the parts of marketing orientation which least change the status quo.

(iv) *Change under negative pressure.* Managers decide that the organisation is likely to go into liquidation unless (temporarily) some other approach is tried to try and redeem customer sales.

(v) *Lack of skills.* The firm does not have the right people with the right skills in the right jobs to make the marketing orientation work effectively.

(vi) *Wrong time.* The new orientation may be introduced at the wrong time such that planning is not possible or the firm is forced to adapt in a rushed fashion. This may lead to a lack of belief in the new approach.

(vii) *Inexperience relative to competitors.* If the market is highly competitive then other firms may well be far more effective at market orientation because of their length of time of practice. This may lead to a temporary loss of business as staff become experienced in the new practices.

## 4 GREEN MARKETING

*Tutorial note.* This solution is very long and detailed. You would be expected to make only the most obvious points in an examination.

'Green marketing' brings the *environment* into the 'triangle' involving company, customers and competitor to create a 'magic diamond'. There are strong reasons for bringing the environment into the business equation, but the strongest reason is the 'green consumer' or growing public awareness of the issues involved. Since customer reaction is the ultimate determinant of market success and profitability, green marketing must be taken seriously by even the most sceptical businessman, since his customers now consider it to be important.

Green consumption can be defined as the decisions directly or indirectly related to consumer choice and usage which involve environmentally-related beliefs, values, attitudes, behaviour or choice criteria. That this is important is evident from:

(a) surveys which indicate increased levels of environmental awareness and concern;
(b) increasing demand for and availability of information on environmental issues;

(c) green product concepts and green substitute products;
(d) value shifts from consumption to conservation;
(e) effective PR and marketing campaigns by environmental charities and causes.

Nevertheless, of course, levels of greenness vary across the population. The market can be segmented. Profiles of green consumers show that the force of green concern varies according to product class, prevailing market conditions, attitudes and beliefs about the product in question.

A behaviourally-based *psychographic typology* by Ogilvy and Mather involves a range of factors.

*Activists* (16%) are:

(a) aware of the issues;
(b) likely to buy green products;
(c) concerned for their children;
(d) optimistic about technological change;
(e) people oriented;
(f) home owners with children;
(g) Conservative voters;
(h) likely to be upmarket consumers.

*Realists* (34%):

(a) are the youngest group - those with young children;
(b) are worried about the environment;
(c) consider profit and environmental protection as conflicting;
(d) are pessimistic about a solution;
(e) are sceptical about a 'green bandwagon';
(f) vote Labour.

*Complacents* (28%):

(a) are upmarket consumers with older children;
(b) are optimistic - about mankind, business and government;
(c) see this as someone else's problem;
(d) are not very conscious of green issues;
(e) are right wing politically.

*Alienated* (22%):

(a) are less well educated, downmarket consumers;
(b) are young families/senior citizens;
(c) are unaware of green issues;
(d) see greenness as a fashion or a fad;
(e) are pessimistic about a solution;
(f) are left wing politically.

Green marketing argues that marketing *as such* is not environmentally unfriendly, and that the products and services with which it deals will necessarily become greener to reflect more general awareness of the need to counter the effects of environmental degradation and develop sustainable management strategies.

A new, green, managerial orientation is involved. This will include:

(a) rethinking the balance between efficiency and effectiveness;
(b) rethinking attitudes to and relationships with customers;
(c) rethinking the balance between our needs and our wants;
(d) redefining 'customer satisfaction';
(e) refocusing onto the long term objective, rather than short or medium term;
(f) 'less is more';
(g) rethinking the value chain;
(h) new corporate culture(s).

*Marketing information*

At the heart of green marketing is an appreciation and thorough understanding of the ways in which the company impacts on the customer, the society and the environment. An audit of company performance is therefore essential.

Customer needs, and their sensitivities to particular environmental issues, need to be closely researched, along with the activities, strategies and policies of competitors. A typical mode of analysis, such as the SCEPTICAL list, could be applied to green issues.

*Marketing planning*

Marketing plans need to be re-considered in the light of new environmental priorities. Those areas which will require re-definition include:

(a) financial, strategic product/market and technical objectives;

(b) markets;

(c) strategies and action plans, including market share, customer satisfactions and competitor comparisons;

(d) performance and technical aspects of product performance and quality.

*Performance*

All of these aspects will have to be fitted within a view of the company's performance which takes account of environmental responsibilities. In addition, the traditional criteria for evaluating success or failure, and the parameters within which they operate, may well have to be re-drawn.

*Time*

Timescales also have to be lengthened considerably, since products are now evaluated in terms of their long term effects, as well as the impact of the processes by means of which they have been produced. Programmes designed to clean up environmental impacts often take a long time to become fully operational.

*Judging success*

Getting marketing's four Ps (price, place, promotion and product) right leads to profit, according to orthodox ideas. Green marketing insists that the mix must be evaluated in terms of four Ss.

Satisfaction of customer needs

Safety of products and production for customers, workers, society and the environment

Social acceptability of a product, its production and other activities of the company

Sustainability of the products, their production and the other activities of the company

*Competitors and suppliers*

Since greenness will be an important competitive factor, it will be important for companies to have information about their performance here in comparison with major competitors and to be assured that their suppliers are meeting green standards.

*A model of the green marketing process*

Like conventional marketing, green marketing needs to sort out not the four Ps of the conventional mix but a blend of internal and external factors. Peattie (1992) describes these as internal and external 'green Ps', to be used as a checklist to diagnose how well the company is succeeding in living up to targets for green performance.

Inside the company, marketers need to attend to the following 'internal green Ps'.

(a) *Products.* A green audit needs to look at how safe products are in use, how safe they are when disposed of, how long they last, and what are the environmental consequences of materials used in manufacturing and packaging the product.

(b) *Promotion.* Using green messages in promotion. Establishing standards of accuracy and reliability.

(c) *Price.* Prices set for green products must reflect differences in demand; price sensitivity is also an important issue.

(d) *Place.* How green are the methods by which distribution takes place?

(e) *Providing information.* This needs to be related to internal and external issues bearing on environmental performance.

(f) *Processes.* Energy consumed, waste produced.

(g) *Policies.* Do they motivate the workforce, monitor and react to environmental performance?

(h) *People.* Do they understand environmental issues and how the company performs in relation to these issues?

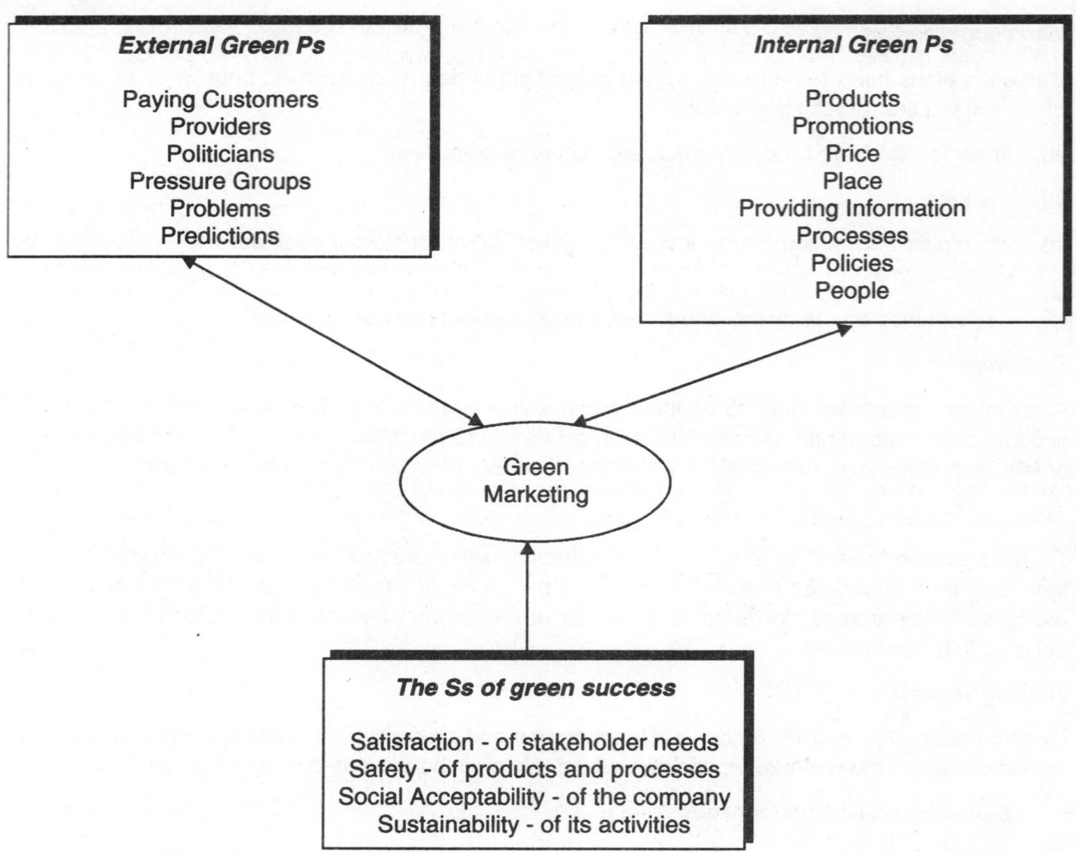


Outside the company, a different set of factors need to be addressed. These might be referred to as 'external green Ps'.

(a) *Paying customers.* What are their needs in relation to green products and services? What information are they receiving about green products?

(b) *Providers.* How green are suppliers of services and materials to the company?

(c) *Politicians.* Public awareness and concern over green issues is beginning to have a strong influence on the legislation which appears and this directly impacts on the conduct of business. A modern organisation must make this part of its concerns.

(d) *Pressure groups.* What are the main issues of concern? Which groups are involved and what new issues are likely to concern them?

(e) *Problems.* Which environmental issues have been a problem for the company, or part of the area in which it works, in the past?

(f) *Predictions.* What environmental problems loom in the future? Awareness of scientific research can be strategically vital.

(g) *Partners.* How green are my allies? How are business partners perceived? Will this pose problems?

Being able to predict problems can produce great strategic advantages, but also some odd results. The problem of CFCs from aerosols, and their effects on the ozone layer, was known about from the early 1970s and Johnson & Johnson abandoned the use of them in their products back in 1976. Consumer reacts to the product began in the late 1980s and of course the firm were well prepared but found themselves in a very strange position, having to attach 'ozone friendly' labels to products which had, in fact, been modified more than ten years before!

This illustrates green marketing problems very well - action is vital at the time when public *perceptions* threaten a product, rather than the manufacturer simply dealing with the environmental dangers which the product may pose. There are still problems, however. A number of barriers have to be overcome.

*Costs* are likely to be incurred with the need to develop new products and services.

*Technical and organisational barriers* have to be overcome in developing, for instance, practical applications of green energy sources and in reshaping organisations and their workforces into new ways of carrying out their workroles and promoting new attitudes to their jobs.

At the moment, many of the problems which will need to be addressed are highly *complex*, and there seem to be conflicts between the various alternatives available.

Many of the policies pursued by a particular enterprise will have implications for the environment in countries *beyond national boundaries*. Conversely, changes which promote beneficial effects, for example on the ozone layer, may well *not have visible effects*, and may be resisted as a consequence. The fact that problems are generally created, and have to be treated, over a relatively *long time scale* also creates difficulties in promoting policies and mobilising groups to implement them.

One of the main problems faced by those seeking to implement these green policies is the *lack of certainty* about the *nature* of the problem, about the *effectiveness* of the remedies proposed, and about the *reactions* of the publics towards which these policies are ultimately directed. In some cases, companies have introduced supposedly environmentally friendly policies and products simply as a means of paying token allegiance to the idea, or to try to garner extra sales from the gullible. One consequence of this is *moral fatigue* - as with other issues in the past, the public may become jaundiced and disenchanted with the whole idea, or sceptical about claims to greenness which are made, in various ways, by almost every manufacturer or service provider.

## 5 ENVIRONMENTAL FACTORS

*Tutorial note.* This question has in fact been answered in much broader terms than just the environment in a 'green' sense.

A specific choice of industry is required. Then you should seek to adopt the following approach.

The environment should be sub-divided into micro or internal environment and macro or external environment. You could comment that internal (or intrinsic) influences are largely within the control of the firm and external (or extrinsic) influences are largely outside the control of the firm. The firm makes strategic responses:

(a) to the internal factors through management processes and policies;
(b) to the external factors through the corporate planning activity.

You should then proceed to define the types of influences within each, all of which shape and influence marketing activity.

*Internal influences*

(a) *The corporate culture.* 'The attitudes, behaviours and values of the workforce'. This will determine ultimately the quality of the work and the degree of competitiveness attained.

(b) *The management style.* This will influence the type of culture which develops and how the work gets done. The more participative the approach, the greater the motivation of the staff.

(c) *Size and complexity of the organisation.* This will influence the degree of efficiency with which the work gets done and the speed and responsiveness to customer needs and/or major change. Usually, the bigger and more complex the organisation, the slower and more bureaucratic the work processes.

*External influences*

These, as far as marketing is concerned, should exceed in number the internal influences, and they may include the following.

(a) *Quality of supplier relations.* High quality relationships need to be developed with the right type of suppliers. Reciprocity (suppliers who are also customers) would strengthen this relationship. When supplier relations fail, customers suffer and may place their business elsewhere.

(b) *Competitiveness of market.* The more competitive the industry, the greater is the requirement for both organisational efficiency and market orientation if profitability is to continue and the firm survive.

(c) *Nature of customer base (type of market).* If the market is brand-sensitive then the firm will have to invest heavily in a promotional mix to build and retain brand loyalty. If the market is subject to regular change, the firm will need to commit itself to high levels of market and customer research in order to maintain a competitive position.

(d) *Impact of regulatory processes.* Where the market is highly regulated (such as financial services) firms may find they have to invest considerable sums of money to stay within new regulations.

(e) *Impact of social change.* Where the industry is subject to changes in taste or fashion, then the firm could perceive such change as an opportunity rather than a constraint (eg the environmental or 'green movement'), it could proceed to develop or modify products and services to meet such change.

(f) *The impact of technical change.* New technology facilitates the opportunity to increase competitiveness through providing opportunities for increased speed, greater flexibility and better quality. It is important for the firm to keep up-dated in developments in its industry so competitors do not reap the benefits of such technology.

(g) *Impact of economic and political change.* The impact of rising and falling interest, tax and government spending rates can significantly undermine or assist the firm's marketing planning, as can the development of the economic cycle. Through a process of forward planning and research, the firm can be more proactive so that impending political or economic change can to some extent be in-built to business predictions, though no-one can predict the nature of economic or political crises.

All the above factors should be built into a periodic PEST and SWOT analysis which will themselves be part of the periodic marketing planning process.

## 6 OBJECTIVES, STRATEGIES AND CONTROL

The product chosen to illustrate the annual marketing plan is washing powder.

The annual marketing plan is the operational plan that is based on the longer term strategic marketing plan. Annual plans explain the way in which the company is aiming for the objectives of the strategic marketing plan. There are a number of reasons why it is important to formulate annual marketing plans.

(a) They explain what the present situation is and what is expected in the year ahead
(b) They indicate the resources that are necessary to fulfil the objectives
(c) They specify expectations so that the company can anticipate where it will be in a year's time
(d) They describe the course of action over the next year
(e) They allow performance to be monitored

The basic marketing planning process can be shown in diagrammatic form for a given year.

*The annual marketing plan*

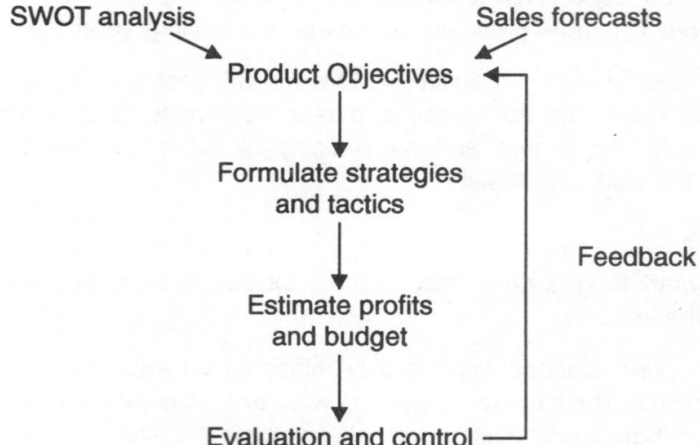


Here, we will concentrate on three areas of the planning process using washing powder as an example.

*Objectives*

Objectives in the annual plan concentrate on product rather than strategic applications. The SWOT (strengths and weaknesses/opportunities and threats) analysis would indicate a number of implications for the washing powder manufacturer. There may be a new competitor in the market, or new product attributes sought by the consumer, for example more environmentally 'friendly' powders.

The objectives for the brand of washing powder over the next year can now be defined. One could be to improve market share by a certain percentage, but with a new competitor the company might be pleased if it maintains market share for this year. A certain sales volume may be specified depending, of course, on the company's assessment of opportunities in the market. Profits will be another objective of the company and are often stated in terms of return on investment (net profits divided by total investment). The company may have to decide whether the return on investment is substantial enough or whether it could do better investing elsewhere. The annual marketing plan should also set objectives for the marketing mix variables. These objectives are necessary in order to satisfy the broader objectives of market share etc. For example, if the washing powder manufacturer wishes to increase market share by 5% over the year, then this will have implications for the marketing mix objectives. Promotional effort will probably have to be increased in order to take market share from other companies, as there would be few new users to target.

*Strategy*

There are many levels in the organisation where strategies can be developed. *Corporate strategy* deals with the overall development of an organisation's business activities whilst *marketing strategy* looks at the organisation's activities in the markets served. This can be long term or short term as in the case of annual marketing planning. Going back to the above model, when product objectives have been formulated then the marketing strategy that should allow these objectives to be met can be developed. There may be refinements to be made as to the target market the company is aiming for.

Perhaps the washing powder brand has slipped downmarket over time. A decision has to be made whether to fully address this target market or to reposition the powder. Marketing mix variables can then be developed to accomplish these objectives. If the objective is to increase sales by a certain percentage then a promotion of a money off coupon may be used to increase sales. If the objective is to build brand awareness then an extensive advertising campaign can be used. Different objectives will have different implications for the marketing mix strategy that is most appropriate.

*Control*

The purpose of *control* of the annual marketing plan is to examine whether the objectives have been achieved. Control of marketing planning should not simply be left to the end of the year evaluation of the success of the product, but be reviewed throughout the year. The results of evaluation and control should be included in the formulation of the annual plan in the following year.

If sales of the washing powder are below those that were indicated in the objectives then reasons for this should be analysed. It may be that during the year the introduction of liquid detergents for washing clothes and heavy promotion of these products detracted from the company's brand. In this case a decision should be made whether to sit back and see if this was just a short-term phenomenon or whether to promote the powder aggressively. One way in which control can be managed by a company is through 'management by objectives'. Management set short-term goals (monthly or quarterly), performance against these goals is analysed, and if these are not met then the reasons are analysed and corrective action taken. Usually sales analysis, market share analysis, marketing expenses to sales analysis, financial analysis and customer attitudes are used to control the annual marketing plan. The main responsibility for annual marketing plan control is with top or middle management.

## 7 PRIMARY AND SECONDARY RESEARCH

Research can be classified as either primary or secondary. Secondary research consists of existing research material and is often termed *desk research*. Primary research is new original data collected specifically for a purpose.

*Secondary research*

Secondary research is often conducted before primary research because of the high cost of primary research and the time it takes to conduct. Secondary sources include the following.

(a) *Internal data sources*, for example, sales figures, financial data, customer complaints and past research reports. Internal data sources are often a neglected area of marketing research. Sometimes the way the data is collected can make an important difference to their use in marketing research.

(b) *Government sources*. There are many publications from government departments that are useful secondary research sources. The *Guide to Official Statistics* (HMSO) and *Regional Statistics* (HMSO) are useful publications that will aid the researcher to discover what statistics are available and where they can be found. Government departments also publish data that may be of use to the market researcher: for example, *Housing and Construction Statistics* and *Family Expenditure Survey Reports*. Government departments in other countries also publish statistical data, as do organisations such as the EU.

(c) *Other publications*. There is a vast array of additional data sources available to the researcher. Many trade associations publish data for the industry. Yearbooks and directories are published in many industries. Professional institutions also provide members with information. The general and trade press also can be useful sources of information on trends and competitors. There are a number of commercial research companies that can also be used. Well known examples in this area are Mintel, MEAL (Media Expenditure Analysis), Euromonitor and the Economist Intelligence Group. Industry surveys from a financial viewpoint are conducted by some brokerage firms.

Secondary research can be expensive if all these reports are purchased. It may be in the company's best interests to join one of the main commercial libraries for example at London or Manchester Business School. Secondary data has a number of limitations which will be dealt with later, first we will turn our attention to primary research.

*Primary research*

Primary research can be classified into three areas: experimentation, observation and questionnaires/interviewing. Experimentation is often used in the fields of scientific or technical research, as it usually involves testing in a laboratory situation where variables can be controlled. Within marketing, however, this is very difficult to do as there are many behavioural and situational variables that affect purchase decisions. Experimental research in marketing involves the testing of changes to one aspect of the marketing mix to monitor response. A supermarket may be contemplating the introduction of a new dessert and therefore introduce it in a representative sample of outlets to observe sales. Price sensitivity can be monitored using experimental research, as can the acceptability and effectiveness of advertisements.

Observing consumers' buying behaviour can also be a useful primary data collection method. Bias in the research is kept to a minimum in this method because of the distance between researcher and subject. Audits can be made of products in stock in sales outlets, or traffic and pedestrian flows can be monitored to assess the viability of sites. Consumers' shopping behaviour can be monitored using video cameras, EPOS systems and personal observation. Also of importance when assessing the level of service the company is providing is observing the behaviour of staff.

Questionnaires and interviewing are the most common methods of primary data collection. Questionnaires can be structured and administered by post or by person or semi-structured and administered verbally either face to face or by telephone. Interviews are usually based on a semi-structured questionnaire and can be individual or in groups. Great care is needed on the design of questionnaires to make sure that the information gained is what was really required.

*Summary*

To be successful, research should ideally use more than one technique. Secondary data can be used, for example, as an industry overview and to suggest areas where primary research is required. Although comparatively cheap, secondary research does have limitations. It can give an overview of an industry but many of the details that are important to marketing management are missing. There may not be a great deal of secondary information available in certain industry sectors, so primary research becomes more important. If there is data available for the industry as a whole it is not specific to any one company. In practice some of the secondary data sources can be quite difficult to obtain. The choice of research methods obviously depends on the objectives of the research. If you wish to find out the consumer attitudes to your product, secondary internal sources can be used to a certain degree, but primary research would give a more detailed and useful picture. Primary research is not without problems though, as specialist staff need to be used to administer and analyse primary data. However, the main limitation of secondary research is that it does not specifically relate to the company's consumers.

## 8 THE MARKET RESEARCH PLAN

There are a number of factors that have to be considered before a research plan can be designed. Whether or not the research should be done in house or through an agency will depend on the capabilities of the marketing department. The budget that is available will determine the methodology chosen to a certain degree. Any time constraints will also have an effect on the method chosen. The research plan should firstly set out clear objectives. In this case the objective will be 'to investigate the opinions and attitudes towards our trade competitors'.

Secondary research would have to be undertaken in order to assess the marketplace.

*Secondary research - sources of information*

Before an analysis of competitors can be started they have first to be identified. This can be done by looking at directories and yearbooks, asking present and past customers, keeping a 'weather eye' on trade press and asking sales representatives. Company profiles can then be used to give descriptions of the company in terms of size, profitability, past performance, corporate culture and image. Information that will be required to draw up these profiles can be found in annual reports (available from Companies House), trade press and published commercial reports in the area.

*Primary research*

The primary research should cover three areas. It should make an assessment of awareness of your company and its competitors. The image, opinions and attitude towards competitors (include your company also to get a comparative picture) should then be investigated. It should also look at the buying practices of the respondent, although not in a great deal of detail, simply enough to make recommendations in this area. Sales representatives could be used to gain information on competing firms although they will not really have the necessary skills to do this adequately and would probably not be objective.

The internal capabilities of the company should be taken into account when deciding whether to undertake the research in house or to employ a specialist marketing research company. The sample selected will depend greatly on the type of industry the company competes in. If the industry is dominated by a small number of large firms, a different sampling method should be used than for an industry characterised by a large number of small firms. If there are only a few buyers of the product in the market, then it is possible to research all the buyers. If there are a large number, then a representative sample must be chosen.

The primary research recommended is a questionnaire that would be administered by an interviewer. If the budget did not allow for this, then questionnaires could be mailed. However, when asking about awareness it is better that an interviewer is present. Also the responses to the first section (on awareness) will determine the companies that will be asked about in the second section (comparing attributes). Many firms will not be averse to discussing competitors in this way as they see it as encouraging competition. Before the interviewer calls, it is necessary to discover in each company who the right person to interview would be. This person should be an important member of the buying group, who will have the authority to answer questions. Researchers should telephone beforehand to make an appointment with the correct person. The identification of respondents can be made either by telephone or by consulting sales representatives.

The questionnaire should be designed with care and should include the following.

(a) A section evaluating the respondent's awareness of competitors in the industry and your own company.

(b) A section to give information on the opinions on your company and competitors. This should be scaled; for example, a rating from poor to excellent can be used for the companies the respondent is aware of along the following dimensions.

    (i) Quality of service (pre-sale)
    (ii) Quality of after sales service
    (iii) Delivery time
    (iv) Delivery reliability
    (v) Product range
    (vi) Price
    (vii) Value for money

    Following on from this, the competitors' images can be assessed by asking respondents to rate each company along certain dimensions. This can be done by having statements that are scaled from 'agree strongly' to 'disagree strongly' and include statements such as 'the company is a traditional type of supplier' or 'the company follows the market leader'.

(c) A section that analyses the way in which purchases are made for this type of product in the company. Questions that should be asked include: how many people are involved in buying? Is there an informal or formal buying procedure?

*Analysis*

The analysis that is appropriate will depend on the sample size. If a very small number were interviewed, then little statistical analysis can be carried out. For larger samples questionnaires should be coded for ease of analysis. This will also mean that cross tabulations can be performed on data. For example, quality can be cross tabulated with price. General percentages should be analysed before undertaking any advanced quantitative techniques.

*Report preparation*

The research report should then be presented in a way that can be quickly and easily understood. It should not include detailed statistical analysis but should include the pertinent points and conclusions and recommendations.

Included in the research plan should be an envisaged time scale for each aspect of the research as shown below.

*Time scale of research*

| | *Week* |
|---|---|
| Secondary research | 1-2 |
| Design sample frame | 2-3 |
| Primary data collection | 3-6 |
| Analysis | 6-8 |
| Report preparation | 8-10 |

*Limitations*

Limitations of the research should be acknowledged. Budget and time limitations are obviously important. The identification of the sample is another area in which limitations are likely to exist. Unless there are a very small number of competing suppliers there is not going to be a 100% response rate. Including more respondents would alter the findings of the research.

## 9 THE PRODUCT LIFE CYCLE

Product sales and profitability change over time. The pattern of development can be divided into distinct sections. The diagram below shows the typical product life cycle representation.

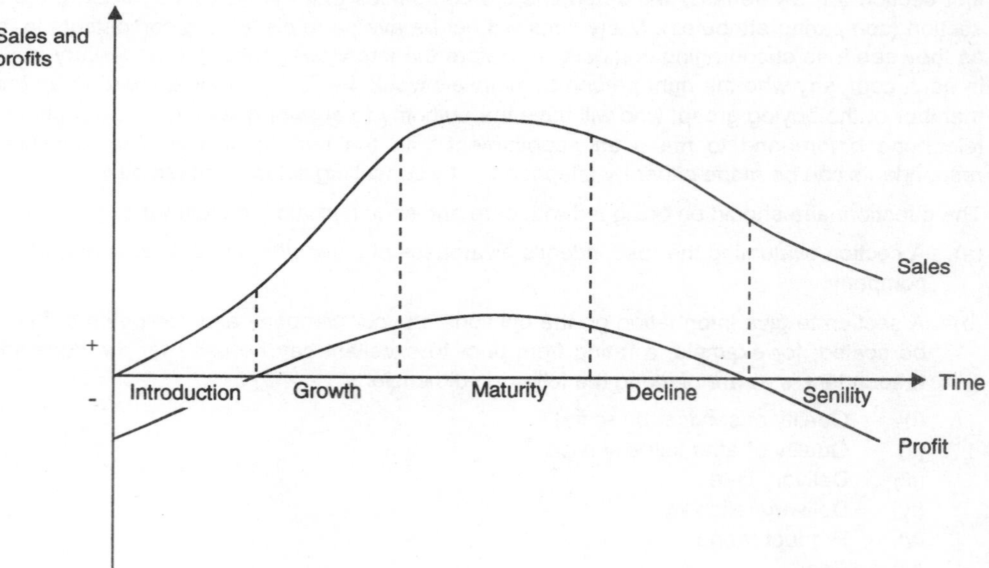


For different types of products and services the length of the life cycle will vary, as will the level of sales at each stage. In the development stage ideas for new products are generated and screened for viability. The new product's profit potential can then be assessed and the decision taken on whether the launch of the product would fit current company strategic objectives. The initial concept can be tested by consumer research, and then a few prototypes of the products can be produced and tested by consumer panels. Before the launch of the product on a nationwide scale test marketing is often used, commonly using a TV region to launch the product in a limited area. Most discussions of the product life cycle concentrate on the four stages after the product has been launched: introduction, growth, maturity and decline.

*Introduction*

In the introductory stage the product takes time to be accepted by consumers so sales growth is slow. Only a few firms sell the product so competition is slack, costs are high because of low output. Camcorders are probably still in their introductory stage in the consumer market. The price for the product will depend on product strategy. A high price can be charged in order to recover high development costs if demand for the product is not thought to be particularly price sensitive. This is *price skimming*. A low initial price strategy is known as *price penetration*. This strategy is suitable when demand is price sensitive and there is a need to stimulate demand for the product. Promotion in the introduction stage will concentrate on building awareness of the product. In consumer markets this is often done by above the line advertising and the use of free samples to encourage trial of the product. The distribution method chosen needs to be carefully assessed if products are to succeed. In this stage of the PLC only a few distribution channels are commonly used. The product itself may go through a period of refinement to match consumer preferences. There is usually a limited variety of product features. Word of mouth recommendations of the product are very important in this stage, and sales are often made to consumers who are willing to take a risk buying a new product. These consumers can be described as *innovators*.

*Growth*

In the growth stage more competitors enter the market with similar products, sometimes with extra features. There is an overall expansion of the market. Competitors learn from the original producer's mistakes. Customers who purchase in this stage are *followers* rather than *leaders*. Dishwashers are in their growth stage of the PLC. There are more product varieties, styles, colours and options available to the market. Distribution networks often become much wider in the growth stage. As competitors enter the market the price is likely to fall. Marketers try to create a *unique selling proposition* (USP) in order to maintain a price premium. This is often achieved by creating a brand image. Promotion in this stage will highlight the differences between the product and competitors and build brand awareness.

*Maturity*

In the maturity stage the market becomes saturated. Demand becomes more stable so producers can match production and consumption more easily. A small number of competitors are left, with fewer new entrants into the market. Consumers are usually buying the products as a replacement rather than for the first time. An example of a product in the mature stage is refrigerators. Prices become more stable, with temporary price promotions boosting sales in the short term. Promotions will remind consumers of the product, brand image and its USP. Established relationships exist in the distribution of the product. Brand image will be well established and hopefully has encouraged consumers to be loyal to the brand. The maturity stage can be the longest of all four stages. In order to extend it as long as possible managers seek to:

(a) find new users for the product;
(b) develop new market segments for the product;
(c) refine the product design.

*Decline*

The final stage of the product life cycle is the decline stage. Demand falls as customers purchase new products that fulfil their needs better. An example could be black and white televisions. The product can still be profitable if enough loyal customers remain. If these customers are not particularly price sensitive then price can remain relatively high. Advertising can be used to remind consumers about the product. One of the main problems is that as sales fall distributors may reduce the allocated shelf space or stop stocking the product. Product improvements do not usually occur at this stage. The decision has to be made whether to withdraw the product from sale.

The discussion above looks at the stages of a 'typical' product life cycle. There are, however, failed products that do not go through all the stages and products that are fads or fashions that do not follow the typical shape. Product life cycle analysis can be used on product categories (eg coffee), product forms (eg instant coffee) and brands (eg Nescafe). In the main brands have shorter life cycles. There have been many criticisms of the PLC concept as a marketing tool. One of the main ones is that the course of the PLC can be affected by marketing strategy so products may be discontinued when they could have been revived.

## 10 PACKAGING

**Report**

To: *The management*
From: *A marketer*
Re: *Packaging*

Packaging is one of the most vital aspects of the marketing mix. It shares its importance with naming the product and with branding which will appear on the package. Packaging forms part of the 'augmented product' which, to be effective, must strengthen the selling potential of the core product.

The package can be defined as the container, label and any further wrapping such as a carton holding a bottle. There are two main considerations in answering the question.

(a) The actual containing of the product for its protection, enabling it to be marketed in certain quantities, including the material from which the package is made.

(b) The use of the package as a means of distinctively identifying and promoting the product.

(a) *The role of packaging in protection*

Where the product has to travel any distance in the chain of distribution, it is important that the packaging is sturdy enough to afford secure protection, particularly if the journey is one to an overseas market where long distances and different distribution systems are involved.

For health and regulatory reasons, with a food product, the packaging must keep the product free from contamination or the manufacturer may face prosecution should a customer pursue a claim.

The packaging should afford ease of handling and convenience to all intermediaries and, with the increasing use of palletisation, be robust enough to withstand mechanical handling procedures. The packaging should be able to withstand the climatic conditions it will experience in transit, so that the product remains 'as new' at all times. The packaging must be of a form that is capable of being labelled, for security, ordering, processing or recognition purposes.

(b) *The role of packaging in promotion*

The package should provide accurate information as to ingredients (if a foodstuff) or instructions of use (if a tool or piece of equipment).

The package could be shaped to enhance the product's 'unique selling proposition' and as a differentiating tool from competitive offerings. Colours, logos and creative design can be used on the package as part of the firm's branding policy.

The package can be used to convey 'additional benefits and added value', for example to notify consumers about competitions, or to provide price offers or gift vouchers to encourage re-purchase.

An absence of complex package (for example, 'no frills' foodstuff range) can help boost price competitiveness or alternatively assist the firm to claim it is 'environmentally friendly' through selling the product without the packaging.

The package can help with 'immediate association'. Cleverly placed next to a market leader in a supermarket, it can influence the consumer to try the retailer's brand rather than the internationally known best seller.

If not effectively designed the packaging can discourage the consumer from purchasing the product; here the augmented product (the packaging) actually serves only to reduce the sales of the core product.

Please raise any queries about this report with me.

A Marketer

## 11 SEGMENTATION

Firstly, you need to identify the objectives of using segmentation as a prelude to suggesting the basis of segmentation of a consumer product.

*The role of segmentation in marketing strategy* is as follows.

(a) To divide the total market into targetable, profitable groupings to whom promotional mixes can be addressed.

(b) To position the firm's product against clearly identified market segments.

There are two approaches to identifying customer groupings.

(a) Market segmentation through an analysis of the characteristics of the customer.
(b) Market segmentation through an analysis of the response of the customer.

Whether the firm is offering a consumer or industrial product to the market, for a strategy of market segmentation to be successful a number of requirements need to be met.

(a) For a segment to be viable, it must be distinguishable from other segments. At the same time the customers within each segment must have a high degree of similarity on the criteria adopted for segmentation. It follows that on the aggregate level customers must be different in some other dimensions, thus allowing segments to be isolated within the overall market.

(b) The criteria used to differentiate between customer groupings (market segments) must be relevant to the purchase situation. These criteria should be related to differences in market demand.

(c) The segment must be of sufficient potential size to ensure that any marketing investment made within it will result in an adequate return.

(d) An identified market segment can only be exploited if it can be reached. It must be possible to direct a separate marketing strategy to each segment. This means that the customers within each segment will respond to differing promotional tools and will have differing buying behavioural attributes (true within consumer markets and across the industrial/consumer market divisions). They will also respond differently to pricing strategies, to personal selling and will have different expectations of the product, and different product benefit needs.

*Bases for segmentation of a consumer product*

(a) *Age*: people buy different products at different times during their own life-cycle.

(b) *Sex*: some products are particularly required by females, others by males.

(c) *Family size:* some products, eg large cars and caravans, are more suited to the needs of large families than to couples or individuals.

(d) *Family life cycles:* the stage of development of the family will influence what families want and what families do. Products are developed to satisfy these needs.

(e) *Social class:* one's place in the 'social strata' will determine in part product needs, eg type of holiday taken, hobbies and interests followed.

(f) *Geo-demographic factors* (eg ACORN classification): how must earning potential people have, and where they live can influence the types of products and services they are willing to pay for. Firms should only therefore segment against *effective demand.*

(g) *Education*: the complexity of the consumer in terms of his mindset, thinking and educational background will influence purchase decisions, the newspapers he reads and his responsiveness to promotional effort.

(h) *Benefit/lifestyle segmentation*: consumers can be segmented against the kinds of benefits they seek (how they will use them and what they wish products and services to provide) from the products and services they are willing to pay for. For example, financial services: some people want security, others return on investment, others insurance against life threatening illness, theft or fire.

(i) *Loyalty status:* consumers can be segmented against their acceptability to branding and the degree to which they are likely to stay loyal to the brand or the firm once committed. For example, those people who will 'always buy Nescafé' or those who will always 'buy Ford cars' or 'shop at Marks & Spencer'.

*Bases for segmentation of an industrial product or service*

(a) *Size of firms.* Some products or services may only be useful to firms of a specific size (eg specific manufacturing plant).

(b) *Type of industry.* Some products or services may be industry specific and not used outside that industry.

(c) *Geographical region.* Some firms may find their markets being highly concentrated into specific areas where there are a large number of similarly characterised firms, all of whom are likely to want similar products and services.

(d) *Type of buying organisation.* Some firms may want to focus their selling activities towards centralised buyers - units which buy for the whole firm, thus larger sales become possible, rather than towards decentralised buyers who must be approached individually.

(e) *The use of the end product being marketed.* Where products have a multi-use, some firms may prefer to target such buyers in the hope of gaining sales of related products.

## 12 PRICING

(a) *Cost plus pricing*

Costs are the most important influence on pricing decisions. Many firms base their pricing policy on simple cost plus rules. This means that costs are estimated and then a profit margin is added to arrive at the price. This method of pricing is relatively easy for management to implement and affords some degree of stability over pricing. There are two main types of cost based pricing. The first is *full cost.* Although it is not appropriate to go into this in detail here it is worthwhile pointing out the differences between full and cost plus pricing. Full cost pricing takes account of the full average costs of production including an allocation for overheads. The profit margin is then added to determine the price. The problem with full cost pricing is that if the company produces many brands the allocation of overheads costs can be difficult to determine. *Cost plus pricing* on the other hand only uses the direct cost components; for example, labour and raw materials are used to calculate unit costs. An additional margin is then added that includes profit and an overhead charge. Cost plus pricing is used extensively in the UK retailing sector, where the mark up price includes a fixed margin that varies between product classes. The percentage margin may also vary according to demand factors. The problems of cost plus pricing arise out of the difficulties in calculating direct costs and the allocation of overhead costs. The cost plus approach leads to price stability because in the main prices change due to cost changes.

(b) *Market skimming pricing*

Market skimming involves setting a high initial price for a new product. If a new product has a high value to consumers then a high price can be charged. The strategy is initially to command a premium price and then gradually to reduce the price to penetrate the more price sensitive segments of the market. One advantage of this method of pricing is that it is easier to reduce prices if a mistake has been made than it is to increase prices. A high price also creates an image of a quality product, especially if other aspects of the marketing mix reflect this. In order for this strategy to be successful there must be enough consumers who are not price sensitive. The costs of producing the small volumes of premium price products should not be greater than the advantage gained by charging the higher price. The strategy will only work if the higher price does not stimulate competition, so is suitable for markets that have high entry barriers, for example, high development costs or high promotional costs.

(c) *Marginal cost pricing*

Marginal cost pricing is the setting of the price of one unit at the cost of producing an extra unit (marginal cost). From an economics viewpoint marginal cost pricing is the most efficient pricing method. This is because when price is equal to marginal cost it is allocatively efficient. In a perfectly competitive market the market mechanism ensures that price does equal marginal cost if profits are maximised. However, perfect competition never occurs in the real world. Profits are maximised instead when price is greater than the marginal cost of producing the good. If this is the case it is allocatively inefficient; that is, too little of a good is being produced to keep the price high, so consumption is below the optimum level. In theory nationalised industries were supposed to set their price equal to marginal costs but have recently been under instruction to price in a more commercial manner. In practice, marginal cost pricing is difficult because of problems in calculation. Again, there will be problems in the allocation of overheads and the additional problem of whether to set prices equal to long run or short run marginal costs.

(d) *Market penetration pricing*

In a market penetration pricing strategy the company sets a low price for the product in order to stimulate growth in the market or to obtain a larger market share. This strategy is only successful if demand is price sensitive and economies of scale can be achieved. That is, unit costs of production and distribution fall with increased output. So companies set a low price in the belief that consumers will value this and their market share can then increase. The low price strategy should also deter competitors from entering the market. The low price approach is often used with heavy promotional effort to penetrate mass markets and take market share. If the firm needs to recoup high development costs in a short time this may not be the most appropriate pricing strategy. If there are high barriers to entry, including a high degree of branding, the market may not be suitable for penetration pricing. Low prices, however, are not likely to be effective if the product is in the decline stage of the PLC, as customers are usually changing to substitute products.

## 13 PRICING POLICY

**Report**

To: *The management*
From: *A Marketer*
Re: *Pricing policy of a product line*

A product line can be defined in terms of a 'broad group of products whose uses and characteristics are basically similar'. Such products can be differentiated by:

(a) Price
(b) Packaging
(c) Targeted customer
(d) Distribution channel used

A firm may have a line of products because it wishes to target a number of segments of the market, all of whom require different benefits. The following are the considerations you might make when detailing the influences on pricing of a product line.

(a) *Product quality.* If the firm is seeking a niche upper market segment and a reputation for quality then it may decide a high price is necessary (for example, the Caribbean cruise holiday market). This price may hold for all products in the line, yet there may be special offers for block bookings or during certain times in the year when demand falls.

(b) *Company image.* The firm may be seeking an exclusive image in the market place and may use pricing strategy in conjunction with public relations to achieve this, for example Marks & Spencer.

(c) *Costs of production.* The firm will want to meet the full costs of production and make sustainable profits so pricing must reflect this. The bigger the operation, the bigger the scale economies available from production and marketing, particularly where products are very similar (thus permitting bulk manufacture/purchase of parts). This situation would help secure lower prices and increased competitiveness in a mass market.

(d) *Degree of standardisation of products.* An extension of (c) above, this implies that where products in a line are quite different in order to meet consumer needs, then the costs of the product and, therefore, the price, will have to be higher.

(e) *Desired level of profit.* A firm may willingly take losses on one line of product as long as the range of products meets the forecast profits target. It may price, therefore, to achieve this goal.

(f) *Desired level of market share.* A firm may set or alter prices as a promotional tool to realise market share goals.

(g) *To manage the portfolio effectively.* The firm may have a number of product lines in the market (or different markets) at the same times. Portfolio analysis may indicate that price changes to specific products in specific lines at specific times may realise more revenue from life-cycles; the firm is thus able to use pricing to manage profitability.

(h) *To market diversify.* The firm may be able, through lowering or increasing the price, to take its product line into a different market (upper or lower in income grouping). Some changes to the line (apart from price) would also probably be necessary in order to do this.

(i) *As a promotional tool.* A firm may use its pricing structure as a promotional tool to bring 'value for money' to the customer's attention. In order to increase added value it may additionally offer 'free servicing' as an added incentive.

(j) *To capitalise on novelty.* If the product line is new, and the market largely untapped, a firm may be able to 'harvest' significant profits from the market over the short term by pricing up the whole line. Innovative products will command this competitive advantage until other, like products enter the market when the firm will need to reduce its profits to stay competitive. Such 'pricing up' over the short term will additionally help cover the heavy research and development costs of innovation.

Please raise any queries regarding this report with me.

A Marketer

## 14 DISTRIBUTION

A major element in distribution strategy is the degree of market coverage that is desired for a product. Linked to this question is the required support the distribution strategy needs from the producer. In order to serve existing and future customers to the required standard the company must decide how many outlets should be established in an area and what services channel members can offer. Market coverage is often termed 'distribution intensity' and refers to the number and size of outlets in a particular area. There are three basic choices in the method of distribution: selective, intensive and exclusive.

*Exclusive distribution*

Exclusive distribution means appointing outlets for an area to distribute your goods exclusively. Exclusive distribution restricts the number of outlets where the goods are available. This exclusivity can be in the overall type of channel chosen, for example selecting department stores rather than supermarkets, and/or choosing a certain department store, eg Rackhams rather than another, eg Debenhams. It is used in a number of circumstances. If customers are willing to exert some effort in searching for the product or service then exclusive distribution is possible. There may be an aim to restrict outlets providing your product to encourage a high quality image (the perfume industry offers a good example). This can be beneficial for the supplier and the store which sells the product. The producers may adopt exclusive distribution if there is a high degree of service or after sales support required from the product. Exclusive distribution allows the producer more control of the marketing mix at the point of sale and minimises channel conflict. There is necessarily a close relationship between channel members in an exclusive distribution system.

*Intensive distribution*

Intensive distribution is the opposite of exclusive distribution. Here the aim is to cover the market as intensively as possible. Many intermediaries are used to bring the products to as many people as possible, both within one geographical area and throughout many areas. This coverage method is often used for goods and services that either consumers or organisational buyers purchase frequently. It can be typified by convenience goods that the buyer will not want to put any effort into purchasing. Examples include food, washing powder, tobacco and in organisational markets, office supplies. Outlets for these goods have to be easily accessible and to have a choice of readily available brands.

*Selective distribution*

Selective distribution is somewhere between exclusive and intensive distribution. It is suitable for products that consumers are willing to put some effort into purchasing. This method is chosen when brands are important to consumers or the outlets are important to consumers (for example Harrods). The reasons for adopting this type of channel strategy are similar to those outlined in our discussion of exclusive distribution.

*Choice of strategy: factors*

There are four main factors that determine the choice of distribution strategy.

(a) *Customers*

Target customer groups have a major impact on market coverage decisions. Social class, income and geographic area are important market segmentation variables that have an influence on channel decisions. Consumer behaviour also plays an important part in market coverage decisions. How consumers view stores and products will influence the most appropriate distribution strategy to undertake.

(b) *Products*

The actual product characteristics are important in determining appropriate market coverage. A relatively cheap, frequently bought product will be better suited to intensive distribution. An expensive product that is purchased infrequently may be better distributed exclusively or selectively.

(c) *Outlets*

Too few or too many outlets in an area may affect the choice of distribution strategy. If an organisation has too few outlets in an area then sales targets will be difficult to achieve. If the organisation has too many outlets, this may not be efficient. When a reseller is unable to perform some marketing functions, for example after sales service when an intensive strategy has been adopted, then this will determine the future of the distribution strategy.

(d) *Control*

The level of desired control over how the product is presented to the public is a major determining factor in formulating a distribution strategy. If an intensive distribution strategy is adopted, then the supplier usually gives up some of its control over the marketing of the product. For instance, if the product is sold in nationwide supermarket chains then display and final pricing is usually determined by the supermarket. If an exclusive distribution strategy is adopted then control is less likely to be relinquished.

## 15 MAIL ORDER SELLING

Mail order shopping has developed from small beginnings in the nineteenth century to a major industry. It grew substantially in the early twentieth century because in the Depression consumers wanted to spread the cost of purchases over time. Traditional mail order shopping has four key characteristics.

(a) *Commission*. The company pays a certain percentage of sales (often 10%) to agents.

(b) *Convenience*. Shopping in the home is promoted as more convenient than spending time and energy visiting stores.

(c) *Comprehensive*. Catalogues have a great variety of products available.

(d) *Credit*. Payment can be spread over a period of time.

In the 1950s and 1960s mail order shopping extended rapidly, although by the early 1980s it was suffering from a slowdown in growth, mainly due to a staid and downmarket image. In the late 1980s, however, mail order shopping underwent a transformation and correspondingly grew in profitability and popularity. The main reason for the growth in recent times has been the adoption of marketing principles. This includes the adoption of market segmentation techniques, customer service and image building.

*Mail order market*

The five main mail order companies in the UK at present are Great Universal Stores (GUS), Littlewoods, Freemans, Grattan and Empire Stores. These have a 97% share of the market. The rest of the market is made up of specialist mail order companies that have developed niche markets. Many companies have developed mail order services to increase the number of customers they can serve without expensive store expansion. Examples include Habitat, Selfridges and Lakeland Plastics. In the past, catalogues were run on an agency level, but this has now developed into direct catalogues (shorter than agency catalogues) and 'specialogues'. The agency networks have become less effective over the past decade with many 'agents' using catalogues only for themselves and their immediate family rather than a wider network of family, friends, neighbours and colleagues.

*Mail order vs traditional retailers*

Until recently mail order companies were being left behind by high street retailers in marketing techniques. One of their main competitive advantages was the availability of credit but this was eroded by the high street retailers developing credit systems. There has recently been a blurring of the distinctions between mail order and traditional store retailing. Charge cards have aided the stores in developing mail order services. Retailer involvement has helped the image of mail order companies, as this has increased the perceived quality of products. For example, Next merged with Grattan, Freemans with Sears and there are close links between Top Shop and Empire Stores. The 'Direct' catalogues have increased significantly. Examples of these include 'You and Yours' (Grattan) and 'Family Album' (GUS). 'Specialogues' have been developed to break away from the traditional downmarket image. They are excellent examples of how mail order companies have taken on board the theory and practice of market segmentation. Consumers have been segmented into the different groupings according to whichever basis of market segmentation is used. These consumers can be targeted by providing certain types of products and promotion that appeals to them. The positioning of new products and services can then be implemented using the media and other promotional tools suitable for this segment.

*Computerisation*

Computerised databases can be used to increase efficiency, reduce paperwork and, perhaps most importantly, to profile customers. Mail order companies have vast amounts of information on each customer and these can be used to target potential customers of the 'specialogues'. In addition to the general demographic information that can be found in databases, such as age, profession, sex and location, there is a whole history of past products purchased and products returned. So, for example, if a customer has purchased a number of items of clothing in a large size, then they may be suitable candidates for a 'specialogue' in this area.

*'Next' Directory*

The introduction in the late 1980s of the Next Directory certainly made mail order companies rethink their marketing strategies. The glossy catalogue with fabric samples and 48 hour delivery was aimed at the AB social groupings, rather than CDs. Many mail order companies responded by improving their catalogue presentation and introducing 'specialogues' aimed at higher social classes. For example, Freemans introduced 'Bymail' which had clothes designed by Jeff Banks.

*New developments*

There are a number of new developments in the industry. There is increased internationalisation of the market with many European retailers now having significant shares in the UK mail order companies. Home shopping services have been developing. These include teleshopping which most mail order companies undertake to some degree. Orders can be placed by telephone, customers can be told immediately if goods are in stock and so these orders can be processed much quicker than those placed by mail. In the future there may be more home shopping facilities developed in this area, for example, videotext sales.

*Summary*

The main reason for the growth of mail order is the response to competitive pressures from the high street. Mail order companies have used their technology to become closer to the consumer, given tailored products and promotions to certain customer groups, rethought their image and replaced the traditional USP of credit with a new emphasis on convenience and customer service.

## 16 PHYSICAL DISTRIBUTION MANAGEMENT

In order that goods move from producer to consumer efficiently and effectively the movement of these goods need to be managed. To get products to the right place at the right time in the right quantities takes a good deal of management skill. The physical flow of goods and materials coming into the company and going out of the company to the final consumer is usually termed 'logistics management'. *Logistics management* comprises materials management and physical distribution. *Materials management* is the flow of goods and materials into the company. This includes all the raw materials that go into the production of the final goods. *Physical distribution* on the other hand concerns the movement of finished goods to the customers. We will concentrate on the physical distribution aspect of logistics.

The output of a distribution system is a level of customer service. Physical distribution managers have to balance the desired level of service with their decisions on transport, warehousing and inventory management.

*Warehousing*

It is usual in manufacturing that the most cost effective means of production is centralised. Warehousing is therefore very important to store finished goods. Managers need to keep an adequate stock of goods to allow for market fluctuations. They also need to calculate how many warehouses are needed, the type of warehouses required and the positioning of warehouses in the most efficient locations. Warehousing provides two important functions. The first concerns the movement of goods. Large amounts of products flow into the warehouse, then they are broken down in to smaller units and go out of the warehouse. The second main function of warehousing is the storage of goods to cope with demand fluctuations. There are two main types of warehousing facilities: *private*, that is owned by the firm, and *public*. Public warehouses are often categorised by the type of goods they store, for example cold storage warehousing. Distribution centres have developed from private warehousing and are used primarily for the movement of goods and not their storage. These are often used by large supermarket chains who want an efficient movement of many goods at frequent intervals. Private and public warehousing systems have advantages and disadvantages and need to be assessed for the individual firm.

*Inventory management*

Inventory management involves finding a balance between keeping inventory costs as a whole as low as possible and providing customers with a good service. Costs come from the holding of inventories, ordering inventory and the risks that stocks will run out. So the main management roles concerning inventory management are to decide how many goods to order, when to order and how to balance keeping adequate stocks without running out of the goods. How much to order can be assessed using specific formulae and/or the skill and experience of management. Sales forecasts can be used in order to ascertain when to reorder stocks. Sales forecasts are, of course, subject to some amount of error. If this was not so there would never be occasion to run out of goods. An estimate of this error can be used to provide the company with a buffer stock to use if demand is greater than expected.

*Physical distribution management*

Physical distribution management is often thought of in simple transportation terms. Although we have seen that there is much more to this management task, transportation is still a very important aspect. If transportation is not handled efficiently then stocks can build up and inventory costs soar, in addition to the adverse effects on customer service. There are many ways in which goods can be transported from one place to another. Management must choose the most suitable method for the product in question according to:

(a) speed;
(b) dependability;
(c) availability;
(d) frequency;
(e) capability;
(f) cost.

There are five main transportation methods available to management: rail, road, sea, air and pipeline. Each of these can be assessed according to the six criteria outlined above. The 'best' method of transporting goods will depend on the product characteristics. For example, oil is suitable for pipeline transportation whilst coal is suitable for rail transportation.

*Conclusion*

Successful physical distribution management is a key factor in the success of a company. It is one of the most obvious ways in which marketing management can build a high level of customer service into their product offering as it concerns the actual delivery of the product to the consumer. The desired level of customer service needs to be balanced against the costs of physical distribution management. An effective physical distribution system should be developed by management and incorporated into the overall logistics management of the business.

## 17 WHOLESALER

This simply calls for you to adopt the role of a wholesaler and to write imaginatively and creatively about the services you provide. Within your writing, you should include most of the following.

(a) Wholesalers bridge the gap between small retailers, who have limited capital and limited knowledge of sources of supply, and manufacturers. who are always looking for new opportunities to expand the sale of their products. The knowledge wholesalers command is useful to both retailers and manufacturers who are looking for new business.

(b) Wholesalers provide warehousing for large stocks of product and save retailers and manufacturers money in so doing.

(c) Wholesalers buy in advance of demand. The wholesale trade will anticipate what customers will be seeking to buy in the coming months. This means accepting the risks of being wrong. Buying ahead also helps provide a steady market for manufacturers.

(d) The wholesaler helps to finance trade and keep the market buoyant by buying from manufacturers and so keeping their resources liquid and by giving generous trade credit to retailers.

(e) As an expert buyer, the wholesale will try to buy when prices are low, storing goods until they are less plentiful and then selling at a profit. Individual customers, with some planning, are thus able to take advantage of price variations. It could be argued that wholesalers in some small way help to even out the buying cycle between surpluses and shortages.

(f) In some trades, the wholesaler grades, sorts, prepares and packs the goods (for example, foodstuffs). He may even sell goods under his own brand label.

(g) Since the wholesaler is in touch with both retailers and manufacturers, he is in an ideal position to pass back information about what products are selling and what criticisms are being made. Wholesalers could therefore be labelled as 'order influencers' as changes to products may be made upon a wholesaler's recommendation.

(h) Wholesale firms can combine with distribution firms to form a joint channel direct to customers.

(i) Large 'super warehouses' now exist where customers can 'buy direct off the pallet'. This form of 'no frills' retailing has turned wholesale warehouses into shops.

(j) Wholesalers, through their activities, add value to products and assist small producers who lack specialist skills and expertise (for example, in exporting to Europe).

(k) Some wholesalers now provide promotional material which actively assists in the marketing of their services; they have become more proactive than in the past.

(l) Wholesalers are more accessible than manufacturers and computerisation has increased their quality of service provision and their response times to customers.

## 18 SALES PROMOTION

*Recommendations on appropriate sales promotions*

To support the launch of Chico it will be necessary to use some form of sales promotion to support our above the line advertising campaign. The main objective of the sales promotions recommended is to stimulate trial of Chico by our target consumers.

*Free sample*

The first sales promotion recommended is a free sample of Chico attached to a monthly magazine. The use of impregnated paper in the pages of the magazine could be considered but this is usually the approach of the higher priced perfumes in glossy magazines. It is recommended that a phial of Chico be attached as a free gift to the full circulation of a monthly woman's magazine that is read by our target market. The magazine 'Essentials' has been chosen because the readership is from our target group social class and age bracket. The magazine has also run this type of promotion before and would be willing to co-operate.

The aim of this promotion is to enable potential customers to try our product without having to ask to test it in a store. This can also be combined with advertising copy within the magazine describing the type of woman that wears Chico.

*Competition*

In addition to the free phial of Chico on the outside of the magazine it is recommended that we include a competition inside the magazine. The first 200 postcards to be drawn on a certain date win a full sized bottle of Chico.

*Timing*

The timing of this sales promotion will be crucial. Stores must already have adequate stocks of Chico so that as sales have been stimulated consumers are actually able to buy the product. It should also coincide with the above the line advertising campaign. This method of promotion should only be used once, preferably in the November issue of the magazine as this might encourage purchases for Christmas. A special Christmas promotional offer could be run in the stores at this time. This could be a special gift pack of perfume, talcum powder and body lotion in Chico.

*Image*

This sales promotion method will stimulate trial of Chico without any adverse effects on the image. Care has to be taken that the image we present during sales promotion does not conflict with the image from our media advertising. The image we want to build for Chico is elegant, sophisticated yet at the same time fun-loving and young. Any direct price promotions would 'cheapen' the image of Chico and should be avoided. The promotion method chosen for the launch should get over the buying inertia many women feel towards buying perfume and take the risk out of purchasing the product. As perfume can only really be tested on an individual's skin and then should be allowed to develop for a while before testing this method would be ideal in the circumstances.

After the initial launch further sales can be stimulated using another method of sales promotion. This could take the form of a competition, the details on a leaflet given with purchase, backed up of course with advertising. An appropriate prize would be an exotic holiday.

*Evaluation*

To evaluate the sales promotion effectiveness a number of methods can be used. Firstly the number of responses to the free draw for Chico should be analysed. Sales data before the promotion should be noted and compared with sales data during and after the promotion. As perfume is not purchased frequently there may be a drop in sales after the sales promotion. The market share Chico has gained needs to be monitored. It may also be necessary to hold consumer panels to see if people responded to the promotion and in what way. A survey could be carried out to evaluate the impact of the promotion on consumer purchase behaviour.

## 19 NOTES ON PROMOTION

(a) *Unique selling propositions*

The unique selling proposition theory says that consumers remember one main point from advertising. If advertising tries to tell consumers too much then it may fail. Another approach to unique selling propositions is the idea of building a strong brand image. Companies can identify an appropriate USP by analysing the reasons why goods are purchased and then focusing their marketing communications on one of the benefits associated with buying the product. Many marketers favour the approach of one message. Common USPs are 'lowest price', 'best service', 'highest technology' or 'quickest service'. This message can then be incorporated throughout the company's marketing communications. Advertising, sales promotion and public relations can all reinforce the chosen USP. A company's USP can also be thought of as the bundle of messages that combine to make the image of the company. For example the Halifax Building Society's USP can be thought of as large, safe, traditional, market leader. When designing the message in marketing communications there are three main approaches. The first is the rational approach that tries to appeal to consumers' best interests: for example, an advert that says 'if you can buy cheaper we will refund the difference' will be promoting a low price USP in a rational way. The emotional approach uses emotional stimuli to motivate purchase. For example, toothpaste is often advertised to stimulate fear of tooth decay, stained teeth or bad breath. The moral approach tries to appeal to the consumer's sense of right and wrong. A recent example of this type of campaign is the promotion of the environmental benefits of using certain products.

(b) *The promotional mix*

The promotional mix is the combination of marketing communication strategies. It is one of the 'Four Ps' of the marketing mix and includes advertising, sales promotion, publicity and personal selling. Through promotional mix, companies communicate product benefits and the reasons why consumers should purchase a product. The most important aspect of the promotional mix is communication. An effective promotional mix should take into account the suitability of each aspect of the mix in fulfilling promotional objectives. Advertising is paid, ongoing non-personal communication that uses mass media such as television, press or radio. Advertising's main function is to create awareness, stimulate purchase and keep consumers aware of the product in the long term. Sales promotions are usually short term and are inducements for consumers to purchase the product. Sales promotional tools include the use of coupons, competitions, money off packs and free samples. It can be used to stimulate interest from consumers who do not usually purchase the product or to increase sales to existing consumers. Personal selling is the face to face communication between the company's employees and the consumer and is an important element of the promotional mix. Publicity is the unpaid communication about the company, so press articles concerning the company come under publicity. Marketing managers must decide on the overall objectives of the promotional mix and allocate resources for each element depending on the promotional mix chosen.

(c) *Point of sales display*

Point of sales displays include the displays for the product in the store, for example, advertising signs, window displays or in-store displays. Within the promotional mix they come under sales promotion. They are used at the point of purchase and are most effective when combined with advertising. Retailers are often unwilling to co-operate with point of sales displays that are bulky and take up valuable floor space. Smaller stores may be more co-operative than large supermarket chains regarding the siting of point of sales displays. The main point of sales displays in supermarkets are at the checkouts (where confectionery and magazines are displayed in racks) and occasionally at the end of aisles. Smaller stores may be more co-operative in the placing of window displays and advertising posters because they may see this as a way to promote themselves. This can be used in conjunction with other sales promotion techniques. For example, if a competition is running then the point of sales display can promote this. In industrial markets in store displays can be given to dealers, for example display items in car showrooms. If the company owns the point of purchase or if it is more powerful than the channel member at the point of purchase then there is much more control over this element of the promotional mix.

(d) *Publicity*

Publicity is an important aspect of the promotional mix. Although it is essentially free communication in the media, this does not mean to say the company has no control in this area. It is an effective means of communication for positive news about the company and can also be of use in lessening the effects of negative news. The main advantage of publicity over advertising is that it is seen as a truthful and credible source of information. It is also inexpensive, because of the non-paid nature. There are some costs involved in the successful management of publicity though, such as the production of press releases, or recruiting staff in the area of public relations. It can also support other elements of the marketing mix. However, there are problems in using publicity. A company may give information to the press but the press can do as they wish with it. They may or may not print a story, and it may be presented in either a positive or a negative light. The timing of publicity is also difficult to control. Company communications and press releases are not the only elements in publicity. Special events such as the sponsorship of events are reported in the press or seen on television. The effectiveness of publicity can be assessed by the amount of publicity it receives and the number of people it reaches.

## 20 PUBLIC RELATIONS

Public relations is the planned and sustained effort to encourage goodwill between an organisation and its publics. A company's publics include shareholders, customers, government and other businesses. The aim of public relations is to present a positive image of the company to these publics or at least to promote some form of understanding. Public relations is a long-term effort by the firm to improve or sustain this image and should be a two way communication between the company and its publics.

The way in which public relations can be seen to reduce the effects of a corporate crisis on the publics can be looked at in terms of the transfer model below.

*Transfer model*

| *The corporate crisis causes* | *If public relations has been successful then this will change to* |
|---|---|
| Hostility | Sympathy |
| Prejudice | Acceptance |
| Apathy | Interest |
| Ignorance | Knowledge |

As can be seen above in the face of a corporate crisis the company can achieve understanding through public relations rather than a positive image. In order for public relations to work, trends must be monitored so that PR management is prepared if a problem arises. Here we will concentrate on how public relations can help to change the four negative aspects in the above model to the positive achievements.

We will assume that the company is a chemical factory and the crisis a chemical spillage into a local river. The publics involved will be the local community, local anglers, employees, customers, suppliers, government (the Department of the Environment), the local authority, the National Rivers Authority, shareholders, the money markets, distributors and environmentalist groups. As can be seen the list of publics the company must address can be extensive.

Some assessment has to be made about the scale of hostility present in the various publics. Some of this may be based on a lack of information or a misunderstanding of information. However, there may be in this case a very urgent need to satisfy the publics' desire for information. Direct communication should be made with all official bodies concerned with, of course, complete honesty. If there is false information given out at the beginning of the incident then this makes the matter much worse for public relations managers in the future. Misinformation will mean that credibility will be damaged if, or more probably when, it is found out. Other publics can be reached by holding a press conference or a public meeting.

Converting prejudice into acceptance is more difficult in this type of crisis, as many people will think their prejudices have been confirmed. If, however, the situation is handled well and communicated through effective PR then this prejudice might be lessened. Changing apathy to interest will not be as applicable in this example of a crisis. The organisation itself may be accused of apathy. The change from ignorance to knowledge will be more important. Publics will want to know exactly what has been leaked into the river, how it happened, could it happen again, where it was leaked, how much was leaked, what the effects might be and whether there are long-term implications. The role of public relations will be to answer these questions. In the event of the leakage the media should be given the opportunity to discuss with the company the effects of the pollution. If a question cannot be answered reasons should be given. The company should do all in its power to speak with one voice and avoid conflicting statements.

The various general techniques that public relations management can use include the following.

(a) Open days or organised visits to the company
(b) Sponsorship
(c) Community projects
(d) Company publications including annual reports
(e) Videos
(f) Press releases
(g) Community meetings

Many of these techniques would not be appropriate to manage the crisis the company faces in the short term. However, as stated earlier, PR concerns the long term and in the future, after the initial crisis has been handled, these tools and techniques can be used to help the image and understanding of the company. For example, having open days for the local community will help alleviate fears of the incident recurring.

However, we have discussed public relations here in a reactive role, that is, reacting to a crisis that has already occurred. There is also a role for public relations in the prevention of, and preparation for crises. The PR manager is responsible for the goodwill felt towards the company and so should in some respect act as watchdog regarding the practices of the organisation. The preventative role in PR should concentrate on what could possibly go wrong in the organisation. Then some preparation needs to be undertaken for crises. A committee should be set up of interested parties in the organisation, perhaps including top management, safety officers, works manager and the PR manager. This committee need to agree on the responses to any incident that would be desirable by the firm. The provision of information needs to be discussed and adequate information needs to be kept up to date and close to hand.

## 21 AGENCY/CLIENT RELATIONSHIPS

When developing an advertising programme the advertising objectives should be assessed. These can vary but common ones are outlined below.

(a) To create awareness of a new product
(b) To create awareness of new features of a product
(c) To ensure exposure
(d) To increase sales and profits
(e) To increase response, for example for a charity
(f) To improve the company image
(g) To change attitudes or behaviour, eg the AIDS prevention campaign
(h) To generate enquiries from potential customers

Advertising can have long or short term effects. The above objectives are rather general. Specific objectives of an advertising campaign might be to communicate certain information about a product, or to highlight a particular Unique Selling Proposition.

Advertising also plays a role in industrial markets. It can be used to promote the corporate image, to communicate technical specifications or to make the company more 'legitimate' in the eyes of its buyers. The advertising campaign should be planned through the following stages.

ADVERTISING OBJECTIVES
↓
THE MESSAGE
↓
MEDIA SELECTION
↓
THE FREQUENCY OF DISPLAY
↓
STYLE OF THE MESSAGE
↓
BUDGET
↓
EVALUATION

Most large scale advertising does not simply concern the advertiser and the media owner. In many cases an advertising agency is involved. The role of the advertising agency is to advise the client on the various media forms on behalf of the client. There are a number of different types of agencies. Creative agencies specialise in the more creative side of advertising, for example designing television advertisements. There are also media buyers who specialise in buying air time and media space and smaller agencies who specialise in industrial advertising.

There are many advantages of using an agency. The media owners find it more efficient if they only deal with a small number of organisations. For the organisation advertising, it is cheaper to employ the services of an agency than to set up a specialist advertising department and recruit highly skilled staff. Agencies also have close links with services such as printers and their employees usually have a wide experience of advertising. When choosing an agency the company can either approach an agency whose work it likes or ask for a competitive presentation. This is where one or more agencies give a presentation on either the market generally or a specific campaign proposal.

In order that the campaign is effective, that is, that it fulfils the objectives stated at the beginning of the advertising planning process, there must be good communications between the agency and client. If the client is vague about the objectives of the campaign or the agency misinterprets the aims, then the success of the campaign is doomed from the start. The advertising manager of the company that is going to advertise (client) must be familiar with the techniques and workings of advertising. He must also give the agency as much information about the company as is required, for example on the future objectives of the company. The advertising manager should be involved with all the negotiations between in house specialists and the advertising agency. In house specialists include individual product managers or brand managers.

The relationship between the agency and client varies to a great degree. As stated earlier some agencies' main role is to sell advertising space. However, the agencies that have extended their role look upon their clients as partners in a long-term relationship. One aspect of this is that if a client wishes to get the most from the agency it must disclose a certain amount of confidential information. The relationship between agency and client can therefore be very close and be of mutual benefit. Advertisers are known by the agency and over time the agency knows the type of approach the client likes and the type it dislikes.

## 22 PULL TECHNIQUES

A 'pull effect' is when the intended target audience is very familiar with a product and asks for the brand by its name, thus acting as an attraction for retailers and wholesalers to stock it. In effect, the consumers' demand 'pulls' the product through the chain of distribution. There are various 'pull techniques' used to encourage such a reaction in consumers.

(a) *Price reductions.* Made by the manufacturer, retailer or wholesaler, these 'offers' are usually 'timescaled' to encourage intention to buy. Examples are kitchen and household furnishings products.

(b) *Coupons.* These usually have to be collected by consumers so the tactic acts as an encouragement to re-buy and to engender loyalty. A gift, entry to a competition with a major price at stake or 'free product' is usually the outcome of saving the coupons.

(c) *Loss leaders.* Where some products (perhaps the least successful performances) are sold off deliberately at a loss to illicit interest in other products in the range (eg the 'star performers'). A good example here is holidays.

(d) *Competitions.* The incentive to compete, and the desire for materialism, is always strong within human nature. Firms realise this and often offer luxury products such as exclusive foreign holidays or new cars as prizes in competitions, entry to which is possible by purchasing the product.

(e) *Testimonials.* Well known and well liked show business or sporting personalities are used to endorse the product. Consumers are sub-consciously made to associate their lifestyle and successes with those of the personality through using the product.

(f) *Free samples.* These are often used as part of in-store demonstrations (for example, foods and wines) where the consumer is invited to try the product free and may be given special discounts if the product is purchased that day.

(g) *Merchandising and point of sale displays.* Usually consisting of large posters, cardboard displays with lots of colour and major promotional incentives, these are used in stores to inform and persuade the customer to try the product.

(h) *Packaging.* Through uniqueness of design, use of colour or logos, and through placing effectively on in-store shelving, packaging can be used to build brand image and as a product differentiator.

(i) *Corporate sponsorship* (for example, sporting events). This can be used to illicit interest in products (but more commonly services) and if made accessible to television exposure can be very useful in illiciting interest in a company's range of products or indeed in promoting the image of the company itself.

(j) *Trade-in facilities.* Often associated with 'white' or kitchen goods, and also cars, these can be used to persuade the customer to 'buy new' when in fact there may still be a long life in their existing purchase. Trade-in facilities usually offer a fairly attractive cash reduction on the new product.

(k) *Credit facilities.* Used widely nowadays (particularly with cars and electrical goods), credit facilities allow customers to extend the payment period over many months or even years. The firm is able to offer these deals through agreements with banks and finance houses. Increasingly 'zero interest' or 'free finance' adaptations to these offers have made them very attractive as incentives to purchase.

(l) *Guarantees.* These are additions to statutory rights made by firms to add value through differentiating themselves from competitors. Examples are where the firm offers to extend the statutory 'guarantee period' or guarantees to refund the cost of the product if the customer can buy it cheaper elsewhere.

## 23 SERVICES MARKETING

Services are more important today because of the growth of service sectors in advanced industrial societies and increasingly market-orientated trends within service-providing organisations (eg 'internal markets', 'market testing' and so on). The extension of the service sector and the application of 'market principles' across what were previously publicly-owned utilities has made a large number of service providers much more marketing conscious.

The definitions offered of services are:

> '... those separately identifiable but intangible activities that provide want-satisfaction, and that are not, of necessity, tied to, or inextricable from, the sale of a product or another service. To produce a service may or may not require the use of tangible goods or assets. However, where such use is required, there is no transfer of title (permanent ownership) to these tangible goods'. (Donald Cowell, *The Marketing of Services)*

> '... any activity of benefit that one party can offer to another that is essentially intangible and does not result in the ownership of anything. Its production may or may not be tied to a physical product'. (P Kotler, *Social Marketing)*

Services marketing differs from the marketing of other goods but it is difficult to make a judgement which encompasses the wide variety within service types and situations. Broadly, however, the *marketing characteristics of services* which make them distinctive from the marketing of goods involves five major differences.

(a) Intangibility
(b) Inseparability
(c) Heterogeneity
(d) Perishability
(e) Ownership

*Intangibility*

Refers to the lack of substance which is involved with service delivery. Unlike a good, there is no substantial material or physical aspects of a service: no taste, feel, visible presence and so on. Clearly this creates difficulties and can inhibit the propensity to consume a service, since customers are not sure what they have.

In fact it would be incorrect to make this a 'black or white' phenomenon. Shostack has suggested viewing insubstantiality not as an 'either/or' issue but rather as a continuum.

Marketers and consumers need to try to overcome this problem and typically seek to do so in a number of different ways, and of course for different reasons. The consumer needs information to avoid making a mistake, to form some grounds for judgement and to cut down risk. The marketer wishes to make the choice of the product 'safer' and make the consumer feel more comfortable about paying for something they do not then own and which has no physical form.

*Inseparability*

Service often cannot be separated off from the provider. The creation, or the performance, of a service often occurs at the same instant a full or partial consumption of it occurs. Goods in the vast majority of cases have to be produced, then sold, then consumed, in that order. Services are only a promise at the time they are sold: most services are sold and then they are produced and consumed simultaneously. Think of having dental treatment or a journey. Neither exists until they are actually being experienced/consumed by the person who has bought them.

Creation of many services is coterminous with consumption. Services may have to be, at the same time:

(a) made available;
(b) sold;
(c) produced; and
(d) consumed.

*Heterogeneity*

Many services face a problem of maintaining consistency in the standard of output. Variability of quality in delivery is inevitable, because of the number of factors which may influence it. This may create problems of operation management, for example, it may be difficult or impossible to attain *precise standardisation of the service offered* or *influence or control over perceptions of what is good or bad customer service.*

This points up the need to constantly monitor customer reactions. A common way addressing this problem involves applying a system to deliver a service which may be *franchised* to operators. The problem remains, however, and almost the only way to address it is by constant monitoring and response to problems.

*Perishability*

Services cannot be stored, of course. They are innately *perishable*. Seats on a bus or the services of a chiropodist consist in their availability for periods of time, and if they are not occupied, the service they offer cannot be used 'later'.

This presents specific marketing problems. Meeting customer needs in these operations depends on staff being available as and when they are need. This must be balanced against the need for a firm to minimise unnecessary expenditure on staff wages. Anticipating and responding to levels of demand is, therefore, a key planning priority.

*Ownership*

Services suffer from a fundamental difference compared to consumer goods. They do not result in the transfer of property. The purchase of a service only confers on the customer access to or right to use a facility, not ownership. Payment is for the use of, access to or the hire of particular items. Often there are tight constraints on the length of time involved in such usage. In the case of purchasing a product there is transfer of title and control over the use of an item.

This may well lessen the perceived customer value of a service and consequently make for unfavourable comparisons with tangible alternatives.

*The importance of service*

The *service dimension* has become the focus of a new approach for organisations providing products as well as services. Most of the ideas in this approach are well-established from the marketing approach, the 'quality movement' or 'TQM'. Tom Peters argues for a radical review of managerial approaches, insisting that the delivery of extra 'added value' through the service dimension is a critical competitive factor in marketplaces which are becoming more crowded and more competitive by the day. Theodore Levitt's *total product concept* is used to analyse systematically the value process through the service dimension.

Levitt proposes that we see products as composed of a number of different layers. This runs from an inner core to an outer ring of layers.

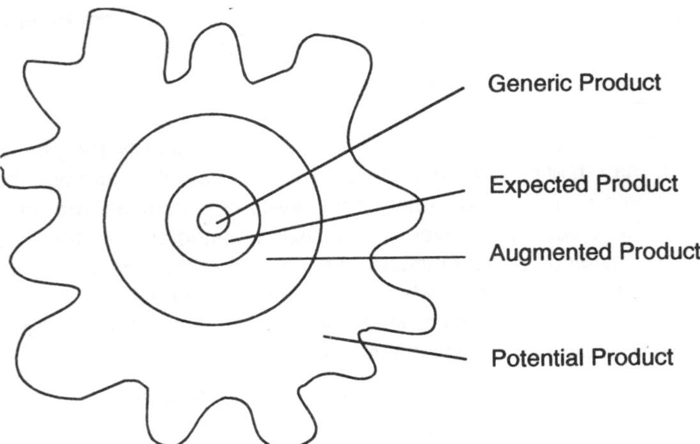


Levitt's total product concept is explained as follows.

(a) The *generic product* (eg washing powder or bread or clothes) is at the centre.

(b) The *expected product* (eg the format used, the functions it fulfils, the fact that it does what it is supposed to do) comes next. How white does it wash? How well does it fit? Clearly some products will do what they are expected to do better than others.

(c) The *augmented product* refers to the extra elements which aim to provide additional customer satisfaction, such as helpful and well-trained salespeople, range of products provided, guarantees of delivery and responsiveness to customer needs; having 'just the right' flavour, colour, price and so on.

(d) The *potential product* refers to the extra service dimensions of customer care which companies develop, for instance, no quibble refund, return-anything policies, extra high quality decor or extra value provided in service encounters by, for example, music, flowers, entertainment in the service environment; sensitivity to customer needs and empowerment of staff to deal with them without referring to higher levels of management. These are all aspects of 'potential product'.

Peters argues that companies pursuing a customer care strategy are creating totally new products by concentrating on the two outer rings of the Levitt TPC.

*The Customer Care Product* *Traditional Thinking on the Product*

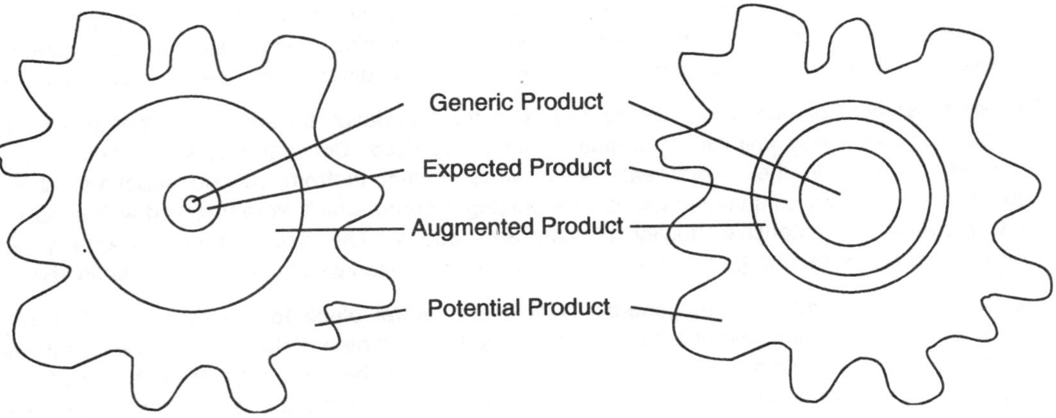


Peters believes that attention should be focused on *repositioning* the product in order to create whole new markets by emphasising the two outer (Levitt) rings, developed through the service dimension. He argues that this is becoming ever more important as competition increases, marketplaces become heavily overcrowded and the need to differentiate on generic or expected qualities becomes ever more problematic.

> 'The value of this advice is rising from "useful" to "essential" - service added is increasingly becoming the competitive battleground in every market. That is, traditional strategic thinking, in retailing and manufacturing, can be depicted (as in the previous diagram) as "generic" dominated. The effective organisation of tomorrow - will ... emphasise service added via the "augmented" and "potential" rings.' (Tom Peters, *Thriving on Chaos)*

## 24 CUSTOMER CARE

Customer care and TQM are closely related to each other. Quality programmes, however, cover many topics other than dealing with customers. Customer care programmes focus on gaining deep knowledge of customers and aim to identify their needs and improve care provided for them. Care is the outcome of this process, however, and 'satisfied customers' are the focus of customer care programmes. The challenge is to maintain this emphasis throughout a quality process. While customer care should be the way in which customers experience the delivery of the product or service, it is quality programmes which direct the processes constituting the services or products which they are experiencing and to which they are responding.

Common elements in customer care and TQM programmes include:

(a) an emphasis on process;
(b) an emphasis on the details of the system;
(c) the need to establish fundamental changes in:
    (i) attitude;
    (ii) focus;
    (iii) orientation;
(d) the idea of a 'core philosophy' which transforms practice;
(e) the derivation of the concept of quality for this particular product/service from customer perceptions, attitudes, expectations and needs.

Briefly, *quality* in management can be defined as combining the satisfaction of customer needs with the achievement of company objectives. Within the terms of this analysis, *systems* aim to achieve success and profitably by placing the customer at the centre of all enterprise activities, by providing the right amount of:

(a) quality;
(b) availability (at launch and afterwards);
(c) service;
(d) support;
(e) reliability;
(f) cost/value for money.

These systems must be *total*, reaching forward to distributors down the chain and back to suppliers in the case of manufactured goods, to assure the quality of raw materials and the condition of the product which reaches the ultimate consumer. Hence, total quality management.

The customer-supplier relationship is very important indeed within the TQM philosophy, which sees business as a long chain of such customer-supplier relationships. Each customer is a supplier to someone further down the chain, so that it makes no sense to differentiate one role from the other.

The establishment of TQM programmes has been the foundation for startling corporate success stories, such as those enjoyed by Jaguar Motors and Ford. Consumer surveys showed large numbers of faults in the components which were bought in from outside suppliers. Quality programmes installed as a consequence used testing systems which were installed with suppliers, and implemented extensive quality studies and audits. The improvement in quality and performance within the marketplace as a consequence has been widely admired and analysed.

As with quality programmes in general, TQM gives central place to the customer. Satisfying customers is the first principle of TQM since they are the guarantee of the organisation's continued existence. Gaining custom means winning a competition for the patronage of each individual or corporate buyer - and satisfying the particular needs of that individual is the competitive edge which wins survival and prosperity, rather than extinction.

Customer-supplier relationships under TQM are guided by:

(a) recognition of the strategic importance of customers and suppliers;
(b) development of win-win relationships between customers and suppliers; and
(c) establishing relationships based on trust.

These principles are translated into practice by:

(a) constantly collecting information on customer expectations;
(b) disseminating this information widely within the organisation; and
(c) using this information to design, produce and deliver the organisation's product and services.

TQM programmes demand the following.

(a) Total involvement from staff
(b) A customer orientation
(c) Defining customer requirements and obligations
(d) Measurement
(e) Commitment from the top management
(f) Adherence to standard processes and procedures
(g) Paying customer objectives

The corporate *mission* and the values which underlie organisational objectives, must always be clearly and directly related to the formulation of such objectives. If they are not, then TQM programmes will not accord with the strategic direction which has been agreed.

**MINI-CASE**

(a) The company's managers presently have a very wide product mix which they are attempting to sell into the market for office furniture. Additionally they seek to penetrate an up-market position and see their business as a quality leader and therefore presumably a *price maker* rather than a *price taker*. They also hold a whole range of spare parts and accessories which can be held in stock for a number of years.

As the business is small, the managers should recognise that they clearly cannot command the level of financial resources to pursue this policy in the medium term. They are therefore faced with strategic choices.

(i) To seek and acquire provider quality and reliable suppliers of all the existing range on a just in time basis, obviating the need to hold and finance stocks for such a long periods.

(ii) To operate the same product mix on a sale or return basis from manufacturers. This again will facilitate the current range being maintained.

(iii) To seek an alternative distribution policy, for example joint ventures with major DIY stores or a merger with a competitor for specified strategic purposes.

(iv) To rationalise and cut down the product range specialising in only the highest selling complimentary products (this will allow marketing economies to be achieved).

In consideration of these options the firm should adopt portfolio analysis to evaluate the contribution made by each product to the range. Additionally, market research and product life cycle management will help the firm adopt a planning approach which will provide information to reduce the uncertainties of strategic decision-making.

The two major dimensions to the product portfolio which a good answer should highlight are therefore as follows.

(i) *The width of the portfolio* which is a measure of the number of different markets addressed.

(ii) *The depth of the portfolio* which refers to the total number of products carried, and relates to market segments addressed.

The balance to the product mix must also concern the *volumes of sales* achieved by the different lines; what may appear to be a wide and deep portfolio may be an illusion if just one product within it produces 80% of the total sales; the same is true in relation to profit. An effective and well-managed product mix will therefore show a balanced profit contribution from each line.

The key questions you should therefore highlight in your answer are the following.

(i) What segments of what markets is the firm currently targeting? What segments does market research indicate *should* be targeted?

(ii) What is the current profit contribution made per product to the profitability of the portfolio over the last year?

(iii) What are the forecast sales in volume terms for each product over the next year?

(iv) What items in the current product mix could be removed to increase profitability and reduce costs?

It is probably fair to conclude that some kind of *line rationalisation* is called for, which may not necessarily need to be accompanied by a move down market which would impact the company's image in a negative manner. To be known as 'a specialist quality provider of ...' would certainly be more effective than that of an unrealistic 'quality provider of everything'. The changes decided upon would have to be accompanied by a promotional campaign, but the option of slimming down some lines whilst increasing quality on the 'portfolio leaders' would seem best advice business-wise and image-wise.

(b) In any business situation there are costs accruing from:

(i) buying in stock;
(ii) holding stock;
(iii) using stock; and
(iv) running out of stock.

At the moment, the case study would imply that Fine Furnishings has very high stock holding costs, particularly since it has to service so many lines and sees fit to hold some stocks for such a long period of time (years). This longevity may also cause problems in terms of the responsiveness of the company to changes in customer needs - it may find it is holding on to stock that nobody wants to buy.

The company should seek to identify the comparative costs of holding stocks of the different items for different lines. This information could then be fed into the portfolio analysis process to determine the value added per product to company profitability. Within this process the firm should seek to identify:

(i) the warehouse costs per stocked item;
(ii) the labour costs per stocked item; and
(iii) the insurance, processing and administration costs per stocked item.

You would be seeking to argue for the adoption of a full stock control programme which would, through an analysis of current purchasing policy, determine how effectively the firm is managing stock. Such a control programme would:

(i) identify how long it takes stock to arrive and turnover;
(ii) identify the costs of stock management; and
(iii) provide clues for improvements.

For example, such a process may reveal it is possible to make products more acceptable to users or intermediaries by packaging them into different sized units such as shrink-wrapped bulk packs, pallet loads or container loads. It is often possible to win substantial cost savings in terms of handling or warehousing by considering such approaches to stock management.

The firm would need first to identify what customers want before making any changes. *Market and customer research* would determine needs and stock management policy should adapt in response to these needs. The adoption of a computerised customer information system developed from a corporate management information system should assist the firm:

(i) to provide customers with the products and information they want when they want it;

(ii) to help provide quality service which would add value to the quality products;

(iii) to help information flow for business planning purposes; and

(iv) to provide a quick response to stock management difficulties such as a failure of suppliers or excess demand in any one period.

A good answer would include many of these points as well as stating the need to reduce stockholding to free up capital.

(c) In order to continue to be successful Fine Furnishings will need to communicate with *existing* as well as *potential* customers. It can do this in the following ways.

(i) *Directly*, by using a professional sales force or part-time appointed agents
(ii) *Indirectly*, using advertising and point of sales displays

The choice of the *promotional mix* (and if public relations are included, the *communications mix*) should be made on the basis of what is going to be most effective in generating increased sales whilst keeping costs to minimum (thus you should point to a *mutuality of objectives* - cost efficiency and cost effectiveness).

Within this question you should cite possible successful *promotional methods* within the promotional mix. To do this you will need to demonstrate a knowledge of promotional planning which you would argue and should link into the marketing plan. Relevant comments could be as follows.

(i) Using promotion in line with product life cycles.
(ii) Using promotion in line with demand fluctuations in the trading year.
(iii) Using promotion in to meet marketing objectives.

Making reference to office furniture as an industrial product is necessary only in so far as it clarifies that promotional methods need to address the buying behaviour of industrial buyers - therefore you should point to the use of:

(i) trade fairs and exhibitions;
(ii) direct sales force representatives and catalogues;
(iii) relationship marketing through technical service;
(iv) corporate advertising in magazines; and
(v) demonstrations.

A well-researched promotional plan will help the firm:

(i) to increase sales and profits;

(ii) to be more proactive rather than reactive to markets;

(iii) to promote itself through its products;

(iv) to help determine the most appropriate product mix;

(v) to help determine the most appropriate stockholding policy; and

(vi) to provide the most effective channel for the development of a successful product/market strategy.

*Promotional activity*

| *Stage of buying decision* | *Purpose of your communication* | *Typical promotional methods to employ* |
|---|---|---|
| Becoming aware of a need and interested in a solution | Creating awareness<br>Arousing interest | Advertising<br>Samples<br>Direct mail<br>Exhibitions |
| Understanding alternative solutions<br>Forming attitudes towards solutions offered | Emphasising customer benefits | Advertising<br>Sales calls<br>Demonstrations |
| Deciding to buy | Reinforcing benefits<br>Handling customers' doubts and objections<br>Reminding | Point-of-sale displays<br>Posters<br>Packaging<br>Sales calls<br>Sales promotion |
| Experiencing and perceiving the product in use | Reinforcing benefits and choice<br>Sorting out difficulties in use | Advertising<br>Direct mail<br>Sales calls<br>Technical service |
| Evaluating alternatives.<br>Re-forming attitudes | Suggesting alternative uses<br>Handling doubts and objections | Advertising<br>Telephone calls<br>Sales calls |
| Deciding to re-purchase | Reminding about benefits<br>Providing incentive to re-purchase | Advertising<br>Telephone calls<br>Sales calls<br>Sales promotion |

# *Glossary and Index*

> ***Tutorial note.*** In this subject, it is not always easy to arrive at exact definitions of certain words, as different authors use them in different ways. So treat this glossary as a memory jogger, not as the definite answer to your query. If in any doubt after you have used this glossary, consult the index and go back to the relevant section of this Study Text.

**4 Ps** See marketing mix.

**ACORN** A categorisation of Residential Neighbourhoods.

**Adoption process** Similar to buyer behaviour ie the process of deciding to buy a product. Adopter categories can indicate the extent to which people are prepared to innovate and try out new products.

**Advertising** Any paid form of non-personal presentation and promotion of ideas, goods or services by an identifiable sponsor.

**AIDA** Acronym denoting elements of a marketing communications strategy (to generate awareness, arouse interest, stir up desire and trigger action).

**Ansoff matrix** Approach to product-market strategies based on new or existing products and new or existing markets.

**BCG matrix** See Boston classification.

**Benchmarking** Technique by which a company tries to emulate or exceed standards achieved or processes adopted by another company.

**Boston classification** A classification developed by the Boston Consulting Group to analyse products and businesses by market share and market growth. 'In this, *cash cow* refers to a product of business with high market share and low market growth, *dog* refers to one with a low market share and low growth, *problem child* (or *question mark*) has low market share and high growth and a *star* has high growth and high market share' (CIMA).

**Brand** A name, term, symbol or design (or combination) which is intended to signify the goods or services of one seller or group of sellers and to differentiate them from those of competitors. Also, a particular make of a product form.

**Breakeven point** The level of activity at which there is neither profit nor loss (CIMA).

**Breakeven (cost-volume-profit (CVP)) analysis** The study of the interrelationships between costs, volume and profit at various levels of activity.

**BS EN ISO 9000** A standard of quality assurance (formerly BS 5750).

**BS7750** A standard of environmental management systems.

**Budget** A plan expressed in money. It is prepared and approved prior to the budget period and may show income, expenditure, and the capital to be employed. May be drawn up showing incremental effects on former budgeted or actual figures, or be compiled by zero-based budgeting (CIMA).

**Business strategy** How to approach a particular product and/or market.

**CAD** Computer aided design; the use of information technology in product design.

**CAM** Computer aided manufacturing, the physical control of the production process or part of it by computers, as applied in robots, computer numerical control tools.

**Cash cow** See Boston classification.

**Concentrated marketing** Sell your product in one segment only.

**Competitive advantage** Factor which enables a firm to compete successfully with competitors on a sustained basis

**Competitor analysis** Analysis of competitors' strengths and weaknesses, strategies, assumptions, market positioning, etc from all available sources of information in order to identify suitable strategies.

**Consumer goods** Goods made for the household consumer, which can be used without any further commercial processing. Convenience goods are generally purchased in small units or low value (eg milk). Shopping goods have higher unit values and are bought less frequently (eg clothes, furniture). Speciality goods are those of high value which a customer will know by name and go out of his or her way to purchase. These distinctions are broad and blurry; there is no point in logic-chopping.

**Consumer** The end user of a product service. May or may not be the customer.

**Consumers' Association** UK interest group representing consumers; conducts product tests and comparisons, lobbies government etc.

**Corporate appraisal** A critical assessment of the strengths and weaknesses, opportunities and threats (*SWOT analysis*) in relation to the internal and environmental factors affecting an entity in order to establish its condition prior to the preparation of the long-term plan (CIMA).

**Corporate culture** Culture residing in an organisation.

**Corporate objectives** Objectives for the firm as a whole.

**Corporate strategy** Strategy for the business as a whole (Johnson and Scholes).

**Culture** The sum total of beliefs, knowledge, attitudes of mind and custom to which people are exposed in their social conditioning.

**Customer** The purchaser of a product/service. May or may not be the consumer.

**Customer care** A fundamental approach to the standards of service quality. It covers every aspect of a company's operations, from the design of a product or service to how it is packaged, delivered and serviced (Clutterbuck).

**Decline** Stage of the product life cycle characterised by declining sales volumes and profits.

**Demand function** Mathematical expression which shows how sales demand for a product is dependent on several factors.

**Desk research** The collection of secondary data in marketing research.

**Differentiated marketing** Introduce several versions of a product, each tailored to a particular segment.

**Direct distribution** Supply of goods to customers without an intermediary (eg direct sales, mail order in some cases).

**Direct exporting** Exporting to overseas customers, who might be wholesalers, retailers or users, without the use of export houses etc. See also indirect exporting.

**Direct mail** Means of promotion, whereby selected customers are sent advertising material addressed specifically to them (eg by post and/or fax).

**Direct selling** The use of a salesperson to sell a product, as opposed to advertising etc.

**Distribution channel** Means of getting the goods to the consumer.

**Diversification** Extension of a firm's activities to new products and/or new markets.

**DMU** Decision-making unit ie the people in a business who decide whether to buy a product.

**Dog** See Boston classification.

**Emergent strategy** Strategy developed out of a pattern of behaviour not consciously imposed by senior management.

**Entry barriers** These discourage firms from entering an industry.

**Environmentalism** An ethos which puts fundamental importance on the relationship between human beings and their actions with the physical environment (ecology).

**EU (European Union)** Political and economic association comprising 15 European countries.

**Exit barriers** These make it difficult for firms to withdraw from an industry.

**External green Ps** An addition to the marketing mix's 4 Ps to cover environmental factors outside the business: Paying customers, Providers, Politicians, Pressure groups, Problems, Predictions, Partners.

**Family life cycle (FLC)** A summary demographic variables, combining the effects of age, marital status, career status (income) and presence/absence of children.

**Field research** The collection of primary data in market research.

**Flexibility** Ability to respond to change, new circumstances etc.

**Forecasting** The identification of factors and quantification of their effect on an entity, as a basis for planning.

**Franchising** Popular in retail and service industries, the franchisee supplies capital and the franchiser supplies expertise, a brand name and national promotion.

**Gap analysis** The comparison of an entity's ultimate objective with the sum of projection and already planned projects, identifying how the consequent gap might be filled.

**General Electric Business Screen** A product for portfolio analysis that overcomes some of the limitations of the growth/share matrix [the Boston classification] (Economist Pocket Marketing).

**Growth** Stage of product life cycle characterised by increasing sales volumes, profitability and competition.

**Indirect distribution** The use of intermediaries, such as wholesalers and retailers, to supply a product to the customer.

**Indirect exporting** Use of intermediaries such as export houses, specialist export management firms, complementary exporting (ie using other companies' products to pull your own into an overseas market); ie the outsourcing of the exporting function to a third party.

**Industrial markets** Business-to-business market (eg the sale of machine tools, consultancy advice etc).

**Inspection review** Inspection of products after manufacture is held to be wasteful. Defective production is a waste of materials, time, working capital. See TQM.

**Internal green Ps** An extension of the marketing mix's 4 Ps to include environmental matters. The 7 Ps are: Product, Promotion, Place, Price, Providing information, Processes, Policies, People.

**Introduction** Stage of the product life cycle; sometimes referred to as launch. Product sells in small volumes, and sales promotion is expensive.

**JIT (just in time)** A technique for the organisation of work flows to allow rapid, high quality, flexible production whilst minimising manufacturing waste and stock levels. An item should not be made or purchased until it is needed by the customer or as input to the production process.

**Joint venture** An arrangement of two or more firms to develop and/or market a product/service; each firm provides a share of the funding and has a say in management.

**Management buy-out** A transaction in which the executive managers of a business join with financing institutions to buy the business from the entity which currently owns it.

**Marginal costing** The accounting system in which variable costs are charged to cost units and fixed costs of the period are written-off in full against the aggregate contribution. Its special value is in decision-making.

**Marginal cost plus pricing/mark-up pricing** Method of determining the sales price by adding a profit margin onto either marginal cost of production or marginal cost of sales.

**Market** A group of consumers who share some particular characteristic which affects their needs or wants, and which makes them potential buyers of a product (Economist Pocket Marketing).

**Market positioning** 'The attempt by marketers to give the product a distinct identity or image so that it will be perceived to have distinctive features or benefits relative to competing products' (Economist Pocket Marketing).

**Market research** Sometimes used synonymously with marketing research; strictly speaking, however, it refers to the acquisition of primary data about customers and customer attitudes for example, by asking a sample of individuals to complete a questionnaire.

**Market segmentation** See segmentation.

**Market share** One entity's sales of a product or service in a specified market expressed as a percentage of total sales by all entities offering that product or service. A planning tool and a performance assessment ratio.

**Marketing** The management process which identifies, anticipates and supplies customer requirements efficiently and profitably.

**Marketing audit** Part of the position audit which reviews the organisation's products, markets, customers and market environment: 'a comprehensive, systematic, independent and periodic examination of a company's or business unit's marketing environment, objectives, strategies and activities, with a view to determining problem areas and opportunities and recommending a plan of action to improve the company's marketing performance' (Kotler).

**Marketing mix** The set of controllable variables and their levels that the firm uses to influence the target market. The mix comprises product, place, price, promotion (the 4 Ps). In service industries, this can be expanded to include people, processes, and physical evidence.

**Marketing orientation** A commitment to the needs of customers; 'marketing (focuses) on the idea of satisfying the needs of the customer by means of the product and the whole cluster of things associated with creating, delivering and finally consuming it' (Levitt).

**Marketing research** The objective gathering, recording and analysing of all facts about problems relating to the transfer and sales of goods and services from producer to consumer or user. Includes market research, price research etc. Marketing research involves the use of secondary data (eg government surveys) in desk research as well as field research (which the firm undertakes itself) to acquire primary data.

**Maturity** Stage of product life cycle characterised by relatively stable sales volumes and profitability.

**Me Too** A product modelled consciously on a successful competitor: the type of product that appears on a market with no differentiating features from already-existing products (Economist Pocket Marketing).

**Media** Non-personal means of communication (eg TV, newspapers etc).

**Merger** The amalgamation of two or more entities.

**Mission** An organisation's rationale for existing at all and/or its long term strategic direction and/or its values.

**Mission statement** Document in which the mission is formally stated.

**MKIS** Marketing information system.

**Non profit marketing** Marketing activities undertaken by non profit making organisations such as charities, government departments etc.

**Own brand** Brand created and supported by a retailer (eg Marks and Spencer's St Michael brand), or generic term covering goods sold under the retailer's name (eg Safeway baked beans).

**Pareto (80/20) distribution** 'A frequency distribution with a small proportion (say 20 per cent) of the items accounting for a large proportion (say 80 per cent) of the value/resources' (CIMA).

**People** Marketing mix element for services, to highlight the fact that the quality of many services depends on the quality of the people delivering it (eg a play can be ruined by bad acting).

**Personal selling** The presentation of goods or services in person by a sales representative.

**PEST factors** Factors in an organisation's environment (political-legal, economic, social-cultural, technological).

**Physical evidence** Marketing mix element for services denoting the environment in which the service is delivered (eg seating comfort and lighting in a restaurant).

**Pilot** A trial undertaken on a modest scale in order to test the feasibility of something much bigger (Economist Pocket Marketing).

**Place** Element of the marketing mix detailing how the product/service is supplied to the customer (distribution).

**Planning** The establishment of objectives, and the formulation, evaluation and selection of the policies, strategies, tactics and action required to achieve them. Planning comprises long-term/strategic planning, and short-term operation planning. The latter is usually for a period of one year.

**Planning horizon** 'The furthest time ahead for which plans can be quantified. It need not be the planning period' (CIMA).

**Positioning** See market positioning.

**Primary data** In market research, this is data collected specifically for the study under consideration (eg by questionnaire).

**Problem child** See Boston classification.

**Process research** Research into the ways goods/services are produced.

**Processes** Marketing mix element for services denoting how the service is actually delivered.

**Product** Anything that can be offered to a market that might satisfy a need or a want. It may be an object, a service, a place, an organisation, or an ideal (Economist Pocket Marketing.)

**Product class** Broad category of product (eg cars).

**Product life cycle** A model which suggests that sales of a product grow and mature and then decline as the product becomes obsolete and customer demands change. Applicable in some cases (eg horse-drawn transportation) but perhaps less so in others (eg corn flakes); use with caution. It is defined in the CIMA Official Terminology as 'the pattern of demand for a product over time'.

**Promotion** Element of the marketing mix which includes all communications with the customer, thus including advertising, publicity, PR, sales promotion etc.

**Protectionism** Discouraging imports by raising tariff barriers, imposing quotas etc.

**Public relations** The means by which an organisation tries to develop a mutual understanding between itself and its public (Institute of Public Relations).

**Quality** The totality of features and characteristics of a product or service which bears on its ability to meet stated or implied needs; fitness for use.

**Quality assurance** Arrangement whereby a supply guarantees quality of goods supplied by enabling the customer to review the production process or suggest techniques, or by adoption of an externally monitored quality standard such as BS5750.

**Quality management** Ensuring products are made to design specification.

**Quality related costs** 'The costs of ensuring and assuring quality, as well ass loss incurred when quality is not achieved. Quality costs are classified as prevention cost, appraisal cost, internal failure cost and external failure cost (BS6143)' (CIMA).

**Question marks** See Boston classification.

**Questionnaire** The primary tool of market research, a device for delivering questions to respondents and recording their answers (Economist Pocket Marketing).

**Retailer** Trader selling directly to households.

**Sales orientation** Customers have to be persuaded to buy a product.

**Sales promotion** Marketing activities other than personal selling, advertising and publicity aimed to stimulate purchasing by customers. Examples include money-off coupons, free flights, competitions etc.

**Sampling** Taking a limited number of a large poplulation so that by studying the part something may be learnt about the whole. The 'population' is all those people who have the characteristics in which the researcher is interested (Economist Pocket Marketing).

**SCEPTICAL list** A model of analysis.

**Secondary data** In marketing research, data neither collected directly by the user nor specifically for the user, often under conditions not known to the user. Examples include government reports.

**Segmentation (market segmentation)** The subdividing of the market into distinct and increasingly homogeneous sub groups of customers, where any subgroup can be selected as a target market to be met with a distinct marketing mix.

**Services** Distinguished from products because they are generally produced as they are consumed, and cannot be stored or taken away. For example, a bus is a product which is used to provide a service (transportation); the service is provided as you are consuming it (ie your trip from A to B). Also the standard of service differs each time it is produced (eg one bus driver may be a better or faster driver than another).

**Societal marketing concept** Concept that holds that the organisation's task is 'to determine the needs, desired satisfactions are more effectively and efficiently than competitors in a way that preserves or enhances the consumer's and the society's well-being' (Kotler).

**Sole trader** 'A person carrying on a business with sole legal responsibility for his actions, not in partnership nor as a company' (CIMA) (ie the business has no separate legal existence).

**Stakeholder** Person or group with an interest in organisational activities (eg shareholders, employees, customers, government etc).

**Stars** See Boston classification.

**Strategy** A course of action, including the specification of resources required, to achieve a desired objective. Note that different authors use the word to mean different things.

**Substitute product** Product that can stand in for another product (eg, in fast food, fish and chips might a substitute product for doner kebabs and vice versa).

**Sustainability** Developing strategies so that the business or entity only uses resources at a rate which allows them to be replenished in order to ensure that they will continue to be available.

**SWOT analysis** See Corporate appraisal.

**Take-over/acquisition** 'The acquiring, by a company, of a controlling interest in the voting share capital of assets of a company'

(CIMA). Note, sometimes sole traders, who are not companies, take over other sole traders' business assets and so perhaps the first half of this definition is a bit restrictive.

**Target market** Market, or market segment to which an organisation offers goods/services; one or more segments selected for special attention by a business.

**Test marketing** Samples of a proposed new product are tried out in areas which are supposed to be representative of the market as a whole.

**TQM (Total quality management)** An approach to production, and also management, aimed to prevent defective manufacture and to promote continuous improvement. CIMA defines it as 'the continuous improvement in quality, productivity and effectiveness obtained by establishing management responsibility for processes as well as outputs. In this, every process has a process owner and every person in an entity operates within a process and contributes to its improvement'.

**Trade/retail audits** Marketing research technique, where inspectors are sent to selected shops/outlets to count stock and deliveries, hence to estimate throughput.

**Undifferentiated marketing** Hope as many people as possible will buy the product, therefore do not segment.

**Unique selling proposition (USP)** The idea that a product should have at least one unique feature that differentiates it from all its competitors, and that can be easily communicated to customers through advertising (Economist Pocket Marketing)

**Wholesaler** Intermediary between manufacturers and retailers.

**World class manufacturing** Term covering diverse issues such as JIT, TQM, human resources management, etc.

**World trade organisation (WTO)** Set up under the 1993 GATT agreement, the WTO is a body which adjudicates between countries who have disputes over trade.

Above-the-line, 195
Absorption costing
  justifications for using, 159
  marginal costing, 161
Acid rain, 34
ACORN, 109, 116
Administered marketing system, 174
Advantages of agencies, 202
Advertiser and the agency, 202
Advertising, 194
  agencies, 202
  budget decision, 81
After sales service/technical advice, 171
AIDA model, 194
Allocation of costs, 81
American Marketing Association, 94, 194
Analysis, 18
Annual Abstract of Statistics, 94
Ansoff's Product/Market matrix, 69, 106
Association of British Insurers, 95
Assumptions and limitations of the product life cycle concept, 233
Audits of Great Britain (AGB), 102
Awareness building, 196

Barksdale and Harris, 234
Bases for segmentation, 71
BCG matrix, 127
Below-the-line advertising, 195
Bennett and Cooper, 13
Body language, 189
Body Shop, 37
Booz, Allen and Hamilton, 132
Borden, Neil, 17, 27
Boston Consulting Group (BCG) growth-share matrix, 127, 234
Bottom up planning, 63, 80
Brand, 75, 137, 203
  extension, 205
  image, 203
  life cycles, 123
  name, 154, 203
  vs generic advertising, 195
Branding, 203
Breakeven analysis, 162
Breakeven point, 162
British Business, 94
British Institute of Management, 48, 95
British Standards Institution, 39, 49
Brown, 257
BS EN ISO 9000, 60
BS4778, 49
Bulletins, 191
Business system, 15

Cannibalisation, 106
Cannon, Tom, 70
Capacity, 80
Capacity utilisation, 249
Cash cow, 128
Census of Population, 94
Census of Production, 94
Census Statistics, 110
CFCs, 46
Chain of distribution, 168
Channel design decisions, 170
Channel dynamics, 174
Chartered Institute of Marketing, 95
City Business Library, 95
Classification of respondents, 99
Cluster sampling, 97
Clutterbuck, 258
Communicating, 191
  with customers, 185
Communications mix, 185
Company mission statement, 64
Competition, 23, 146
  analysis, 27
Competitive advantage, 68
Competitive bidding, 147
Competitive effectiveness, 24
Competitive positioning, 78
Competitive pricing, 155
Competitive scope, 68
Competitive strategies, 68
Competitors' actions and reactions, 151
Comprehension building, 196
Concentrated marketing, 74
Consumer, 23
  mobility, 237
  panels, 99
  promotions, 207
  surplus, 148
Consumerism, 149
Contract manufacturing, 239
Contractual marketing systems, 174
Control, 18, 81
Controllables, 28
Controlled test marketing, 101
Cook, 122
Copy research, 101
Corey, Professor, 155
Corporate culture, 24
Corporate marketing systems, 174

Corporate mission, 264
Corporate objectives and strategies, 265
Corporate philosophies, 9
Corporate strategic plans, 62
Cost, 200
Cost leadership, 69
Cost-plus pricing, 145, 153
Cowell, 242
Criticisms of the product life cycle, 122, 123
Crosby, 54
Cultural factors, 240
Customer care, 257, 260
  shortcomings, 263
Customer database, 116
Customer orientation, 6
Customisation, 171
Customs, 240

Data Research Institute, 95
Database marketing, 115
Decision support systems, 18, 102
Decline stage, 230
Deliberate strategies, 63
Demand, 145, 148, 156
Deming, 50
  Chain Reaction, 51
  system, 51
  14 points, 51
Demographic segmentation, 108
Department of Employment Gazette, 94
Department of Trade and Industry, 94
Desk research, 94
Development of marketing departments, 18
Dhalla, 123
Differential pricing, 148
Differentiated marketing, 74
Differentiation, 69, 228
Diffusion of innovation, 134
Digest of UK Energy Statistics, 94
Direct attitude survey, 149
Direct distribution, 169
Direct mailing, 117
Direct observation, 96
Direct selling, 172
Display, 167
Distribution channels, 237
Distribution research, 90
Distribution strategy, 174
Distribution system, 15
Distributive network, 23
Distributor characteristics, 171
Diversification, 69
Divestment or liquidation, 231
Divisional marketing organisation, 20
Dog, 128
Doyle, Peter, 5, 9
Drucker, Peter, 7, 43

Early cash recovery objective, 153
Ecology, 32
Economic environment, 25
Economic review, 91
Economic Trends, 94
Economies of scale, 236
Effective, 63
Effective communication, 186
Effectiveness, 63
Efficiency, 63
Efficient reminding, 196
Elasticity, 156
Elements of the marketing mix, 17
Elkington and Burke, 35
Emergent strategies, 63
Ennew, Watkins and Wright, 68
Entry modes, 238
Environment, 22
Environment Business Supplement, 39
Environmental issues, 33
Environmental risk screening, 36
Environmental standard BS7750, 38
EPOS, 102
Establishing objectives within the not for profit sector, 249
Ethical investment, 36
Ethics/consumerism, 27
Euromonitor, 95
European Eco-Management and Audit regulation, 39
Evaluating data, 102
Exclusive distribution, 174
Exhibitions, 210
Exit barriers, 231
Experimentation, 95
Exporting, 238
Extel Group, 95
External agencies, 92
External green Ps, 46
Eye camera, 96

Family branding, 205
Family life cycle (FLC), 111
Family type, 110
Fast Moving Consumer Goods, 47

Feedback, 190
Feigenbaum, 55
Field research, 95
Financial Statistics, 94
Financial Times, 95
Financial Times Business Information Service, 95
Flow of influence, 16
Focus/nicheing, 69
Ford, 52, 101
Four Ps, 28, 44
Four Ss, 44
Fragmented industries, 78
Franchising, 171, 239
Friedman, Milton, 37
Full cost pricing, 144
Full costing, 161
Functional organisation, 19

Gap analysis, 57
Gap in the market, 76
General Electric, 50
  Business Screen, 127, 129, 234
General Motors, 12
Genetic diversity, 34
Geo-demographic segmentation, 116
Geographic segmentation, 108
Geographical organisation, 19
Geographical remoteness, 240
Gift purchases, 154
Galbraith, J K, 13
Goals down - plans up, 80
Going rate pricing, 154
Goods and services, 242
Government, 94
  controls, 28
Graham, 178
Grayson, 39
Green agenda, 33
Green consumer, 40
Green economics, 33
Green marketing practices, 42
Green movement, 32
Green pressures, 35
Growth stage, 225
Growth strategies, 69

Hall-Jones Scale, 108
Harvesting, 128, 231
Heterogeneity, 246
High- and low-contact service systems, 245
HM Statistical Service, 109
Housing and Construction statistics, 94
Human and animal welfare, 35

Improving the standard of customer care, 262
Inappropriate marketing processes, 266
Income effects, 152
Indirect distribution, 169
Industrial and consumer distribution channels, 173
Industrial marketing, 196
Industrial Marketing Research Association, 95
Industrial Productivity in the USA, 50
Industrial promotions, 207
Inelastic demand, 157
Inflation, 151
Information system, 16
Informative advertising, 195
In-house marketing research, 92
Initial concept testing, 133
Inseparability, 245
Institute of Practitioners in Advertising, 95
Intangibility, 243
Interest groups, 23
Intermediaries, 172
  objectives, 151
Intermediate customers, 153
Internal environment, 24
Internal green Ps, 45
International channels, 176
International marketing practice, 235
International Telephone and Telegraph (ITT), 54
Introduction stage, 223
Inventory Audit of Retail Sales, 100
Investment overseas, 239
ISO9000, 39, 184

JICNARS scale, 108, 200
JICPAS, 200
Johnson & Johnson, 46
Joint products, 155
Joint ventures, 239
Jones, Sir John Harvey, 264
Juran, 52
Just in time, 177

Kanban, 179
Kotler, 77, 143, 195, 242

**L**aboratory tests, 101
Laggards, 120
Lancaster, 177, 241
Lanzilotti, 144
Lead generation, 196
Legitimisation, 196
Levitt, Theodore, 6, 11, 233
Liaison, 190
Licensing, 239
Lifestyle segmentation, 114
Likert scales, 102
Local knowledge, 167
Logistics management, 176
Loss leader, 152, 155

**M**acro environment, 25
Maintenance, 231
Making the channel decision, 171
Malcolm Baldridge National Quality Award, 260
Management contracts, 239
Managing customer contact, 249
Managing the product portfolio, 126
Marginal costing, 160, 161
  and absorption costing compared, 161
Marginal costing, 160
Market development, 69, 106
Market environment, 22
Market forecast, 91
Market intelligence, 190
Market level plans, 66
Market management, 20
Market orientation, 6
Market penetration, 69, 106
  objective, 152
Market research, 18, 89, 91
Market segmentation, 66, 70, 106
Market skimming objective, 153
Market test, 149
Marketing, 27, 236
  audits, 24, 82
  budget, 80
  capabilities, 24
  characteristics of services, 242
  concept, 3, 4
  Diagnostics, 41
  flow, 16
  information system, 18, 66, 103
  management, 18
  mix, 223, 226, 235
  Myopia, 11
  orientated strategy, 11
  orientation, 4
  planning, 44, 62, 64, 79
  research, 89
  Science Institute, 123
  strategies, 62
Marks & Spencer, 204
Massingham, 241
Matrix management, 20
Maturity stage, 226
McKenna, 177, 183
Media habits, 199
Media problems, 241
Merchandising, 208
Micro environment, 22, 24
Mintel, 95
MIT Commission, 50
Monitor, 246
Monopoly, 143
Monthly Digest of Statistics, 94
Morden, 243
Mothercare, 74
Motivation of consumers, 27
Motivational research, 101
Multi-branding, 205
Multi-channel decisions, 173
Multiple products, 152
Multistage sampling, 97

**N**ader, Ralph, 13
New product development, 130
New product pricing, 152
Niche, 231
Nielsen Index, 100
Non-random sampling, 97
Not-for-profit organisations, 5

**O**akland, 56
Objectives of advertising, 195
Observation, 95
Odd number pricing, 154
OECD, 34
Ogilvy and Mather, 41
Ogilvy, Benson, Mather, 101
Oligopoly, 143, 159
Oliver, 179
One coin purchase, 154
Organising marketing departments, 19
Ownership, 247
Ozone depletion, 35

Packaging, 137
Peattie, 35, 45
Penetration, 224
People, 249
and customer service, 249
Perceptual map, 76
Perfect competition, 143
Performance evaluation, 24
Perishability, 171, 247
Personal selling, 249
Persuasive advertising, 195
PEST factors, 16
Peters, Tom, 178, 263
Physical evidence, 249, 250
Pilot testing, 99
Place, 47, 224, 226, 229, 232, 237
Place of availability, 249
Planning, 18
a promotion campaign, 197
cycle, 63
Political/legal environment, 25
Polli, 122
Polluter pays principle, 34
Pollution concerns, 34
Porter, Michael, 68
Positioning products, 75
Post-testing, 102
Practical processes for a customer care programme, 269
Price, 47, 141, 224, 226, 229, 232, 241
determination, 142
discrimination (or differential pricing), 148, 154
elasticity, 143, 156
leadership, 156
perception, 151
research, 90
setting in practice, 144
Pricing, 141
policy, 150
Primary data, 95
Problem child, 128
Product, 47, 117, 224, 225, 228, 231, 236
adaptation, 237
characteristics, 171
development, 69, 106
differentiation, 74, 195
life cycle, 118, 123, 222
line pricing, 154
line promotion objective, 153
mix, 126
offer, 142
portfolio planning, 126
research, 89, 90
standardisation, 236
testing, 133
Product/service portfolio, 106
Product-based organisation, 20
Profit maximisation, 8
Profit/volume or P/V ratio, 161
Profitable survivor, 231
Promotion, 48, 167, 185, 224, 226, 229, 232, 240
Promotional mix, 186, 193
Psychogalvanometer, 96
Psychographic segmentation, 114
Public relations, 211
Publicity, 211
Push and pull effects, 193

Quality, 228, 259
and British Standards, 60
and customer care, 248
connotations, 151
Control Handbook, 52
gaps, 57
management, 259
Movement, 49
policy, 133
programme, 59
Quantum price, 154
Questionnaire design, 99
Questionnaires, 98
Quota sampling, 97

RAJAR, 200
Random sampling, 96
Ratings tests, 101
Reassurance, 196
Recommended retail price, 153
Recording data about attitudes, 102
Recycling, 35
Registrar General's Classification, 108
Reliability of sample data, 102
Reminding advertising, 195
Repositioning, 198
Research and development, 236
Resource allocation, 66
Resource depletion, 34
Retailer or middleman promotions, 207
Retailers, 174
Reuters, 95
Rolls Royce, 74

**S**ales conferences, 191
Sales force promotions, 207
Sales forecasts, 92
Sales manuals, 191
Sales meetings, 191
Sales orientation, 6
Sales promotion research, 90
Sales promotions, 194, 207
Salesperson's image, 190
Sampling, 96
Scope of marketing, 17
Screen Advertisers' Association, 200
Screening new product ideas, 132
Secondary data, 93
Segmentation by age, 108
Segmenting the green market, 41
Selective distribution, 174
Selling function, 185
Semantic differential scales, 102
Sensitivity, 152
Services, 136
  economy, 242
Shostack, 243
Simulated store technique, 101
Situation analysis, 66
Skimming, 224
Social responsibility, 36
Social/cultural environment, 26
Society of Motor Manufacturers and Trades (SMMT), 95
Socio-economic groups, 108
Sole ownership, 240
Specific market research, 91
Sponsorship, 211
St Michael, 204
Stages in strategic planning, 64
Star, 128
Stock holding and storage, 167
Stone & Young, 267
Strategic implications of the product life cycle, 124
Strategic marketing plan, 18
Strategy development, 66
Strategy formulation, 66
Stratified sampling, 97
Strong, 194
Successful advertising, 201
Successful customer care, 269
Supplier characteristics, 171
Suppliers, 23, 151
Sustainability, 36, 38
SWOT analysis, 66
Synchronisation, 179
Systematic sampling, 97

**T**achitoscope, 96
Target markets, 74
Target pricing, 153
Techniques of market research, 91
Technological complexity, 237
Technological environment, 26
Television, 199
Test marketing, 101, 134
Theory of diminishing returns, 81
Thomas, 257
Timex, 227
Top down planning, 64, 80
Total market demand, 91
Total quality management (TQM), 43, 55, 259
Trade audits or retail audits, 100
Trade fairs, 210
Trade motivation, 27
Trademarks, 206
Trademarks Act 1994, 206
Transport, 167
Turnkey construction contracts, 239

**U**ncontrollables, 28
Undifferentiated marketing, 74
Unique selling proposition, 16, 143
Unsafe at Any Speed, 13

**V**ertical marketing system, 174

**W**aste, 35
Wensley, 118
Western Electric, 52
Which? magazine, 35
Wholesalers, 174
Wind, 75

**Y**uspeh, 123

## ORDER FORM

If you want more question practice for this exam, use our companion Practice & Revision Kit. Published in February 1998, the Kit is packed with past exam questions, including the December 1997 paper. Each question has a full suggested solution prepared by an experienced tutor. A new edition will be published in February 1999.

To order your Kit, you can phone us on 0181 740 2211, email us at *publishing@bpp.co.uk*, fax this form to 0181 740 1184 or cut it out and post it to the address below.

**To: BPP Publishing Ltd, Aldine House, Aldine Place, London W12 8AW**

**Tel: 0181 740 2211**
**Fax: 0181 740 1184**

Forenames (Mr / Ms): ____________________ Surname: ____________________

Address: ________________________________________

________________________________________

Post code: ______________ Date of exam (month/year): ______________

| **Please send me the following books:** | *Quantity* | *Price* | *Total* |
|---|---|---|---|
| CIM Advanced Certificate *Marketing Fundamentals and Sales* Practice & Revision Kit | .............. | £7.95 | .............. |
| **Postage and packaging:** | | | |
| **UK:** Kits £2.00 for first plus £1.00 for each extra | .............. | | .............. |
| **Europe (inc ROI & CI):** Kits £2.50 for first plus £1.00 for each extra | .............. | | .............. |
| **Rest of the World:** Kits £5.00 for first plus £3.00 for each extra | .............. | | .............. |
| | | | ________ |

**I enclose a cheque for £ ________ or charge to Access/Visa/Switch**

**Card number** | | | | | | | | | | | | | | | | | | | |

**Start date (Switch only)** ________ **Expiry date** ________ **Issue no. (Switch only)**________

**Signature** ____________________

To order any further titles in the CIM range, please use the form overleaf.

## ORDER FORM

To order your CIM books, you can phone us on 0181 740 2211, email us at *publishing@bpp.co.uk*, fax this form to 0181 740 1184, or cut this form out and post it to the address below.

**To: BPP Publishing Ltd, Aldine House, Aldine Place, London W12 8AW** **Tel: 0181 740 2211 Fax: 0181 740 1184**

Forenames (Mr / Ms): ______________________Surname: ______________

Address: ________________________________________________

________________________________________________________

Post code: ________________ Date of exam (month/year):______________

**Please send me the following books:**

| | Price | | Quantity | | Total |
|---|---|---|---|---|---|
| | 4/98 Text | 2/98 Kit | Text | Kit | £ |
| **Certificate** | £ | £ | | | |
| Marketing Environment | 16.95 | 7.95 | ......... | ......... | ......... |
| Understanding Customers | 16.95 | 7.95 | ......... | ......... | ......... |
| Business Communications | 16.95 | 7.95 | ......... | ......... | ......... |
| Marketing Fundamentals | 16.95 | 7.95 | ......... | ......... | ......... |
| **Advanced Certificate** | | | | | |
| Promotional Practice | 16.95 | 7.95 | ......... | ......... | ......... |
| Management Information for Marketing and Sales | 16.95 | 7.95 | ......... | ......... | ......... |
| Effective Management for Marketing | 16.95 | 7.95 | ......... | ......... | ......... |
| Marketing Operations | 16.95 | 7.95 | ......... | ......... | ......... |
| **Diploma** | | | | | |
| Marketing Communications Strategy | 17.95 | 8.95 | ......... | ......... | ......... |
| International Marketing Strategy | 17.95 | 8.95 | ......... | ......... | ......... |
| Strategic Marketing Management: Planning and Control | 17.95 | 8.95 | ......... | ......... | ......... |
| Strategic Marketing Management: Analysis and Decision | 24.95 | - | ......... | ......... | ......... |

**Postage and packaging:**

| | Total |
|---|---|
| **UK:** Texts £3.00 for first plus £2.00 for each extra | ......... |
| Kits £2.00 for first plus £1.00 for each extra | ......... |
| **Europe (inc ROI & CI):** Texts £5.00 for first plus £4.00 for each extra | ......... |
| Kits £2.50 for first plus £1.00 for each extra | ......... |
| **Rest of the World:** Texts £8.00 for first plus £6.00 for each extra | ......... |
| Kits £5.00 for first plus £3.00 for each extra | ......... |
| | ______ |

**I enclose a cheque for £ _________ or charge to Access/Visa/Switch**

**Card number** | | | | | | | | | | | | | | | | | | | |

**Start date (Switch only)** ________ **Expiry date** ____________ **Issue no. (Switch only)**___

**Signature** ____________________

## REVIEW FORM & FREE PRIZE DRAW

All original review forms from the entire BPP range, completed with genuine comments, will be entered into one of two draws on 31 July 1998 and 31 January 1999. The names on the first four forms picked out on each occasion will be sent a cheque for £50.

**Name:** ______________________ **Address**: ______________________

______________________

______________________

**How have you used this Text?**
*(Tick one box only)*

- ☐ Home study (book only)
- ☐ On a course: college ______________
- ☐ With 'correspondence' package
- ☐ Other ______________

**Why did you decide to purchase this Text?**
*(Tick one box only)*

- ☐ Have used companion Kit
- ☐ Have used BPP Texts in the past
- ☐ Recommendation by friend/colleague
- ☐ Recommendation by a lecturer at college
- ☐ Saw advertising
- ☐ Other ______________

**During the past six months do you recall seeing/receiving any of the following?**
*(Tick as many boxes as are relevant)*

- ☐ Our advertisement in the *Marketing Success*
- ☐ Our advertisement in *Marketing Business*
- ☐ Our brochure with a letter through the post
- ☐ Our brochure with *Marketing Business*

**Which (if any) aspects of our advertising do you find useful?**
*(Tick as many boxes as are relevant)*

- ☐ Prices and publication dates of new editions
- ☐ Information on Text content
- ☐ Facility to order books off-the-page
- ☐ None of the above

**Have you used the companion Practice & Revision Kit for this subject?** ☐ Yes ☐ No

**Your ratings, comments and suggestions would be appreciated on the following areas.**

| | *Very useful* | *Useful* | *Not useful* |
|---|---|---|---|
| *Introductory section (How to use this text, study checklist, etc)* | ☐ | ☐ | ☐ |
| *Introductions to chapters* | ☐ | ☐ | ☐ |
| *Syllabus coverage* | ☐ | ☐ | ☐ |
| *Exercises and examples* | ☐ | ☐ | ☐ |
| *Chapter roundups* | ☐ | ☐ | ☐ |
| *Test your knowledge quizzes* | ☐ | ☐ | ☐ |
| *Illustrative questions* | ☐ | ☐ | ☐ |
| *Content of suggested solutions* | ☐ | ☐ | ☐ |
| *Glossary and index* | ☐ | ☐ | ☐ |
| *Structure and presentation* | ☐ | ☐ | ☐ |

| | *Excellent* | *Good* | *Adequate* | *Poor* |
|---|---|---|---|---|
| *Overall opinion of this Text* | ☐ | ☐ | ☐ | ☐ |

**Do you intend to continue using BPP Study Texts/Kits?** ☐ Yes ☐ No

**Please note any further comments and suggestions/errors on the reverse of this page.**

**Please return to: Edmund Hewson, BPP Publishing Ltd, FREEPOST, London, W12 8BR**

## REVIEW FORM & FREE PRIZE DRAW (continued)

**Please note any further comments and suggestions/errors below.**

### FREE PRIZE DRAW RULES

1 Closing date for 31 July 1998 draw is 30 June 1998. Closing date for 31 January 1999 draw is 31 December 1998.

2 Restricted to entries with UK and Eire addresses only. BPP employees, their families and business associates are excluded.

3 No purchase necessary. Entry forms are available upon request from BPP Publishing. No more than one entry per title, per person. Draw restricted to persons aged 16 and over.

4 Winners will be notified by post and receive their cheques not later than 6 weeks after the relevant draw date. Lists of winners will be published in BPP's *focus* newsletter following the relevant draw.

5 The decision of the promoter in all matters is final and binding. No correspondence will be entered into.